Richard Green

Works of John And Charles Wesley

A Bibliography: Containing an Exact Account of all the Publications

Richard Green

Works of John And Charles Wesley
A Bibliography: Containing an Exact Account of all the Publications

ISBN/EAN: 9783337141370

Printed in Europe, USA, Canada, Australia, Japan

Cover: Foto ©Thomas Meinert / pixelio.de

More available books at **www.hansebooks.com**

THE WORKS

OF

JOHN AND CHARLES WESLEY.

A BIBLIOGRAPHY:

CONTAINING AN EXACT ACCOUNT OF ALL THE PUBLICATIONS

ISSUED BY

THE BROTHERS WESLEY

ARRANGED IN CHRONOLOGICAL ORDER, WITH A LIST OF THE

EARLY EDITIONS, AND

DESCRIPTIVE AND ILLUSTRATIVE NOTES:

BY THE

REV. RICHARD GREEN,

DIDSBURY COLLEGE, MANCHESTER;

Author of *Life of John Wesley; The Mission of Methodism* (The Fernley Lecture for 1890); etc.

LONDON:
Published for the Author by C. H. KELLY, 2, Castle Street, City Road,
and 66, Paternoster Row.
1896.

TO THE MEMBERS OF

THE WESLEY HISTORICAL SOCIETY

THE FOLLOWING PAGES

ARE

RESPECTFULLY INSCRIBED.

PREFACE.

IT is not too much to say, that, while Wesley's Theological teaching cannot be thoroughly understood without a careful study of his numerous writings, so neither can his indefatigable labours, nor the difficulties and oppositions in the face of which he toiled, be duly estimated.

The following pages will show how varied were his literary productions; and they can hardly fail to excite surprise that, in the midst of his ceaseless evangelistic activity, he could write so much. It is indeed he who deserves the credit of having been the first in this country to provide and diffuse cheap popular literature of a useful kind.

The works are placed in the precise order in which they were published, as far as that order, by the most careful inquiry, can be ascertained. The only variations being that, for convenience of reference, the Poetical Works issued in any year are placed at the end of the list for that year.

The *full title-page* of the *first edition* of each work is given,* and the name of publisher and date of issue of all known editions to the end of the century. Differences in spelling in title-pages are reproduced. They were due mainly to the fact that Wesley seldom had the opportunity of correcting the press proofs. A brief description of each book and pamphlet generally follows, and a statement of the occasion on which it was written. Where they can be discovered, the titles of works which Wesley combatted or condensed are inserted, and illustrative extracts from the Journals of the two brothers and from other writings are added, the whole forming a view of the literary labours of these remarkable men such as has not hitherto appeared.

It will be observed that there is much confusion in the numbering of the Editions. It is a common characteristic; and probably arose from the books having been published in different towns and by different printers.

---

* Except only in a very few instances where the author has not been able to see the first edition.

PREFACE.

Every available source of information has been searched in order to make this list as full and accurate as possible. It was Wesley's practice to append to his publications lists of all previous works issued by him. These have been carefully examined. Advantage has been taken of the labours of previous compilers, particularly of the First Part of Dr. Osborn's valuable *Outlines of Wesleyan Bibliography* (London: Wesleyan Conference Office, 1869); the *Chronological List of the Writings of John and Charles Wesley*, by Alexander Heylin, appended to Tegg's Edition of Stevens' *History of Methodism* (London: Wm. Tegg, 1864); *List of Works revised and abridged from various authors* and *List of Poetical Works published by John and Charles Wesley*, in Smith's *History of Wesleyan Methodism*, vol. I; and the references in Tyerman's *Life and Times of John Wesley*; etc., etc.

In addition to the use of his own almost complete collection of the earliest editions of all the Works published by John and Charles Wesley, the author has freely consulted the Allan and the Wesleyan Book-Room libraries, and the large collection of Wesley's publications made by the Rev. Samuel Romilly Hall, and now in Didsbury College Library; while the help of many correspondents has been very kindly given, and is most gratefully acknowledged. He is particularly indebted to his friend and colleague, the Rev. R. Waddy Moss, for much help and counsel.

RICHARD GREEN.

DIDSBURY COLLEGE,
JANUARY, 1896.

BIBLIOGRAPHY.

1733.

1. A COLLECTION OF FORMS OF PRAYER FOR EVERY DAY IN THE WEEK. 12mo. 1733.

With preface and questions for self-examination. There is some difficulty in determining the original title of this pamphlet. It does not appear that an early edition was in the hands of any of the compilers of the lists of Wesley's works. A fifth edition (1740), the earliest seen by Dr. Osborn, had neither the original preface nor the questions for self-examination inserted by Wesley; but hymns were added which were first published in 1739-40. It was so in the sixth edition (1742). But in a (so-called) fifth edition, published in Bristol, 1755, the pamphlet is evidently restored to its original character. There is no author's name on the title-page. This is in accord with the preface in which the writer hides himself under the designation, "the collector of these prayers." The preface and questions for self-examination are given, and, besides the omission of the hymns, there are certain marked similarities between this edition and the republication by Wesley in his collected works, making it highly probable that the printer in Bristol (J. Palmer) had before him a copy of the original edition.

A COLLECTION OF FORMS OF PRAYER FOR EVERY DAY IN THE WEEK. The Fifth Edition, Bristol: printed and sold by J. Palmer in Wine Street; by G. Woodfall, near Charing Cross, London; A. Dodd, at the Peacock in the Strand; J. Robinson, Ludgate-street; and T. Trye, near Gray's Inn, 1755, 12mo., pp. 76.

Fifth edition, London; Strahan, 1740; Sixth, Bristol: F. Farley, 1742; Sixth, London: Hawes, 1775; Seventh, Newcastle: Gooding, no date; Eighth, 1745; Eighth, London: H. Cock, 1755; Ninth, Dublin: 1748.

This is the first work John Wesley printed; as he informs us in his Journal under date May 14th, 1765, "In the same year (1733) I printed (the first time I ventured to print anything) for the use of my pupils, *A Collection of Forms of Prayer*."

1734.

2. A TREATISE ON CHRISTIAN PRUDENCE. Extracted from Mr. Norris. By John Wesley, M.A., Fellow of Lincoln College, Oxon. The second edition. London: printed by W. Strahan, and sold by Thomas Harris, at the Looking Glass and Bible, on London-Bridge; by Thos. Trye, at Grey's-Inn Gate, and at the Foundery, near Upper-Moor-Fields. 1742. (Price threepence), 12mo., pp. 35.

The first edition was published in 1734, see following letter; but a copy of it has not been found. Third edition, Bristol: F. Farley, 1749; Fourth edition, London: 1784.

"I published a Collection of Forms of Prayer for everyday, in 1733—An Abridgment of Mr. Norris' Christian Prudence, and Reflection on the Conduct of our Understanding, in 1734—An edition of the Christian Pattern, a Sermon on Job iii. 17, and Advice to a Young Clergyman (written by my father) in 1735—A Collection of Psalms and Hymns in 1736 [? 1737]—A Sermon on Salvation by Faith, An Extract from ye Homilies on ye same, and ye Life of Mr. Haliburton, in 1738—A Sermon on Free Grace, an abridgment of Nicodemus or a Treatise on ye fear of Man, and a Collection of Hymns and Sacred Poems, in 1739. Dated at Bristol, March 15, 1739-40.—JOHN WESLEY." See Rawlinson's Continuation of Wood's *Athenæ Oxonienses*, in the Bodleian MSS., Oxford. This is sufficient authority for the dates assigned to Nos. 1, 2, 4, 5 and 7.

1735.

3. THE CHRISTIAN'S PATTERN: OR A TREATISE OF THE IMITATION OF CHRIST. Written originally in Latin, by Thomas a Kempis. With a Preface containing an account of the Usefulness of this Treatise; Directions for reading it with advantage; and likewise an Account of this Edition. Compared with the Original, and corrected throughout, by John Wesley, M.A., Fellow of Lincoln College, Oxon. London: Printed for C. Rivington, at the Bible and Crown in St. Paul's Churchyard. 1735. Pp. xxxix., 319. 8vo. [Five copperplate engravings.]

A beautiful little pocket-edition (24mo., pp. xvi. 344) was published in the same year. The title page is slightly altered, and there is "a new preface, giving some plain directions how to read this (or, indeed, any other religious book) with improvement." An engraving of the Crucifixion is placed opposite the title-page. This engraving reversed was on one of the earliest Tickets of the Society.

A second edition, 24mo., was published in 1750. No other edition of the complete treatise was published by Wesley; but it was re-printed (with some omissions) by Cordeux: 1815. 12mo., pp. 252.

In a notice of the larger edition, inserted in the smaller one, it is affirmed, "This edition is a closer translation of the original than any hitherto published; being as literal as is consistent with elegance, and divided, like the Latin, into distinct sentences."

"Sometimes I slipped into his [Fletcher's] study on other days. I rarely saw any book before him besides the Bible and Christian Pattern."—Wesley's *Life of Fletcher*.

"He was dissatisfied with Dean Stanhope's translation, and determined to give a full view of the self-denying purity of his favourite guide."—H. Moore, *L. of Wesley*, ii, 401.

4. ADVICE TO A YOUNG CLERGYMAN: In a Letter to him, concerning.—I. His Intention; II. Converse and Demeanour; III. Reading Prayers; IV. Studies; V. Preaching and Catechising; VI. Administering the Sacrament; Lastly, Discipline. By a Divine of the

1737.] **Nos. 5-6.**

Church of England. London : Printed for C. Rivington, at the Bible and Crown in St. Paul's Church-Yard, and sold by J. Roberts in Warwick-Lane. [Price one shilling.] 12mo., pp. iv.. 69.

Signed at the end :—S. W. It was written by Samuel Wesley, sen. The preface is by John Wesley.

Heylin gives April as the date for the Christian's Pattern and October for the Advice ; on what authority is not stated.

The author's copy has this manuscript note, "This letter was written by Mr. Wesley for the use of Mr. Nathaniel Hoole his . . . . in his curacy, 1724. I had the same put into my hands in MS. by Mr. Wesley.—John Pennington." "I took some pains a year or two since in drawing up some advices to Mr. Hoole's brother, then to be my curate at Epworth."—Let. S. W. to J. W. "Some advices I drew up for Mr. Hoole, my curate, may not be unuseful to you. Pray let no one but yourself see them."—Let. S. W. to J. W., Wroot, January 26, 1724-5.—*Life of S. W.*, pp. 391-2.

5 A SERMON preached at St. Mary's in Oxford, on Sunday, September 21, 1735. By John Wesley, M.A., Fellow of Lincoln College, Oxon. Publish'd at the request of several of the hearers. London : Printed for C. Rivington, at the Bible and Crown, in St. Paul's Church-Yard ; and J. Roberts in Warwick-Lane, 1735. 12mo.. pp. 26.

This sermon is founded on Job iii. 17. Jackson says, "This appears to have been the first sermon that Mr. Wesley ever committed to the press." It was first republished in 1816 in a volume of sermons by Charles Wesley. The original has no title, but one was supplied by Jackson, " The trouble and rest of good men."

A SERMON on "The Pleasantness of a Religious Life" (Proverbs iii. 17). By John Wesley. 8vo., 1735.

Heylin says, "This I give on the authority of Watts' *Bibliotheca Britannica*. I have never seen it, and it appears in no edition of Wesley's sermons or works." Both Lettsome and Cooke mention it in the *Preacher's Assistant* ; but they evidently copy from Watts, and all three omit the sermon on Job iii. 17. It is not in the list that Wesley gave of the books he had written (see No. 2), nor is it in any list or catalogue published by him. It is probably a mistake for the preceding sermon, which is not mentioned in any of the authorities given by Heylin. There is not the slightest probability of the existence of the latter sermon.

1737.

6. A COLLECTION OF PSALMS AND HYMNS. Charlestown : Printed by Lewis Timothy, 1737, 12mo., pp. 74.

This book contains the earliest of John Wesley's translations of German hymns. It was reprinted (1882) with preface by the Rev. G. Osborn, D.D. (London : T. Woolmer, 2, Castle-Street, City-Road, E.C.) It is not, as described on the title-page, a "*fac-simile* reprint," the first two pages only being in *fac-simile*. It is not dated. See note under No. 2.

I I

There is only one copy of this edition now known. It was purchased in London, for a few shillings; some years afterwards it was sold for £5; subsequently £24 were bidden for it at a sale by auction (1894), and refused.

1738.

7. A COLLECTION OF PSALMS AND HYMNS. London: Printed in the year 1738, 12mo., pp. 84.

No author's or printer's name.
This very rare volume is fully described in Osborn's *Outlines of Wesleyan Bibliography*, and in *The Poetical Works of J. and C. Wesley*, vol. ii. It has never been republished. There is a copy in the Didsbury College Library; and another in the Archiepiscopal Library at Lambeth. No others are known.

8. A SERMON ON SALVATION BY FAITH. By John Wesley, M.A., Fellow of Lincoln College, Oxford. London: Printed for James Hutton at the Bible and Sun, next the Rose-Tavern, without Temple-Bar, 1738, 12mo., pp. 23.

Third edition, 1740; Fourth, London: Strahan, 1741; Fifth, London: W. Strahan, 1741; Sixth, Newcastle: Gooding, 1743; Ninth, Newcastle: Gooding, 1745; An edition, Dublin, 1747; Ninth, London: H. Cock. 1750; An edition in French, "Imprimé à Londres, par Strahan," 1759; Ninth, Hawes, 1773; Tenth, 1776; Unnumbered, Farley, 1763; Ditto, 1783; Lon. Paramore, 1783; London: Paramore, 1791.

This was Wesley's first publication after his "conversion." It stands, where such a sermon should, at the beginning of his collection of his published works. He preached a sermon on the same text in the last year of his life after an interval of 53 years.
"Among the curious mistakes made by Wesley respecting his own writings, one of the most curious respects the date at which this celebrated sermon was preached. His Journal shows that he left England for Germany on Tuesday, June 13, just five days before the Sunday on which in all editions of his works he is said to have preached before the University of Oxford. The 11th is doubtless the true date."—OSBORN. "Having preached faith in Christ there [Stanton Harcourt] on Sunday, 11, I went on to Oxford; and thence on Monday to London. We went on board the next day, Tuesday, 13, and fell down to Gravesend that night."—*Journal*, June, 1738. The error began probably in an anonymous edition of the sermon printed in Dublin, 1747—the first, if not the only, edition on which any date appears. Wesley did not add the date until 1771.

1739.

9. THE DOCTRINE OF SALVATION, FAITH, AND GOOD WORKS. Extracted from the Homilies of the Church of England. London: Printed for James Hutton, at the Bible and Sun, without Temple-Bar, 1739, 12mo., pp. 23.

Third edition, 1755; Fourth, London: Strahan, 1741; Sixth, Strahan, 1744; Ninth, Newcastle: Gooding, 1749; Ninth, Dublin: Powell, 1747; Tenth, Bristol: Farley, 1748; Eleventh, Bristol. 1762: Eleventh, Bristol: Pine, 1770; Twelfth, Bristol: Pine, 1767; Thirteenth, Bristol: Pine, 1770.

"In the following week, I began more narrowly to inquire what the doctrine of the Church of England is, concerning the much controverted point of justification by faith; and the sum of what I found in the Homilies, I extracted and printed for the use of others."—*Journal*, November 12, 1738. The work would not be published till 1739.

10. An Abstract of the Life and Death of the Reverend Learned and Pious Mr. Thomas Halyburton, M.A., Professor of Divinity in the University of St. Andrews (Acts xiii. 41). London : Printed for John Oswald, at the Rose and Crown in the Poultry, near Stocks Market, 1739, (price, bound in plain sheep, one shilling,) 12mo., pp. xii., 107.

The Recommendatory Epistle, signed George Whitefield, London, February 5, 1738-9. *The Preface*, signed John Wesley, London, February, 9, 1738-9. At end :—" N. B.—The Life of Mr. Haliburton at large, with Dr. Watts' Preface, may be had for 2s. 6d. bound."

An Extract of the Life and Death of Mr. Thomas Haliburton (Acts xiii. 41). London : Printed by W. Strahan, and sold at the Foundery, near Upper-Moor-Fields ; at James Hutton's, Bookseller, at the Bible and Sun, without Temple Bar ; and at John Lewis's, in Bartholomew Close. 1741, [Price, stitch'd, sixpence], 12mo., pp. 92.

Contents and preface unpaged.

Second edition, Bristol : F. Farley, 1747 ; Third, Bristol : Pine, 1768 ; Third (*sic*) Lon : Paramore, 1795 ; Fourth, Bristol: Pine, 1773 ; Fifth, Bristol : 1742 ; Fifth, London : Hawes, 1777 ; A Fifth, London : Cordeux, 1813 ; Ninth, Newcastle : Gooding, 1749 ; Eleventh, Bristol : Pine, 1762.

These two pamphlets are one and the same—the first, being called an Abstract, and having Whitefield's letter in it ; the second and all following editions not having the letter and being called an Extract, a term frequently used afterwards by Wesley. For some interesting facts respecting this pamphlet see Jackson's *Life of C. Wesley*, i. 129.

This is an abridgement of "*Memoirs of the Life of the Reverend, Learned and Pious Mr. Thomas Haliburton, Professor of Divinity in the University of St. Andrews in Scotland:* In four parts, whereof three were drawn up by himself, the fourth collected by his friends from his private papers and his dying lips." A second edition was published in London, by R. Cuttenden, in 1718, with a " Large Recommendatory Epistle by J. Watts," dated May 1, 1718 ; a Dedication by his wife, and a " Preface to the Reader " by another hand. Wesley abridged it to one-fourth its original size.

Wesley's estimate of these memoirs was very high. He says, in the preface, " This work of God in the soul of man is so described in the following treatise, as I have not seen it in any other, either ancient or modern, in our own or any other language. So that I cannot but value it next to the Holy Scriptures, above any other human composition, excepting only the *Christian Pattern*, and the small remains of Clemens Romanus, Polycarp and Ignatius."

Haliburton passed through very severe struggles but the reader is left without definite knowledge of the nature of them, the style being enigmatical and but comparatively few of the incidents of his history being given. It was published by Wesley in the early period of his career, which may account for the mystic element that is left in it.

"I cannot but look upon his life as the most perfect copy of his blessed Master's that I have yet seen,"—Whitefield's letter. But see Southey's *Life of Wesley*, Bohn's Ed., p 156 and note.

11. FREE GRACE: A Sermon preach'd at Bristol. By John Wesley, M.A., Fellow of Lincoln-College, Oxford. Bristol: Printed by S. and F. Farley. 1739, 12mo., pp. 35.

Hymn on *Universal Redemption*, thirty-six stanzas, appended.

Second edition (not so called), London: Strahan, 1740; On page 4 of this is a curious "Advertisement" relating to a pamphlet, entitled, *Free Grace Indeed*, written against this sermon. Third, 1741; Fourth, London: Printed and sold at the Foundery, 1754; Bristol: Pine, 1765; London: 1809.

Tyerman says of this sermon: "It led to the division which Whitefield so devoutly deprecates; also to the organisation of Lady Huntingdon's Connexion, and to the founding of the Calvinistic Methodists in Wales; and finally culminated in the fierce controversy of 1770 and the publication of Fletcher's unequalled *Checks*, which so effectually silenced the Calvinian heresy that its voice has scarce been heard from that time to this. Viewed in such a light, the difference between Wesley and Whitefield was really one of the greatest events in the history of Wesley, and even of the religion of the age."—*Life of Wesley*, i. 317. "It is one of the most able and eloquent of all his discourses, a triumphant specimen of impassioned argument."—Southey's *L. of Wesley*, 486.

12. NICODEMUS: or, a Treatise on the Fear of Man. Written in German by August Herman Frank. Abridg'd by John Wesley, M.A., Fellow of Lincoln College, Oxford. Bristol: S. and F. Farley, 1739. 8vo., pp. viii. 40.

Second Edition (not so called), London: W. Strahan, 1740, pp. viii. and 32. Third, Newcastle: Gooding, 1744; Fourth, Bristol: Farley, 1749; Another fourth, Dublin: Powell, 1749; Fifth, Bristol: Pine, 1767; Sixth, London: 1766; Another, London: Paramore, 1786; Seventh, London: Whitfield, 1798.

The preface, or dedication, to the original edition is dated "At Glaucha, by Hall, 1701." The same preface in Wesley's edition is dated October 26, 1731. The Treatise was written by August Herman Franke, Minister of Glaucha, and Professor of Divinity at the University of Hall (Halle), in 1701. It was translated in Scotland soon after. A second edition was published in Edinburgh, 1731. Wesley's appears to have been taken from this edition, but it is considerably abridged. It was a suitable pamphlet for the early Methodists.

13. AN EXTRACT OF THE REV. MR. JOHN WESLEY'S JOURNAL, from his embarking for Georgia to his return to London. (Rom. ix. 30, 31.) Bristol: Printed by S. and F. Farley, and sold at the New School-House in the Horse-Fair; and by the Booksellers in Town and Country. 12mo.; pp. iv. xxiv. 75. [No. i.]

Printed this year or the preceding, but the first edition has no date. The last paragraph of the Journal, No. I., was written in February, 1738, and No. II. of the Journal was published in 1740.

The beginning of Wesley's most interesting work. It embraces the Missionary period of his life.

  Second Edition, Bristol: Felix Farley, 1743; Third, Bristol, 1765; Fifth, London: Hawes, 1775

14. TWO TREATISES. The first, On Justification by Faith only, according to the Doctrine of the Eleventh Article of the Church of England. The second, On the Sinfulness of Man's natural Will, and his utter Inability to do Works acceptable to God, until he be justify'd and born again of the Spirit of God, according to the Doctrine of our Ninth, Tenth, Twelfth, and Thirteenth Articles. They are a Part of the Works of the Learned and Judicious Dr. Barnes, who had been for many years famous as a great Reviver of Learning in the University of Cambridge; he afterwards became a Protestant, and was martyr'd for the Faith in Smithfield in the Year 1541. To which is prefix'd a preface containing Some Account of the Life and Death of Dr. Barnes: Extracted from the Book of Martyrs. By John Wesley, A.M., Fellow of Lincoln College, Oxford. London: Printed and sold by John Lewis (Printer to the Religious Societies), in Bartholomew Close, near West Smithfield. 1739. 12mo., pp. 99.

Does not appear to have been reprinted.

15. HYMNS AND SACRED POEMS. Published by John Wesley, M.A., Fellow of Lincoln College, Oxford; and Charles Wesley, M.A., Student of Christ Church, Oxford. (Coloss. iii. 16.) London: Printed by William Strahan; and sold by James Hutton, Bookseller, at the Bible and Sun, without Temple-Bar; and at Mr. Bray's, a Brazier, in Little-Britain. 1739. 12mo., pp. xvi. 223.

  Second Edition, London: Strahan, 1739, pp. viii. 160 (differs from the first edition); Third, London: Strahan, 1739, pp. xvi. 223 (unabridged, almost a *fac-simile* of the first edition); Fourth, Bristol: Farley, 1743, pp. vi. 316, with contents and index; Another, Dublin: 1747; Fifth, London: 1756, pp. vi, 317, with contents and index.

This volume is on many accounts most interesting, chiefly as it contains the first printed hymns written by Charles Wesley. It is the first of four different books having the same title.

The preface is curious. It states that "some of the verses in the collection were wrote upon the scheme of the mystic divines;" and the confession is made, "These we once had in veneration as the best explainers of the Gospel of Christ; but we are now convinced we therein greatly erred, not knowing the Scriptures nor the power of God."

1740.

16. SERIOUS CONSIDERATIONS CONCERNING THE DOCTRINES OF ELECTION AND REPROBATION. Extracted from a late Author [Dr. Watts]. London : Printed in the year 1740. 12mo., pp. 12.

No name of author, editor, or printer.

Second edition, London : 1752 ; Third edition, Bristol : 1769 ; another, miscalled the third, London : Hawes, 1778 ; Sixth, London : Cordeux, 1813.

It has been doubted if the preface *To the Reader* is by John Wesley. It is not thought to be in his style ; it is not reprinted in Jackson's edition of the collected works ; but it is in Wesley's own edition (1771).

17. THE NATURE AND DESIGN OF CHRISTIANITY. Extracted from a late Author [W. Law]. London : printed by W. Strahan in the year 1740, 12mo., pp. 19.

Another, 1740, 16mo., pp. 23 ; Second edition, 1741 ; Third, 1742 ; Fourth, Newcastle-upon-Tyne : Gooding, 1743 ; Fifth, 1746 ; Sixth, London : Cock, 1769 ; Seventh, Foundery, 1754 ; Dublin : 1757 ; Seventh, London : J. Richardson, 1758 [Price 2d. or 12s. a hundred to those that give them away] ; another, London : Paramore, 1784 ; Eighth, 1755 ; another Eighth, Bristol : 1768 ; another, Bristol : Farley, n. d. ; Ninth, Bristol : 1771 ; Tenth, London : Hawes, n. d. ; Eleventh, 1793 ; Nineteenth, 1785 ; others, 1796 ; 1804 ; Louth, n. d. ; Dublin, n. d. ; an edition in French is dated Bristol : Chez Madame Farley, dans l'an 1758.

This is an abridgement of the first chapter of Law's *Practical Treatise upon Christian Perfection*, and is therefore an instalment of the abridgement of the entire work, published by Wesley in 1743 (No. 45).

18. AN EXTRACT OF THE REV. MR. JOHN WESLEY'S JOURNAL, from Feb. 1, 1737-8, to his Return from Germany. (1 Timothy i. 16.) London : printed by W. Strahan ; and sold at the Foundery, near Upper Moor-Fields ; and at James Hutton's, at the Bible and Sun without Temple-Bar. 1740. 12mo., pp. 90. [No. ii.]

Second edition, Bristol : F. Farley, 1743 ; Third, Bristol, 1765 ; Fifth, London : Hawes, 1775.

The Preface, dated London, Sep. 29, 1740, and signed John Wesley, contains a statement of his views respecting some of the doctrines of the Moravian Church. The Journal relates mainly to his religious experience previously to and immediately after his "conversion," which incident is narrated. It also contains an account of his visit to the Moravians in Germany.

19. HYMNS AND SACRED POEMS. Published by John Wesley, M.A., Fellow of Lincoln College, Oxford ; and Charles Wesley, M.A., Student of Christ-Church, Oxford. (Col. iii., 16.) London : Printed by W. Strahan ; and sold by

James Hutton, Bookseller, at the Bible and Sun without Temple-Bar, and at the Foundery, near Upper-Moor-Fields. 1740. 12mo., pp. xi. 207, iv.

Distinguished in early catalogues as Vol. II. Not republished separately, but incorporated with the Fourth (1743) and Fifth (1756) editions of the 1739 book, (No. 15). "Contains several admirable translations from the German, which doubtless came from the pen of John. The original hymns, among which are some of the finest in the English language, display a deep pathos with all the energy and daring of Charles's genius. The most remarkable hymn in the volume is one entitled, 'The just shall live by faith,' which describes Mr. Charles Wesley's religious history up to this period of his life."—Jackson's *Life of C. W.*, i. 243.

The volume is divided into two parts; the first comprising forty-one hymns, the second sixty-four. In the former appears for the first time, "Jesu, lover of my soul." The preface is peculiar. It relates to the way of salvation, which is the chief subject of the hymns; but some expressions in it, Wesley saw occasion afterwards to modify.—See *Plain Account of Christian Perfection*, pp. 27-30 (No. 238).

1741.

20. AN EXTRACT FROM THE REV. MR. JOHN WESLEY'S JOURNAL with regard to the Affidavit made by Captain Robert Williams. (John vii., 51.) London: printed in the year 1741. 12mo., pp. 12.

The affidavit is mentioned in the preface to the *Journal*, (*Works*, i. 3). See also Tyerman's *Life of Wesley*, i. 429-30.

This very rare tract consists of such portions of Wesley's Journal printed in 1739 (see No. 14) as relate to the accusation and trial of Wesley for refusing the Sacrament of the Lord's Supper to a communicant in Savannah. The first date given (p. 2) is June 25, 1736: it should be 1737. Not a little scurrilous writing appeared in reference to this event. Whitefield, in *The Weekly History*, very stoutly defends his friend, after having made careful enquiries into the circumstances on the spot.

21. AN EXTRACT OF THE LIFE OF MONSIEUR DE RENTY, a late Nobleman of France. Published by John Wesley, M.A., Fellow of Lincoln College, Oxford. (Gal. v. 6; James ii. 22.) London: Printed by W. Strahan; and sold at the Foundery, near Upper Moorfields; at James Hutton's, Bookseller, at the Bible and Sun without Temple Bar; and at John Lewis's in Bartholomew Close. 1741. [Price Stitch'd, Four-pence.] 12mo., pp. 67.

Second edition, Bristol: Farley, 1746; Third, Bristol: Grabham and Pine, 1760; Fourth, London, 1778; Fifth, London, 1788; Sixth, London: Whitfield, 1796; another, Dublin: J. Jones, 1802.

This is extracted from "*The Holy Life of Monr. De Renty, a late Nobleman of France and sometimes Councellor to King Lewis the 13th*. Written in French by John Baptist S. Jure, and faithfully translated into English, by E. S. Gent. London: John Crook, at the Sign of the Ship in St. Paul's Church-yard, 1658." The 358 pages of this translation are carefully abridged to 67.

Nos. 22-23-24. [1741.

"I ended the 'Abridgment of Mr. De Renty's Life.' O that such a life should be related by such an historian ! who by inserting all, if not more than all, the weak things that holy man ever said, or did . . . has cast the shade of superstition and folly over one of the brightest patterns of Heavenly Wisdom."—*Journal*, Jan. 6, 1738.

22. SERIOUS CONSIDERATIONS ON ABSOLUTE PREDESTINATION. Extracted from a late author, [R. Barclay.] Bristol: Printed by S. and F. Farley, in Castle Green. 1741. 12mo., pp. 24.

Editions unnumbered,—Bristol: 1770; London: 1790; London: Cordeux, 1816.

"We presented a thousand of Barclay to Mr. Whitefield's congregation on Sunday. On Sunday next I propose to distribute a thousand more at the Foundery."—Letter to C. W. *Works*, xii. 107.

23. A SHORT ACCOUNT OF THE DEATH OF MRS. HANNAH RICHARDSON. Published by Charles Wesley, M.A., Student of Christ-Church, Oxon. n.d. Half-title, 12mo., pp. 8.

No printer's name. Dated at beginning, Saturday, April 19, 1741.

Was often reprinted. Fifth edition, Newcastle : Gooding, 1743 ; Sixth, Bristol : F. Farley, 1748 ; Seventh, Foundery : 1754 ; Ninth, 1766 ; Tenth, 1775.

Some interesting particulars of the death and burial of this young woman are given in C. Wesley's *Journal* (April 17—21, 1741.) A hymn is appended which was sung at the funeral and was probably composed for the occasion. It appeared in a volume published the following year : see No. 40, page 131. "One of the most striking and effective antidotes to the peculiarities which were taught by Molther [the ' still ' heresy], that the brothers ever published. The entire tract, giving an account of her life and end, is written with singular terseness and spirit. It quickly passed through many editions, and ought never to be out of print. "—Jackson's *Life of C. Wesley*, i. 275.

24. A DIALOGUE BETWEEN A PREDESTINARIAN AND HIS FRIEND. Published by John Wesley, M.A., Fellow of Lincoln College, Oxford. London : Printed by W. Strahan, in the year 1741. 12mo., pp. 7.

The second edition, corrected and enlarged : "Out of Thine own Mouth !" added :—London : Strahan, 1741, pp. 12, preface added ; Third edition, Bristol : 1741 ; Third, Bristol : F. Farley, 1742 ; London : Cordeux, 1815 ; Another, 1816.

Joseph Gurney in 1778 affirmed that this was taken without acknowledgement from *A Dialogue between a Presbyterian and a Baptist*, by Grantham, 1696. Tyerman supports the accusation. Heylin says : " I have compared the two, and find that the charge is altogether groundless."

25. Reflections upon the Conduct of Human Life with reference to Learning and Knowledge. Extracted from Mr. Norris. 12mo., pp. 36.

Generally assigned to this year; but no compiler appears to have seen a copy of the first edition.

Second edition, London: Strahan, pp. 36, 1741; Third, London: Cock, 1755; Fourth, London: Hawes, 1776.

In this extract twenty-five chapters of the original work are omitted. At the end of the third edition is appended "A Scheme of Books suited to the preceding Reflections": see also *Works*, 1771, vol. viii.

26. An Extract of the Christian's Pattern: or, a Treatise of the Imitation of Christ. Written in Latin by Thomas a Kempis. Published by John Wesley, M.A., Fellow of Lincoln College, Oxford. London: Printed by W. Strahan, and sold at the Foundery, near Upper-Moor-Fields; at James Hutton's, Bookseller, at the Bible and Sun without Temple Bar; and at John Lewis's, in Bartholomew Close, 1741. [Price, stitch'd, eightpence.] 12mo., pp. 130

Other editions 1744; Bristol: F. Farley, 1746; Bristol: Grabham, 1759; London: Hawes, 1777; London: Paramore, 1780; one printed in the year 1788; London: Story, 1800. Frequently printed in 24 mo.

This is an abridgement of No. 3. Eight chapters are omitted from Book I, seventeen from Book III, and three from Book IV. The preface and the contents are also omitted.

"The Societies are not half supplied with books; not even with 'Kempis' . . . which ought to be in every house."—*Large Minutes*, 1763, page 23, (No. 221).

27. The Scripture Doctrine Concerning Predestination, Election, and Reprobation. Extracted from a late Author. By John Wesley, M.A., Fellow of Lincoln College, Oxford (1 Tim. iv. 10). London: Printed by W. Strahan; and sold by Thomas Harris, at the Looking-Glass and Bible on London Bridge; and at the Foundery, near Upper-Moor-Fields. 1741. 12mo., pp. 16.

Other editions, London: Hawes, 1775; Hawes: 1776; London: Paramore, 1782; New York: 1789, appended to "The Articles of Religion as received and taught in the Methodist Episcopal Church throughout the United States of America;" London: Cordeux, 1812; London: Mason, 1833.

Incorporated in the *Preservative against Unsettled Notions in Religion*, 1758, (No. 191).

Nos. 28-29-30. [1741.

28. THE ALMOST CHRISTIAN: a Sermon preached at St. Mary's, Oxford, before the University, on July 25, 1741. By John Wesley, M.A., Fellow of Lincoln College, Oxon. London: Printed by W. Strahan. 1741. [Price twopence.] 12mo., pp. 21.

Sixth edition, Sheffield: John Garnett, 1744; Sixth, Bristol: Farley, 1747; Seventh, Bristol: Farley, 1748; Ninth, Bristol: Grabham, 1758; Tenth, Bristol: 1762; Eleventh, Bristol: 1766; Twelfth, Bristol: Pine, 1770; Fifteenth, London: Hawes, 1780; others 1782, 1787.

"It being my turn (which comes about once in three years), I preached at St. Mary's, before the University. The harvest truly is plenteous. So numerous a congregation (from whatever motives they came) I have seldom seen at Oxford. My text was the confession of poor Agrippa, ' Almost thou persuadest me to be a Christian.' I have ' cast my bread upon the waters.' Let me ' find it again after many days.' "—*Journal*, Saturday, July 25, 1741.
"We met at ten to pray for a blessing on my brother's sermon, which he is preaching at this hour before the University."—Charles Wesley's *Journal*, same date. See curious note respecting this sermon in Tyerman's *Life of Wesley*, i. 362-3.

29. CHRISTIAN PERFECTION: a Sermon preached by John Wesley, M.A., Fellow of Lincoln-College, Oxford. London: Printed by W. Strahan, and sold by Thomas Harris, at the Looking-Glass and Bible on London Bridge, and at the Foundery, near Upper-Moor-Fields. 1741. [Price sixpence.] 12mo., pp. 48.

Appended is a hymn of 28 stanzas entitled " The Promise of Sanctification: Ezekiel xxxvi. 25, &c. By the Reverend Mr. Charles Wesley." It was afterwards published in *Hymns and Sacred Poems* of John and Charles Wesley, 1742, page 258.

Second edition, Newcastle: Gooding, 1743.

"I think it was in the latter end of the year 1740 that I had a conversation with Dr. Gibson, then Bishop of London, at Whitehall. He asked me what I meant by *perfection*. I told him without any disguise or reserve. When I ceased speaking he said, ' Mr. Wesley, if this be all you mean, publish it to all the world.' I answered, ' My lord, I will,' and accordingly wrote and published the sermon on *Christian Perfection*."—*Plain Account of Christian Perfection*, page 19; No. 238. Tyerman thinks this was Wesley's first publication this year; but it does not appear in a catalogue at the end of *The Almost Christian*, in which nearly every other publication of the year is mentioned.

30. A COLLECTION OF PSALMS AND HYMNS. Published by John Wesley, M.A., Fellow of Lincoln College, Oxford. London: Printed by W. Strahan; and sold at the Foundery near Upper Moorfields; at James Hutton's, Bookseller, at the Bible and Sun without Temple-Bar; and at John Lewis's in Bartholomew-Close. 1741. [Price, bound, One Shilling.] 12mo., pp. iv. 126.

Divided into two parts: Part I containing 77 Psalms and Hymns; Part II, 75. A title is prefixed to each Psalm or Hymn; some of the Hymns are divided into two, or more, parts. The table of contents is inaccurate.

Second edition, enlarged, London: Strahan, 1743, pp. 138. "Charles Wesley, M.A., Student of Christ-Church, Oxford," is inserted on the title page. Though this edition is said to be "enlarged," the total number of Psalms and Hymns is less than in the first edition. There are 68 in Part I, and 62 in Part II. Several additional psalms are inserted, but fewer hymns. The number of pages is greater. Several changes are made in the arrangement. The third edition varies from the second. Third edition, enlarged, London: 1744; Fourth, enlarged, Bristol: 1748; Fifth, London: II. Cock, 1751; Fifth, Bristol: Grabham, 1760; Sixth, London: 1756, no printer's name; Ditto, Bristol: Pine, 1762; Seventh, Bristol: Pine, 1765; Eighth, Bristol: Pine, 1773; Ninth, London: Hawes, 1776; Tenth, London: Hawes, 1779; Eleventh, London: Paramore, 1789; London: Printed in the year 1791; Twelfth, London: Paramore, 1794; Thirteenth, London: G. Story, 1808; Fourteenth, London: Cordeux, 1813; Fifteenth, 1818; Sixteenth, London: Cordeux, 1815, long 12mo.; Another, 1823; Eighteenth, London: Cordeux, 1818, long 12mo.; Seventeenth, London: J. Kershaw (printed by J. Nichols), 1824, long 12mo; Eighteenth, London: 1825, 24mo.

"The Eighteenth edition, 24mo., 1825, was the last published. There were, however, at least twenty-three editions, as I have seen that number, and probably there were more."—Heylin.

An abridged edition was bound up with the *Sunday Service* (see Nos. 376, 378).

This is the third book published with this title.

31. HYMNS ON GOD'S EVERLASTING LOVE. To which is added the Cry of a Reprobate, and the Horrible Decree. Bristol: printed by S. and F. Farley, at Shakespear's Head, in Castle Green. 1741. 12mo., pp. 36.

Contains 18 hymns, neither hymns nor verses numbered. Four verses of the 14th hymn are omitted in the *Poetical Works* (iii. 31). The weird "Cry of a Reprobate" was republished in Jackson's *Life of C. Wesley*.

32. HYMNS ON GOD'S EVERLASTING LOVE. London: printed by W. Strahan: and sold by T. Harris, at the Bible and Looking Glass on London Bridge and at the Foundery, near Upper Moor Fields. Price fourpence. No date. 12mo., pp. 60.

Contains 28 hymns. Of the first 17, 16 are numbered, the 14th being unnumbered. After them are eleven hymns under the title *Gloria Patri*, numbered consecutively, 1 to 11.

A second edition of the first (though not numbered as such) was published at Bristol the same year, probably to meet the great demand in London; see *Works*, xii. 107. The two tracts were published together in 1756 without any author's or printer's name; and having the title, "HYMNS ON GOD'S EVERLASTING LOVE. In two parts. The Second edition. London: printed in the year 1756." 12mo., pp. 84. This edition differs from the First thus:—Part I., Four verses are omitted from hymn 14; Part II., Hymns 12 and 13 are omitted; and from *Gloria Patri*, Nos. 2, 7, 8, 9, 10, and 11.

No. 33. [1742.

Third, Bristol: Pine, 1770; 17th hymn omitted from this and subsequent editions. Fourth, London: Hawes, 1779; Another, Paramore, 1792.

"This is the blasphemy clearly contained in the *horrible decree* of predestination, and here I fix my foot."—Sermon on Free Grace, (No. 11). Wesley did not coin the phrase *The Horrible Decree*. A work had previously appeared with the following title, *Fate and Destiny inconsistent with Christianity: or*, THE HORRID DECREE *of Absolute, Unconditional Election and Reprobation fully detected. Showing the grand error of asserting that Christ did not die for all men, but for an elect number only. In eight Conferences between Epenetus and Eutychus.* By Edward Bird. London: Rivington, 1726. (See also, Calvin's use of the term, quoted in *Poetical Works of J. and C. Wesley*, Vol. iii. pref. note xviii).

This being the first anonymous publication of hymns by the Wesleys, it may be proper to refer to the fact that the brothers agreed not to distinguish their hymns. The editor of the *Poetical Works* says that any distinction now attempted must be to a great extent, if not wholly, conjectural. But his own inquiries have led him to think it likely that John Wesley contributed more largely to these joint publications than is commonly supposed; and that the habit of attributing almost everything found in them to his brother, is scarcely consistent with a due regard to accuracy.—(Adv. vol. viii. p. xv.)

1742.

33. A SERMON preach'd on Sunday, April 4, 1742; before the University of Oxford. By Charles Wesley, M.A., Student of Christ-Church. London: Printed by W. Strahan, and sold by Thomas Harris, at the Looking Glass and Bible, on London Bridge; by Tho. Trye, at Gray's-Inn-Gate, Holborn; and at the Foundery, near Upper-Moor-Fields, 1742. [Price Two-pence.] 12mo., pp. 29. [Text, Ephesians, v. 14.]

The Second edition, London: Strahan, 1742; Third, London: Strahan, 1742; Fifth, Bristol: F. Farley, 1743; Fifth, Newcastle; Seventh, 1745; Tenth, Bristol: 1745; Twelfth, Bristol: Farley, 1749; Thirteenth, Bristol: Grabham, n.d.; Fifteenth, London: 1749; Sixteenth, London: Cock, 1749; Nineteenth, Bristol: Pine, 1761; Twentieth, London: H. Fenwick, 1763; Twentieth, Bristol: 1763; Twenty-first, London: 1767; Twenty-first, Bristol: W. Pine, 1770; Twenty-second, London: 1771; Twenty-third, 1775; Twenty-sixth, London: Paramore, 1780; Twenty-sixth, London: 1782; Twenty-seventh, London: Hindmarsh, 1782; London: Paramore, 1783, with the words "This Sermon is not to be sold, but given away," on the title-page; Another in 1784; Twenty-seventh, 1786; Another, 1789; Twenty-ninth, 1790.

The Sermon was advertised as "Recommended by Mr. Whitefield," in *The Weekly History* (London: Lewis, Saty., May 8, 1742).

John Wesley writes in his Journal (*Works*, i. 364), "About two in the afternoon, being the time my brother was preaching at Oxford, before the University, I desired a few persons to meet with me, and join in prayer. We continued herein much longer than we at first designed, and believed we had the petition we asked of God."

"It is doubtful whether any Sermon in the English language, or in any language upon earth, has passed through so many editions, or has been a means of so much spiritual good." (See Jackson's *Life of C. Wesley*, i., 310; also for other particulars.)

34. THE CHARACTER OF A METHODIST. By John Wesley, M.A., Fellow of Lincoln College in Oxford. ("Not as though I had already attained.") Bristol: printed by Felix Farley, and sold at his Printing Office, in Castle-Green, and by J. Wilson, in Wine-street; in London: by Thomas Trye, near Gray's-Inn-Gate, and Thomas Harris, on the Bridge and at the Foundery. 1742. 12mo., pp. 20.

On pp. 18-20 is a hymn of sixteen stanzas entitled, "The Whole Armour of God," afterwards published in Charles Wesley's Hymns and Sacred Poems, vol. I., p. 236 (No. 138). The hymn appears to have been omitted after the second edition.

Second edition, Bristol: F. Farley, 1742, precisely as first edition; Another, London: 1742; Third, Newcastle: Gooding, 1743; London: 1743, (*French*); Fifth, London: 1745; Another, Dublin: S. Powell, 1747; Seventh, Bristol: Farley, 1751; Seventh, London: Cock, 1751; Eighth, Bristol: 1763; Ninth, London: 1765; Ninth, Bristol: W. Pine, 1769; Tenth, London: Paramore, 1786; Thirteenth, London: Story, 1802; Sixteenth, London: Cordeux, 1814; Another, London: Mason, 1835.

The greater part of this tract is incorporated, in a condensed form, in the *Plain Account of Christian Perfection*, 1765 (No. 238); and of it Wesley says, "These are the very words, wherein I largely declared, for the first time, my sentiments of Christian Perfection," *ib*. p. 17. He had previously, to some extent, treated of the subject in the *Sermon on Christian Perfection* (No. 29).

35. THE PRINCIPLES OF A METHODIST. By John Wesley, M.A., Fellow of Lincoln-College, Oxford. Occasioned by a late Pamphlet, intitled, "A Brief History of the Principles of Methodism." [By Rev. Joseph Tucker, Vicar of All Saints, Bristol.] Bristol: Printed by Felix Farley, and sold at his shop in Castle Green, and by John Wilson, in Wine Street: in London, by Thomas Trye, near Gray's-Inn-Gate, and Thomas Harris, on the Bridge; and at the Foundery, Upper-Moor-Fields. 1742. 12mo., pp. ii. 32.

Second edition, Bristol: Felix Farley, 1746; Edition not numbered, Dublin: S. Powell, 1747; Third, London: 1756; Fourth, London: R. Hawes, 1777; Unnumbered, London, for the Author, 1789; London: Whitfield, 1796.

The date on the title page is 1742. The pamphlet which "occasioned" it not having been published till July, 1742, it is clear that the book cannot have been issued before this year; and, therefore, that the date of 1740, given in all the editions of *Wesley's Works*, must be an error. It does not appear in any catalogue before 1742.

Wesley says: "I have often wrote on controversial points before, but not with any particular person, so that this is the first time I have appeared in controversy properly so called. I now tread an untried path with fear and trembling; fear not of my adversary, but of myself."—Preface to the reader. It is a brave defence of his teaching.

36. A COMPANION FOR THE ALTAR. Extracted from Thomas a Kempis. By John Wesley, M.A., Fellow of Lincoln-College, Oxon. Bristol: F. Farley. 1742. 12mo., pp. 24.

Second edition, Bristol: Felix Farley, 1742; Third, London: W. Strahan, 1744; Fourth, London: 1750; Fourth, Dublin: Powell, 1748; Fifth, London: Cock, 1755; Sixth, Bristol: 1761; Another, Bristol: 1765; Another, Bristol: Pine, 1769; Another, called the Eighth, London: Hawes, 1769.

This is taken from Book iv. of *The Christian's Pattern* (No. 3) as it appears in *The Extract* of the same (No. 26); but it is a little further condensed. It was kept constantly on sale.

37. AN EXTRACT OF THE REVD. MR. JOHN WESLEY'S JOURNAL, from August 12, 1738, to Nov. 1, 1739. (Acts v. 38, 39.) Bristol: Printed by Felix Farley, and sold at his shop in Castle-Green, and by John Wilson, in Wine-Street; In London, by Thomas Trye, near Grey's-Inn-Gate, and Thomas Harris, on the Bridge; and at the Foundery, in Upper-Moor-Fields. 1742. 12mo., pp. iv., 98. [No. iii.]

Second edition, Bristol: Felix Farley, 1748; Third, 1748; Unnumbered, London: Sold at the New Chapel, City-Road, 1788; Another, London: 1805.

Both Wesley and his work were greatly traduced from the beginning. In defence he published these extracts from his extensive MS. Journals, and so was led to give to the world one of the most interesting and instructive records of ministerial labour ever written.

"What I design in the following extract is openly to declare to all mankind, what it is that the Methodists (so-called) have done and are doing now,"—*Preface*.

38. A COLLECTION OF TUNES SET TO MUSIC, AS THEY ARE COMMONLY SUNG AT THE FOUNDERY. London: Printed by A. Pearson, and sold by T. Harris, at the Looking-Glass and Bible, on London-Bridge; T. Trye, at Gray's-Inn-Gate, Holborn, and at the Foundery, near Upper-Moor-Fields. 1742. 12mo., pp. 36.

There are 42 Tunes, the melody only is printed, with a verse of a hymn interlined. At the head of each tune is its name, with a reference to the page in vol. I., II., or III., of *Hymns and Sacred Poems* (Nos. 15, 19, 40,) from which the hymn is taken. The notation is very curious.

This is the first Methodist Tune-book. On this account, and from the character of the tunes, it is full of interest. These are really *the* "Old Methodist Tunes."

It was reproduced in *fac-simile*, with a preface by Osborn; (London: Woolmer, 1882).

39. AN ELEGY ON THE DEATH OF ROBERT JONES, ESQ., OF FONMON-CASTLE, IN GLAMORGANSHIRE, SOUTH-WALES. (Wisdom of Solomon V., 3, 4, 5). By Charles Wesley, M.A., Student of Christ-Church, Oxford. Bristol: Printed by F. Farley, and sold at his shop in Castle-Green. 1742. 4to., pp. 26.

Second edition, Bristol: F. Farley, 1748, (12mo., pp. 22); another, not numbered, London: Printed and sold at New Chapel, 1789. Reprinted in *A Collection of Moral and Sacred Poems*, published by Wesley, 1744, in three vols. (No. 58); in Charles Wesley's Journal, 1849; and in *Bards of Epworth*, 1856.

In this elegy on a fellow-collegian, a convert under his ministry and an attached friend, Charles Wesley "describes Mr. Jones's early life, conversion, subsequent piety, exemplary conduct as a husband and a father, his attachment to the Church of England, catholic spirit, fidelity to his Christian profession, and triumphant death," –*Life of C. W.*, i. 314. In spirited verse his friend endeavours to

"Bring back his virtues into open day,
The sinner, convert, friend, and dying saint display."

40. HYMNS AND SACRED POEMS. Published by John Wesley, M.A., Fellow of Lincoln-College, Oxford, and Charles Wesley, M.A., Student of Christ Church, Oxford. (Titus ii. 11-14.) Bristol: Printed and sold by Felix Farley, in Castle-Green; J. Wilson, in Wine-Street; and at the School-Room in the Horse-Fair; in Bath by W. Frederick, Bookseller; and in London by T. Harris, on the Bridge; also at the Foundery, in Upper-Moor-Fields. 1742. 12mo. pp. xii. 304. viii., and one page of *errata*.

The preface, on Christian Perfection, "the subject of many of the verses," is evidently by John Wesley.

Second edition bears date 1743; another 1745, both Bristol: Farley. The former was sold "also by A. Bradford, in Philadelphia." Third edition, London: Printed in the year 1756.

This is the third volume having the same title, and is called Vol. III. in some early catalogues. It is divided into Parts I and II; the former containing fifty-one hymns, the latter one hundred and ten, of which seven are "Hymns for Children." "Five of these, with four from other sources and some prayers, appear to have been soon after published in a separate form, without title, name, or date," (Osborn): see also No. 99.

In this volume "Gentle Jesus, meek and mild, Look upon a little child," and "Wrestling Jacob," appear for the first time.

41. A COLLECTION OF HYMNS published by John Wesley, M.A., Fellow of Lincoln-College, Oxford; and Charles Wesley, M.A., Student of Christ-Church, Oxford. [Price Three-pence.] London: Printed by W. Strahan. 1742. 12mo., pp. 36.

Another edition, London : Strahan, 1743, with the additional words on the title-page, "Extracted from the First volume of Hymns and Sacred Poems" (No. 15); Another Dublin : S. Powell, 1749 ; Another Belfast : James Magee, 1750. One of the editions is said to be priced two-pence.

"Another beautiful illustration of Wesley's desire to elevate the poor is found in the publication of this tract. The book from which it was extracted sold for two-and-sixpence, and was out of their reach. He therefore selected twenty-four of the choicest pieces contained in it, and sold them at three-pence, a tenth part of the price of the volume."—Osborn, *Meth. Bib.*, p. 12.

1743.

42. THOUGHTS ON MARRIAGE AND A SINGLE LIFE. By John Wesley, M.A., Fellow of Lincoln College, Oxon. Bristol: Printed by Felix Farley ; and sold by the Booksellers of Bristol, Bath, London, Newcastle upon Tyne, and Exeter; as also by A. Bradford in Philadelphia. 1743. 12mo., pp. 12.

Second edition, Bristol : F. Farley, 1743.

A short and thoughtful tract, written in Wesley's condensed style, in reply to a question frequently asked of him, "Which is to be preferred, a married state or a single life," and because he had never seen " any treatise upon it that was just and agreeable to Holy Writ, and at the same time short and so plain that every reader of a common capacity might understand it."

It is sometimes named in catalogues, *Thoughts on Marriage and Celibacy.*

43. THE NATURE, DESIGN, AND GENERAL RULES OF THE UNITED SOCIETIES, IN LONDON, BRISTOL, KING'S-WOOD, AND NEWCASTLE UPON TYNE. Printed by John Gooding, on the Side. [Price one penny.] 1743, 12mo., pp. 12.

Signed by John Wesley only, and dated February 22, 1742-3. A hymn of eighteen verses, entitled, " A Prayer for those who are Convinced of Sin," follows the Rules in this edition, and in several of those published during the lifetime of Wesley.

Second edition, Bristol : Farley, dated May 1, 1743; the " I " in paragraph 7, page 9, is exchanged for " We," and the name of Charles Wesley is added, as in all subsequent editions. Third, Bristol : Farley, 1743 ; Fourth, London : Strahan, 1744, (on the title-page of this edition are added the words "To which are subjoin'd the Rules of the Band Societies"); Fifth, Bristol : Farley, 1747 ; Fifth, Dublin : 1747 ; Sixth, Dublin : Powell, 1758, (two hymns) ; Sixth, London : 1750 ; Seventh, London : T. Pasham, 1755 ; Eighth, London : 1756 ; Eighth, London : 1764 ; Ninth, London : 1766 ; also Bristol, 1769 ; Tenth, Bristol : Pine, 1770 ; Tenth, London : 1772, (dated at the end May 1, 1764) ; Eleventh, London : Hawes, 1774 ; Sixteenth, London : Hawes, 1776 ; Seventeenth, London : Paramore, 1781 ; Eighteenth, London : Paramore, 1782 ; Nineteenth, London : Paramore, 1787 ; another Nineteenth, 1785 ; Twenty-first, London : 1790 ; Twenty-second, London : Paramore, 1793 ; Twenty-third, London : Paramore, 1794 ; another, 1796 ; one not numbered, London : G. Story, 1800 ; many subsequently.

1743.] **Nos. 44-45.**

In some editions the following curious addition is made to the rule forbidding the wearing of costly apparel,—" particularly the wearing of Calashes, Highheads, or enormous Bonnets." From the twenty-third edition (1794), "To receive what they are willing to give *toward the relief of the poor*," is changed, as to the latter phrase, into, "*for the support of the Gospel.*" Towards the close of the century, the wording of the Rules was for some time much altered.

In the fourth edition (1744) are added "THE RULES OF THE BAND SOCIETIES, drawn up Dec. 25, 1738," together with "DIRECTIONS GIVEN TO THE BAND SOCIETIES, Dec. 25, 1744." The hymn is omitted. The fifth edition is restored to the original form. These Rules and Directions were afterwards often reprinted as a separate pamphlet, (12mo., pp. 4) : see No. 57, also *Min. Conf.* 1749, page 4. (No. 136).

44. A WORD IN SEASON : or, Advice to a Soldier. (1. Tim. vi. 12.) Newcastle upon Tyne : Printed by John Gooding, on the Side. Sold by R. Akenhead, on Tyne Bridge, Newcastle ; by T. Trye, at Gray's-Inn-Gate, Holbourn ; at the Foundery, near Moor-Fields, London ; and at the New School in the Horse Fair, Bristol, 1744. [Price one penny.] 12mo., pp. 8.

The above is a copy of the title-page of the earliest edition I have seen. The book, however, must have been written in this year or sooner ; for Charles Wesley mentions his giving a copy to the captain of the mob at Sheffield, May 25, 1743,—*Journal*, vol. i., p. 328. It is frequently mentioned in the early catalogues under the heading "Books published by Mr. John Wesley," but for the first time in 1743. It was also issued with the title *Advice to a Sailor*. No copy appears with the writer's name ; but the style is sufficient evidence of the authorship.

An edition, London : 1756 ; another, London : 1789.

This is the first of a number of "WORDS" addressed to various classes of people, published at different times, and generally of four pages in extent.

45. A PRACTICAL TREATISE ON CHRISTIAN PERFECTION. Extracted from a late Author [W. Law] by John Wesley, M.A., Fellow of Lincoln College, Oxon. Newcastle upon Tyne : Printed by John Gooding, on the Side ; sold by R. Akenhead, on Tyne-Bridge, Newcastle ; by T. Trye, at Gray's-Inn-Gate, Holbourn ; at the Foundery, near Upper-Moor-Fields, London ; and at the New School in the Horse-Fair, Bristol. 1743. [Price One Shilling]. 12mo., pp. 115.

This is a very carefully prepared extract from *A Practical Treatise upon Christian Perfection*, by William Law, A.M. (London : Innys, 1726. 8vo., pp. 546). The influence of Law's writings upon Wesley's mind was very great, although he did not wholly agree with his views. He says "In 1727 I read Mr. Law's 'Christian Perfection,' and 'Serious Call,' and more explicitly resolved to be all devoted to God, in body, soul and spirit."—Letter in *Journal*, May 14, 1765. See also *Works*, i. 99, x. 403, &c.

Nos. 46-47-48. [1744.

46. THE PILGRIM'S PROGRESS from this World to that which is to come. Abridged by John Wesley, M.A., Fellow of Lincoln College, Oxford. (1 Cor. i. 27.) Newcastle upon Tyne: Printed by John Gooding, on the Side; sold by R. Akenhead, on Tyne-Bridge, Newcastle; by T. Trye, at Gray's-Inn-Gate, Holbourn; at the Foundery, near Upper-Moor-Fields, London; and at the New School in the Horse Fair, Bristol. 1743. [Price Fourpence.] 12mo., pp. 49.

Second edition, Newcastle: Gooding, 1744; another Second, London: 1745; Third, Bristol: Farley, 1748; Fourth, London: Trye, 1758; Fifth, Bristol: Pine, 1766; Sixth, London: Paramore, 1787; Eighth, London: Story, 1802.

This abridgement was prepared doubtless for the benefit of the poor. The allegory is compressed to the utmost degree, and thereby of course the picturesque quaintness of the inimitable original is sacrificed. Works of art will not bear such treatment. It cannot be called one of Wesley's successful works, however good his aim may have been.

47. AN EARNEST APPEAL TO MEN OF REASON AND RELIGION. By John Wesley, M.A., Fellow of Lincoln-College, Oxford. (John vii. 51.) Newcastle upon Tyne. Printed by John Gooding, on the Side. [Price Sixpence.] 1743, 12mo., pp. 59.

Second edition, Bristol: F. Farley, 1743. On page 53 of this edition is found a hymn entitled "Primitive Christianity," of two parts, of fourteen and sixteen stanzas respectively. Third edition, Bristol: Farley, 1744; Another, miscalled the third, Bristol: Farley, 1749, has appended a second hymn, "For a Person called forth to bear his Testimony"; Fourth, Dublin: S. Powell, 1747; Fifth, Dublin: Powell, 1750; Sixth, Bristol: 1765; Another Sixth, Bristol: Pine, 1771; Another, also called the Sixth, 1775; Seventh, London: Paramore, 1786; Eighth, 1796.

Wesley describes it to be, "a plain account both of our principles and our actions." He dwells on the nature and reasonableness of true religion, addressing himself chiefly to "those who do not receive the Christian system as of God." He then enters upon a defence of Scriptural principles, which he applies in fervent appeals to religious professors, especially to members of the Church of England. See also Telford's *Life of John Wesley*, pp. 327-8.

In his collected works (1772), Wesley says this was published in 1744. This is plainly a mistake, for both the first and second editions bear date 1743; and it is in more than one catalogue of that year. As he quotes the rhyme, which is not appended to the first edition, it is probable he had a later one before him.

1744.

48. A SERIOUS CALL TO A HOLY LIFE. Extracted from a late Author [W. Law.] By John Wesley, M.A., Fellow of Lincoln College, Oxford. Newcastle-upon-Tyne: Printed by John Gooding, on the Side; sold by R. Akenhead, on Tyne-Bridge, Newcastle; by T. Trye, at

1744.]　　　　　　　　　　　　　　　　　　　　　　　　**Nos. 49-50.**

Gray's Inn Gate, Holbourn; at the Foundery, near Upper-Moor Fields, London; and at the New School in the Horse-Fair, Bristol. 1744. [Price Two Shillings.] 12mo., pp. iv. 230.

An edition, presumably the second, but not so called, London: Paramore, 1784. In this are the words, often inserted at that time, "This book not to be sold, but given away." Third edition, entitled "An Abridgment of Mr. Law's Serious Call to a Holy Life." London: G. Story, 1804.

"A treatise which will hardly be excelled, if it be equalled, in the English tongue, either for beauty of expression, or for justness and depth of thought."—Wesley's *Works*, vii. 297. "The most famous, if not the greatest of all Law's Works. Next to the Bible it contributed more than any other book to the rise and spread of the great evangelical revival of the eighteenth century."—Canon Overton's *Life of Law*, p. 109.

The "Extract of the Christian's Pattern," the "Treatise on Christian Perfection," and the "Serious Call" were sometimes bound together in one volume.

49.　THE DISTINGUISHING MARKS OF A WORK OF THE SPIRIT OF GOD. Extracted from Mr. Edwards, Minister of Northampton, in New-England. By John Wesley, M A., Fellow of Lincoln-College, Oxford. London: Printed by W. Strahan; and sold by T. Trye, near Gray's-Inn-Gate, Holbourn; and at the Foundery, near Upper Moor Fields. 1744. [Price Four-pence.] 12mo., pp. 48.

Second edition, London: Cock, 1755; Third edition, London: Paramore, 1795.

The work from which this is extracted is thus advertised in the *Weekly History*, May 15, 1742:—

"*The Distinguishing Marks of a Work of the Spirit of God*, applied to that uncommon operation that has lately appeared on the minds of many of the people in New-England. With a particular consideration of the Extraordinary Circumstances with which this work is attended. By Jonathan Edwards, A.M., Pastor of the Church of Christ, at Northampton; which was lately re-printed in London and recommended by the Rev. Dr. J. Watts, with a Preface by the Rev. Mr. Cooper, of Boston, giving some account of the present work of God in those parts, and some Letters of Dr. Coleman to Dr. Watts. Boston: 1741. London: re-printed for S. Mason, 1742.

N. B.—The above Discourse is earnestly recommended (by the Rev. Mr. Whitefield, and the Rev. Mr. Wesley) to the serious perusal of all Christians of all Denominations, especially to Ministers."

50.　EXTRACT OF COUNT ZINZENDORF'S DISCOURSES on the Redemption of Man by the Death of Christ. By John Wesley, M.A., Fellow of Lincoln College, Oxford. Newcastle-upon-Tyne: Printed by John Gooding, on the Side; sold by R. Akenhead, on Tyne Bridge, Newcastle;

Nos. 51-52. [1744.

by T. Trye, at Gray's-Inn-Gate, Holbourn, at the Foundery, near Upper-Moor-Fields, London ; and at the New-School in the Horse-Fair, Bristol. 1744. [Price Six-pence.] 12mo., pp. 78.

Extracted from "Sixteen Discourses upon Luther's Explanation of the Second Article of the Creed." Wesley, at first much impressed by the Moravians, and deeply indebted to several of them for help in one period of his spiritual life, was obliged, at length, to separate entirely from them. See Preface to Fourth Extract from Journal (No. 53). Never re-printed.

51. THE LIFE OF GOD IN THE SOUL OF MAN; or, the Nature and Excellency of the Christian Religion. Abridged by John Wesley, M A., Fellow of Lincoln College, Oxford (Eph. iv. 18, Gal. ii. 20, Rom. viii. 14). Newcastle-upon-Tyne : Printed by John Gooding, on the Side ; sold by R. Akenhead, on Tyne Bridge, Newcastle ; by T. Trye, at Gray's-Inn-Gate, Holbourn ; at the Foundery, near Upper-Moor-Fields, London ; and at the New-School in the Horse-Fair, Bristol. 1744. [Price fourpence.] 12mo., pp. 48.

Second edition, Bristol : F. Farley, 1748, evidently printed from the same type as the first edition, except the title-page ; another, Dublin : Powell, 1748 ; Third, London : Printed in the year 1756 ; Third, Bristol : Pine, 1770 ; Fourth, London : 1777 ; Fifth, London : 1790 ; Sixth, London : Whitfield, 1797.

This treatise was written by Henry Scougall, A.M., Sometime Professor of Divinity in King's College, Aberdeen. He was the son of Bishop Scougall, and died in the year 1678. The book was first published in 1677, without the author's name, by Bishop Burnet. It was a favourite with the Wesleys when at Oxford. Charles Wesley lent it to Whitefield, who says of it, "Though I had fasted, watched and prayed, and received the Sacrament so long, yet I never knew what *true religion* was till God sent me that excellent treatise by the hand of my never-to-be-forgotten friend."—Tyerman's *L. of Whitefield*, i. 17. Wesley recommended it to all his preachers.

52. A BRIEF ACCOUNT OF THE OCCASION, PROCESS, AND ISSUE OF A LATE TRYAL at the Assize, held at Gloucester, the third of March, 1743. Between some of the people call'd Methodists, Plaintiffs, and certain Persons of the Town of Minchin-Hampton, in the said county, Defendants. Extracted from Mr. Whitefield's Letter. By John Wesley, A.M., Fellow of Lincoln College, Oxford. (Acts xix. 35—40,) [Preface is signed by John Wesley and dated May 1, 1744.] Bristol. 1744. 12mo., pp. 12.

Another, Bristol : Farley, 1748, unnumbered.

A hymn of ten stanzas, entitled "A prayer for His Majesty King George," was appended. It was afterwards printed in *Hymns for Times of Trouble and Persecution*, (No. 59).

This is from an account of an action commenced by Whitefield against the ringleaders of a mob that assailed him and his congregation in Minchin-Hampton. It was published by him in *A Letter to a Friend* (London : J. Robinson, 1744. 8vo., pp. 15).

53. AN EXTRACT OF THE REVEREND MR. JOHN WESLEY'S JOURNAL, from November 1, 1739, to September 3, 1741. (Job. xxxii. 16, 17, 21, 22.) London : Printed by W. Strahan ; and sold by T. Trye, at Gray's-Inn-Gate, Holbourn ; and at the Foundery, near Upper-Moor Fields. 1744. [Price One Shilling.] 12mo., pp. 120. [No. iv].

Second edition, Bristol : Felix Farley, 1749.

Prefixed is a letter to the Moravian Church, " more especially that part of it now or lately residing in England." It is signed by John Wesley, and dated June 24, 1744. The same date appears at the end of the Journal. Two hymns are appended.

The special interest of this Extract arises from its containing exact accounts of Wesley's relations with the Moravians. In the letter prefixed he speaks with much plainness and openness, not hesitating to tell them, in a fraternal spirit, both what he approved and what he disapproved in their opinions and conduct.

54. A NARRATIVE OF THE LATE WORK OF GOD AT AND NEAR NORTHAMPTON, IN NEW ENGLAND. Extracted from Mr. Edwards's Letter to Dr. Coleman. By John Wesley, M.A., Fellow of Lincoln College, Oxford. Bristol : Printed by Felix Farley, and sold by him at his house in Castle Green ; at the Schoolroom in the Horse Fair, and by J. Wilson in Wine Street. In London : by T. Trye, near Gray's Inn Gate, Holborn ; Henry Butler, at the corner of Bow Churchyard, and at the Foundery, near Moorfields. In Exeter by B. Thorne and E. Score ; as also at the several societies in England. n.d. 12mo., pp. 48.

Second edition, London : H. Cock, 1755.

Wesley writes in his Journal, Oct. 9, 1738, "I set out for Oxford. In walking, I read the truly-surprising narrative of the conversions lately wrought in and about the town of Northampton, in New England." He sent an extract to a friend, whose reply threw him into great perplexity, and led him to much heart-searching, which is recorded at some length in his Journal, (see *Works*, i. 160-3).

I am quite unable to assign the precise date of the publication of this pamphlet. There is no date upon the title-page, nor any that affords any clue in the body of the work. There is one—Friday, June 27, 1743 ; but this is obviously an error : it should be 1740. It was certainly not published for some considerable time after Wesley read the account in 1738. Osborn and Tyerman assign it to 1742 ; Heylin to 1744. It does not appear in any catalogue till 1745. Probably 1744 is the proper date.

55. SCRIPTURAL CHRISTIANITY. A Sermon preached August 24, 1744, at St. Mary's Church in Oxford, before the University. By John Wesley, M.A., Fellow of Lincoln College (Ezek. xxxiii. 4). London: Printed by W. Strahan, and sold by T. Trye, near Gray's-Inn-Gate, Holbourn, Henry Butler, at the corner of Bow Church-Yard; and at the Foundery near Upper Moorfields. 1744. (Price Threepence). 12mo., pp. 31.

Preface to the Reader is dated Octob. 20, 1744, and signed John Wesley.

Fourth edition, London: Strahan, 1744; Fifth, London: 1744; another, not numbered, Newcastle: Gooding, 1744; Fifth, Newcastle: 1745; Sixth, Bristol: F. Farley, 1748; Sixth, Bristol: 1748; Sixth, Dublin: 1749; another, London: Hawes, 1775; London: Whitfield, 1798.

In the Preface, Wesley says he should not have printed the sermon, but for the false and scurrilous accounts of it which had been published in every corner of the nation.

"Friday, August 24 (St. Bartholomew's Day). I preached, I suppose the last time, at St. Mary's. Be it so. I am now clear of the blood of these men. I have fully delivered my own soul. . . . It was determined that when my next turn to preach came, they would pay another person to preach for me. And so they did twice or thrice, even to the time that I resigned my Fellowship."—*Eccles. Hist.*, iv., 187 (No. 355).

"At ten I walked with my brother, and Mr. Piers and Meriton, to St. Mary's, where my brother bore his testimony before a crowded audience, much increased by the racers. Never have I seen a more attentive congregation. They did not let a word slip them. Some of the Heads stood up the whole time and fixed their eyes on him. If they can endure sound doctrine like this, he will surely leave a blessing behind him. The Vice-Chancellor sent after him and desired his notes; which he sealed up and sent immediately."—C. Wesley's *Journal*. See also Jackson's *Life of C. Wesley*, i. 402-3.

56. THE CASE OF JOHN NELSON. Written by Himself. (Amos iii. 8.) London: Printed in the year 1745. 12mo. pp. 36.

Second edition, London: 1745; Third, Newcastle: 1744; Fourth, London: 1755; Fifth, Leeds: 1761; Sixth, Bristol: 1761.

This book, though not written by Wesley, was edited and published by him. The above is not given as the title-page of the earliest edition, about which there is some uncertainty, but of the earliest I have seen. Heylin and Tyerman, but not Osborn, date the first edition 1744. Soon after Nelson was liberated from the army, July 28, 1744, Wesley summoned him to London. The "Case" may have been written there, and at once published under Wesley's direction. It is a touching story of brave endurance in the cause of righteousness, and a painful exposure of the condition of English life at the time. It casts much light on the early struggles of Methodism. "It being our thanksgiving day, I read John Nelson's Case, a plain accomplishment of the promise, I will give you a mouth and wisdom, &c."—C. Wesley's *Journal*, Bristol, Sept. 17, 1744.

57. RULES OF THE BAND SOCIETIES. Drawn up December 25, 1738. DIRECTIONS GIVEN TO THE BAND SOCIETIES, December 25, 1744. 22mo., pp. 3.

The above appear together in a pamphlet, without date or name of printer. They were frequently reprinted.

Under No. 43 it is stated that in the Fourth edition of the "Rules of the United Societies," published 1744, the "Rules of the Band Societies" are given. This seems to have been the first time the Band Rules appeared in print.

For an account of the origin of the "Band Societies," see Wesley's *Works*, viii. 255-6. The Band Society in London was begun May 1, 1738, (*ibid.* viii. 380). "The meeting called 'the bands,' or 'the body band,' consists of as many persons as belong to any or all the bands in that society."—See Crowther's *Portraiture of Meth.* 1815, page 282.

In the *Minutes of Conference*, 1744, (No. 136), page 4, the question is asked, —"Q. 4. What are the Rules of the Bands? A. They are these (which were read and considered)." To these were added the *Directions*, and they were published together at the end of 1744.

58. A COLLECTION OF MORAL AND SACRED POEMS. From the most celebrated English Authors. By John Wesley, M.A., Fellow of Lincoln-College, Oxford. In Three Volumes. Bristol: Printed by Felix Farley. Sold also by J. Wilson, in Wine-Street; in London, by T. Trye, near Gray's-Inn-Gate; H. Butler, near Bow-Church; and at the Foundery, Upper-Moor-Fields; in Exeter by Mr. Score and Mr. Thorne. 1744. [Price, unbound, 7s. 6d.] Vol. I. 12mo., pp. vii., 347.

Vols. II. and III. A COLLECTION OF MORAL AND SACRED POEMS, publish'd by John Wesley, M.A., Fellow of Lincoln-College, Oxford. Bristol: Printed by Felix Farley, 1744; and sold by the Booksellers of London, Newcastle, Bristol, Bath, Exeter, &c. 12mo., pp. 373 and 288.

The Dedication to "The Right Honourable the Countess of Huntingdon," who suggested the publication, is dated Oxford, Aug. 1744, and is signed by John Wesley.

There is neither index nor table of contents. A few only of the authors' names are given. On page 206 of Vol. III. we read, "The poems that follow are by the Revd. Mr. John and Charles Wesley." The first of these is entitled "God's Greatness," and was first published in *Hymns and Sacred Poems*, 1739, page 161, (No. 15). The second is the *Elegy on the Death of R. Jones.*—(See No. 39). The remaining fifteen appear here for the first time.

In the Dedication Wesley says he had long had the design of attempting something of this kind, and that he revised all the English poems that he knew, and selected what appeared most valuable in them, omitting only Spenser's Works, "because scarce intelligible to the generality of modern readers."

These volumes were never reprinted.

Nos. 59-60-61-62. [1744-5.

59. HYMNS FOR TIMES OF TROUBLE AND PERSECUTION. (Micah vi. 9.) London: Printed in the year 1744. 12mo., pp. 47.

This consists of three parts:—1. Hymns for Times of Trouble; thirteen hymns. 2. Hymns in Time of Persecution; sixteen hymns. 3. Hymns to be sung in a Tumult; four hymns. The hymns in each part are separately numbered, and only seven have titles.

> The Second edition is enlarged by the addition of 15 hymns, under the title of *Hymns for Times of Trouble, For the Year 1745.* The passage of Scripture on the title-page is changed to Isaiah i. 19, 20. The names of the authors are added,—"By John and Charles Wesley, Presbyters of the Church of England;" also, to the former date, "Re-printed at Bristol, by Felix Farley, 1745." [Price sixpence.] It is paged continuously, and the number of pages is increased to 69. Third edition, enlarged, London: 1756 (see No. 60).

60. HYMNS FOR TIMES OF TROUBLE. (Isaiah xxiv. 15.) 12mo. pp. 12.

This small tract is without date, or author's or printer's name. There is much uncertainty as to the time of its first publication. Osborn inserts it under 1745, "because it was certainly written about this time." Heylin assigns it to the same year. It does not appear in the catalogues until 1746. It is inserted here on account of its connection with the previous publication. It contains only 6 hymns, numbered but untitled. It was incorporated with the Third edition of No. 59, making in all five parts and 54 hymns, 12mo. pp. 82.

"In these very spirited compositions the national sins are confessed and lamented; the mercy of God is earnestly implored in behalf of a guilty people; civil war is deprecated as a great and terrible calamity; the preservation of the Protestant religion, and a revival of its primitive spirit, are both solicited as the most important of all blessings; and the king is specially commended to the divine protection, not as the creature of the popular will, but as God's vicegerent and his minister for good to the people."—*Life of C. Wesley*, i. 360: see also pp. 359-408. The hymns were written in a time of great national disquiet, and of much violent persecution of the Methodists.

61. A HYMN AT THE SACRAMENT. 12mo., pp. 4.

This hymn contains ten stanzas. It was republished amongst the "Miscellaneous Hymns and Poems" (*Poetical Works of J. and C. Wesley*, viii. 441), with this note appended, "Published separately as a tract of four pages without name or date, but probably before 1745." It is No. 910 in the New Supplement in the Methodist Hymn Book now in use. The fifth and eighth verses are omitted. It is there attributed to Charles Wesley.

1745.

62. INSTRUCTIONS FOR CHILDREN. London: Printed for M. Cooper, at the Globe, in Paternoster Row. 1745. Price 3d., or 20s. a hundred to those who give them away. 12mo., pp. 39.

Second edition, London : M. Cooper, 1745, pp. 38. Appended is the tract "Swear not at all," (No. 78), one of the "Words" to be mentioned afterwards. Another edition, unnumbered, Newcastle : Gooding, 1746; Third, 1747; Fourth, Dublin : Powell, 1749; Fourth, London : 1755; Seventh, London : Cock, 1760; London : Mason, n.d., 24mo.

Chiefly translated from the French of Abbé Fleury and M. Poiret. "Although the great truths herein contained are more immediately addrest to Children, yet are they worthy the deepest consideration both of the oldest and wisest of men."—Preface, addressed "To all Parents and Schoolmasters." "I despair of seeing any [tracts] in the English tongue superior to those extracts from Abbé Fleury and M. Poiret, published under the title of 'Instructions for Children.' I have never yet seen anything comparable to them, either for depth of sense, or plainness of language."—Wesley's *Works*, xi., 339. "Monday, July 4 (1743), and the following days, I had time to finish the 'Instructions for Children.'"—*Journal*. It is not mentioned in Catalogues until 1745.

The book was subsequently translated into Latin for use in the School at Kingswood, and published as *Instructiones Pueriles* (No. 117).

63. A FARTHER APPEAL TO MEN OF REASON AND RELIGION. By John Wesley, M.A., Fellow of Lincoln College, Oxford. (Psalm cxli. 5.) [Part I.] London : Printed by W. Strahan ; and sold by T. Trye, near Gray's-Inn-Gate, Holbourn ; Henry Butler, at the corner of Bow Church-Yard ; and at the Foundery, near Upper-Moor fields. 1745. [Price, bound, one shilling.] 12mo., pp. 106.

At the end is a letter addressed to the Reverend Mr. Thomas Church, dated London, Decem. 22, 1744. It begins, "Since this was in the press." The Appeal must, therefore, have been published early in 1745. It appears in the catalogues of that year. It is distinguished as Part I. on the third page, not on the title. Appended is a hymn of four stanzas, entitled "An Act of Devotion."

Fourth edition, Bristol: Grabham, 1758 ; Fifth, London : Hawes, 1778 ; Another Fifth, London : 1786.

The first part of the *Farther Appeal* was written in reply to several hostile pamphlets, particularly one by the Bishop of London, and one by the Bishop of Lichfield and Coventry, in which Wesley's doctrines and his field-preaching and its effects are assailed. He vindicates his teaching as being in harmony with Scripture and the doctrines of the Church of England, his method as lawful, and the effects as not being "such as had been weakly and wickedly reported."

64. A FARTHER APPEAL TO MEN OF REASON AND RELIGION. By John Wesley, M.A., Fellow of Lincoln College, Oxford. (Psalm cxli. 5.) London : Printed by W. Strahan ; and sold by T. Trye, near Gray's-Inn-Gate, Holbourn ; Henry Butler, in Bow Church-Yard ; and at the Foundery, near Upper-Moor-Fields. 1745. [Price, unbound, one shilling.] 12mo., pp. 78.

This is Part II., but is not so distinguished on the title-page, but on page 3.

DITTO, DITTO. Part III. (Luke xix. 41, 42.) London : Strahan, &c. 1745.

It is paged in continuation of Part II., together pp. 139 (wrongly printed 239). Dated at end, London, Dec. 18, 1745, a year later than No. 63. It must therefore have been published either at the close of 1745 or early in 1746. It is placed here for convenience. These two parts appear always to have been published together.

Third edition, Bristol : Farley, 1746; Fourth, London : Strahan, 1746; another Fourth, Bristol : Pine, 1765; Sixth, 1786.

"I retired to Newington in order to finish the *Farther Appeal*, the state of the public affairs loudly demanding that whatever was done should be done quickly."—*Journal*, Nov. 25, 1745.

Wesley presented a copy of Parts II. and III. to every clergyman and alderman of Leeds.

Part II. is an earnest appeal indeed, addressed to members of the Church of England first, and to others, on the moral state of the nation. Part III. is a defence of the whole Methodist work, and an account of the brutal treatment the Methodists had received in many parts of the country.

"I waited on Mr. B—e, Rector of—, who had sent to me as soon as he had read the 'Farther Appeal.' He said, 'Sir, all this is sad truth. But what can we do to help it?' I went afterwards to another clergyman, who had likewise sent and desired to speak with me. How is this? I thought the publication of this tract would have enraged the world beyond measure. And, on the contrary, it seems nothing ever was published which softened them so much."—*Journal*, Jan. 8, 1746.

65. AN ANSWER TO THE REV. MR. CHURCH'S REMARKS on the Rev. John Wesley's Journal. In a Letter to that Gentleman. By John Wesley, M.A., Fellow of Lincoln College, Oxford. (1 Kings xx. 11.) Bristol : Printed by Felix Farley, and sold by him at his house in Castle Green, at the School-Room in the Horse-Fair, and by J. Wilson, in Wine Street; in London by T. Trye, near Grey's-Inn-Gate, Holborn ; Henry Butler, at the Corner of Bow Church-Yard ; and at the Foundery, near Moor Fields : and in Exeter by B. Thorne and E. Score. [Price 4d.] 12mo., pp. 46.

Dated at the end Bristol, Feb. 2, 1744-5, and signed John Wesley. It is in the 1745 catalogues.

Second edition, London : Strahan, 1745.

In the letter named in No. 63, reference is made to Mr. Church's remarks on Wesley's last Journal ; and Wesley promises "attentively to consider the points therein objected to." This is his reply to Church, whose pamphlet is entitled, "*Remarks on the Rev. Mr. John Wesley's last Journal, wherein he gives an account of the tenets and proceedings of the Moravians, especially those in England, and of the divisions and perplexities of the Methodists, &c, &c.* In a letter to that Gentleman. By Thomas Church, A.M., Vicar of Battersea, and Prebendary of St. Paul's." London : 1745, 8vo., pp. 76.

Wesley pursues his accuser throughout all his assertions, answering him sentence by sentence with extreme care; for he acknowledged him, as he afterward said, to be "a gentleman, a scholar, and a Christian ; (adding) and as such he both spoke and wrote."

66. Thoughts Concerning the Present Revival of Religion in New England. By Jonathan Edwards, A.M., Pastor of the Church of Christ at Northampton. Abridg'd by John Wesley, A.M., Fellow of Lincoln-College, Oxford. (Isaiah xl. 3.) London: Printed by W. Strahan, and sold by T. Trye, near Gray's-Inn-Gate, Holborn; Henry Butler, in Bow Church-Yard; and at the Foundery, near Upper-Moor-Fields. 1745. [Price 8d., unbound.] 12mo., pp. 124.

In old Catalogues sometimes called *New England Narrative*. It is an abridgement of "*Some Thoughts concerning the Present Revival of Religion, in New England*, and the way in which it ought to be acknowledged and promoted. Humbly offered to the public in a Treatise on that subject. In Five Parts. By Jonathan Edwards, A.M., Pastor of the Church of Christ, at Northampton." Boston: Printed (1742); Edinburgh: Reprinted 1743, 8vo., pp. 221. The Preface is omitted, each part is carefully abridged, and the whole reduced by more than one-half.

"The most ingenious Calvinist that ever wrote against free-will is, I think, Mr. Edwards of New England."—Fletcher's *Works*, ii. 38.

67. An Extract of Mr. Richard Baxter's Aphorisms of Justification. Publish'd by John Wesley, M.A., Fellow of Lincoln College, Oxford. Newcastle upon Tyne: Printed by John Gooding, on the Side; sold by R. Akenhead, on Tyne Bridge, Newcastle; by T. Trye, at Gray's Inn Gate, Holbourn; at the Foundery, near Upper Moor Fields, London; and at the New-School in the Horse-Fair, Bristol. 1745. [Price Threepence.] 12mo., pp. iv. 36.

Preface to the Reader, an interesting composition, is dated Newcastle upon Tyne, March 25, 1745, and signed by John Wesley.

Second edition, London: W. Strahan, 1745; Third, London: Paramore, 1784; Fourth, London: 1797.

Extracted from "*Aphorismes of Justification. With their explanation annexed, wherein also is opened the Nature of the Covenants, Satisfaction, Righteousness, Faith, Works, etc.* Published especially for the use of the Church of Kederminster in Worcestershire. By their unworthy Teacher, Ri. Baxter. (Heb. ix. 11)." London: 1648.

Wesley's attention was directed to this work by a bookseller. He immediately determined to print the substance of it, though objecting to some of its expressions. He thought it "a powerful antidote against the spreading poison of antinomianism." "Q. 4. Shall we read over together Mr. Baxter's Aphorisms concerning justification? A. By all means: which were accordingly read. And it was desired, that each person present would in the afternoon consult the Scriptures cited therein, and bring what objections might occur the next morning."—*Minutes of Conference*, Bristol, Aug. 1, 1745.

68. A Short View of the Difference between the Moravian Brethren, lately in England, and the Reverend Mr. John and Charles Wesley. Extracted chiefly from a late Journal. London: Printed by W. Strahan; and sold by T. Trye, near Gray's-Inn-Gate, Holburn; Henry Butler, at the corner of Bow-Church-Yard; and at the Foundary, near Upper Moorfields. 1745. [Price Twopence.] 12mo., pp. 24.

An Edition, not numbered, Dublin: 1747; Second (so called), Bristol: 1748.

The extracts from the Journal extend from Nov. 7, 1739, to August 28, 1740, and occupy nearly eleven pages; then follows a short and distinct statement of the "difference between the Moravian doctrine and ours," signed by the two brothers, and dated London, May 20, 1745. Six hymns are appended, which were most likely written for the occasion. They are highly characteristic of the authors.

In a letter dated Oct. 8, 1860, the late Dr. George Morley, who was a careful collector of Wesleyana, states that he had traced certain hymns to "a tract published 1741, entitled *A Short View of the Difference between the Moravians Now in England, and the Rev. Mr. John and Charles Wesley.*" It is possible that such a tract was published by Wesley in 1741. It was the year after he had separated from the Moravians; and the year in which he "had a conversation of several hours with P. Böhler and M. Spangenberg," and a long conversation, in Latin, with Count Zinzendorf, in each case on subjects treated of in the above tract—No. 68; in which some expressions occur similar to those used in both conversations.

The pamphlet of 1841 may have been a part of the pamphlet named above, which is expressly dated May 20, 1745, and signed by John and Charles Wesley; and is said to be "extracted chiefly from a late Journal." This Journal was not published until 1744;—the preface is dated June 24 of that year, and is addressed to "the Moravian Church, more especially that part of it now or lately residing in England." If, therefore, the earlier pamphlet was also an extract from the Journal, Wesley must, contrary to his usage, have quoted from his unpublished MS. Journal. Mr. C. D. Hardcastle, who is my informant, examined the tract at Dr. Morley's house many years ago, noting the date and the peculiarity of the title, and that the hymns were the same as those in the larger tract. He does not think it contained all that the later one does. After long inquiry, I have failed to find a copy, and have no more information concerning it than is given above. It is not named in any catalogue. The later tract would supersede it.

An abridgement of the pamphlet was inserted by Wesley in his *Preservative against Unsettled Notions in Religion*, (No. 191), published in 1758, and this has been included in two editions of his Works.

69. A COLLECTION OF RECEITS FOR THE USE OF THE POOR. (*Homo sum: Humani nihil à me alienum puto.*—TER.) Bristol: Printed by F. Farley. Price Twopence. 12mo., pp. 17.

Another edition, Newcastle-upon-Tyne, printed by John Gooding, 1745, [Price Two-pence], 12 mo., pp. 16. It is difficult to determine which of these was first published. Wesley was in Bristol, August 1st, at the "Second Conference," and he stayed some days, visiting the "little societies in Wiltshire and Somerset." He spent from Sept. 18 to Nov. 4 in Newcastle. The order given is probably the correct one.

No date on title, nor author's name; but a characteristic Advertisement, on the reverse of the title, is dated August, 1745. In this advertisement he says, "I suppose there are very few *infallible* medicines; but believe most of those which follow will fail as seldom as any, and much more seldom than the costly ones in common use. From a vast number, I have selected those, which are not only *cheap*, but *safe*: very few of them, if they do no good, being likely to do much harm. For most distempers, I have set down several. If one does not help, another may. And they may generally be tried one (at some distance) after another, using the easiest and simplest first."

For an Ague six different remedies are given. One is curious, "Spread soft wax, about the thickness of a crown piece, large enough to cover the wrist. On this spread the leaves of the tops of Rue, not yet fully open'd. Let this plaister lie on the wrist five or six days." One for St. Anthony's Fire is, "A cloth dipped in blood, and laid on moist." For the Gout, "Use little flesh, no strong drink, and much exercise." For Head-ache, "Wear Green hemlock that is tender, thickly spread on the soles of your feet. Shift it every day." Etc., etc.

70. A Dialogue Between an Antinomian and his Friend. By John Wesley, M.A., Fellow of Lincoln-College, Oxford. London: Printed by W. Strahan, and sold by T. Trye, near Gray's-Inn-Gate, Holbourn; Henry Butler, at the corner of Bow-Church-Yard; and at the Foundary, near Upper-Moorfields. 1745. [Price One-penny.] 12mo., pp. 12.

A Second edition, London: Strahan, 1745; Third, 1745.

71. A Second Dialogue, &c. (Rom. iii., ult.), London, &c., as above, but with the spelling, "Holborn" and "Foundery." 12mo., pp. 12.

Dated at the end, London, Aug. 24. 1745.

Second edition, London: Foundery, 1755; Third, Bristol: 1745; Third, London: Hawes, 1778; Third, (including both dialogues), London: Whitfield, 1798.

The words of the Antinomian are taken from various authors, and are printed in italics. The origin of the Dialogues is shown in the Minutes of a Conference held at Bristol, Aug. 2nd., 1745, when the question was asked, "What can we do to stop the progress of Antinomianism? Ans. 1st, Pray without ceasing, that God will speak for himself. 2d, Write one or two more dialogues."

An extract from each is given in the *Preservative against Unsettled Notions in Religion*, (No. 191).

72. Modern Christianity: exemplified at Wednesbury and other adjacent Places in Staffordshire. (*Tua res agitur paries quum proximus ardet.*) Publish'd by John Wesley, M.A., Fellow of Lincoln College, Oxford. Newcastle-upon-Tyne: Printed by John Gooding, on the Side; sold by R. Akenhead, on Tyne-Bridge, Newcastle;

No. 73. [1745.

by T. Trye, at Gray's-Inn-Gate, Holbourn; at the Foundery, near Upper-Moorfields, London; and at the New-School in the Horse-Fair, Bristol. 1745. [Price Two-pence.] 12mo., pp. 26.

Second edition, London: Strahan, 1745.

At the end before the last paragraph is the date Oct. 22, 1743. The last paragraph may have been added at the time of publication. The pamphlet was obviously not printed at the time it was written. It does not appear in the catalogues for 1743, 1744, or the earlier 1745. In an advertisement prefixed, Wesley says, "It was our desire and design that the following accounts, drawn up long since, should have slept for ever; but the gross misrepresentations of these facts, which are still spread abroad from day to day, constrain us at length to speak the naked truth," &c. In an old catalogue the title is altered to, *Sufferings of the Primitive Methodists at Wednesbury (which ought never to be forgot)*. This describes the character of the pamphlet. It is a precise and painful account of a brutal persecution of the Methodists by the mobs of Wednesbury and Walsall, in which Wesley and several others had nearly lost their lives. "I received a full account of the terrible riots which had been in Staffordshire. I was not surprised at all: neither should I have wondered if, after the advices they had so often received from the pulpit, as well as from the episcopal chair, the zealous high churchmen had rose, and cut all that were Methodists to pieces. Resolving to assist them as far as I could, I set out early in the morning."—*Journal*, June, 18, 19, 1743.

On an inner page, dated September 9, 1745, are "proposals for printing, by subscription, Three Volumes of Sermons, by John Wesley, M.A."

73. ADVICE TO THE PEOPLE CALLED METHODISTS. (*Disce, docendus adhuc quæ censet amiculus* [misprinted *amicutus*]—HOR.) Printed in the year 1745. [Price One Penny.] 12mo., pp. 11.

Dated at end, October 10, 1745.

Second edition, London: 1746; Fourth, Bristol: 1746; Fifth, Bristol: F. Farley, 1746; Another, Dublin: S. Powell, 1748; London: 1751; London: Paramore, 1787; London: Cordeux, 1818.

The Methodists had been very unjustly treated in many parts of the country, and they greatly needed encouragement and help. But their assailants had not always been careful to distinguish between them and others who were classed with them. As the Methodists showed more earnestness in attention to religious duties than most of their neighbours, the term became applied to any persons who displayed more than ordinary religious fervour and was even attached to the wildest fanatics, for whose extravagancies Wesley was unwilling his people should be blamed. He, therefore, first specifies whom he means "by this ambiguous term." He says, "By Methodists I mean, a people who profess to pursue (in whatsoever measure they have attained) holiness of heart and life, inward and outward conformity in all things to the revealed will of God: who place religion in uniform resemblance of the great Object of it; in a steady imitation of Him they worship, in all His inimitable perfection; more particularly, in Justice, Mercy and Truth, or universal Love filling the heart and governing the life." To such he writes this very seasonable pamphlet. It contains tender advice to the Methodists to consider the circumstances in which they stood and their liability to give offence, to trust in God, to be true to their principles, and not to talk much of their persecutions.

74. A Collection of Prayers for Families. Publish'd by John Wesley, M.A., Fellow of Lincoln College, Oxford. Half-title, 12mo., pp. 24.

No date or printer's name. [Price Twopence] at the end.
Many editions. A twenty-seventh, London: Mason, 1843, is noted.

Found in a 1745 Catalogue, and therefore inserted here. Probably not written by Wesley, but extracted by him from some unmentioned author. It is reprinted in the several editions of his works, and in the second edition of the *Christian Library* (No. 131). It contains a morning and evening prayer for each day of a week. This devotional manual is admirably suited to its high purpose. The prayers are comprehensive, but brief, each covering about a page and a half. They are written in plain and appropriate language,—the language of humility, thankfulness and faith. The petitions and the intermingled thanksgivings are most fitly expressed. It is a little compilation well adapted to aid a family in the offering of its daily devotions. If Wesley did not write it, he was at great pains to adapt it to general use.

75. A Letter to the Author of the Craftsman concerning Real Christianity, Disparag'd under the name of Methodism. By John Wesley, M.A., Fellow of Lincoln College, Oxford. London: Printed in the year 1745. 12mo., pp. 4.

Signed at the end John Wesley.

This is very scarce. It is not named by Osborn. A copy is in the Didsbury College Library, and one in the Wesleyan Conference Office Library. It is in the last edition of the collected Works, but not in the first. It is not mentioned in the catalogues, nor does it appear to have been republished separately.

"Another attack on Methodism was one published in the *Craftsman* of June 22, and copied in the *London Magazine* and other periodicals of the period. It was, in fact, an onslaught upon the government of the day, entitled 'Ministerial Methodism, or Methodists in Politics'; but in castigating ministers of state, it grossly calumniates ministers of Christ. The article, though neatly written, was supremely silly: Wesley at the urgent request of his friends, answered it."—Tyerman's *Life of Wesley*, i. 475.

76. A Word in Season; or, Advice to an Englishman. 12mo., pp. 6 or 8.

No name of writer, or of place or date of printing.
Under date Tuesday, Oct. 15, 1745, Wesley says in his *Journal*, "I wrote 'A Word in Season; or Advice to an Englishman.'" He was then in Sheffield. In a week he was in Newcastle.

That this tract was published in 1745 is evident; but where it was first printed cannot be told, neither can the first edition be distinguished. An edition called the third, pp. 11, has two hymns annexed,—one, "Regard, thou righteous God, and true," and one, "For His Majesty King George." Many editions were issued, some with, others without, the hymns. An eighth is noted, with John Wesley, Fellow of Lincoln College, on title-page, London: Strahan 1745, pp. 8, with the two hymns. Whether the hymns were in the first edition is uncertain, though it is most likely they were. In the collected Works (1771) this note is added, "This was published at the beginning of the late rebellion."

Nos. 77-78-79-80-81. [1745.

77. A WORD TO A DRUNKARD. 12mo., pp. 4.

No date or name.
"I wrote 'A Word to a Drunkard.'"—*Journal*, Nov. 28, 1745.
This is an appropriate place in which to notice several of these "WORDS." They were addressed to different classes of people, and directed against some of the prevalent vices of the day. They were mostly of four pages, written in courteous but earnest language; convenient, little, effective appeals, that were scattered broadcast by the itinerant evangelists. They are without date, or name of writer or printer. The following are generally supposed to have been published about this time.

78. "SWEAR NOT AT ALL." 12mo., pp. 4.

Half-title. Sometimes the title is "Swear not at all, saith the Lord God of heaven and earth"; sometimes "A Word to a Swearer."
This appears as an appendix of two pages to an edition of *Instructions for Children* (No. 62), bearing date 1745. It also appears in a 1745 catalogue.

79. A WORD TO A SABBATH BREAKER. 12mo., pp. 4.

This was generally published with the title, "Remember the Sabbath Day to keep it holy." In a 1745 catalogue it is called "An earnest Persuasive to keep the Sabbath holy," and, like all these "Words," is priced at "2s. a hundred."

80. A WORD TO A STREET WALKER. 12mo., pp. 4.

Also published as "A word to an Unhappy Woman," which is the title given to the tract in the collected Works, ix. 290, (No. 276). One edition was printed in the year 1748; another, London, 1761. It afterwards bore the title (as did another tract to be noticed), "A Word to whom it may concern," printed by J. Paramore, at the Foundery, Upper-Moor-Fields, 1784; also "A Word to a Prostitute." When the first edition was published is uncertain. It is not in the catalogues of 1746, but is in those of 1749.

81. A WORD TO A CONDEMNED MALEFACTOR. 12mo., pp. 4.

Half-title; neither name nor date. Reprinted at the end of *Prayers for Condemned Malefactors*, 1785, (No. 384).
This, like the two preceding "Words," is written in a very tender but earnest spirit. The language is striking and pungent, calculated to carry conviction to the heart of the reader and to arouse to thought and consideration. Wesley seems to have written these brief pieces with the utmost care. The folly, the sinfulness, the danger of the practices which he condemns are very faithfully exposed. But, while not abating in the slightest degree the consequences of evil doing, he opens in each tract a path of hope to the penitent. His interest was very great in the class for whom this particular tract was designed. He and his brother and their "Helpers" visited the prisons, and accompanied many "a condemned malefactor" to the gallows.

82. A WORD TO A PROTESTANT. 12mo., pp. 4.

First edition, small type, no hymns.

It is so described by Osborn and placed under this year. It is much longer than the other "Words," and sometimes occupies six pages, or with the hymns, twelve pages.

One title-page is as follows :—

A WORD TO A PROTESTANT. By John Wesley, M.A., Fellow of Lincoln College, Oxford. The Eighth edition, London: Printed by W. Strahan, and sold by T. Trye, near Gray's-Inn-Gate, Holbourn; H. Butler, in Bow-Church-Yard; and at the Foundery, near Upper-Moor-Fields. 1745. [Price One Penny.] Three hymns are appended, "Where have I been so long?" "Forgive me, O Thou jealous God," "O Thou who seest what is in man." 12mo., pp. 12. Eight editions in one year!

Another edition, Bristol: Felix Farley, 1746; Another, Dublin: Powell, 1749; Another, Bristol: Farley, n.d.

He first explains the word Papists, and then states some of the errors held by them, those "which defile the purity of Christianity" and those that "strike at its very root;" particularly "the grand Popish doctrines of Merit, Idolatry, and Persecution." He then explains the word Protestant, and proceeds to exhort the would-be Protestant to avoid the errors against which he professedly protests. "Be a real Protestant . . . . Cast away all trust in your own righteousness, all hope of being saved by your own works . . . . Put away the idols out of your heart . . . . And if you love God love your brother also . . . . Let this be your truly Protestant zeal: While you abhor every kind and degree of persecution, let your heart burn with love to all mankind, to friends and enemies, neighbours and strangers, to Christians, Heathens, Jews, Turks, Papists, Heretics; to every soul which God hath made." This tract was called for by the wild and virulent treatment which the Methodists received at the hands of excited mobs and professedly Protestant teachers, as is shown in one of the publications of this year, entitled *Modern Christianity, exemplified at Wednesbury*, (No. 72).

In the collected Works, 1771, ix. 324, (No. 276), a note says: "This was wrote during the late rebellion."

Other *Words* were published subsequently.

83. HYMNS ON THE LORD'S SUPPER. By John Wesley, M.A., Fellow of Lincoln College, Oxford, and Charles Wesley, M.A., Student of Christ-Church, Oxford. With a preface concerning The Christian Sacrament and Sacrifice. Extracted from Dr. Brevint. (1 Cor. xi. 24.) Bristol: Printed by Felix Farley. 1745. 12mo., pp. xxxii. 141.

Second edition, Bristol: F. Farley, 1747; Third, London: H. Cock, 1751: This and some other editions have "by John and Charles Wesley, Presbyters of the Church of England," on title-page; Fourth, London: 1757; Another, Bristol: Grabham; Fifth, London: 1755; Fifth, Bristol: 1762; Sixth, Bristol: 1771; Seventh, Bristol: 1775; Seventh, London: 1776; Ninth, London, Paramore: 1786; Tenth, London: Paramore, 1794; Eleventh, London: Kershaw, 1825.

Contains 166 hymns in five numbered sections, with an additional section, entitled "After the Sacrament."

The Preface was sometimes published separately. It is taken from *The Christian Sacrament and Sacrifice. By way of Discourse, Meditation and Prayer upon the Nature, Parts and Blessings of the Holy Communion.* By Daniel Brevint, D.D., Dean of Lincoln. "The Epistle," which is prefixed, is addressed to the Right Honourable the Lady Elizabeth Carteret, and is dated, Durham, Jan. 24, 1673, and signed " Dan. Brevint." The book was for some time out of print and a third edition was published in 1739. Wesley has abridged it in his usual style. He has omitted the "Epistle." The eight sections are preserved as in the original, but the work is reduced from 134 to 32 slightly larger pages. See "Advertisement," *Poetical Works*, iii. page 183: Jackson's *Life of C. Wesley*, i. 421-2.

The volume was in great demand, as is shown by the number of editions published. Wesley taught his people by precept and his own practice the importance of frequent communion. The Sacrament of the Lord's Supper was administered to the Societies in London every Sabbath Day.

In 1871 a volume was published entitled "THE EUCHARISTIC MANUALS of John and Charles Wesley, reprinted from the original editions of 1748-57-94, edited, with an introduction, by W. E. Dutton." It contained *A Companion for the Altar*, (No. 36), Brevint's Preface and the *Hymns on the Lord's Supper*. The object of the publication was to attempt to prove that Wesley held High Church doctrine on this Sacrament.

84. HYMNS FOR THE NATIVITY OF OUR LORD. 12mo., pp. 24.

The First edition has no name, date, or place. The title as above occupies the first page; the hymns begin on the second.

Second edition, Bristol: Felix Farley, 1745, 12mo., pp. 24;* Third, Dublin: Powell, 1747;* Fourth, Dublin: 1751; Fourth, Bristol: F. Farley, 1750; Tenth, London: 1750; Eleventh, 1755; Fifth, Bristol: Farley, 1756;* Sixth, Bristol: Pine, 1761;* Bristol: Pine, 1764; Ditto, 1768; Ditto, 1772; London: Paramore, 1782; London: Hawes, n.d.; London: Cordeux, 1815, together with Hymns for New Year's Day, paged consecutively; Ditto, 1816; Eleventh, London: J. Kelshaw, 1825. Ten other editions have been noted, dated 1762-6-8, 1770-7, 1782-4-7, 1801-9.

"Pray tell R. Sheen that I am hugely displeased at his reprinting the Nativity Hymns, and omitting the very best hymn in the collection—'All glory to God in the sky.' I beg they may never more be printed without it. Omit one or two and I will thank you. They are *namby-pambical*. I wish you would give us two or three invitatory hymns. We want such exceedingly."—Letter from J. W. to C. W., dated, Dec. 26, 1761 : *Works*, xii. 115.

From those marked with an asterisk the eighteenth hymn was omitted.

Mr. Hardcastle thinks this was printed first in 1744, his authority being the late Mr. Love, a large collector of Wesleyan Hymn-books. But it is not mentioned in either of two 1745 catalogues, one of them dated September 9.

1746.

85. LESSONS FOR CHILDREN. Printed in the year 1746. [Price 6d.] 12mo., pp. 76.

The Preface, addressed "To All Parents and School-Masters," is dated February 24, 1745-6. No name of author or printer. The vignette is the same as appears in the first edition of *Hymns on the Lord's Supper*, printed by Felix Farley, Bristol, (No. 83).

The complete work was issued in four parts at different intervals. This is Part I. It consists entirely of extracts from the Scriptures and the Apocrypha, with a few explanatory footnotes and references. The whole work when completed formed a volume of nearly 400 pages. It was prepared with much painstaking and care, and it forms a really valuable lesson-book for the young. "The most useful portions of Scripture, such as children may the most easily understand, and such as it most concerns them to know, are set down in the same order and (generally) the same words" as in Holy Scripture. The exhortation to the teacher is well worthy of reproduction. It is as follows:—
"I cannot but earnestly intreat you to take good heed, how you teach these deep things of God. Beware of that common, but accursed way of making children parrots, instead of Christians. Labour that, as far as possible, they may understand every single sentence which they read. Therefore, do not make haste. Regard not *how much* but *how well*, or to how good purpose, they read. Turn each sentence every way, propose it in every light, and question them continually on every point; if by any means they may not only *read*, but *inwardly digest* the words of eternal life." Thus the teacher of men sought to provide for the instruction of little children.

86. A WORD OF ADVICE TO SAINTS AND SINNERS. London: Printed in the year 1746. 12mo., pp. 12.

Extracted from the Works of Thomas Willcocks.

Third edition, Dublin, 1748; Third and Fourth, Bristol, 1748; Fourth, Newcastle, 1750; Fourth, Dublin: Powell, 1759; Fifth, London, 1755; Sixth, Bristol: Pine, 1764; Seventh, Bristol: Pine, 1768; Eighth, 1777; Tenth, London: Paramore, 1782. Many subsequent editions.

This is a very searching appeal to the two classes named, not merely to partake of ordinances and to make profession of religion, but also to be earnest and careful in seeking the reality of inward godliness.

87. THE PRINCIPLES OF A METHODIST FARTHER EXPLAIN'D: Occasioned by the Reverend Mr. Church's Second Letter to Mr. Wesley: In a Second Letter to that Gentleman. By John Wesley, M.A., Fellow of Lincoln-College, Oxford. London: Printed by W. Strahan; and sold by T. Trye, near Gray's-Inn-Gate, Holbourn; H. Butler, in Bow-Church-Yard, Cheapside; and at the Foundery, near Upper-Moorfields. 1746. [Price Eightpence.] 12mo., pp. 79.

Dated at the end June 17, 1746. Signed, John Wesley.

Second edition, Bristol: Farley, 1746; Third, Dublin: Powell, 1747.

Church's letter is entitled, *Some Farther Remarks on the Rev. Mr. John Wesley's Last Journal, together with a few Considerations on his Farther Appeal.* It is an octavo volume of 143 pages, and is divided into two parts. In the former the writer attempts to show the inconsistency of Wesley's conduct and sentiments with the constitution and doctrines of the Church of England, dwelling particularly on his divergence from Article xi., which relates to Justification. The latter part contains a Vindication of the former "Remarks," and a Reply to the Answer to them, which Wesley had written the year before, (see No. 65).

Nos. 88-89-90. [1746.

88. SERMONS ON SEVERAL OCCASIONS. In Three Volumes. By John Wesley, M.A., Fellow of Lincoln College, Oxford. Vol. I. London : Printed by W. Strahan ; and sold by T. Trye, near Gray's-Inn Gate, Holbourn ; and at the Foundery, near Upper Moorfields. 1746. 12mo., pp. xii., 250.

Second edition, London: W. Bowyer, 1745 (identical with First edition); Third, Bristol: W. Pine, 1769; Fifth, 1796.

In the proposals for printing Three Volumes of Sermons by subscription, dated Sep. 7, 1745, the price is stated to be 2s. 6d. each vol. "in quires"; and the hope is expressed that the first volume will be in the press about Michaelmas, and delivered to the subscribers at or before Christmas. This cannot have been accomplished, for this (the first volume) bears date 1746. It contains 12 sermons.

In the preface, wherein is one of the most impressive paragraphs Wesley ever wrote, it is stated : "The following sermons contain the substance of what I have been preaching for between eight and nine years last past. During that time I have frequently spoken in public on every subject in the ensuing collection : and I am not conscious that there is any one point of doctrine, on which I am accustomed to speak in public, which is not here, incidentally, if not professedly, laid before every Christian reader."

89. A SHORT ACCOUNT OF THE DEATH OF SAMUEL HITCHENS. By James Hitchens, Tinner. (Job i. 21.) London : Printed in the year 1746. 12mo., pp. 11.

Third edition, Newcastle upon Tyne : Gooding, 1746 ; Fifth, 1747 ; Sixth, 1747.

This, like a similar account of Thomas Hitchens, to be afterwards noticed, was a great favourite, and often reprinted. It was written by their father, another hand contributing ; and it appears to have been revised by Wesley.

90. HYMNS FOR OUR LORD'S RESURRECTION. London : Printed by W. Strahan, and sold by T. Trye, near Gray's-Inn-Gate, Holborn ; Henry Butler, in Bow Church-Yard ; and at the Foundery, near Upper-Moor-Fields. 1746. 12mo., pp. 20.

No name of writer is given.

Second edition, Bristol : 1746 ; Third, Dublin : Powell, 1747 ; Third, Bristol : F. Farley, 1748 ; Fourth, Dublin : 1752 ; London : Cock, 1754 ; Fourth, Bristol : Pine, 1764 ; Fifth, Bristol : Pine, 1769 ; Fifth, London : 1774 ; Sixth, London : Hawes, 1777 ; Others variously numbered, or not at all, 1753, 1754, 1767, 1769, 1787, 1791, 1801, 1804, 1809, 1813.

A tract of sixteen hymns ; the seventh and sixteenth only having titles, the latter "For Ascension Day." Two only and part of a third are in the Large Hymn Book. C. Wesley's great Easter-hymn, "Christ the Lord is risen to-day," is not included. It was first published in 1739, (No. 15).

1746.] **Nos. 91-92-93-94.**

91. HYMNS FOR ASCENSION DAY. Bristol: Printed by Felix Farley. 1746. 12mo., pp. 12.

Seven hymns only: three of which are in the large Hymn-book. No name of writer.

Second edition, Bristol: Farley, 1747; Third, Dublin: Powell, 1747; London: H. Cock, 1753; Bristol: Pine, 1761; Others, 1771; 1775; 1784; 1789; 1798; 1822.

92. HYMNS OF PETITION AND THANKSGIVING FOR THE PROMISE OF THE FATHER. By the Reverend Mr. John and Charles Wesley. Bristol: Printed by Felix Farley. 1746. 12mo., pp. 36.

Second edition, Bristol: F. Farley, 1747, apparently from the same type as first edition; Third, Dublin: Powell, 1747; London: H. Cock, 1753; Bristol: Pine, 1760; another, 1768; Dublin: M. Joyce, 1781; Others, 1775; 1779; 1786; 1793; 1801; 1813.

On the third page they are entitled, *Hymns for Whit-Sunday.* Seven of the hymns and parts of three others are in the large Hymn-book (No. 345).

93. GLORIA PATRI, &c., or Hymns to the Trinity. London: Printed in the year 1746. 12mo., pp. 11.

Second edition, Bristol: F. Farley, 1749; Third, London: H. Cock, 1753; Fourth, London: 1757; Fourth, Bristol: Pine, 1764; Fifth, London: 1757; Fifth, Bristol: 1771; Sixth, London: 1775.

Twenty-four Hymns, mostly of one or two verses each. Probably printed by Strahan, as the wood-cut on the title-page is often found in his publications. In the year 1767, a volume entitled *Hymns on the Trinity* (No. 246), was published. It is quite a distinct work from the above.

The hymn-tracts on the Christian Festivals, of which this is the last, were often sold bound together. Both John and Charles Wesley punctually observed these festivals. "Everywhere avail yourself of the great festivals by preaching on the occasion, and singing the hymns, which you should take care to have in readiness."—*Large Minutes*, fifth edition, 1780 (No. 344).

94. HYMNS ON THE GREAT FESTIVALS, and other Occasions. London: Printed for M. Cooper, at the Globe in Paternoster Row; and sold by T. Trye, near Gray's-Inn-Gate, Holborn; Henry Butler, in Bow Church-Yard; The Booksellers of Bristol, Bath, Newcastle upon Tyne, and Exeter, and at the Musick-shops. 1746. 4to. pp. ii. 66, with 24 tunes interleaved.

Second edition, 1753: Sold at Mrs. Lampe's lodging in Broad Court, Bow Street, Covent Garden.

This is not an additional Hymn-book, but a selection of twenty-four hymns, taken from several of the festival hymn-tracts already mentioned, and from *Hymns on the Lord's Supper* (No. 83), *Funeral Hymns* (No. 96), and others; together with three not previously published, but which afterwards appeared in *Hymns and Sacred Poems*, 1749, (No. 139). To each hymn an original tune is added, composed by John F. Lampe, a musical composer, engaged at the Covent Garden Theatre. Lampe underwent a great spiritual change through the instrumentality of the Wesleys, and one of Charles Wesley's most beautiful Funeral hymns was written on his death. See John Wesley's *Journal*, Nov. 29, 1745; Charles Wesley's *Journal*, ii. 37, 174; and Jackson's *L. of C. Wesley*, i. 432-5.

"Not only did the Wesleys sanction the use of their Hymns in this manner, but as soon as the book was published they endeavoured to promote the use of it by referring publicly to the Tunes it contained. Thus the 'Redemption Hymns' (No. 105), published next year, are so arranged that the first twenty-four correspond in metre to the twenty-four tunes contained in this volume; and a note on the first page indicates where the corresponding tune may be found. A similar reference is carried through the collection of 'Graces before and after Meat,' (No. 98). Twelve of these tunes afterwards found a place in the collection of tunes authorised by Wesley; and more than one are understood to have been among his favourite tunes, particularly the short metre with which this collection opens, and which was afterwards called by the name ot the composer."—Osborn, *Wes. Bib.* p. 21.

95. HYMNS FOR THE PUBLIC THANKSGIVING-DAY, October 9, 1746. London: Printed in the year 1746. 12mo., pp. 12.

Seven hymns probably printed by Strahan, but quite anonymous. Another edition printed in the year 1746; another, Bristol: Pine, 1769.

"A comparison of the woodcuts of different copies leaves no doubt that these hymns were published simultaneously at London and Bristol, or that a second edition appeared in the latter city the same year."—Osborn.

"The day of Public Thanksgiving for the victory at Culloden was to us a day of solemn joy."—*Journal*, Oct. 9, 1746.

96. FUNERAL HYMNS. [First Series.] (Rev. xiv. 13.) 12mo., pp. 24. n.d.

The title of the first edition contains only the words given above.
There are sixteen hymns numbered, five of them having titles.

Second, n.d.; Third, Dublin: Powell, 1747; Third, London: H. Cock, 1753; Another, 1759; Another, 1769; Fifth, London, 1770; Fifth, Bristol: Pine, 1770; Sixth, London: Hawes, and sold at the Foundry, 1776; Seventh, London: Paramore, 1784; Eighth, London: Whitfield, 1798; Ninth, London: Cordeux, n. d.; Another, not numbered, 1817.

The first and second editions have no date. Stevenson, following Heylin, gives 1744 (see Julian's *Hymnology*); but no reason is assigned and the date is probably wrong. The year 1744 was one of the most eventful and laborious in C. Wesley's life. It was the year of the great persecutions, of which he wrote in *Hymns for Times of Trouble and Persecution*, (Nos. 59 and 60). He was from home almost the whole year travelling and preaching; his labours were excessive. But in the beginning of 1745 he visited many dying persons in London and elsewhere; and some of the expressions and incidents recorded in his Journal at that time are strikingly similar to passages in some of the hymns. Such prominence is given to the subject in this part of the Journal as is not elsewhere to be found in the same space. Further, this pamphlet is not named in the 1745 catalogues; nor even in 1746, when the other hymn-tracts are announced. It was probably written partly before but chiefly in the early months of 1745, and published towards the close of the year, or in the beginning of 1746, to which year Osborn assigns it. A writer of Notes on Hymn-Books in the *Keighley Visitor*, 1861, speaks of it thus, "1744, Funeral Hymns. 24 pages, 16 hymns. No date, but probably 1744, as the *Second edition is 1745*." The last statement is not warranted; and if it were correct, it would scarcely be a sufficient ground for the assumption founded upon it.

A second pamphlet, having the same title as the above, was published in the year 1759, (No. 197). In Vol. VI. of the *Poetical Works* a "Third Series" is given. This is only a grouping together by the Editor of various hymns on the subject, some of which were left in manuscript by the author. They were never published together as a separate pamphlet.

97. HYMNS FOR THE WATCHNIGHT. 12mo., pp. 12.

The title occupies about half the first page, which is without date or name. There are eleven hymns, numbered, but without titles. The popular hymn, "Come let us anew, Our journey pursue," which has been sung by thousands every year for a century and a half, was not then written.

Heylin places this tract under 1744; but it does not appear in either the 1745 or the 1746 catalogues.

98. GRACES BEFORE MEAT. 12mo., pp. 12.

It was reprinted in Dublin, by S. Powell, in 1747, together with *Gloria Patri*; and in separate form many times. Twenty-six short hymns numbered. To each is assigned a tune from *Hymns for the Great Festivals* (No. 94). No name or date is ever found on this Tract except in one edition, nor has it any title beyond two lines in larger type than the rest, on page 1. Graces "at or after Meat" commence on page 6.

99. HYMNS FOR CHILDREN.

Nine hymns and four prayers.

See reference to this under No. 40. Heylin and Stevenson assign it to this date. I have not seen a copy.

N.B.—HYMNS FOR TIMES OF TROUBLE. (Isaiah xxiv. 15.) 12mo., pp. 12. Should probably appear here, or in the later part of 1745, to which Osborn hesitatingly assigns it. See No. 60.

1747.

100. LESSONS FOR CHILDREN. Part II. Printed in the year 1747. [Price 6d.] 12mo., pp. 108.

Biblical lessons reaching from the death of Moses to the death of Manasseh—a continuous history written in plain language, mostly in the words of Holy Scripture. "Most of this week I spent at Lewisham in writing 'Lessons for Children,' consisting of the most practical Scriptures, with a very few explanatory notes."—*Journal*, Dec. 15, 1746. See No. 85.

Nos. 101-102. [1747.

101. PRIMITIVE PHYSICK; or an Easy and Natural Method of Curing most Diseases. London: Printed and sold by Thomas Trye, near Gray's-Inn-Gate, Holborn, 1747. 12mo., pp. 119.

Preface dated London: June 11, 1747.

Second edition, Bristol: G. Woodall, n.d.; Another, not numbered, Dublin: 1754; Fifth, Bristol: Palmer, 1755, "corrected and enlarged," also additional Preface, dated Bristol, Oct. 16, 1755; Eighth, Bristol: Grabham, 1759; Ninth, London: Strahan, 1761; Tenth, Bristol: W. Pine, 1762; Twelfth, Bristol: W. Pine, 1765; Thirteenth, Bristol: Pine, 1768; Another, Bristol: 1770; Sixteenth, London: Hawes, 1774; Twentieth, London: Paramore, 1781; Twenty-first, London: Paramore, 1785; Twenty-third, London: 1791.

It was further enlarged and revised through successive editions down to the twenty-third, which was the last published during Wesley's life.

Subsequent editions are the Twenty-fourth, London: Paramore, 1792; Twenty-fifth, London: Story, 1801; Thirty-second, London: Mason, 1828.

In the Ninth edition the Preface, dated London, Nov. 10, 1760, was further enlarged, and special attention called to Electricity, which the Author affirms "comes nearest an Universal Medicine of any known in the World." The word "tried" is added to those remedies which are "found to be of the greatest efficiency"; and on the title-page are the words "*Homo sum: humani nihil a me alienum puto.*"

This book has excited the mirth of many persons by the curious nature of some of the remedies recommended. It consists of 725 receipts for 243 of the various ills to which flesh is heir. Whatever may be said of the remedies, the advices on cold-bathing and the witty and sagacious preface deserve to be read and pondered, especially the "few plain, easy Rules" on the preservation of the health, which are chiefly transcribed from Dr. Cheyne. "Without any concern about the obliging or disobliging any man living, a mean hand has made here some little attempt towards a plain and easy way of curing most diseases." As an encouragement and guide to the use of some of the receipts the following note is given, "I have subjoin'd the letter 'I' to those medicines, which are said to be infallible."

102. A SHORT ACCOUNT OF THE DEATH OF THOMAS HITCHENS. By James Hitchens, Tinner. Printed in the year 1747. 12mo., pp. 12.

Third edition, printed in the year 1747; Fourth, having the words, "The Lord gave, and the Lord hath taken away, blessed be the Name of the Lord," on the title-page, and printed at Leedes: by James Lister at New-Street-End, 1747; another Fourth, London: H. Cock, 1751; Another edition, Bristol: Pine, 1771.

Samuel Hitchens died at Bisveal, near Redruth, on Aug. 16, (see No. 89). His brother Thomas died on Sep. 12, 1746. On the following Sunday Wesley was preaching in Gwennap "to an immense multitude of people," and he says, "In the close of my sermon I read them the account of Thomas Hitchens's death, and they could not conceal their desire to go to him and be with Christ." —*Journal.*

103. A LETTER TO THE RIGHT REVEREND THE LORD BISHOP OF LONDON : Occasioned by his Lordship's last Charge to his Clergy. By John Wesley, M.A., Fellow of Lincoln College, Oxford. (Job. xxxii. 21, 22.) London: Printed by W. Strahan. Sold by T. Trye, near Gray's-Inn-Gate, Holborn ; and at the Foundery, Upper-Moor-Fields. 1747. [Price twopence.] 12mo., pp. iii., 32.

Dated at the end, London, June 11, 1747, and signed John Wesley. A hymn by Charles Wesley appended, (entitled, but not in the pamphlet, "For one called forth to bear his testimony"). Jackson describes the hymn as of "almost unparalleled sublimity and force ;" adding, " Nothing could give so perfect a view of the spirit in which he had exercised his ministry, from the time at which he began his glorious career in Moor-Fields and Kennington Common to this period of his life."—*Life of C. Wesley*, i. 543.

Second edition, Bristol : Farley, 1749 ; another, Dublin : 1748.

In the Bishop's Charge are several very severe strictures on the teaching of Wesley, the Moravians, and Whitefield. Wesley answers for himself and his friends pithily, and with great plainness and force. It is one of many pamphlets he had occasion to write in defence of his work and his doctrine. His closing words are, " But I must draw to a conclusion. Your lordship has without doubt had some success in *opposing* this doctrine. Very many have, by your lordship's unwearied *endeavours*, been deterred from hearing it at all ; and have thereby probably escaped the being *seduced* into holiness, have lived and died in their sins. My Lord, the time is short. I am past the noon of life, and my remaining years flee as a shadow. Your lordship is old and full of days, having past the usual age of man. It cannot therefore be long before we shall both drop this house of earth, and stand naked before God ; no, nor before we shall see the great white throne coming down from heaven, and Him that sitteth thereon. On his left hand shall be those who are shortly to dwell in everlasting fire prepared for the devil and his angels. In that number will be all who died in their sins, and among the rest those whom you *preserved* from repentance. Will you then rejoice in your success ? The Lord God grant it may not be said in that hour, ' These have perished in their iniquity, but their blood I require at thy hands.'" See also Moore, *L. of Wesley*, ii. 415.

104. A WORD TO A FREEHOLDER, &C. 12mo, pp. 4.

The earliest edition recorded is dated 1748. It has a woodcut on the title-page—a large swan, with a coronet and chain.

Another edition, London : 1767 ; another, printed in the year 1767 ; another London : Paramore, 1783.

" We reached Colestock, dropping wet, before seven. The rain ceased while we were in the house, but began when we took horse, and attended us all the way to Exeter. While we stayed here to-day to dry our clothes, I took the opportunity of writing ' A Word to a Freeholder.' "—*Journal*, June 24, 1747.

It was written on the eve of an election, against bribery, and in favour of that " Parliament man" who loved his God, his King, and his country. At the Conference of 1767 Wesley advised his preachers to " read everywhere the *Word to a Freeholder*, and disperse it as it were with both hands."

Nos. 105-106. [1747.

105. HYMNS FOR THOSE THAT SEEK, AND THOSE THAT HAVE, REDEMPTION IN THE BLOOD OF JESUS CHRIST. London : Printed by W. Strahan, and sold by Thomas Trye, near Gray's-Inn-Gate, in Holbourn ; and at the Foundery, near Upper-Moor-Fields. 1747. [Price Six-pence.] 12mo., pp. 70.

Eight lines of *errata* at the end. No name of author : no index. To all the hymns but one a tune is assigned from *Hymns on the Great Festivals* (No. 94). A few of the hymns have titles prefixed.

Second edition, Bristol : Farley, 1747 ; another, not numbered, Dublin : Powell, 1747 ; Third, Bristol : Farley, 1749 ; Third, Newcastle : Gooding, 1751 ; another, Dublin : 1750 ; Fourth, London : Cock, 1755 ; Fourth, London : 1765 ; Fifth, London : 1756 ; Sixth, London : 1761 ; Seventh, Bristol : Pine, 1765 ; Eighth, Bristol : Pine, 1768 ; Ninth, London : Hawes, 1776 ; Tenth, London : Hawes, 1779 ; another, London : Paramore, 1788.

This little volume was written by Charles Wesley amidst peculiar circumstances. Its author was in the hey-day of his strength and his evangelistic labours. At no time in his life did he work harder in seeking to promote the redemption from evil of the poor, ignorant, and degraded multitudes then to be found in the land. His Journal at this period is one continuous record of toil and endurance, for it was the time of the fiercest opposition to the uprising Methodism on the part of the mobs, instigated in many instances by their mistaken clergy.

The persecution he endured assumed the utmost violence and brought him often into the greatest peril. Yet he appears to have toiled on in a spirit of glad exultation and fervent praise. His ministry was wondrously successful. Very many persons in all parts of the country were led to seek, and many found, the Redemption of which he sang. For he was not merely the poet of the evangelical revival. As a preacher he was equal to any of his companions in the impassioned fervour of his appeals and in his success. The hymns reflect the condition amidst which they were written, although there are no direct references to the circumstances of the writer. They answer to the title they bear. They are words of penitent inquiry and of earnest prayer, of exhortation and help ; words setting forth the excellency of the Redeemer and of His great Redemption,—words to encourage to hope, to patience, and to faith.

The little volume deserves the highest place amongst the group of hymn-pamphlets, of which it may be regarded as the last. It contains fifty-two hymns, some of them being equal to any of the productions of their author's facile pen. An evidence to John Wesley's estimate of their value is found in the fact that he selected twenty-four of them for his large Hymn-book.

106. HYMNS AND SACRED POEMS, published by John Wesley, M.A., Fellow of Lincoln College, Oxford, and Charles Wesley, M.A., Student of Christ Church, Oxford. (Col. iii. 16.) Dublin : Printed in the Year 1747. 12mo., pp. 60.

This contains thirty-seven hymns, selected almost exclusively from *Hymns and Sacred Poems*, 1739, (No. 15), the first book published by Wesley with that title.

It is not known by whom, or with whose authority, this was published. It is exceedingly scarce.

1748.]   **Nos. 107-108-109.**

1748.

107. SERMONS ON SEVERAL OCCASIONS. In Three Volumes. By John Wesley, M.A., Fellow of Lincoln College, Oxford. Vol. II. London: Printed by W. Strahan: and sold by T. Trye, near Gray's-Inn Gate, Holbourn; and at the Foundery, near Upper-Moor-Fields. 1748. 12mo., pp. 312.

    Second edition, Bristol: John Grabham. No date. Identical with the First edition.

    Twelve Sermons, all of which are in Volume ii. of the collected Works, 1771, (No. 276). Nine of the sermons in this volume are entitled *Discourses on our Lord's Sermon on the Mount;* four others with the same title are in Volume iii. These discourses are amongst the most beautiful examples of ethical teaching that Wesley ever penned. They deserve to be very widely read. They are the best antidote Wesley prepared for the Antinomianism which was rife in his day, and against which he wrote and preached so vigorously. The contents of this volume are unchanged in all the editions of the Sermons published during Wesley's life, excepting that in his own edition of the collected Works (No. 276) one sermon is inserted with the title, *The Lord our Righteousness.*

    This is the second of the four volumes to which reference is made in the Methodist Trust Deeds as constituting, with Wesley's Notes on the New Testament (No. 172), the standard doctrinal writings of the Methodist Church.

108. A LETTER TO A PERSON LATELY JOIN'D WITH THE PEOPLE CALL'D QUAKERS. In answer to a Letter wrote by him. Printed in the year 1748. 12mo., pp. 15.

    Dated at the beginning, Bristol, Feb. 10, 1747-8. No name or initials signed.

    Second edition printed in the year 1748; Third edition, 1748; Reprinted in the *Preservative against Unsettled Notions in Religion*, 1758, (No. 191).

    The letter begins, "You ask me, 'Is there any difference between Quakerism and Christianity?' I think there is. What that difference is, I will tell you as plainly as I can." What "Quakerism" is, he shows by extracts from Robert Barclay's work. He distinguishes between "the people commonly call'd Quakers" and their opinions. "I do by no means intend to deny that many Quakers (so termed) are real Christians; men who have the mind that was in Christ. With some of them I count it a blessing to converse, and cannot but esteem them very highly in love." Wesley described Barclay's book as "that solemn trifle."—*Works*, i. 495.

109. A WORD TO A METHODIST, written by John Wesley, February 27th, 1748. Translated into Welsh, and printed under the title of Gair I'r Methodist, O waith, Mr. J. Wesley, 1748.

    Reprinted at Dublin 1751, 16mo., pp. 8.

"Mr. Swindells informed me that Mr. E. would take it a favour if I would write some little thing, to advise the Methodists not to leave the Church, and not to rail at their ministers. I sat down immediately and wrote 'A Word to a Methodist,' which Mr. E. translated into Welsh, and printed."—*Journal*, Feb. 27, 1748. Every trace of this seems to have been lost. It is not even known whether the Dublin edition was in Welsh or English.

At this time there was a strong tendency amongst the Methodists in Wales to leave the Establishment. Between 1740 and 1780 many pamphlets were published on the subject.

110. A LETTER TO A CLERGYMAN. Dublin: Printed by S. Powell, Crane Lane. 1748. 12mo., pp. 8.

Dated at the beginning Tullamore, May 4, 1748. Signed J. W.

Another, "Dublin printed: Reprinted at London," 1748; Third edition, Bristol: Pine, 1766.

Wesley had held a conversation with a clergyman, whose name is not given, on persons being allowed to preach who had not received a University education and permission from a properly constituted authority. This applying to Wesley's lay-preachers, he undertakes to defend them. He imagines a physician who, having received a medical training and authority to practise, nevertheless fails to effect any cures; he asks what objection can be raised to an unlearned man who has some little knowledge of medicine, using his power, if he prove himself able to effect cures and does actually effect them; and he quotes the indisputable maxim, *Medicus est qui medetur*. He then applies the same method to "Physicians of the soul," and evidently with some inefficient clergymen in view, who, though having had a University training, yet turned no sinners from the error of their ways, he presses home an appeal to his opponent on behalf of the men who, though they lacked an academical training, were able to lead men from sin to righteousness, and had actually done so. The spirit of the whole is expressed in one sentence: "Every Christian, if he is able to do it, has authority to save a dying soul."

111. LESSONS FOR CHILDREN. Part III. Printed in the year 1748. 12mo., pp. 124.

See Nos. 85 and 100.
The same vignette is used in each of the first three parts.
The Biblical Lessons, published in this and the two preceding parts, reach to the end of the Book of Proverbs. The fourth part was not published until after an interval of six years.

112. A SHORT LATIN GRAMMAR. Bristol: Printed by Felix Farley. 1748. 12mo., pp. 37.

The second edition, corrected and enlarged, Bristol: W. Pine, 1763, pp. 48; Fourth, 1788; Fifth, London: Blanshard, 1813.

"I read over Mr. Holmes's 'Latin Grammar,' and extracted from it what was needful to perfect our own."—*Journal*, Oct. 15, 1750. This must have been for the second edition.

113. A Short English Grammar. Bristol: Printed by Felix Farley. 1748. 12mo., pp. 12.

Second edition, Bristol: 1761; Third edition, London: Hawes, 1778.

Short enough to delight the heart of the laziest schoolboy. An English Grammar of only nine 12mo pages is a curiosity. As may be supposed, it is very rudimentary. It was sold for one penny. Certainly Wesley strove to provide for the youngest, the poorest, and the most illiterate.

114. Thomæ a Kempis de Christo Imitando. Libri Tres. Interprete Sebast. Castellione. In Usum Juventutis Christianæ. Edidit Ecclesiæ Anglicanæ Presbyter. Bristoliæ: Typis F. Farley. Anno Salutis, 1748. 12mo., pp. 143.

This is an abridgement of the *Imitation*, similar to the *Extract of the Christian's Pattern*, (No. 26). It and the other Latin books and the Grammars were prepared for use in the Kingswood School. It is not included in any edition of Wesley's Works.

It has no preface or introduction of any kind. It displays very careful editing. Probably Wesley himself carried this and all the Latin books through the press. Copies of it are seldom seen.

No reprint of this beautiful little book is known.

115. Mathurini Corderii Colloquia Selecta. In Usum Juventutis Christianæ. Edidit Ecclesiæ Anglicanæ Presbyter. Bristoliæ: Typis F. Farley. Anno 1748. 12mo., pp. 51.

Another, Londini: Cordeux, Anno Salutis, 1813.

The conversations are arranged in four sections according to their difficulty to the beginner in Latin. The earliest consists of very short questions with equally simple replies, and the subjects throughout are of a moral, religious, or ecclesiastical character.

116. Historiæ et Præcepta Selecta. In Usum Juventutis Christianæ. Edidit Ecclesiæ Anglicanæ Presbyter. Bristoliæ: Typis F. Farley. Anno Salutis, 1748. 12mo., pp. 79.

These are arranged in five books, of which the subjects are respectively God, prudence, justice, courage, and temperance. The contents are only slightly argumentative, chiefly moral advice varied with anecdote. Crisp maxims abound, especially at the headings of the various chapters, such as, "It does not matter how many, but how good are the books you read," and "The will to sin is itself sin."

117. Instructiones Pueriles. In Usum Juventutis Christianæ. Edidit Ecclesiæ Anglicanæ Presbyter. Bristoliæ: Typis Felix Farley. Anno Salutis, 1748. 12mo., pp. 39.

Second edition, Bristoliæ: Typis Gulielmi Pine, Anno Salutis 1765; Another, Londini: Cordeux, 1812; Another, Bristoliæ: Pine, 1791.

This is divided into six sections of six or seven pages each. Everything is put in a pithy and compact form, few sentences occupying more than a couple of lines. And the tone throughout is dogmatic and certain, as though the writer was of opinion that boys should listen and obey, and were best trained by imperatives. It is substantially a translation of the *Instructions for Children* noticed already under No. 62.

The whole book is divided into Prælectiones, and is sometimes entitled *Prælectiones Pueriles*: see Short Account of Kingswood School, p. 2, (No. 127).

118. A SERIOUS ANSWER TO DR. TRAPP'S FOUR SERMONS on the Sin, Folly, and Danger of being Righteous overmuch. Extracted from Mr. Law. By John Westley, M.A., Fellow of Lincoln College, Oxford. Cork: Printed by George Harrison, 1748. 12mo., pp. 60.

A hymn of 25 stanzas, headed Isaiah lxiv., is appended, taken from *Hymns and Sacred Poems*, 1740, (No. 19).

Another, London: 1749, 12mo., pp. 48; Another, Dublin: S. Powell, 1749, no hymn.

There is a little uncertainty about the date of this publication. All the authorities give 1749; but Harrison's is plainly dated 1748. Wesley was much in Ireland in both years.

Dr. Trapp's pamphlet was entitled *The Nature, Folly, Sin, and Danger of being Righteous overmuch; with a particular view to the Doctrines and Practices of certain Modern Enthusiasts. Being the substance of Four Discourses lately preached in the Parish-Churches of Christchurch and St. Lawrence Jewry, London: and St. Martin's in the Field, Westminster.* By Joseph Trapp, D.D. London: 1739. 8vo., pp. 69. Three editions were issued in the course of the year. The Sermons were mainly directed against Law's *Serious Call to a Holy Life*, and *A Practical Treatise upon Christian Perfection*; against Whitefield's *Journal*,—"that rhapsody of madness, spiritual pride and little less than blasphemy"; and against the irregular services of the Methodists, particularly the field-preaching which had then begun. "We have heard of Field-Conventicles in Scotland among the Enthusiasts of that country. We have in former times had something of this nature in England, as practised by Brownists, Anabaptists, Quakers, Ranters, or such like. But for a Clergyman of the Church of England to pray and preach in the fields, in the country, or in the streets in the city, is perfectly new, never heard of before; a fresh honour to the blessed age in which we have the happiness to live. To pray, preach and sing psalms in the streets and fields, is worse, if possible, than intruding into pulpits by downright violence and breach of the peace. I could say much here; but am quite ashamed to speak upon a subject which is a shame and reproach, not only to our Church and country, but to human nature itself."—pp. 57, 58.

To this, Law replied with calmness and dignity, urging upon all, and upon the clergy in particular, the necessity of holiness in heart and life. Free from all severity and harshness, his book is a perfect contrast both in spirit and diction to the work of his opponent. It has been styled, "As grand a piece of writing as can be found in the English language."

Wesley, in his extract has included the substance of Law's reply, carefully editing the whole according to his usual method. He has even given some of Law's peculiar and mystic views, but he has drawn attention to the fact that they are not supported by Scripture.

119. A Letter to a Friend concerning Tea. *Homo sum : Humani nihil à me alienum puto.* By John Wesley, M.A., Fellow of Lincoln-College, Oxford. London: Printed by W. Strahan, in the year 1748. 12mo., pp. 16.

Dated at the beginning Newington, Dec. 10, 1748.

Second edition, Bristol: Farley, 1749.

Wesley describes the ill-effects upon himself and others of the use of *(strong green)* tea; and urges its abandonment, on the grounds of health and economy, by many cogent and well-sustained arguments. Two years before issuing this tract he had talked "largely" with both the men and women leaders on the use of tea. They agreed it would save great expense, as well of health as of time and money, if the poorer people of the Society could be persuaded to abandon its use; and they resolved to begin and set the example. The effect upon himself of "breaking off a custom of six and twenty years' standing" was strange enough. He says, "The first three days my head ached, more or less, all day long, and I was half asleep from morning to night. The third day my memory failed almost entirely." But he persevered, and sought his "remedy in prayer." His headache passed away; his memory became strong as ever, and he found no further inconvenience. But twelve years after, "at the close of a consumption," he recommenced its use, under medical advice. The explanation of the injurious effects of the tea is to be found mainly in the character of the tea itself. He mentions a number of other drinks which he recommends in preference to tea.

1749.

120. An Extract of the Revd. Mr. John Wesley's Journal, from Sept. 3, 1741, to October 27, 1743. [No. v.] Bristol: Printed by Felix Farley, and sold at the School Room in the Horse-Fair; also by T. Trye, near Gray's-Inn-Gate, Holborn; and at the Foundery, near Upper-Moor-Fields, London. 1749. 12mo, pp. 123.

Another, Dublin: Powell, 1749; Another, Bristol: Pine, 1769; London: Paramore, 1797.

This little volume contains accounts of unwearied labour in travelling and preaching, of physical suffering, of exposure to danger through the violence of opposing mobs, of diligent visitation of poor prisoners in their cells and of the members of his societies in their homes, of the institution of his class-meetings and the holding of his first love-feasts in London, of discomforts arising from the defection of some of his people, the unkindness of false friends and the bitterness of controversies into which he was unwillingly led, of singular incidents which some might, as he feared, ascribe to mere enthusiasm and extravagance, and, withal, of the increasing success of his preaching and toil. It also records the death of his mother and his preaching her funeral sermon in Bunhill-Fields, to "an almost innumerable company of people," his preaching from his father's tomb in Epworth and being denied the Sacrament of the Lord's Supper by the curate of the parish. And it closes with a brief but vivid account of the extremely violent treatment that he received at the hands of an infuriated mob in Wednesbury and the neighbourhood. The whole forms a striking illustration of the great and varied difficulties amidst which Methodism in its earlier years grew up.

121. A LETTER TO THE REVEREND DOCTOR CONYERS MIDDLETON, Occasioned by his late Free Enquiry. The Second edition. Bristol: Printed by Felix Farley, and sold at the School-Room in the Horse-Fair; also by T. Trye, near Gray's-Inn-Gate, Holborn; and at the Foundery near Upper-Moor-Fields, London, 1749. 12mo., pp. 102.

Dated at the beginning, January 4, 1748-9, and at the end, January 24, 1748-9.

Dr. Middleton's book, a quarto volume of nearly 400 pages, was entitled *A Free Inquiry into the Miraculous Powers, which are supposed to have subsisted in the Christian Church, from the Earliest Ages, through several successive centuries. By which it is shewn that we have no sufficient reason to believe, upon the Authority of the primitive Fathers, that any such powers were continued to the Church after the days of the Apostles.* By Conyers Middleton, D.D. London: Manby and Cox, 1749, 4to., pp. cxli., 232, xx.

Wesley makes this severe charge, "In your late Enquiry you endeavour to prove—First, That there were no miracles wrought in the primitive Church; Secondly, that all the primitive Fathers were fools or knaves; and most of them both one and the other. And it is easy to observe, the whole tenour of your argument tends to prove, Thirdly, That no miracles were wrought by Christ or his Apostles; and, Fourthly, That these, too, were fools or knaves, or both." Wesley plies him with the severest logic.

"I had designed to set out with a friend for Rotterdam; but being much pressed to answer Dr. Middleton's book against the Fathers, I postponed my voyage, and spent almost 20 days in that unpleasing employment."—*Journal*, Jan. 2, 1749. "I looked over the celebrated tract of Mr. Daillé, 'On the Right Use of the Fathers.' I soon saw what occasion that good man had given to the enemies of God to blaspheme: and that Dr. Middleton, in particular, had largely used that work in order to overthrow the whole Christian system."—*Ibid*, Jan. 28.

"He took but little notice of the Doctor's flippant remarks on what he called the Methodistical Miracles. But when he essayed his great power to sap the foundations of that religion which he had bound himself, by every sacred obligation, to maintain and enforce, Mr. Wesley ceased, comparatively, from his great labours for *nearly twenty days* (as he informs us), and in that time produced a reply to the Doctor's ponderous volume against the Miracles of the Primitive Church. There were but few men, even of those who knew Mr. Wesley, that could imagine that so many months, as the days he has mentioned, would suffice to wade through the Fathers of the three first centuries, and produce such a triumphant refutation."—Moore's *Life of J. Wesley*, ii. 413, 414.

122. A PLAIN ACCOUNT OF GENUINE CHRISTIANITY. Dublin: Printed by S. Powell, in Crane Lane. 1753. 12mo., pp. 16.

Another, Bristol: E. Farley, 1755; Bristol: Pine, 1761; Bristol: Pine, 1768; London: Paramore, 1779; London: 1788.

This tract is taken entirely and without any change from the close of the previous publication, the last page only being omitted. In it Wesley considered, "1. What is a Christian indeed? 2. What is real, genuine Christianity? 3. What is the surest and most accessible evidence that it is of God?" It was kept in constant circulation, many editions of it being issued. When the first edition was published is not known. Its appropriate place seems to be immediately after the book from which it was taken. "Perhaps the most beautiful of all Mr. Wesley's tracts."—Wesley's *Works*, 1829, Pref. xi.

123. THE MANNERS OF THE ANTIENT CHRISTIANS. Extracted from a French Author [Fleury] by John Wesley, M.A., Fellow of Lincoln-College, Oxford. Bristol: Printed by Felix Farley, and sold at the School-Room in the Horse-Fair; also by T. Trye, near Grays-Inn-Gate, Holborn; and at the Foundry near Upper-Moor-Fields, London, 1749. 12mo., pp. 24. [Price Two-pence.]

Second edition, Bristol: F. Farley, 1749; Third, Bristol: Pine, 1767; Fourth, Bristol: Pine, 1771; Fifth, London: 1791; Sixth, London: Whitfield, 1798.

Contains a brief description of the character of Christ, the condition of the Church at Jerusalem, and the state of the heathen before their conversion; then of the habits of the Christians, particularly their prayers, reading of the Scriptures, and fasting, their general demeanour, their marriages, public assemblies, care for the poor and sick, and their hospitality. A very useful tract.
Included in the collected Works, 1771, (No. 276).

124. A TOKEN FOR CHILDREN. Extracted from a late Author [see No. 63] by John Wesley, M.A., Fellow of Lincoln College, Oxford. (Luke x. 14.) [*Should be Mark.*] Bristol: Printed by Felix Farley. 1749. 12mo., pp. 34.

Second edition, Bristol, 1749; Another second, Bristol: Grabham, 1759.

This is an interesting, almost curious, instance of the care with which Wesley, in his desire to provide for the religious wants of all classes, utilised whatever fell in his way. It is a series of extracts taken from *A Token for Children: Being an exact account of the Conversion, holy and exemplary lives, and joyful deaths, of several young Children:* by James Janeway, Minister of the Gospel. Ten examples are given and carefully abridged, and published without preface or comment. Wesley's care for the young may be seen on turning to 'Children,' &c., in the Index to his collected Works.

125. DIRECTIONS CONCERNING PRONUNCIATION AND GESTURE. Bristol: Printed and sold by Felix Farley, at the Printing-Office in Castle-Green: Sold also by T. Trye, near Gray's-Inn Gate, Holborn, London. 1749. [Price One Penny.] 12mo., pp. 12.

Another, Bristol: Pine, 1770; Another, London: 1811.

Referred to in the Journals and some catalogues under the title of *Rules for Action and Utterance*.

The following are some of the Rules for Gesture ; " 1. Never clap your hands, nor thump the pulpit. 2. Use the right hand most, and when you use the left let it be only to accompany the other. 3. The right hand may be gently applied to the breast, when you speak of your own faculties, heart or conscience. 4. You must begin your action with your speech, and end it when you make an end of speaking. 5. The hands should seldom be lifted up higher than the eyes, nor let down lower than the breast. 6. Your eyes should have your hands in view, so that they you speak to may see your eyes, your mouth, and your hands all moving in concert with each other, and expressing the same thing. 7. Seldom stretch out your arms sideways, more than half a foot from the trunk of your body. 8. Your hands are not to be in perpetual motion. This the antients call'd the babbling of the hands." These, with others in the same tract, will convey some idea of Wesley's own manner when preaching. He sometimes collected as many of his preachers together as he could, and read to them these rules : see *Jour.*, Feb. 23, 1749.

"I read Mr. Sheridan's 'Lectures on Elocution' . . . and was disappointed. There is more matter in the penny tract, 'On Action and Utterance,' abundantly more, than in all Mr. S.'s book, though he seems to think himself a mere phœnix."—*Jour.*, Aug. 10, 1775.

126. A PLAIN ACCOUNT OF THE PEOPLE CALLED METHODISTS. In a letter to the Rev. Mr Perronet, Vicar of Shoreham in Kent. Bristol : Printed by F. Farley. 1749. 12mo., pp. 34.

Signed by John Wesley.

Another, Dublin : Powell, 1749 ; Second edition, London : Strahan, 1749 ; Fifth, London : II. Cock, 1755 ; Sixth, Bristol : Pine, 1764 ; Eighth, London : 1786 ; Ninth, London : Paramore, 1795.

This is a brief account of the " whole Œconomy " of the early Methodists, " not only their *practice* on every head, but likewise the *reasons* whereon it is grounded, the *occasion* of every step they have taken, and the *advantages* reaped thereby."—*Works*, ii. 167-8. " In that little tract, ' A Plain Account of the People called Methodists,' you see our whole plan. We have but one point in view, to be altogether Christians ; scriptural, rational Christians : for which we well know not only the world, but the almost Christians, will never forgive us."—Letter by J. W., *Meth. Mag.*, 1825, p. 653.

" I have not merely read, but I have devoured your letter addressed to Mr. Perronet, entitled, *A Plain Account, &c.* . . . I will, as speedily as possible, translate and publish that letter."—Letter from John de Koker ; Rotterdam, Oct. 10, 1749. See Wesley's *Works*, ii. 168.

127. A SHORT ACCOUNT OF THE SCHOOL IN KINGSWOOD, near Bristol. Bristol : Printed by Felix Farley. 1749. 12mo. pp. 8.

Second edition, Bristol : Pine, 1758.

This is a short account of the internal management of the school, the books used, the hours, the food, the habits, &c.

An edition was printed in Bristol (Pine, 1768, pp. 12), in which is added a Method of study extending over four years for "those who design to go through a course of academical learning." At the end it is affirmed, "Whosoever carefully goes through this course will be a better scholar than nine in ten of the graduates at Oxford or Cambridge."

Another short "Account of the Case of the School" is given in the *Journal*, June 22, 1751.

The several Latin books and grammars of different languages already named and others to be mentioned were all prepared for use in this school. Wesley had long desired to erect a Christian school which should not disgrace the Apostolic age. But he was hindered by want of funds, until a lady hearing of his design gave him £500 and subsequently £300 more. He gave much time and attention to this school for many years. There had already been a small school for the children of the colliers at Kingswood. It was begun by Whitefield, though the burden of it fell upon Wesley. But the new school, called the Large School, was intended for the children of the more respectable members of his societies. It was opened in June, 1748, with six masters and 285 scholars. Wesley says, "From the very beginning I met with all sorts of discouragements. Cavillers and prophets of evil were on every side. An hundred objections were made both to the whole design and every particular branch of it; especially by those from whom I had reason to expect better things. Notwithstanding which, through God's help I went on; wrote an *English*, a *Latin*, a *Greek*, a *Hebrew*, and a *French Grammar*, and printed *Prælectiones Pueriles*, with many other books for the use of the school; and God gave a manifest blessing."—*Journal*, June 22, 1751.

But in two years the school was in confusion, and the number of scholars reduced to eighteen. Wesley determined to purge the house thoroughly; and at the time the account just quoted was written there were in it only "two Masters, the house-keeper, a maid, and eleven children." After a few years a considerable portion of the school was appropriated to the education of the preachers' sons. They were instructed, boarded, and clothed. The school passed through various vicissitudes. It often fell below the expectations of its founder; nor did it reach a condition entirely satisfactory to him until nearly the close of his life. An interesting account of the school is given in Tyerman's *Life of John Wesley*, ii., 7-11.

128. Caii Sallustii Crispi Bellum Catilinarum et Jugurthinum. In Usum Juventutis Christianæ. Edidit Ecclesiæ Anglicanæ Presbyter. Bristoliæ: Typis F. Farley. Anno Salutis, 1749. 12mo., pp. 110.

A short life of Sallust in Latin is prefixed. The text is divided into rather more sections than is usual, the object being apparently sometimes to secure greater equality in length, sometimes to let a speech exactly fill a section. But there is no consistency in either respect.

129. Cornelii Nepotis Excellentium Imperatorum Vitæ. In Usum Juventutis Christianæ. Edidit Ecclesiæ Anglicanæ Presbyter. Bristoliæ: Typis F. Farley. Anno Salutis, 1749. 12mo., pp. 100.

In this impression, the Milan quarto edition of *Æmilius Probus de Viris Illustribus* is followed, though the text has benefited from the care of later revisers. The lives of Cato and Atticus are included; the editor evidently sides with the critics who attribute all the biographies to Nepos himself. A sketch of the life of Nepos in fourteen lines is prefixed.

130. EXCERPTA EX OVIDIO, VIRGILIO, HORATIO, JUVENALI, PERSIO, ET MARTIALI. In Usum Juventutis Christianæ. Edidit Ecclesiæ Anglicanæ Presbyter. Bristoliæ : Typis F. Farley. Anno Salutis, 1749. 12mo., pp. 242.

The lion's share, considerably more than half of the book, is naturally assigned to Horace, all whose works are laid under contribution. More than three-quarters of the Ars Poetica is given. Four pages are considered enough for Persius, and seven for Ovid. There are no indices, or tables of contents; but most of the pages are furnished with short but useful explanatory footnotes in Latin.

"I travelled with him [Wesley] in what might be called his home circuit, the counties of Norfolk, Kent, Oxford, and other parts during the winter, and was never absent from him in those excursions, night or day. He had always books with him in the carriage, and used sometimes to read his own *excerpta* of the classics to me."—Smith's *Life of Henry Moore*, p. 82.

131. A CHRISTIAN LIBRARY: Consisting of Extracts from, and Abridgements of, the Choicest Pieces of Practical Divinity which have been publish'd in the English Tongue. In Fifty Volumes. By John Wesley, M.A., Fellow of Lincoln College, Oxford. Vol. I. Bristol: Printed by Felix Farley, 1749. 12mo., pp. vi. iv. 296, iv.

Preface dated, Kingswood-School, March 25, 1749.

This, the largest of Wesley's publications, was issued at intervals from 1749 to 1755. Only one volume was published in 1749; Eleven in 1751; Seven in 1752; Fourteen in 1753; Eight in 1754; and Nine in 1755.

Reprinted in thirty volumes, 8vo., 1819-1827, with Wesley's corrections and eleven additional pieces which he had previously published separately.

"I have had some thoughts of printing, on a finer paper, not only all that we have published already, but, it may be, all that is most valuable in the English tongue, in threescore or fourscore volumes, in order to provide a complete library for those that fear God," &c.—Letter to Mr. Blackwell, dated Newcastle, Aug. 14, 1748: *Works*, xii. 156. The work consists exclusively of pieces of "Practical Divinity," beginning with the "Epistles of the Apostolical Fathers." The rest is selected from well-known English and a few Continental writers. It is impossible to read over the list of authors and subjects without being impressed with the wide range from which the extracts are taken. The labour of condensation must have been very great. Many a folio has been brought down to the limits of Wesley's favourite handy duodecimo.

This laborious and expensive undertaking was not remunerative. Wesley writes, "In the remaining part of this and in the following month, I prepared the rest of the books for the 'Christian Library;' a work by which I lost above 200 pounds. Perhaps the next generation may know the value of it."—*Journal*, Dec. 6, 1752. The work was prepared for the press just as he could snatch time in travelling. He did not transcribe the passages, but only marked with his pen those which he wished to be printed, altering or adding a few words here and there. As he could not correct for the press, that duty fell upon others; and he tells us that a hundred passages were left in that he had scratched out; so that the work cannot be taken as an authoritative statement of Wesley's doctrinal teaching.

"I set upon cleansing Augeas's stable; upon purging that huge work, Mr. Fox's 'Acts and Monuments,' from all the trash which that honest, injudicious writer has heaped together, and mingled with those venerable records, which are worthy to be had in everlasting remembrance."—*Journal*, Jan. 17, 1751. This is a good example of his labour. He reduced the "huge work" of three great folios to four duodecimos.

"I desire the Assistants will take care that all the large Societies provide the 'Christian Library' for the use of the preachers."—*Min. Conf.*, 1766.

"I wish all our preachers, both in England and Ireland, would herein follow my example, and frequently read in public, and enforce select portions of the 'Christian Library.'"—*Journal*, May 13, 1754. See also *Works*, x. 381; xiii. 352; Tyerman's *Life of Wesley*, ii. 65-7; Stevens' *Hist. of Meth.* Bk. vi. ch. 5.

The contents of this volume comprise the *Epistles* of S. Clement to the Corinthians and S. Polycarp to the Philippians, to which brief foot-notes are added; the *Epistles* of S. Ignatius to the Ephesians, the Magnesians, the Trallians, the Romans, the Philadelphians, and the Smyrnæans, and to S. Polycarp; also the *Martyrdom of S. Ignatius*, and the *Martyrdom of S. Polycarp*, extracted from the *Epistle* of the Church of Smyrna; together with the *Homilies* of Macarius, and an Extract of sixteen chapters from the first book of John Arndt's *True Christianity*.

132. AN ANSWER TO A LETTER PUBLISHED IN THE BATH JOURNAL, April 17, 1749, sign'd N. D. Bristol: Printed by Felix Farley. n. d. 12mo., pp. 4.

Dated Limerick, May 27, 1749, and signed John Wesley.

Three editions published in 1749.

This short but trenchant defence of his people against unfounded accusations is inserted in *Journal*, no. vii, 122, (No. 166).

An anonymous letter signed N. D., had appeared in the *Bath Journal*, in which various unfounded charges of gross immorality were brought against the Methodists. In the letter a reference is made to an accusation brought against Wesley by Dr. Conyers Middleton, to whom Wesley had recently written a letter in refutation of certain views Middleton had propounded: see No. 121. Wesley answers the charges, and, having good reason to suspect who the writer was, adds, "I no longer wonder at your so readily answering for Dr. Middleton. I am persuaded none has a better right so to do: No, not the Gentleman who lately printed in the publick papers a letter to the Lord Bishop of Exeter. Well, sir, you may now lay aside the mask. I do not require you to style yourself my *Fellow-Christian*. But we are fellow-creatures, at least fellow-servants of the great Lord of Heaven and Earth. May we both serve Him faithfully."

133. A SHORT ADDRESS TO THE INHABITANTS OF IRELAND. Occasioned by some late Occurrences. By John Wesley, M.A., Fellow of Lincoln College, Oxon. Dublin, 1749. 12mo., pp. 8.

Dated at end, Dublin, July 6, 1749.

Second edition, London: Cock, 1749.

The Address opens thus: "There has lately appeared (as you cannot be ignorant), a set of men preaching up and down in several parts of this kingdom, who for ten or twelve years have been known in England by the title of Methodists. The vulgar in Ireland term them Swaddlers." It is a calm and beautiful description of the work done by these people; and a tender inquiry as to the manner in which "a man of religion, a man of reason, a lover of mankind, and a lover of his country" ought to act towards them and their work.

"One I observed crying 'Swaddler! Swaddler!'—our usual title here. We dined with a gentleman who explained our name to us. It seems we are beholden to Mr. Cennick for it, who abounds in such-like expressions as, 'I curse and blaspheme all the gods in heaven, but the Babe that lay in the manger; the Babe that lay in Mary's lap; the Babe that lay in swaddling clouts': hence they nicknamed him Swaddler, or Swaddling John; and the word sticks to us all, not excepting the clergy."—*Life C. W.*, i. 473. This strange title, first given to the Methodists in Dublin, was afterwards used in other parts of the country.

134. A LETTER TO A ROMAN CATHOLICK. Dublin: Printed by S. Powell, in Crane-lane, 1749. 12mo., pp. 12.

Dated at end, Dublin, July 18th, 1749.

Second edition, London: Sold at the Foundery, 1755; Another, Dublin: S. Powell, 1750.

This is a tender, fraternal letter. Deploring the want of good feeling between Protestants and Catholics, Wesley inquires if nothing can be done to give "a check to this flood of unkindness", and to restore "at least some small degree of love among our neighbours and countrymen." He then briefly states the essentials of the faith and practice of true Protestants; and asks, "Now is there anything wrong in this? Is there any one point which you do not believe as well as we? But you think we ought to believe more. We will not now enter into the dispute," &c., &c.

Then on the practice of a true Protestant he adds, "I say a true Protestant: for I disclaim all common swearers, Sabbath-breakers, drunkards; all whoremongers, liars, cheats, extortioners; in a word, all that live in open sin. These are no Protestants: they are no Christians at all. Give them their own name: they are open heathens. They are the curse of the nation, the bane of society, the shame of mankind, the scum of the earth."

135. MINUTES OF SOME LATE CONVERSATIONS BETWEEN THE REVD. M. WESLEYS AND OTHERS. Dublin: Printed by S. Powell, in Crane-lane. 1749. 12mo., pp. 30.

136. MINUTES OF SOME LATE CONVERSATIONS BETWEEN THE REVD. M. WESLEYS AND OTHERS. Dublin: Printed by S. Powell, in Crane-lane. 1749. 12mo., pp. 32.

Neither of these was re-printed separately. THESE ARE THE FIRST PRINTED MINUTES OF THE CONFERENCE. They are Wesley's abridgement and re-arrangement of the MS. Minutes of the meetings of the Conference, 1744-8. The former relates to "Conversations" held at the Conferences of

1744-7, and as the conversations were mainly on questions of doctrine, the pamphlet was afterwards called "The Doctrinal Minutes." The latter embraces the Conferences of 1744-8; and as it contains the regulations on discipline, it was called "The Disciplinary Minutes."

"Up to this time (1749) all that had been recorded of the several Conferences previously held was preserved and circulated in MS. No printed Minutes of an earlier date than these have yet been discovered. It is remarkable that while the first of these two Tracts was largely circulated at the time, and even reprinted by Mr. Wesley in his own edition of his Works, vol. xv., the second, which contains the Minutes of the first Conferences on the subject of discipline, was suffered to become so scarce, that when it was reprinted, in 1862, only two copies beside that put before the printer, were known to exist. Historically it is of great value still. Probably the circumstance of its being printed in Ireland contributed to its extreme scarcity; though in the case of the smaller tract that circumstance did not operate. Possibly also Mr. Wesley considered it superseded by the subsequent publications, technically called 'The Large Minutes.'"—Osborn.

A manuscript copy written by John Bennet, one of the "Helpers" who was present at most of these early Conferences, has lately been found; and is about to be printed under the auspices of the Wesley Historical Society.

In Wesley's own copy of the latter pamphlet he has changed the word "Assistants," in the first instance to "Preachers or Helpers," and afterwards to "Helpers." And, to the list of books ordered to be kept "for our own use at London, Bristol, and Newcastle," he has added the *Christian Library* and *Wesley's Hymns and Poems*.

These rare pamphlets are reprinted in Vol. I. of the revised 8vo. edition of the *Minutes of Conference*, (London: Mason, 1862). They are placed there as the first *Minutes*, in lieu of the compilation to be found in the original 8vo. edition, 1812 (prepared by order of the Conference of that year by Mr. Benson), which compilation seems to have been made from the "Doctrinal Minutes" (No. 135), and from the second edition of the *Large Minutes* (1763), to be noticed hereafter.

There were no other annual *Minutes* printed until 1765. The only known records of the intervening Conferences are the short notices of them in Wesley's *Journal;* a few MS. memoranda by different persons, most of which are published in the revised *Minutes;* a brief account of the Conference of 1749 contained in the first edition of the *Large Minutes* (1753); and extracts from the decisions of other Conferences, embodied in the second edition of the *Large Minutes* (1763).

137. HYMNS COMPOSED FOR THE USE OF THE BRETHREN. By the Right Reverend and Most Illustrious C.Z. Published for the Benefit of all Mankind, in the year 1749. 12mo., pp. 12.

No name of author or printer given.

On the reverse of the title is this address, "To the Reader. The following hymns are copied from a Collection printed some months since for James Hutton, in Fetter Lane, London. You will easily observe, That they have no affinity at all to that old Book called *The Bible*: the Illustrious Author soaring as far above this, as above the beggarly elements of *Reason* and *Common-Sense*."

A foot-note cut from an old book reads as follows: "See a Collection of Moravian Hymns, published by Mr. Westley; and printed for Mr. Lewis, in Paternoster Row." In a Catalogue of Wesley's, of this year, is mentioned "Moravian Hymns, price 1d." That the "Brethren" felt themselves compromised by the Count's hymns is obvious from the action taken in

No. 138. [1749.

reference to his hymn-book.—See *Life of Zinzendorf*, by Rev. August Gottlieb Spangenberg; London: Holdsworth, 1838. Perhaps the less said about these so-called hymns the better. They have their place in the history of the very painful discussions of that time; but they have long been expunged from the Hymn-book of the Moravian Church.

138. HYMNS AND SACRED POEMS. In Two Volumes. By Charles Wesley, M.A., Student of Christ-Church, Oxford. Bristol: Printed and sold by Felix Farley. 1749. 12mo. Vol. I., pp. 332, iii.; Vol. II., pp. 336, iii.

"A second edition of these hymns was published in the year 1752: and that without any other alteration, than that of a few literal mistakes."—*Works*, xi. 393. Another, called the second edition, Bristol: F. Farley, 1755 and 1756—a less correct edition. Index to first lines added.

These volumes were published by subscription. The price "in quires" was five shillings, of which half was to be paid on subscribing. The author left a small manuscript volume containing the names of persons who subscribed for 1145 copies of the work. The preachers acted as agents, distributing the books and collecting the subscriptions. Stevenson says, "The work was published by subscription in order to raise money for the author's marriage, and to enable him to commence house-keeping."—*The Meth. Hymn-Book*, p. 21.

The tables of contents are the same in the several editions. Each volume is divided into two parts, and many of the hymns are grouped together under various heads. Most of the hymns have titles prefixed. Hitherto the hymn books have borne the joint names of the two brothers, and no other intimation has been given of their authorship; but these are authenticated as of Charles's composition exclusively.

Many of the hymns in these volumes were suggested by the personal circumstances of the writer. "Some of them are founded upon particular texts of Scripture; others express the author's religious feelings in particular states of mind; not a few were written upon special occasions, as the death of friends, providential deliverances, the success of his ministry, the persecution and opposition with which he had to contend. Several of them are intended for the use of persons in peculiar circumstances, such as ministers of the Gospel, medical practitioners, widows, the afflicted and the dying. More than one-fourth of the second volume consists of 'Hymns for Christian Friends.' Many of these were originally addressed to Sarah Gwynne before his marriage with her, and others after their union; a few verbal alterations being occasionally made, for the purpose of giving them a more general character, and of adapting them to popular use. While these volumes exhibit his piety and genius to great advantage, they throw considerable light upon his personal history, and his prevalent habits of thought. The first volume concludes with a hymn of unusual length and of almost unparalleled sublimity and force. Nothing could give so perfect a view of the spirit in which he had exercised his ministry, from the time at which he began his glorious career in Moorfields and Kennington-Common to this period of his life." The hymn is entitled "For a Person called forth to bear his Testimony." See *Life of C. W.*, i. 542-5: also *The Methodist Hymn Book*, by G. J. Stevenson, p. 20.

"In the year 1749 my brother printed two volumes of 'Hymns and Sacred Poems.' As I did not see these before they were published, there were some things in them that I did not approve of."—J. Wesley's *Works*, xi. 391. That he approved generally of the work is evident, for he extracted 143 hymns from it for his *Collection of Hymns*, (No. 348).

A small tract containing a number of hymns taken from these volumes was issued anonymously in 1759.

1750.

139. SERMONS ON SEVERAL OCCASIONS. In Three Volumes. By John Wesley, M.A., Fellow of Lincoln-College, Oxford. Vol. III. London: Printed by W. Strahan, and sold by T. Trye, near Gray's-Inn Gate, Holbourn; J. Robinson, Ludgate-street; at the Foundery, near Upper Moorfields; and at the School Room in the Horse-Fair, Bristol. 1750. 12mo., pp. 260.

Contains twelve Sermons.

Second Edition, Bristol: W. Pine, no date, one additional sermon; another, Dublin: 1750; 4th Edition, London: Paramore, 1787.

"I retired to Kingswood, to write part of the volume which I had promised to publish this winter."—*Journal*, Oct. 30, 1749. "I retired to Newington once more, and on Saturday, 16, finished my sermons."—*ibid*. Dec. 11, 1749.
Several of the sermons from this and the two preceding volumes (Nos. 88 and 107) were frequently reprinted separately. Among the instances are a pamphlet extracted from this volume and published under the title of *Three Sermons on the Original, Nature, Properties, and Use of the Law; and its Establishment through Faith:* (Isa. xlii, 21.) Bristol: F. Farley, 1751; the sermon on *Catholic Spirit*, published 1755, with hymn on *Catholic Love*, by C. W.; also *A Caution against False Prophets* (Matt. vii., 15-20), *particularly recommended to the people called Methodists*. Bristol: Grabham, 1758.

140. A LETTER TO THE AUTHOR OF THE ENTHUSIASM OF METHODISTS AND PAPISTS COMPAR'D. (*Agedum! Pauca accipe contrà.*—HOR.) London: Printed by H. Cock, and sold by G. Woodfall, near Charing-Cross; A. Dodd, at the Peacock, in the Strand; J. Robinson, in Ludgate-Street; T. Trye, near Gray's Inn; and T. James, under the Royal-Exchange. [Price Four-pence.] 12mo., pp. 45.

Dated, at the end, Canterbury, Feb. 1, 1749-50; and signed, John Wesley. A severe "postscript" on last page.

The anonymous author of the "Comparison" was George Lavington, Bishop of Exeter. His performance was very unworthy either of his ability or his dignity. He first directed his rude assault against Whitefield; then against Wesley. Whitefield replied at once, though he thought that "upon some accounts it did not deserve an answer;" the Rev. Vincent Perronet, Vicar of Shoreham, published three separate, carefully written letters of defence; and Wesley wrote a second Letter at the end of the year. But the Bishop's writing was its own severest condemnation. "Bishop Lavington, the anonymous author, deserves to be coupled with the men who flung dead cats and rotten eggs at the Methodists, not with those who assailed their tenets with arguments, or even serious rebuke."—*John Wesley*, by Julia Wedgwood, p. 313.

141. THE CAUSE AND CURE OF EARTHQUAKES. A Sermon preach'd from Psalm xlvi. 8. London: Printed in the year 1750. 12mo., pp. 24.

No name of writer or printer.

Second edition, London, 1756, states on the title page that it was occasion'd by the earthquake on March 8, 1750, and gives the author's name, Charles Wesley, M.A., late Student of Christ Church, Oxford, but neither printer nor publisher. Osborn thinks it was probably printed by Strahan, whose woodcut appears in the first edition. There were several of the Wesley pamphlets published about this time in London without the name of printer or publisher. It would be interesting to know why.

"This morning (Mar. 8) at a quarter after five we had another shock of an earthquake far more violent than that of February 8th. I was just repeating my text, when it shook the Foundery so violently, that we all expected it to fall upon our heads. A great cry followed from the women and the children. I immediately cried out, 'Therefore will we not fear, though the earth be removed and the hills be carried into the midst of the sea: for the Lord of hosts is with us, the God of Jacob is our refuge.' He filled my heart with faith and my mouth with words, shaking their souls, as well as their bodies."—Letter from C. W. to J. W., *Life of C. W.* i. 549.

"Many flocked to the morning word, and were yet more stirred up thereby. I have scarce ever seen so many at intercession. At the chapel I preached on the occasion, from Psalm xlvi., with very great awakening power."—*Journal* C.W., Mar. 9, 1750. "Fear filled our chapel, occasioned by a prophecy of the earthquake's return this night. I preached my written sermon on the subject with great effect, and gave out several suitable hymns."—*Ibid*, April 4, 1750. (See *Hymns occasioned by the Earthquake*, published in this year, No. 148).

Jackson says the sermon was first published "in all probability within a few weeks of the memorable eighth day of March, 1750, on which the shock of an earthquake was strongly felt in the metropolis of Great Britain, and excited general consternation and alarm. Although this impressive sermon was published anonymously, no doubt can be entertained about its being the production of Mr. Wesley's pen. The sentiments and manner are purely *Wesleyan*, and it is also advertised for sale among his other single sermons in several of Mr. Wesley's old catalogues."—Pref. *Wesley's Sermons*, edited by Thomas Jackson. Two vols., London: Kershaw, 1825. He thus seems to have made the mistake of attributing it to John Wesley. Nor is it ascribed to Charles in the 1829 edition of Wesley's *Works*. It is also attributed to John in a "tract series" of sermons, issued from the Book-room. London: Mason, n.d. But it was certainly written by Charles.

142. A COMPENDIUM OF LOGICK. Bristol: F. Farley. 1750. 12mo., pp. 33.

Second edition, enlarged, London: printed in the year 1756, pp. 42, containing an Appendix, "Of the manner of using Logic, extracted from Bishop Saunderson"; Third, no date, London: pp. 48; Fourth, enlarged, London: Cordeux, 1811.

"We set out at five, and at six came to the sands. But the tide was in, so that we could not pass. So I sat down in a little cottage for three or four hours, and translated Aldrich's Logic."—*Journal*, Mar. 25, 1750.

This was prepared for use in the school at Kingswood. Though Logic was not in the ordinary curriculum, it was prescribed for those "who designed to go through a course of Academical learning."—See *Short Account of Kingswood School*, (No. 127). The Compendium is a mere outline of Aldrich's *Artis Logicæ Compendium*. Wesley was thoroughly tutored in dialectics. He tells us, "For several years I was Moderator in the disputations which were held six times a week at Lincoln College, in Oxford. I could not avoid acquiring hereby some degree of expertness in arguing; and especially in discerning and pointing out well-covered and plausible fallacies. I have since found abundant reason to praise God for giving me this honest art. By this when men have hedged me in by what they call demonstrations, I have been many times able to dash them in pieces; in spite of all its covers, to touch the very point where the fallacy lay; and it flew open in a moment." And he goes on to show how he had been aided by it in particular instances, especially in some of the controversial pieces that have just come under our review.

143. A LETTER TO THE REVD. MR. BAILY, OF CORKE, in Answer to a Letter to the Revd. John Wesley. By J. W., M.A., Fellow of Lincoln College, Oxford. Dublin: Printed by S. Powell, in Crane-Lane. 1750. 12mo., pp. 31.

Dated at the beginning, Limerick, June 8, 1750, not signed.

Second edition, London: J. Robinson, 1750.

"Thursday 14.—Sufficient for this day was the labour thereof. We were on horseback, with but an hour or two's intermission, from five in the morning, till within a quarter of eleven at night. Friday, 15.—We set out at four, and reached Kilkenny about noon—my horse tired in the afternoon, so I left him behind, and borrowed that of my companion. I came to Aymo about eleven, and would very willingly have passed the rest of the night here, but the good woman of the inn was not minded that I should. At last she opened the door just wide enough to let out four dogs upon me. So I rode on to Ballybrittas—about twelve I laid me down. I think this was the longest day's journey I ever rode; being fifty old Irish, that is, about ninety English miles. Saturday, 16.—I rested, and transcribed the 'Letter to Mr. Baily.'"—*Journal*, June 1750. This was a letter of defence in reply to one of great virulence written under the pseudonyms of "George Fisher" and "Philalethes." In Wesley's reply is an account of the rough handling the Methodists received in Cork from the rabble and even from the Corporation.

144. A SHORT ACCOUNT OF GOD'S DEALINGS WITH MR. THOMAS HOGG. Written by Himself in a Letter to his Minister. London: Printed in the Year 1750. 12mo., pp. 10.

Dated Nov., 1741, and signed Thomas Hogg. A hymn is appended with the date, June 29, 1750, and the title, "On the Death of Mr. Thomas Hogg." It is in Vol. vi. of the *Poetical Works*, pp. 209-10. An epitaph follows it.

Another edition. Bristol: Pine, 1769.

"I preached a written sermon at Spitalfields, on my beloved friend and brother Hogg. The chapel was crowded, and the house of mourning was turned to an house of great rejoicing."—C. Wesley's *Journal*, July 11. Hogg was one of the very early Methodists, a member of one of the first select Bands that met at the Foundery, and one of Wesley's stewards.

145. PHÆDRI FABULÆ SELECTÆ. In Usum Juventutis Christianæ. Edidit Ecclesiæ Anglicanæ Presbyter. Bristoliæ: Typis F. Farley. Anno Salutis, 1750. 12mo., pp. 35.

Another of the carefully prepared books designed for use in the School at Kingswood. They were occasionally re-published, and kept on sale until the early part of this century.

Nos. 146-147-148-148a. [1750.

146. DESIDERII ERASMI ROTERODAMI COLLOQUIA SELECTA. In Usum Juventutis Christianæ. Edidit Ecclesiæ Anglicanæ Presbyter. Bristoliæ : Typis F. Farley. Anno Salutis, 1750. 12mo., pp. 85.
    Another, Londini, Cordeux, 1813.

A Latin life of Erasmus occupies the first four pages, and is followed by a table of contents. Twelve of his colloquies have been selected, and each is introduced by a good summary of its contents. There are no notes of any kind, but the text has been carefully read, and is printed from type of unusual excellence for its date.

147. HYMNS FOR NEW YEAR'S DAY, 1750. Bristol : Printed by Felix Farley. [Price One Penny.] 12mo., pp. 11.
Seven Hymns. No date.

    Published also as *Hymns for New Year's Day*, 1752, London : Cock ; and for 1755, London : Printed and sold at the Foundery ; Another for 1758 ; afterwards simply as *Hymns for New Year's Day*. Several editions, 1761-6-9, 1777, 1785, 1791, and others. Sometimes bound up with *Nativity Hymns* (No. 84).

"At four in the morning our room was excessively crowded while I proclaimed the Gospel year of Jubilee. We did not part without a blessing."—C. Wesley's *Journal*, Jan. 1, 1750.

Of the seven hymns in this tract, four have a direct reference to the year of Jubilee, and some of them doubtless were sung for the first time at that service, for which they had been prepared. One, now printed for the first time, was the well-known "Watch-night" hymn—

> Come let us anew
> Our journey pursue,
> Roll round with the year,
> And never stand still till the Master appear.

148. HYMNS OCCASIONED BY THE EARTHQUAKE, March 8, 1750. London: Printed in the year 1750. 12mo., pp. 12.
Six Hymns.

148A. DITTO DITTO. Part II. London : Printed in the year 1750. 12mo., pp. 23.
Thirteen hymns.

    A second edition of Part I. was printed at London in the same year and with the same title-page as the first edition; and in 1756 was published Part I., "The Third Edition," together with Part II., "The Second Edition." The number of Hymns in each part is the same as in the first edition. The parts are not paged consecutively. In the same year an edition, miscalled the second of Part I. and the second of Part II., was printed by E. Farley, Bristol. In this edition, on the title-page of Part I., appear the words : "To which are *(sic)* added an Hymn upon the pouring out of the Seventh Vial, Rev. xvi., xvii., &c.,

1750.] **No. 148.**

occasioned by the destruction of Lisbon;" and on the title-page of Part II, "To which are added an Hymn for the English in America, and another for the year 1756." The former hymn is described as "Written in January, 1756." Together pp. 36; but not consecutively paged.

NOTE A.—

"I prepared a short 'History of England,' for the use of the children; and on Friday and Saturday a short 'Roman History,' as an introduction to the Latin Historians."—*Journal*, Oct. 11, 1750.

This entry in the Journal has led Heylin to place "A Short History of England" and "A Short Roman History" in this year. Tyerman also says: "He also wrote, at this time, his 'Short History of England' and his 'Short Roman History.'"

That the histories here mentioned were ever printed is extremely doubtful. It was Wesley's practice to mark passages to be read in the books used at Kingswood School. "I went into the school and heard half the children their lessons, and then selected passages of the 'Moral and Sacred Poems.'"—*Journal*, Sept. 27, 1750. "I spent most of the day in revising Kennet's 'Antiquities,' and marking what was worth reading in the school."—*ib.* Sept. 29. "I revised, for the use of the children, Archbishop Potter's 'Grecian Antiquities,' a dry, dull, heavy book."—*ib.* Oct. 3. "I revised Mr. Lewis's 'Hebrew Antiquities,' something more entertaining than the other, and abundantly more instructive."—*ib.* Oct. 4. It is probable that he refers, in the extract given above, to such a preparation of a Roman and an English History.

No published "short" History of England is known. It is not mentioned in any list or catalogue, or in the Books of Kingswood School. *A Concise History of England*, in 4 vols., was published afterwards, the preface to which bears date, "London, Aug. 10, 1775," and the Second Volume, 1776: (see No. 313). The earliest *Short Roman History* known was published in 1773: (see No. 289).

NOTE B.—

In this year was also published a pamphlet entitled, "THE CONTENTS OF A FOLIO HISTORY OF THE MORAVIANS OR UNITED BRETHREN, printed in 1749, and privately sold under the title of *Acta Fratrum Unitatis in Anglia*; with suitable Remarks. Humbly address'd to the pious of every Protestant Denomination in Europe and America. By a Lover of the Light." (2 Pet. ii. 19.) London: J. Roberts, 1750. [Price 4d.] 12mo., pp. 60.

Heylin places this under 1751, and says: "The whole of this anonymous pamphlet was not written by John Wesley. I am not aware that it has ever before been attributed to him; but I think it bears internal evidence of having been prepared under his supervision. The preface, unless I am much mistaken, is his. The postscript is signed 'A Methodist'; throughout the pamphlet great prominence is given to the Wesleys and their opinions; and, as a further corroboration, John Wesley was about this very time writing strong things in his Journals against the Moravians. This pamphlet is now exceedingly scarce." The *Acta Fratrum Unitatis in Anglia, 1749,* is a thin folio of 156 pages. An octavo edition was also published. The first part of it relates to a petition presented to the House of Commons by Deputies of the Moravian Churches, praying for permission to settle "in His Majesty's Colonies in America." The petition was referred to a Committee; and the first 58 pages of the folio contain the report of the Committee, together with a copy of the several documents presented by the Petitioners. Some of these are of much historic interest. To this are appended several documents on the Faith, the Liturgy and other matters relating to the Moravian Church.

The pamphlet which Heylin attributes to Wesley contains a "Table of Contents" of the "Acta" and a description of other documents included in the folio volume, together with criticisms severe and keen upon them. At the beginning of the pamphlet some of the hymns in the Brethren's Hymn Book are quoted,—quite an unnecessary work for Wesley to do, for the character of these so-called hymns had already been exposed by him. The postscript is an appeal to "those of the Unitas Fratrum who were once Methodists."

Tyerman, too, gives an account of this pamphlet and of some circumstances which appeared to him to justify its publication. He thinks "there is little doubt that Wesley was its author."—*Life of Wesley*, ii. 96-100.

. There is not a particle of evidence that Wesley wrote this pamphlet, or that he had any hand in it whatever. He was extremely particular in dating his papers, and the preface to this pamphlet is dated, "London, Oct. 2, 1750." Wesley was then in Bristol, and had been for some time. This is conclusive proof, if one were needed, that he did not write it. It is more probable that it was written by the Rev. Vincent Perronet, Vicar of Shoreham, by whose publisher it was printed, and with whose tracts it was sometimes bound up.

1751.

149. THOUGHTS UPON INFANT-BAPTISM. Extracted from a late Writer. Bristol: Printed by Felix Farley. 1751. 12mo., pp. 21, and false title, 2 pp.

Another, 1780; London: Story, 1804; London: Mason, 1837.

The Societies in some parts of the country appear to have been much disturbed by persons who condemned Infant-baptism. Wesley wrote this tract in defence of the rite. He observes that it has been "a troublesome dispute almost ever since the Reformation;" and he confines himself in the tract to a rehearsal of "a few arguments commonly used to vindicate the practice of baptizing children." The tract was taken mainly from *The History of Infant Baptism*: By W. Wall, Vicar of Shoreham.

Anyone having a knowledge of Wall's volumes will be able to estimate the amount of labour required to extract from them a consecutive pamphlet of nineteen pages. Certainly the labour of discovering the source of the pamphlet and tracing the extracts in the original work has proved itself to be not small.

"I made an end of visiting the classes, miserably shattered by the sowers of strange doctrines. At one I preached at Tipton Green, where the Baptists also have been making havoc of the flock; which constrained me in speaking on those words, 'Arise, and be baptized, and wash away thy sins,' to spend near ten minutes in controversy, which is more than I had done in public for many months (perhaps years) before."—*Journal*, April 3, 1751.

The Rev. Vincent Perronet had already (1749) written "*A Defence of Infant Baptism* (In answer to the Objections of the late learned Mr. Gale) In a Letter to the Rev. Mr. John Wesley, A.M., Fellow of Lincoln College, Oxford. To which is added, an Appendix chiefly designed for the benefit of the unlearned reader:" London: J. Roberts. 12mo., pp. 68. But this was not so truly suited to meet the need of "the unlearned reader" as Wesley's pamphlet was.

150. A Short Hebrew Grammar. London: Printed by W. B. [William Bowyer], and sold by T. Trye, near Gray's-Inn-Gate, Holbourn; J. Robinson, Ludgate Street; and by George Englefield, in West Street, near the Seven Dials. 1751. 12mo., pp. 11

Another edition, printed by W. Bowyer and J. Nichols, and sold at the Foundery, near Upper-Moorfields, 1769, 12mo., pp. 23.

On Sunday, Feb. 10, 1751, when walking over London Bridge, Wesley slipped, and sprained his ankle; but he managed to preach at Snowfields and at Seven Dials; and attempted to do so at the Foundery, but could not, the sprain growing worse. He was removed to Threadneedle Street, where he "spent the remainder of the week, partly in prayer, reading, and conversation, partly in writing an 'Hebrew Grammar' and 'Lessons for Children.'" Heylin places both under this year; but there is no record of the printing of the fourth part of the *Lessons for Children* until the year 1754.

151. A Short French Grammar. London: Printed by W. B. [William Bowyer], and sold by T. Trye, near Gray's-Inn-Gate, Holbourn; J. Robinson, Ludgate Street; and by George Englefield, in West-Street, near the Seven Dials. 1751. 12mo., pp. 35.

"I began writing a short French Grammar."—*Journal*, March 6, 1750.

Wesley wrote of the French language thus: "The French is the poorest, meanest language in Europe; it is no more comparable to the German or Spanish than a bagpipe is to an organ; and with regard to poetry in particular, considering the incorrigible uncouthness of their measure, and their always writing in rhyme (to say nothing of their vile double rhymes, nay, and frequent false rhymes), it is as impossible to write a fine poem in French as to make fine music on a Jew's harp."—*Journal*, Oct. 11, 1756. He does not seem to have edited any French books for use in the Kingswood School.

152. A Second Letter to the Author of The Enthusiasm of Methodists and Papists Compar'd. (*Ecce iterum Chrispinus.*—Juv.) London: Printed by H. Cock in Bloomsbury-Market, and sold at the Foundery, near Upper-Moorfields; by J. Robinson, in Ludgate Street; by T. Trye, near Gray's-Inn-Gate, Holborn; by T. James, under the Royal Exchange; and G. Englefield in West-Street, near the Seven Dials. 1751. 12mo., pp. xi. 60.

This contains a prefatory letter addressed to the "Lord Bishop of Exeter," signed John Wesley, and dated Nov. 27, 1750. The anonymous author of "The Enthusiasm" had affirmed, in the third part of his work, published after Wesley's first letter, that certain statements, charging Wesley with gross misconduct, had been made to the "Bishop of Exeter," in the presence of several witnesses. Wesley, knowing the Bishop to be the author of the anonymous production, addresses a letter to him, and prefixes it to his second answer to the anonymous author. The writer of "The Enthusiasm" had undertaken to prove that the whole conduct of the Methodists was but a counterpart of the most wild fanaticisms of Popery, and to support this charge by quotations from their own writings, compared with quotations from Popish authors. Wesley tracks the course of his opponent all through his assertions step by step with the utmost precision, and with relentless severity exposes his errors, until he closes with, "I had occasion once before to say to an opponent, You know not to show mercy. Yet that gentleman did regard truth and justice. But you regard neither mercy, justice, nor truth. To vilify, to blacken is your one point. I pray God it may not be laid to your charge! May He shew you mercy though you shew none!"

This is signed John Wesley, but not dated. In the Journal, however, reference is thus made to it, under date, Nov. 19, 1751, "I began writing a letter to the comparer of the Papists and Methodists. Heavy work such as I should never choose; but sometimes it must be done. Well might the ancient say, 'God made practical divinity necessary, the devil controversial.'" This throws the publication of the letter into the last month of 1751.

The Bishop's publication was apparently put to strange uses. Wesley tells us, "I heard at church, by way of sermon, part of 'Papists and Methodists Compared.' But it did not lessen the congregation at one; on whom I enforced (what they were somewhat more concerned in), 'What shall it profit a man' to 'gain the whole world, and lose his own soul.'"—*Journal*, Aug. 25, 1751.

153. SERIOUS THOUGHTS UPON THE PERSEVERANCE OF THE SAINTS. London: Printed in the year 1751. 12mo., pp. 24.

London: H. Cock, 1751; Dublin: S. Powell, 1752; London: 1779; London: G. Story, 1804; Dublin: Napper, 1813.

This was published quite anonymously; it was not signed nor was the printer's name given; but it was included in Wesley's own edition of his works, and it appears in the catalogues. It is a calm, brief, dispassionate treatment of a solemn subject, concerning which Wesley declares, "I am sensible either side of this question is attended with great difficulties, such as reason alone could never remove. Therefore to the law and the testimony; let the living oracles decide." He gives several Scriptural descriptions of persons termed saints, and shows why he believes that persons so described may fall away and perish everlastingly, answering objections as he proceeds. The style is, as usual, clear, concise, direct, and strictly logical. It would be difficult to find elsewhere so much said on this subject in so few words.

NOTE.—During this year volumes ii.-xii. of the *Christian Library* were published.

Volume ii. contains the remainder of the *Extract of John Arndt's True Christianity*, commenced in vol. i., also the first portion of several pieces entitled, *Acts and Monuments of the Christian Martyrs. Extracted from Mr. John Fox. To which is prefix'd Some Account of his Life.* These extracts extend to the close of volume v. They are preceded by an address *To the Reader*, in which Wesley writes, "After the venerable remains of Ignatius and Polycarp, closed with the artless, yet lively Discourses of Macarius and John Arndt's nervous account of *True Christianity*, worthy of the earliest ages; I believe nothing could be more acceptable to the serious reader, than to see this Christianity reduced to practice, I was therefore easily determined to subjoin to these *The Acts and Monuments of the Christian Martyrs*. Here we see that pure and amiable religion *evidently set forth before our eyes:* assaulted indeed by all the powers of earth and hell, but more than conqueror over all." And he adds, that in abridging this vast work, he had purposely omitted "not only all the secular history, but likewise those Accounts, Writings, and Examinations of the Martyrs, which contained nothing particularly affecting or instructive." The *Life of Mr. John Fox* which is prefixed, was written by his son.

Volume vi. contains *A supplement to Mr. Fox's Acts and Monuments. Extracted from Mr. Clark's General Martyrology.* It is preceded by Samuel Clark's *Address to the Christian Reader.* To each volume is appended a full Table of Contents.

Vols. vii., viii., and part of ix., contain abridgements of *Meditations and Vows, Divine and Moral,* and other writings, By Bishop Hall; and *Extracts from the Works of Robert Bolton, B.D.,* sometime Fellow of Brasen-Nose College, in Oxford; preceded by a short account of *The Life and Death of Mr. Bolton.* In a Preface to the seventh volume, Wesley tells us he thought that after the account of the lives, sufferings, and death of the men "who sealed the antient religion with their blood, nothing would be more agreeable or more profitable to the serious reader than some extracts from the writings of those, who sprung up, as it were, out of their ashes." His desire is to rescue from obscurity, "a few of the most eminent of these: I say, a few, for there is a multitude of them which it would be tedious even to name"; nor does he attempt "to abridge all the works of these few; for some of them are immensely voluminous." Referring to the "blemishes of these excellent writers," he says, "Their language is not so smooth and terse, as that of the present age. Many of their expressions are now quite out of date, and some unintelligible to common readers. Add to this that they are exceedingly verbose, and full of circumlocutions and repetitions." These faults Wesley could not brook, and he proceeds to describe his method of correcting them, a method that he applied in all the writing that he prepared for the press. "The most exceptionable phrases are laid aside, the obsolete and unintelligible expressions altered; abundance of superfluous words are retrenched; the immeasurably long sentences shortened; many tedious circumlocutions are dropt and many needless repetitions omitted." Two other errors, observable in the greater part of the Puritan Writers, he proposes to correct. One of these is, they drag in controversy on every occasion, "nay without any occasion or pretence at all"; the other, "that they generally give a low and imperfect view of sanctification or holiness." The former he finds it easy to remedy "by leaving out all that but glanced upon controversy; the latter is supplied by the following and preceding tracts."

The latter part of vol. ix. and part of vol. x. contain *Extracts from the Works of John Preston, D.D., Chaplain in Ordinary to His Majesty King Charles I. To which is prefix'd some account of his life by the Rev. Mr. Hall.* The extracts from Preston embrace, *The Breast-plate of Faith and Love,* with Sibs' address " to the Christian Reader"; and *The New Covenant or the Saint's Portion.* In the latter part of volume x., are *Extracts from the Works of Richard Sibs, D.D.,* together with some account of his life.

Vol. xi. and part of xii. are devoted to *Extracts from the Works of Tho. Goodwin, Doctor in Divinity;* whose writings alone, Wesley said, "would have sufficed to fill fifty volumes." The remaining portion of vol. xii. is occupied by *Extracts from the Works of William Dell;* and *Sermons on Several Subjects preached about the year 1650, by Thomas Manton, D.D.,* preceded by a brief account of his life.

1752.

154. A SECOND LETTER TO THE LORD BISHOP OF EXETER, in Answer to his Lordship's late Letter. By John Wesley, M.A. London: Printed by H. Cock in

No. 155. [1752.

Bloomsbury-Market; and sold at the Foundery, near Upper-Moorfields; by J. Robinson, in Ludgate Street; by T. Trye, near Gray's-Inn-Gate, Holborn; by T. James, under the Royal-Exchange; and G. Englefield, in West-Street, near the Seven Dials. 1752. 12mo., pp. 12.

Dated at end, Newcastle upon Tyne, May 8, 1752; and signed John Wesley.

Second edition, London: H. Cock, 1752.

Wesley's first letter to Bishop Lavington, of Exeter, was prefixed to the *Second Letter to the Author of the Enthusiasm of Methodists and Papists compar'd:* (see No. 152). In it Wesley defended himself against certain vile aspersions. This second letter is written in answer to his lordship's reply to the first. It has no permanent value save to show how Wesley's good name was traduced, and how he was able to defend it.

155. PREDESTINATION CALMLY CONSIDERED. By John Wesley, M.A.

"That, to the height of this great argument,
I may assert eternal Providence,
And justify the ways of God with man."—MILTON.

London: Printed by W. B. [William Bowyer] and sold at the Foundery, near Upper-Moorfields; by T. Trye, at Gray's-Inn-Gate; and by R. Akenhead, on Tyne Bridge, Newcastle. 1752, [wrongly printed, MDDCCLII]. (Price Eightpence.) 12mo., pp. 83.

Second edition, London: W. B., 1752; Third, London: Cock, 1755; Fourth, Bristol: Pine, 1769; Another, London: W.B., 1772; Fifth, London: Hawes, 1776; Sixth, 1786; Seventh, London: G. Story, 1804; Tenth, London: Cordeux, 1818.

An edition was afterwards published, to which were added 15 metrical stanzas entitled "The Horrible Decree." See No. 31.

This pamphlet was written under peculiar circumstances. At the Conference in Limerick, August 14 and 15, 1752 (the first held in Ireland), the following questions were asked and answers given.—" Q. 6. How far do any of you believe the doctrine of absolute predestination? *A.* None of us believe it at all. Q. 7. Which of you believe absolute election? *A.* Three replied: 'We believe there are some persons who are absolutely elected; but we believe likewise that Christ died for all'; that God willeth not the death of any man, and that thousands are saved that are not absolutely elected. We believe, further, that those who are thus elected cannot finally fall; but we believe that other believers may fall, and that those [of them] who were once justified will perish everlastingly.'" A further question (probably at a subsequent session) was asked, "Can we receive any as a fellow-labourer who does not agree with us both as to doctrine and to discipline? *A.* In no wise. 'How can two walk together unless they be agreed?'"—*Revised Minutes,* 8vo., Vol. I., p. 714. But there was a strange report prevalent amongst the Irish preachers at the time. Wesley, in writing to his brother Charles, says, "They have likewise openly affirmed that you agree with Mr. Whitefield, touching perseverance at least, if not predestination too. Is it not highly expedient that you should write explicitly and strongly on this head likewise? Perhaps the occasion of this latter affirmation was that both you and I have often granted an absolute unconditional election of some, together with a conditional election of all men. I did incline to this scheme for many years; but of late I have doubted it more. First, because," &c., &c.—Quoted in Tyerman's *Life of Wesley*, ii. 144. Tyerman also refers to the intimate friendship subsisting between Charles Wesley and the Countess of Huntingdon, and his frequently preaching and administering the Sacrament in her ladyship's house, as further reasons why this report may have been spread abroad. In addition to the above a pamphlet had been issued by an able writer, Rev. John Gill, D.D., entitled *The Doctrine of the Saints' Final Perseverance Asserted and Vindicated*, in answer to Wesley's pamphlet (No. 153) on the subject published in the previous year. The latter part of the *Predestination Calmly Considered* is a reply to that pamphlet. Plainly it was needful for Wesley to write "calmly" upon this important question.

Tyerman describes the piece as "one of Wesley's most cogent and exhaustive pamphlets." But an abler critic says:—"As a piece of polemic divinity, his 'Predestination Calmly Considered,' is of distinguished excellence. It is a model of controversy, clear and cogent, concise and argumentative, and the more convincing because the spirit in which it is written is as amiable as the reasoning is unanswerable. Perhaps there is not in the English language a treatise which contains, in so small a compass, so full and masterly a refutation of the principle he opposes."—*Life of Wesley*, by John Hampson, A.B., iii. 151.

156. A Short Method of Converting all the Roman Catholics in the Kingdom of Ireland. Humbly proposed to the Bishops and Clergy of this Kingdom. Dublin : Printed in the year 1752. 12mo., pp. 12.

Neither dated nor signed.

Another : London : Re-printed in the year 1753. 12mo., pp. 12.

The grand difficulty of the work of converting the people from Popery, he says, is the strong attachment of the people to the clergy, whom they generally believe to be the holiest and wisest of men. "Here then, we are to begin, we are to strike at the root, and if this bigotry can be removed, whatever is built upon it will fall to the ground." He has one "short and sure method" for accomplishing this. The Papists allow that one set of clergy were holier and wiser even than their own, namely, the Apostles. "Let all the clergy of the Church of Ireland only live like the Apostles, preach like the Apostles, and the thing is done." This gives him the opportunity, which perhaps is what he desired, of declaring how the Apostles lived, and what they preached. He closes with, "Let all the Right Reverend the bishops, and the Reverend the clergy only walk by this rule: Let them thus live, and thus testify with one heart and one voice the Gospel of the Grace of God ; and every Papist within these four seas will soon acknowledge the Truth as it is in Jesus."

It is not included in his own edition of his collected Works, but it is in the later editions.

157. Serious Thoughts concerning Godfathers and Godmothers. 1752. 12mo., pp. 4.

Half-title, no name of author or printer. Dated at end, Athlone, Aug. 6, 1732, obviously an error for Aug. 6, 1752, on which date Wesley was in Athlone.

A brief defence of the antiquity and long-continued use of this office; and a statement, with answers, of some objections to it—one of them being "'But why are those questions inserted, which seem to mean what they really do not?' I answer, I did not insert them, and should not be sorry had they not been inserted at all. I believe the compilers of our Liturgy inserted them because they were used in all the ancient Liturgies. And their deep reverence for the primitive Church made them excuse some impropriety of expression." These, together with an exhortation to fidelity on the part of all who hold the office, make up the little pamphlet. It was inserted in the *Preservative Against Unsettled Notions in Religion*, (No. 191), and in the collected Works.

158. SOME ACCOUNT OF THE LIFE AND DEATH OF MATTHEW LEE, Executed at Tyburn, October 11, 1752, in the 20th Year of his Age. The Second Edition. London: Printed in the year 1752. [Price Twopence.] 12mo., pp. 24.

Two hymns follow the narrative—Psalm li. in Dr. Watts' version, "O Thou that hear'st when sinners cry;" and Austin's Hymn in Wesley's *Psalms and Hymns* (No. 30), "Of Him Who did Salvation bring."

Another edition, Bristol: 1770; Another, G. Whitfield, 1796. The second hymn omitted, and two others substituted for it, entitled "For a Dying Unconverted Sinner": "Now, sinner, now, what is thy hope?" and "And must thou perish in thy blood?" They are Nos. 25 and 26 from *Hymns and Sacred Poems*, (No. 138).

This poor youth, a sad instance of the effect of sin and evil companionship, was convicted of highway robbery. Being visited while in prison he was led to repentance, and obtained salvation through faith in Jesus Christ. He witnessed a good confession for many days in presence of his fellow-prisoners, and died rejoicing in God his Saviour. The hymns appended to the narrative, he was frequently singing during his imprisonment.

Wesley inserted the narrative in his collected Works, which would imply that he wrote it; and if so, that he was the person whose preaching Lee heard in Bridewell, and by whom he was visited both there and in Newgate. Wesley's care for condemned malefactors is known to all readers of his Journals.

I have not seen a copy of the first edition.

NOTE.—Seven volumes (xiii.-xix.) of the *Christian Library* (No. 131) were issued this year.

Vol. xiii. contains two sermons, completing the *Extracts from the Works of Dr. Manton*, begun in volume xii.; also *Extracts from the Works of Isaac Ambrose*, sometime Minister of Garstang, in Lancashire: To which is prefixed some Account of his Life. These include *The Doctrine of Regeneration*, written about the year 1650, and *The Practice of Sanctification; Exemplified in The Believer's Privileges and Duties*. The latter is divided into 32 sections, disposed under the heads,—*The Practice of Sanctification, of Self-Denial, of the Life of Faith, and of Family Duties*.

Vols. xiv. and xv. contain a treatise by the same author, entitled *Looking unto Jesus: or, The Soul's Eyeing of Jesus, as carrying on the Great Work of Man's Salvation*. It is preceded by an Address to the Reader. The Extracts from the writings of Ambrose were subsequently published in two volumes, 8vo.

Vol. xvi. contains *Extracts from the Works of Jer. Taylor, D.D., Chaplain in Ordinary to His Majesty King Charles II.* They comprise *The Rule and Exercise of Holy Living*, in which Wesley has preserved nearly the whole order of chapters and sections, but with considerable abridgement; *The Rules and Exercises of Holy Dying*, which is abridged in every respect throughout; and *Academia Cœlestis: The Heavenly University:* by Francis Rouse, sometime Provost of Eaton-College, with the Address to the Reader and the Preface.

Vol. xvii. contains *The Life of Christ, the Pith and Kernel of all Religion: A Sermon Preached before the Honourable House of Commons, at Westminster, March 31, 1647:* by R. Cudworth, B.D. It is preceded by the *Dedication.* There follow *Extracts from the Works of Nathanael Calverwell*, sometime Fellow of Emanuel-College, Cambridge, including *The Act of Oblivion, The Child's Return, The Panting Soul, Mount Ebal, and Spiritual Opticks;* and *Extracts from the Works of John Owen, D.D.*, sometime Vice-Chancellor of the University of Cambridge: with a brief account of his life. The Extracts embrace *Of the Mortification of Sin in Believers* and *The Nature, Power, Deceit and Prevalency of the Remainder of Indwelling Sin in Believers.* These works are of necessity very considerably abridged, being brought into the compass of 172 duodecimo pages.

In vols. xviii. and xix., extracts from Owen's Works are continued. The former volume comprises a dissertation on *The Nature and Power of Temptation; A Declaration of the Glorious Mystery of the Person of Christ, God and Man*, with the preface; also the first part of a treatise entitled *Of Communion with God the Father, Son, and Holy Ghost.* The second and third parts appear in vol. xix., together with *Extracts from the Works of the Rev. John Smith*, sometime Fellow of Queen's College, Cambridge. The latter follow an Address to the Reader, by John Worthington, dated Cambridge, December 22, 1659; and a brief "Postscript," signed John Wesley and dated March 10, 1752. Then follow abridgements of a discourse on *The True Method of Attaining Divine Knowledge;* two short discourses on *Superstitions*, and on *Atheism;* and others on *The Immortality of the Soul*, and *The Existence and Nature of God.* These Wesley has pruned with care but with unsparing hand. He has removed objectionable phrases, obsolete and unintelligible expressions, superfluous words, long sentences, tedious circumlocutions and needless repetitions, as he had done in some preceding volumes: see p. 75.

1753.

159. AN EXTRACT OF THE LIFE AND DEATH OF MR. JOHN JANEWAY, Fellow of King's College, in Cambridge. By John Wesley, M.A. London: Printed by Henry Cock. 1753. 12mo., pp. 35.

The above is the earliest mentioned by Osborn and Heylin; yet it appears in a 1749 catalogue. Tyerman says "It was also in this [1749] or in a former year, that Wesley published his threepenny tract, entitled, 'An Extract of the Life and Death of Mr. John Janeway,' a young man of remarkable piety, who died at the age of twenty-three, in the year 1657." A tract with precisely the same title as the above, but by James Wheatley, was published in London in 1749. At that time Wheatley was a trusted and faithful Methodist preacher, and it was probably this tract that Wesley mentioned in his catalogue. It is obvious on comparing the two tracts that Wesley's is a slight abridgement of Wheatley's, and probably it was not published until this year.

Nos. 160-161-162. [1753.

The extracts in both cases are from "*Invisibles, Realities, Demonstrated in the Holy Life and Triumphant Death of Mr. John Janeway, Fellow of King's College, in Cambridge.* By James Janeway, Minister of the Gospel."

Another edition, London: R. Hawes, 1775; Another, "not to be sold, but given away," London: Paramore, "at the Foundery," 1783.

Both these were from Wheatley's, not Wesley's Extract. The pamphlet is included in Wesley's own edition of his Works; but it is further abridged, and a few sentences are added from Wheatley's.

160. AN EXTRACT OF THE REVEREND JOHN WESLEY'S JOURNAL, from October 27, 1743, to November 1746. London: Printed by H. Cock, in Bloomsbury-Market; and sold at the Foundery, near Upper-Moorfields; by J. Robinson, in Ludgate-Street; by T. Trye, near Gray's-Inn-Gate, Holborn; by T. James, under the Royal-Exchange; and G. Englefield, in West-Street, near the Seven Dials. 1753. 12mo., pp. 160. [No. vi.]

Second edition, London: Hawes, 1779.

Contains some interesting correspondence, and illustrates an old Methodist custom of meeting at stated times for "the public reading of the letters."

161. THE ADVANTAGE OF THE MEMBERS OF THE CHURCH OF ENGLAND OVER THOSE OF THE CHURCH OF ROME. Bristol: Printed by E. Farley, in Small-Street. 1753. 12mo., pp. 12.

Another, London: 1756.

Reprinted in the *Preservative Against Unsettled Notions in Religion* (No. 191), 1758, and in the collected Works, 1771.

The following principles are laid down: "The more the doctrine of any Church agrees with the Scripture, the more readily ought it to be received; and on the other hand the more the doctrine of any Church differs from the Scripture, the greater cause we have to doubt it . . . That it is a principle of the Church of England that nothing is to be received as an article of faith, which is not read in the Holy Scripture, or to be inferred therefrom by just and plain consequence: That the Church of Rome adds, if she does not prefer, to Holy Scripture, tradition or the doctrine of fathers and councils with the decrees of Popes. . . . Seeing, therefore, the Church of England contends for the Word of God, and the Church of Rome against it, it is easy to discern on which side the advantage lies, with regard to the grand principle of Christianity." This is the drift and substance of this little pamphlet; which, while well proving its point, is not equal in extent or value to a *Roman Catechism with a Reply*, published three years afterwards, (No. 179).

162. THE COMPLETE ENGLISH DICTIONARY, Explaining most of those Hard Words, which are found in the best English Writers. By a Lover of Good English and Common Sense. N.B.—The Author assures you, he thinks this is the best English Dictionary in the World. London: Printed by W. Strahan; and sold by J. Robinson, Ludgate Street; T. Trye, Gray's-Inn-Gate, Holborn; T. James, Royal Exchange; and G. Englefield, West-Street, Seven Dials. 1753. 12mo. pp. 144— unnumbered in all editions.

Although Wesley's name does not appear on the title-page or appended to the preface, there is no doubt as to his authorship. He includes it in the lists of books "published by J. and C. Wesley."

Second edition, Bristol: Pine, 1764; Third, London: R. Hawes, 1777; Another, miscalled second, London: Printed and sold at the New Chapel, City Road, 1790, no date to preface.

The preface, or address, "To the Reader," which is without date, reveals a vein of sarcastic drollery that would scarcely be expected in one engaged in such a work as that which constantly occupied Wesley's mind. He avows, "incredible as it may appear," that this dictionary "is not published to get money, but to assist persons of common sense and no learning, to understand the best English authors, and that with as little expense of either time or money as the nature of the thing would allow;" and, having "so often observed, the only way, according to modern taste, for any author to procure commendation to his book is vehemently to commend it himself," he "in compliance therefore with the taste of the age," adds that "this little dictionary is not only the shortest and the cheapest, but likewise, by many degrees, the most correct which is extant at this day. Many are the mistakes in all the other English dictionaries which I have yet seen. Whereas I can truly say, I know of none in this; and I conceive the reader will believe me; for if I had I should not have left it there. Use then this help, till you find a better."

A Methodist is defined to be, "One that lives according to the method laid down in the Bible."

In the second edition, printed at Bristol, by Wm. Pine, 1764, the above preface is dated Oct., 1753; and two sentences are appended in which the author says he has added "some hundreds of words chiefly from Mr. Johnson's Dictionary," which he had "carefully looked over for that purpose." The preface to the second edition is dated Oct. 20, 1763.

163. DIRECTIONS FOR MARRIED PERSONS; describing the Duties common to both, and peculiar to each of them. By William Whateley. Bristol: Reprinted by F. Farley, in Small Street. 1753. 12mo. pp. 105, ii.

An edition is noted 1760, 12mo., pp. 60; and another, 1768.

This appeared in Vol. xxiv. of the *Christian Library* (No. 131). To it is prefixed a short and characteristic preface, dated London, January 6, 1753, and signed John Wesley, in which he thus commends it: "I have seen nothing on the subject in any, either ancient or modern, tongue, which is in any degree comparable to it. It is so full, so deep, so closely, so strongly wrote, and yet with the most exquisite decency, even where the author touches on points of the most delicate nature that are to be found within the whole compass of divinity."

Farley, who printed the *Christian Library*, reprinted the pamphlet as announced above, at the same time and from the same type; but he did not include Wesley's preface. Whateley, in his address "To the Christian Reader," says, "Marriage hath scarce more that use it, than that accuse it.

Most men enter into this estate, and being entered, complain thereof. They should rather complain of themselves. It is an unjust thing, and a fruit of ignorant pride, to cast the blame of our grievances upon God's ordinances. I had been happy, saith one, had I not been married. Then wast thou foolish both before and since thy marriage. Use it well, it shall add to thine happiness. We make bitter sauce, and cry out that the meat is bitter."

In the fourth volume of *Sermons on Several Occasions*, published 1760, Wesley includes an abridgement of this pamphlet, under the title of *The Duties of Husbands and Wives*, prefixing a single paragraph in commendation of it. He says, "I am persuaded, it is not possible for me to write anything so full, so strong, and so clear on this subject, as has been written near an hundred and fifty years ago, by a person of equal sense and piety." He does not include his own former preface ; but he adds two short papers, entitled *Directions to Children* and *Directions to Servants*. These may be Wesley's; the presumption is that they are.

Osborn assigns the pamphlet to 1760, and describes it to be of sixty pages. If this is the entire work as published in the *Christian Library*, it must be closely printed. But probably it is the abridgement as published in the *Sermons*, for Heylin, who assigns the same date, describes it as including the *Directions to Children and Servants*. I have not seen the edition of 1760.

164. MINUTES OF SEVERAL CONVERSATIONS BETWEEN THE REVEREND MR. JOHN AND CHARLES WESLEY, AND OTHERS. n.d. Half-title; 12mo., pp. 16.

This is the First Edition of the so-called "Large Minutes." It is a digest or compendium of the *Minutes of Conference*, 1744-8, published in 1749 (Nos. 135 and 136), and of the unpublished *Minutes* of the years 1749 and 1753. It was the first of a series of six digests, issued during the life of Wesley, which, being slightly larger than the Annual Minutes, were called in contradistinction, *The Large Minutes*. In the first volume of the revised edition of the *Minutes of Conference*, published in 1862 (London : Mason, 8vo., pp. 727), the six editions of the *Large Minutes* are given in parallel columns, showing the gradual changes and enlargements made in them. In the appendix to this volume are some very interesting memorials of the Conferences of 1749, '52, '53, '55, &c. Those of 1749, '55, and '58 are printed from Wesley's own manuscript copy, and those of 1752 and '53 from notes made by the Rev. Jacob Rowell, who was present. Whatever appears in this first number of the *Large Minutes* that is not taken from the *Minutes* published by Powell, Dublin, 1749 (Nos. 135-6), is to be found in these two MS. records, with the exception of a single sentence relating to the prevention of improper persons entering the society, which sentence cannot be traced.

As many of the entries are taken from 1753 and none from any subsequent record, the presumption is that the little undated tract was printed in this year. Osborn says: "It is supposed to have been published in or about 1753." In the revised edition named above, the date assigned is 1753 or 1757.

165. HYMNS AND SPIRITUAL SONGS, Intended for the Use of Real Christians of all Denominations (Colossians iii. 9-11). London : Printed by William Strahan ; and Sold at the Foundery in Upper-Moorfields, and in the Horsefair, Bristol. 1753. [Price One Shilling.] 12mo., pp. 124, viii. Preface and Index [" INEDX."]

No name of author, until the eighth edition.

1753.] **No. 165.**

Second Edition, London: H. Cock, 1754; Third, Dublin: S. Powell, 1755; Fourth, London: 1756; Fifth, Bristol: Farley and Son, 1758; Seventh, Bristol: Grabham, 1759; Eighth, Bristol: Pine, 1761; in this and subsequent editions appear the words, "By John Wesley, M.A." Ninth, Bristol: Pine, 1760; Another, 1762; Tenth, Bristol: Pine, 1763; Tenth, Edinburgh (enlarged), 1763 (nineteen Hymns of C. Wesley; Watts, two; Addison, one; Cennick, one; Ken, one, added, but by whose authority is not known). Twelfth, Bristol: 1765; Thirteenth, Bristol: Pine, 1767; Fourteenth, Bristol: Pine, 1768, "By John Wesley, M.A., Late Fellow of Lincoln College, Oxford." Another, 1770; Fifteenth, Bristol: Pine 1771, "Published by John and Charles Wesley," and so subsequently. Sixteenth, Bristol: Pine, 1772; Seventeenth, Bristol: Pine, 1773; Eighteenth, London: Hawes, n.d.; Nineteenth, 1775; Twentieth, London: Hawes, 1776; Twenty-first, London: Hawes, 1777; Another, 1782; Twenty-second, London: Paramore, 1781; Another, Dublin: Whitehouse, 1779; Twenty-third, London: Paramore, 1782; Twenty-fourth, London: Paramore, 1786.

This collection, sometimes called *Spiritual Hymns*, consists entirely of hymns from the three volumes of *Hymns and Sacred Poems*, 1739, 1740, and 1742 (Nos. 15, 19 and 40): sixteen from the first, twenty-two from the second, and forty-six from the third, making a total of eighty-four hymns. Twenty-one of the hymns are long, and are divided into two, three, four, or six parts; if each part were counted as a hymn the total number would be 114. To each hymn a title is prefixed. This was the Hymn Book in general use in the congregations from 1753 to 1780, when the *Collection of Hymns for the use of the People called Methodists*, known as "The Large Hymn Book," (No. 348) was compiled; and it was used in the smaller and poorer Societies long after the larger book was published. It was frequently bound up with the *Redemption Hymns* (No. 105), which was largely used in the Class-Meetings and private Bands. Many copies have been found with the Society or Band Ticket pasted on the back, or pinned to the fly-leaf. Wesley tells us in the preface to the large Collection that, when he was importuned to prepare a Hymn Book which might be generally used in the congregations, he replied, "You have such a collection already (entitled *Hymns and Spiritual Songs*), which I extracted several years ago from a variety of Hymn Books." The large number of editions sufficiently attests its popularity whilst it was in use.

NOTE A.—Heylin places in this year SELECT HYMNS FOR THE USE OF CHRISTIANS OF ALL DENOMINATIONS, (No. 208). But he is entirely mistaken, as will be shown in due time. He is equally in error in ascribing to Wesley '*The Trial of the Spirits both in Teachers and Hearers*: extracted by a Member of the Church of England.' This is by C. Perronet.

NOTE B.—The earliest copy of A PLAIN ACCOUNT OF GENUINE CHRISTIANITY, that I can find, bears date 1753. It is placed under 1749, for a special reason. See No. 122.

NOTE C.—During this year fourteen volumes (xx.-xxxiii.) of the *Christian Library* were published.

83

No. 165. [1753.

Vol. xx. contains the remainder of the extracts from the writings of Mr. John Smith, comprising,—*A Discourse of Prophecy: with Rules for the better understanding of Prophetick Writ; A Discourse treating of Legal Righteousness and Evangelical Righteousness, or the Righteousness of Faith; The Difference between the Law and the Gospel, and the Old and New Covenant; The Shortness and Vanity of a Pharisaick Righteousness, or an Account of the False Grounds upon which men are apt to conceit themselves to be Righteous; The Excellency and Nobleness of True Religion;* and *A Christian's Conflicts and Conquests.* These Discourses are divided into chapters as in the original, but each is much abridged. They are followed by a Sermon by Simon Patrick, preached at the Funeral of Mr. Smith. The volume also contains *Memorials of Godliness and Christianity, or, Of Making Religion one's Business,* and *An Appendix applied to the Calling of a Minister,* by Herbert Palmer, B.D., Master of Queen's College, Cambridge.

Vol. xxi. contains *An Extract from the Whole Duty of Man*: first printed in the year 1657. To this is prefixed an Address to the Reader, signed J. Wesley, in which he says, "Whoever reads the following Treatise should consider the time wherein it was wrote. Never was there more talk of Faith in Christ, of Justification by Faith, and of the Fruits of the Spirit. And scarce ever was there less practice of plain moral duties, Justice, Mercy and Truth. At such a time it was peculiarly needful to inculcate what was so generally neglected; and this is well done in the ensuing Tract." Following this is *A Collection of Prayers for Families.* Wesley had already published this in 1745: see No. 74, of which this is an exact reprint.

Vol. xxii. consists of *Directions for Married Persons: Describing the Duties common to both, and peculiar to each of them*: by William Whateley, with a Preface to the Reader, dated London, Jan. 6, 1753, and signed, John Wesley. An account of this is given in No. 163, printed in this year. As both copies were printed from the same type, it is difficult to determine which first appeared. Probably the type was set up for the volume, and the separate pamphlet published afterwards; but it is strange that Wesley's preface, which appears in this volume, was not inserted in the separate publication. The original work was entitled *A Bride Bush, or a Wedding Sermon, compendiously describing the duties of Married Persons:* London: 1617, 4to. This is followed by *Extracts from the Works of Sanderson:* to which is prefixed some account of the life of Dr. Sanderson, sometime Bishop of Lincoln. The extracts embrace four Sermons. Following these is *A Discourse concerning Comparative Religion: or the True and Solid Grounds of Pure and Peaceable Theology,* which is stated to be a subject very important, though hitherto almost wholly neglected. It is a translation from the Latin: but the name of the author is not given.

Vol. xxiii. contains *Thoughts on Religion, and other subjects,* by Monsieur Pascal, with a Preface giving an account of the author, and an Advertisement, relating to the order and method of the Thoughts. Next follows *The Great Duty of Self-Resignation to the Divine Will,* extracted from a treatise by John Worthington, D.D., with a Preface by Bishop Edward Fowler. This subject extends into vol. xxiv., the remaining portion of which contains *Extracts from the Works of Mr. Joseph Allein,* to which is prefixed some account of the Life and Death of the Author—a most interesting and profitable memoir. The extracts comprise *An Alarm to Unconverted Sinners,* and *A Counsel for Personal and Family Godliness.* The *Alarm* was subsequently issued in a carefully abridged form, as a separate publication (No. 362). In it is a form for "a solemn Covenant with God," which Wesley prepared for the use of his Societies, in the Service which he instituted and called "the Renewal of the Covenant,"—a service which is observed annually by the Methodists throughout the world. Vol. xxv. contains the remainder of the extracts from Alleine, namely, *Two Practical Cases of Conscience Resolved;* and also *Extracts from the*

Works of Mr. Samuel Shaw, sometime Minister of Long-Whatton, Leicestershire, with a Short Account of his life. The extract is from *Immanuel: or, A Discovery of True Religion, as it imports a Living Principle in the Minds of Men*: written about the year 1666; and is followed by *Communion with God: A Sermon preached before the Peers,* in the Abbey-Church at Westminster, October 10, 1666, by Seth Ward, then Bishop of Exeter; and *An Exposition of the Church-Catechism,* extracted from Bp. Ken.

In vol. xxvi. is a series of *Lives of Sundry Eminent Persons,* chiefly extracted from Mr. Samuel Clark. The series includes an autobiography of Samuel Clark, Philip Melancthon with preface by Richard Baxter, Peter Martyr, John Calvin, Galeacius Caracciolus the Marquis of Vico, Bernard Gilpin, William Whitaker, Philip de Mornay, John Bruen, Richard Blackerby, Henry Atling, Frederick Spanheim, Sir Philip Sidney, Richard Mather, and John Row. These brief memoirs are given, Wesley says, in a preface, "in order to illustrate, by examples, the Rules already laid down." And he further remarks, with a largeness of charity that well deserves imitation, "Perhaps it may be useful, as well as agreeable, to those who are broke loose from that miserable Bigotry which is too often entailed upon us from our forefathers, to observe how the same Spirit works the same work of grace in men upright of heart, of whatever Denomination. These, how widely soever they differ in opinion, all agree in one Mind, one Temper. How far distant soever they are from each other, with regard to the circumstances of Worship, they all meet in the substance of true Worship, *the Faith that worketh by Love.*"

The extracts from the Lives of Eminent Persons are continued in vol. xxvii. They include Joseph Woodward, Nicholas Leverton, Sir Nathanael Barardiston, Samuel Fairclough, Richard Hooker, Sir Henry Watton, Dr. Donne, George Herbert, Bp. Bedell, and Abp. Usher.

Vol. xxviii. contains *The Spiritual Bee: or a Miscellany of Divine Meditations; Extracts from the Letters of Mr. Samuel Rutherfoord,*—rather more than half of the letters originally published are given by Wesley, each having undergone revision; also *The Happy Ascetic: or the Best Exercise,* together with Prayers suitable to each Exercise: by Dr. Horneck. This is continued in vol. xxix., and is there followed by *A Letter to a Person of Quality concerning the Lives of the Primitive Christians,* by the same author; and by *Extracts from the Works of the Rev. Mr. Hugh Binning,* consisting of Five Sermons, with some Account of the life of the author. In this volume are commenced *Contemplations Moral and Divine,* from the Works of Lord Chief Justice Hale. These extend to vol. xxx., which contains also part of *Vindiciæ Pietatis, or a Vindication of Godliness, in the greatest Strictness and Spirituality of it.* This is from the Works of Richard Allein. In it is the form for the solemn covenanting with God, found also in vol. xxiv., of which, with the exception of a single sentence, it is a verbal reprint, and from which it was doubtless taken.

Vol. xxxi. contains the remainder of the *Vindication; An Extract from the Assembly's Shorter Catechism;* and *Primitive Christianity, or the Religion of the Ancient Christians,* extracted from the writings of Dr. William Cave, in three parts, each divided into chapters. Although this corresponds with the original in the number of parts, yet it is greatly abridged. It was first published in 1672.

Vol. xxxii. contains *A Relation of the Holy War.* In an early period of his literary career (1743) Wesley exercised his talent for abridgement upon Bunyan's inimitable work, *The Pilgrim's Progress,* (see No. 46). That effort cannot be considered in any sense a success. With all his skill, he was not able to improve the work of "the immortal Tinker." In dealing with Bunyan's second great work, *The Holy War,* of which it has been said, "If the Pilgrim's Progress did not exist it would be the best allegory that ever was written" *(Enc. Britt.* Art. *Bunyan),* Wesley has been more sparing of the original than in his former effort. But he has quite failed to produce a more popular book. In fact, as with most artistic works that have been subjected to similar treatment, it has gained nothing in beauty, by what it has lost of originality. Like some other pieces in this large selection, it is given without the name of the author. It occupies little more than a third of the volume. The remainder is devoted to *An Extract of the Christian Sacrifice: A Treatise showing the Necessity, End, and Manner of receiving the Holy Communion, together with suitable Prayers and Meditations*, by Simon Patrick, late Lord Bishop of Ely. This is another example of careful and minute revision, every sentence even having been thoughtfully weighed, and the work of excision most judiciously done. The four Parts into which the treatise is divided are given, and the twelve Meditations, but not arranged for the months of the year as in the original. Those for the special Feasts of the Church are omitted and half of the Additional Prayers. As a devotional manual, it deserves to be reprinted.

The contents of vol. xxxiii. are *A Gospel Glass, or a Call from Heaven to Sinners and Saints by Repentance and Reformation to prepare to meet God*, in thirty-seven chapters; and *An Extract from Mr. Cowley's Essays*, in five parts.

1754.

166. AN EXTRACT FROM THE REVEREND MR. JOHN WESLEY'S JOURNAL, from November 25, 1746, to July 20, 1750 [should be 1749, corrected in *erratum* in No. viii.] London: Printed by H. Cock, in Bloomsbury-Market; and sold at the Foundery, near Upper-Moorfields; by J. Robinson, in Ludgate-Street; and by T. James, under the Royal-Exchange. 1754. 12mo., pp. 139. [No. vii.]

The paging is in the utmost confusion.

Wesley was now fully engaged in his itinerant evangelistic work, of which this " Extract " is a most interesting record. The following are examples of the entries :—

May 9.—" Having not had an hour's sound sleep from the time I lay down till I rose, I was in doubt whether I could preach or not. However, I went to the market-place as usual and found no want of strength till I had fully declared *the Redemption that is in Christ Jesus*. I had designed afterwards to settle the Society thoroughly; but I was not able to sit up so long. Many advised me not to go out at night, the wind being extremely cold and blustering. But I could in no wise consent to spare myself at such a time as this. I preached on *Come unto Me*, &c." " August 12.—In riding to Newcastle I finished the tenth *Iliad* of Homer." " Friday, September 2.—I preached at Wednesbury in the afternoon, and thence rode to Meridan. Riding long stages the next day we reached St. Albans, and the Foundery on Sunday morning." " 25.—Believing my strength would not allow of preaching five times in the day, I desired John Whitworth to preach at five." This was at St. Just, but he rode to Morva, to Zennor, to Newlyn, and to St. Ives, and preached in each place. " Oct. 1.—I preached at Waywick about one, and then rode quietly on to Bristol. I examined the Society the following week, leaving out every careless person, and. everyone who wilfully and obstinately refused to meet his brethren weekly. By this means their number was reduced from 900 to about 730." " April 23.—We had several showers in the afternoon while I was preaching in our garden, and towards the conclusion a vehement shower of hail. But all kept their ground till I concluded." " June 4.—Being extremely hoarse, I could not speak without difficulty. However, I made shift to preach at nine, at two, and at five."

The several numbers of the Journal were not often reprinted separately.

167. AN ANSWER TO ALL WHICH THE REVD. DR. GILL HAS PRINTED ON THE FINAL PERSEVERANCE OF THE SAINTS. By the Revd. Mr. Wesley. London: Printed, and Sold at the Foundery, near Upper-Moorfields; by T. Try, near Gray's Inn-Gate, Holbourn; by J. Robinson, in Ludgate-Street, and by T. James, under the Royal-Exchange. 1754. [Price One Penny.] 12mo., pp. 12.

In 1751 Wesley wrote the *Serious Thoughts on the Perseverance of Saints*, (No. 153); a reply to which was issued in the following year, entitled, *The Doctrine of the Saints' Final Perseverance Asserted and Vindicated*: in answer to a late pamphlet called Serious Thoughts on that subject: By John Gill, D.D., London: 1752. In that year Wesley wrote *Predestination Calmly Considered* (No. 155); the latter part of it being a reply to Dr. Gill, who speedily published a folio volume entitled "*The Doctrine of Predestination Stated, and Set in the Scripture-Light*: in opposition to Mr. Wesley's Predestination Calmly Considered: With a reply to the exceptions of the said writer to *The Doctrine of the Perseverance of the Saints.*" Wesley seems to have deemed the best answer to Dr. Gill was to be found in the poetical tract named above, for he does not in any other way reply to him. And he was probably unwilling to follow his opponent further, who was a very voluminous and, Wesley thought, not conclusive writer; and, moreover, Wesley had already written many things on the great controversy, and was much engrossed with other important work.

This tract of twelve pages consists of thirty-eight stanzas of eight lines each, being the third, the fourth, and part of the fifth hymns (if hymns they are to be called) in the well known *Hymns on God's Everlasting Love* (No. 32), published in 1741. Osborn suggests the query whether the title indicates that the verses were written, not by Charles, but by John Wesley, who was always called the Rev. *Mr.* Wesley. It is to be observed, however, that this is only an extract, and not the original publication.

168. LESSONS FOR CHILDREN. Part IV. London: Printed by Henry Cock. 1754. 12mo., pp. 82.

This is the concluding part of the *Lessons*. It embraces extracts from the books of Ecclesiastes, Isaiah, Jeremiah, Ezekiel, Daniel, The Wisdom of Solomon, and Ecclesiasticus. There are thirty-five lessons or chapters, with short explanations of difficult words and of hidden meanings at the foot of the page, together with references to the text.

A Second edition of the entire work was published in 1816, by Thomas Cordeux, London; with the title *Lessons for Children and Others, Selected from the Holy Scripture*. It was issued also as *Lessons from the Holy Scriptures designed for Domestic Use*, in the same year.

Wesley, in the preface to part I. (see No. 85), tells us that he had endeavoured to select the plainest and most useful portions of Scripture, such as children may the most easily understand, and such as it most concerns them to know. The Lessons in the whole of the four parts are taken exclusively from the Old Testament and the Apocrypha.

NOTE.—In this year eight volumes (xxxiv.—xli.) of the *Christian Library* were published.

Vol. xxxiv. commences with *An Extract from Dr. Goodman's Winter Evening Conference*, in three parts. It is a series of three imaginary and somewhat formal conversations, in which Sebastian reclaims his friend Philander from "the lightnesses of the age," and both together lead Biophilus, a sceptical person, "to deliberate of what before he despised." The conversations are largely interspersed with reflections on religious subjects. To this is added, *An Exposition of the Belief*, taken from the Works of Dr. Robert Leighton, sometime Archbishop of Glasgow. In the succeeding volume (xxxv.) are six *Sermons on Several Occasions*, also from Abp. Leighton's writings. They are followed by ten selected sermons, *Extracts from the Works of Dr. Isaac Barrow, Late Master of Trinity College, Cambridge*. The writings of these two divines in their original form are more condensed in style than those of many already named, yet a keen eye may detect a word or phrase, or part of a sentence, that could be spared without injury to the sense of the passage. But, though there is comparatively so little of needless repetition, yet on every page, if to only a small degree, Wesley has found occasion for the exercise of his powers of abridgement and correction.

Vol. xxxvi. contains *Extracts from the Works of the Reverend Mr. John Brown*, consisting of one piece only, entitled, *Christ the Way, the Truth, and the Life: or a Short Discourse pointing the Way of making Use of Christ for Justification, and more particularly for Sanctification*. This, though styled "a short discourse," extends to 19 chapters. It is followed by *An Extract from a Treatise of Solid Virtue; Written in French*. To this are prefixed an Address to the English Reader by the translator, and a Preface by the Author, Anthoniette Bourignon. The treatise consists of a series of 25 Letters addressed to different persons, but mainly to "My dear child," and chiefly dated from "Holstein, near Gottorp-Castle," in the year 1672-6. The volume contains also *An Extract from a Sermon, preached at Cripplegate*, by Dr. Samuel Annesley, the subject being "How must we reprove, that we may not partake of other men's sins."

Vol. xxxvii. contains *The Saints' Everlasting Rest; or a Treatise of the Blessed State of the Saints in their enjoyment of God in Glory: An Extract from the Works of Mr. Baxter*. It is preceded by a brief Dedication to the Inhabitants of Kidderminster. This is a very considerable abridgement of Baxter's original work. It was republished by Wesley in a separate form in 1776; a description of the extract is given in a Note under that date.

Vol. xxxviii. contains *Devotional Tracts: Translated from the French*. They comprise *Letters to the Duke of Burgundy from M. De Fenelon, Archbishop of Cambray; Letters concerning and from B. Lawrence to the Reverend ——; four Conversations with the same; A Letter to one troubled in Mind*, by Mary Henrics; *Pious Reflections*, in sixteen sections; and *A Mother's Advice to her Daughter*, in five sections. These are followed by *An Extract from a Prospect of Divine Providence*,—a quaint, thoughtful and racy piece of writing, in which a multitude of Scripture and other references are used to illustrate the moral instruction, which is given in a series of Chapters, Sections and Observations; *An Extract from Molinos's Spiritual Guide*, much abridged, in two parts, of six and four chapters respectively; and *An Extract from two Sermons preached at Cripplegate by Dr. Samuel Annesley*, the former on Universal Conscientiousness, and the latter on the Visitation of the Sick.

Vol. xxxix. contains *Extracts from the Sermons of Dr. Henry Moore*, five sermons; and *Extracts from the Works of Steph. Charnock, B.D.*, sometime Fellow of New College, Oxford. The latter are confined to two discourses:— one, "Of the Knowledge of God;" the other, "Of the Knowledge of God in Christ." Wesley prepared the whole of Charnock's Discourses on the Existence and Attributes of God, for the press, but did not publish them. The original, a folio volume with Wesley's manuscript, is in the library at the New Kingswood School, Bath. There follow *An Extract from Dr. Calamy's Sermons*, three in number; and *A Rebuke to Backsliders, and a Spur for Loiterers*, by the author of *Vinditiæ Pietatis* [Richard Alleine]. The last is a discourse on Isa. lxiv. 6, 7, extending through half the volume, although it has undergone a considerable pruning.

An Extract from an Inquiry after Happiness, by Richard Lucas, D.D., in three parts, occupies vol. xl. The original fills two vols. 8vo.; so that the work of condensation must have been great in order to bring it down to little more than a duodecimo. It extends into vol. xli., which also contains *Extracts from the Works of Dr. Reynolds*, sometime Bishop of Norwich, consisting of sermons on "The Vanity of the Creature," "The Sinfulness of Sin," "The Life of Christ," and "The Use of Human Learning."

1755.

169. QUERIES HUMBLY PROPOSED TO THE RIGHT REVEREND AND RIGHT HONOURABLE COUNT ZINZENDORF. London. Sold by J. Robinson in Ludgate-Street, and T. James under the Royal Exchange. 1755. [Price Sixpence.] 8vo., pp. 32.

Another, Dublin: Printed in the year 1755. 12mo., pp. 16.

Inserted in the catalogues amongst the books published by J. and C. Wesley; but not otherwise acknowledged.

Many severe charges had been laid against the "Brethren" in the public Press. James Hutton, one of their number, inserted in the *London Daily Advertiser* of Dec. 31, 1754, a letter calling for these charges to be reduced "into the form of Queries at an Examination," that direct answers might be given to them. It was this challenge that immediately led to the publication of these *Queries*. They contain a terrible indictment, and could not have been written by any man having a spark of Christian good feeling, but under the pressure of a strong conviction of duty or necessity. A letter is prefixed, addressed to Mr. Hutton and dated January 7, 1755. By general consent the pamphlet is attributed to Wesley; and Hutton himself, in a letter written some years afterwards, refers to such a work as having been written by Wesley: see *Memoirs of James Hutton*, pp. 301-2. Some account of the pamphlet is given by Tyerman, *Life of Wesley*, ii. 220-3.

Long afterwards Wesley in his Journal notes: "I met an old friend, James Hutton, whom I had not seen for five-and-twenty years. I felt this made no difference; my heart was quite open; his seemed to be the same, and we conversed just as we did in 1738, when we met in Fetter Lane."—Dec. 21, 1771.

Not a shadow of the imputations contained in this pamphlet rests upon the Moravians of to-day.

170. CATHOLICK SPIRIT. A Sermon on 2 Kings x. 15. By John Wesley, M.A., Late Fellow of Lincoln College, Oxon. London: Printed by H. Cock, in Bloomsbury-Market; and sold at the Foundery, near Upper-Moorfields; by T. Try, near Gray's-Inn-Gate, Holbourn; by J. Robinson, in Ludgate-Street, and by T. James, under the Royal-Exchange. 1755. 12mo., pp. 31.

Another edition. Bristol: Pine, 1770.

Appended is a hymn of seven stanzas of six lines each, entitled *Catholic Love*, and signed at the end of the seventh stanza C.W. It was now published for the first time.

The Sermon appears in the third volume of Sermons, 1750 (No. 139), but with the hymn appended becomes a separate publication. It was worthy of wide dissemination for its truly catholic spirit. It clearly defines, illustrates, and urges real catholicity. Watson says: "No man ever set a better example of Christian charity, and nowhere is the excellence and obligation of that temper more forcibly drawn and inculcated than in his most interesting sermon on 'A Catholic Spirit.'"—*Life of Wesley*, ch. viii. The hymn is the outpouring of a spirit tired of the conflict of bigotry and the strife of words :—

> Weary of all this wordy strife,
> These notions, forms and modes and names,
> To Thee the Way, the Truth, the Life,
> Whose love my simple heart inflames,
> Divinely taught, at last I fly,
> With Thee and Thine to live and die.

171. SERIOUS THOUGHTS OCCASIONED BY THE LATE EARTHQUAKE AT LISBON. *Tua res agitur paries quum proximus ardet.* By John Wesley, M.A. Late Fellow of Lincoln College, Oxford. London: n.d. 8vo., pp. 34.

The first edition must have been published in London, as Wesley was there till the end of the year. Both Heylin and Tyerman imply that this was an 8vo. edition, pp. 34. Osborn mentions a second, London, 1755, but does not describe it. A second was also published in Bristol by E. Farley, 1755, 8vo., pp. 34; and another second in Newcastle, by John White, 12mo., pp. 23, but without date. Sixth edition, London: printed in the year 1756, 12mo., pp. 36.

In the sixth edition, Wesley adds a postscript of fourteen pages, giving an account of the earthquake, as supplied by eye-witnesses, and of some other similar occurrences; also of the very uncommon commotion, both in the inland waters and the neighbouring seas, observed in many parts of Holland, Great Britain and Ireland.

This awful event, in which 60,000 persons perished, occurred on the first and several following days of November, 1755. In fact, there were "shocks, more or less, in some part or other of the world, every day from Nov. 1 to the 31st of December."

Wesley, being, as he tells us, "much importuned thereto," wrote these *Serious Thoughts*, directed, not as he "designed at first, to the small vulgar, but the great; to the learned, rich, and honourable Heathen commonly called Christians."—*Journal*, Nov. 26, 1755.

172. EXPLANATORY NOTES UPON THE NEW TESTAMENT. By John Wesley, M.A., Late Fellow of Lincoln College, Oxford. London: Printed by William Bowyer. 1755. 4to., pp. vi., 759, iii.

Preface dated, Bristol, Hot Wells, Jan. 4, 1754. Last page erroneously numbered 765, and wrongly corrected in *errata*. Portrait, dated 1755.

Second edition, 4to., London: printed in the year 1757; Third, corrected, Bristol: Grabham and Pine, 1760-2, 12mo., 3 vols.; Fourth, 4to., Bristol: Pine, 1768; Fifth, 4to., London: printed for the author, 1788; Fourth (?), 12mo., 3 vols., London: printed and sold at the New

Chapel, City Road, &c., 1789-90; Fifth (?), 12mo., 3 vols., London: Paramore, 1795; Fifth, 3 vols. 8vo., Dublin: John Jones, 1805; Eleventh, 8vo. 2 vols., London: Mason, 1831: (Another example of confusion in numbering the editions). Others not numbered, London, 16mo., 1790; Another 8vo. 2 vols. 1813; Another, Dunfermline: 24mo., 1818; Another, London: Mason, 8vo., 1838; Another, 12mo., 1850; London: Virtue, n.d., 8vo.; London: n.d., 16mo.; Halifax (with additional notes by author of "Helps for the Pulpit"), 8vo., 1870; London: Mason, New Edition, Text and Notes in one volume, 12mo., 1852; Another 1877.

This is one of Wesley's principal works. He had for many years, he tells us, a desire of setting down and laying together what occurred to his own mind in reading, thinking, or conversation, which might assist serious persons, who had not the advantage of learning, in understanding the New Testament. He was often deterred from carrying out his design, partly, he says, by a deep sense of his own inability and of his want of learning for such a work, but much more by his want of experience and wisdom, and, we may add, of time. He adds that being much out of health, he was induced to begin "because he could do nothing else." He went to Bristol to have the benefit of the Hot Well. He says, in his half-quaint way,—"On Sunday (January 6th, 1754) I began writing Notes on the New Testament; a work which I should scarce ever have attempted had I not been so ill as not to be able to travel or preach, and yet so well as to be able to read and write." He plied his pen from five o'clock in the morning until nine at night, "except the time of riding, half-an-hour for each meal, and the hour between five and six in the evening," which was always reserved for devotion. Towards the end of February he was joined by his brother; and they spent several days together in comparing his translation of the Evangelists with the original, and otherwise helping on the work. By the 19th of March, the rough draft being finished, he began transcribing the Notes on the Gospels. In the early part of April he retired to Paddington, giving himself up to writing, and spending only the Sundays at the Foundery. For four months he seems to have been in or near London. Then, "being much out of order," he repairs again to the Hot Well; but in less than a month he is on his way to Cornwall on a preaching tour, returning to London early in October, and retiring to "a little place near Hackney," where he "was as in a College." He remained in London through the winter (1754-5). In April he is at Bristol again: then starts for a three months' evangelistic journey through the North. From July 6 to Aug. 17 he is in London writing and preaching. Then comes another preaching tour in Cornwall until the end of September, when he returns "weary enough" to Bristol, but "preached till all his complaints were gone." He now had "a little leisure to sit still and finish the Notes." The volume was published at the close of the year. How such a work could be written amidst so much labour and distraction is one of the problems of Wesley's life that remain to be solved.

The date of the preface shows that, as was usually his custom, it was written, or the most of it, in anticipation of the work. He says that he first "set down the text in the common English translation," which he judged to be "in general abundantly the best" he had seen; but, while adhering to it as far as possible, he endeavoured to bring it nearer to the original, never altering for altering's sake, "but there and there only where the sense was made better, stronger, clearer, or more consistent with the context," or the phrase better or nearer the original. The notes he made "as short as possible that the comment may not obscure or swallow up the text; and as plain as possible in pursuance of the main design." For the correction of the Greek text, as well as for most of his notes, particularly those on the Apocalypse, and for the analyses of the several books, he is chiefly indebted to the *Gnomon Novi Testamenti* of Bengel,—

"that great Light of the Christian world." He also laid under tribute the *Paraphrase* of Dr. Guyse, the *Theological Lectures* of Dr. Heylin, and the *Family Expositor* of Dr. Doddridge.

Hampson notices the first 4to. edition as "the most elegantly printed book he ever published, and embellished with one of the best of his early prints," of which a curious story is told in the *Journal*, (Nov. 5, 1774). It is an engraving of Williams' portait of Wesley (1742), and shows remarkable fidelity to the original.

"I began reading over the Greek Testament and the Notes, with my brother and several others; carefully comparing the translation with the original, and correcting or enlarging the Notes as we saw occasion."—*Journal*, Dec. 12, 1759. This was for the 3rd edition, 1760-2. "I retired to Rainham, to prepare another edition of the New Testament for the Press."—*ib.*, Dec. 4, 1787. This may have been for the fifth edition, 4to., 1788; or the so-called fourth edition, 12mo., 1789; though more probably for the beautiful, and now rare, pocket edition of the text, with an analysis of the several books and chapters, published in 1790, the last book (excepting the Magazine for the year) that he issued from the press.

Jackson says, "Charles, who was an excellent critic, and possessed a fine taste in composition, afforded his brother more assistance in this work than in any other with which John's name was connected. The revisal of the book, some years after it had been printed, was greatly indebted to his piety, taste, and judgment."—*Life of C. Wesley*, ii. 44. See also H. Moore, *L. of J. Wesley*, ii., 418-20.

173. AN EPISTLE TO THE REVEREND MR. JOHN WESLEY. By Charles Wesley, Presbyter of the Church of England. London: Printed for J. Robinson, in Ludgate-Street. 1755. 8vo., pp. 16.

Another edition, London, reprinted in 1785, 12mo., pp. 12. Reprinted also in Jackson's *Life of Charles Wesley*, Vol. II., pp. 545-551.

A spirited poem addressed to "My first and last unalienable friend," on "the fears and sorrows of a burthen'd heart" concerning

The Church whose cause I serve, whose faith approve,
Whose altars reverence, and whose name I love.

"On Thursday I read my Epistle a second time to a crowded audience, and yesterday at the watch-night."—Letter to Mrs. C. W., May 31, 1735. "The probability is, that he composed it as he travelled on horseback, from Leeds to London, with the three days' debate in the Conference [on separating from the Church] in his recollection, and all the feelings connected with that debate still vivid and strong. Four thousand copies of the tract were printed and immediately put into circulation."—*Life of C. W.* ii. 81-2.

This pamphlet must be read in the light of these controversies. At the Conference of this year all the preachers were desired to speak their minds at large on the question, "Whether we ought to separate from the Church?" For three days whatever could be said for or against was "seriously and calmly considered," and in the "general conclusion," they all agreed—"that (whether it was *lawful* or not) it was in no ways *expedient*." The severity of the struggle and many of its attendant circumstances are well portrayed in Stevens' *History of Methodism*, Book iv., c. iv.; see also Telford's *Life of John Wesley*, 305-6.

1755.]   No. 173.

Note.—During this year the remaining nine volumes (xlii.-l.) of the *Christian Library* were issued.

Vol. xlii. *Extracts from the Works of Dr. Reynolds*, begun in the preceding volume, are continued in this. Two sermons are added to those already published, one on The Rich Man's Charge, and the other on Joy in the Lord. Next comes *Devotions for Every Day of the Week, and the Great Festivals.* No name of author is given. It is a considerable extract from a work familiarly known as *Hickes's Reformed Devotions.* Originally written by John Austin, a Roman Catholic, and more than once "reformed," i.e., revised and expurgated, it found a permanent place in devotional literature under the above title. It was adapted to the English Church by Mrs. Susannah Hopton, for whose work Dr. George Hickes wrote a preface. Wesley has inserted "The Office" for each day of the week, and under the head of *Devotions for the Great Festivals*, the Office of our blessed Saviour, the Office of the Holy Ghost, the Office of the Saints, and the Preparatory Office for Death. Under the head of *Occasional Devotions* are the Office for a Family, two Litanies, and a number of Prayers. Wesley has greatly abridged the original work, reducing it in size to about one fourth. Generally the Psalms written by Austin are given in full in the earlier part, in the latter several are omitted, but there is little or no verbal revision ; a few only of the hymns and of the shorter prayers are given, and the passages of Scripture are not as a rule inserted. " Matins," " Lauds," " Vespers " and "Compline" are changed into "Morning," "Noon," "Afternoon" and "Evening." The Antiphons are omitted. Thus further "reformed," this excellent book is made into a helpful devotional manual, breathing the purest spirit of worship and holy aspiration. But although Wesley detected the value of the work, and prepared it for the benefit of his people, it never came into common use, but remains amidst these volumes of extracts like a buried gem.

Vol. xliii. contains *Extracts from Dr. South's Sermons*, seven in number ; and *An Extract from the Works of Mr. Flavel.* The latter is *Navigation Spiritualized: or, a New Compass for Seamen, Consisting of Thirty-two Points.* To this is prefixed an *Epistle Dedicatory*, addressed *To all Masters, Mariners, and Seamen.*

In vol. xliv. is a second Extract from Flavel's Works,—his more popular, and in every respect better piece, entitled *Husbandry Spiritualized, or The Heavenly Use of Earthly Things*, with a preface by Joseph Caryl. Those who have most admired Flavel's writings have been compelled to acknowledge them as cumbrous in their structure and somewhat heavy. Yet there are portions of them which are enlivened by wit and fancy, and by strokes of true eloquence ; and no one can deny their practical and spiritual character. Wesley has striven, with some success, to divest these two pieces of their overladen verbiage. Here they each present a continuous series of similies, rendered monotonous by want of variety, but full to overflowing of good and wholesome teaching. This volume contains also *A Discourse on the Causes and Cures of Mental Errors*, by the same author. In the Table of Contents, Wesley has given a synopsis of the discourse. *Extracts from two Sermons by Dr. Annesley* on "God's Sovereignty, our support in all worldly distractions," and "The Hindrances and Helps to a good memory in Spiritual Things," complete the volume.

Vol. xlv. contains six *Discourses on Important Subjects*, by Henry Scougal, A.M., to which is prefixed *A Sermon preached at his Funeral*, by G.G., D.D. ; and *An Extract from the Country Parson's Advice to his Parishioners*, in two parts, I. *A Serious Exhortation to a Religious Life ;* II. *Directions how to live accordingly.* These extracts from an anonymous writer, particularly the latter on how to live a godly life, are distinguished by great plainness, clearness and fidelity. They are worthy to take their place amongst the best practical divinity of that age. *An Extract from the Works of Archbishop Tillotson* follows, consisting of two Sermons, the former, " Of the Ordinary Influences or

93

the Holy Ghost on the Minds of Christians," and the latter on "Evil-Speaking," preached before the King and Queen at Whitehall, February 25, 1693-4. To this Wesley prefixes the following laconic address to the reader,—"I have the rather inserted the following Extracts, for the sake of two sorts of people: those who are unreasonably prejudiced for, and those who are unreasonably prejudiced against, this great man. By this small specimen it will abundantly appear, to all who will at length give themselves leave to judge impartially, that the Archbishop was as far from being the worst, as from being the best, of the English writers."

Vol. xlvi. begins with *An Extract from the Works of Mr. E. Young, Fellow of Winchester College, and late Dean of Sarum*. The extract consists of eight sermons and is followed by *An Extract from Thoughts upon Religious and Philosophical Subjects*, by the late Lord Howe. The latter is composed of *Devout Meditations*, originally intended for the private use of the author, and not published until after his death. His reasons for writing them, he says, were—first, to oblige himself frequently to enter into a serious contemplation of God, and of the most proper means to render himself acceptable to Him; and next, that by these reflections he might compare his past and present conditions, and make his life "as uniform as possible in all virtue." They present an admirable example of the way in which a man may profitably reflect on the great questions of life and morals. To this, succeed *Spiritual Letters, Written in Spanish*, by Don Juan D'Avila,—a series of 14 letters rightly termed spiritual, and well calculated to promote spirituality in others. The volume ends with *An Extract from Dr. Annesley's Sermons*—a single sermon on "The adherent vanity of every condition most effectually abated by serious godliness."

Vol. xlvii. contains two pieces:—the first, *An Extract from Thoughts on Religion*, by Dr. Beveridge. Bishop Beveridge's well known work is divided into two parts—Private Thoughts upon Religion: and Private Thoughts on a Christian Life. They were originally two works. Wesley has inserted only the former part. Of this he has given substantially the whole, after the application of his usual process of revision and abridgement, thereby reducing an octavo volume to 175 duodecimo pages. He has appended a synopsis of the Extract. The other piece in the volume is *The Nature and Necessity of Godly Fear, By R. A.* [Richard Alleine]. This is in the form of a discourse, or sermon, founded on the text, "Happy is the man that feareth always;" but, after the method of the author, and indeed the fashion of the time, it is expanded almost into a treatise, as is the case with the other works of the same author already named, and it has undergone a like revision. A synopsis extending over three pages is added.

Vol. xlviii. is almost filled with *An Extract from the Works of the Reverend John Howe, M.A., to which is prefixed Some Account of his Life*. The Life is extended much beyond the limits assigned to those in the previous volumes. The extract is made from *The Living Temple: or, A Design'd Improvement of that Notion, That a Good Man is the Temple of God: In two parts*. This is very considerably reduced. The philosophical and speculative portions are wholly eliminated, and the extract is confined to the most practical parts. The six chapters forming the first part are preserved, but abridged from 204 octavo pages, as in the most recent edition, to 68 duodecimo. In the second part the number of chapters has not been preserved, Wesley's first chapter comprising the first three of Howe's work, but occupying little more than six pages, instead of between 50 and 60 as in the original. Wesley's edition therefore cannot be considered an adequate representation of Howe's great work. It is simply an extract of its moral and religious teaching, which however is almost exclusively given in Howe's own words. A synopsis of the whole is appended. The volume closes with *A Treatise on Self Dedication*, also by Howe.

[1756.] No. 174.

Vols. xlix. and l. contain *Extracts from the lives of Sundry Eminent Persons*. The following is a list :—*The Life of Dr. H. Hammond*, by John Fell, D.D., Dean of Christ Church, Oxford ; *Memoirs of the Life of Mr. James Fraser*, written by himself ; *The Lives of Mr. Tho. Tregoss, and Dr. Samuel Winter*, to which is added *A Short Account of Some Eminent Persons of the Church of Scotland ; The Life of Mr. Tho. Cawton, Sometime Minister of the Gospel at St. Bartholomew's, behind the Royal Exchange, London, and late Preacher to the English Congregation at Rotterdam, in Holland; The Life of Mr. Philip Henry; The Life of the late Reverend Mr. George Trosse, Being an Abridgment of his own Narrative*, in two parts ; *The Life of Mr. Tho. Wilson ; The Life of Mr. John Eliot, The First Preacher of the Gospel to the Indians in America*, by Cotton Mather ; *The Life of Mr. Gregory Lopez, Written originally in Spanish*. To the last Wesley has appended a few foot-notes. For a further account see Note to the year 1785.

At length this work, which from a Bibliographical point of view has great interest, was finished. Wesley seems at first to have designed the work chiefly, if not exclusively, for his preachers. With this end in view he sought the help of the Rev. Dr. Doddridge, whose experience as a Tutor of Nonconformist Ministers was very great and who drew up in reply a long list of books as "a scheme of study for a clergyman." See letter in the Arminian Magazine, i. 419 (No. 333). Wesley's first intention was to print but 100 copies (*Works*, xii. 156). It was a disappointment to him that the work did not sell, though he cheered himself with the vain hope that a subsequent generation would value it ; but, perhaps, an equal, if not greater, disappointment was the fact that the volumes were so inaccurately printed. Being twitted by an opponent upon the obvious contradictions between portions of the *Christian Library* and his other works, he quotes his opponent, " Mr. W. affirms that the *Christian Library* is all agreeable to the word of God," and replies, "I do not : and I am glad I have this public opportunity of explaining myself concerning it. My words are, 'I have made, as I was able, an attempt of this kind. I have endeavoured to extract such a collection of English divinity, as, I believe, is all true, all agreeable to the oracles of God :' (preface, p. 4). I did believe, and I do believe every tract therein to be true, and agreeable to the oracles of God. But I do not roundly affirm this (as Mr. H. asserts), of every sentence contained in the fifty volumes. I could not possibly affirm it for two reasons : (1.) I was obliged to prepare most of those tracts for the press, just as I could snatch time in travelling, not transcribing them ; (none expected it of me ;) but only marking the lines with my pen, and altering or adding a few words here and there, as I had mentioned in the preface. (2.) As it was not in my power to attend the press, that care necessarily devolved on others ; through whose inattention a hundred passages were left in which I had scratched out ; yet not so many as to make up 'forty volumes,' no, nor forty pages. It is probable too, I myself might overlook some sentences which were not suitable to my own principles. It is certain the correctors of the press did this in not a few instances. I shall be much obliged to Mr. H. and his friends if they will point out all those instances ; and I will print them as an *index expurgatorius* to the work, which will make it doubly valuable."—*Remarks on Mr. Hill's Review*, see *Works*, x. 381-2. He cherished the purpose of revising the volumes—" If I live to finish the correction of my own works, I shall then revise the *Christian Library*."—Letter in *Works*, xii. 295. This was ultimately accomplished and a second edition was issued (1819-26) after his death, under the editorship of the Rev. Thomas Jackson. Wesley's corrected copy is in the Library of the Richmond College, Surrey.

1756.

174. A LETTER TO THE REVEREND MR. LAW: Occasioned by some of his late Writings. By John Wesley, M.A., late

No. 175.   [1756.

Fellow of Lincoln College, Oxford. "Unwearied patience, unalterable meekness, are the only proofs that God is in me of a truth."—*Spirit of Prayer.* London: Printed in the year 1756. [Price one shilling.] 8vo., pp. 102.

Dated, at the beginning, Dec. 15, 1755, and at the end, London, Jan. 6, 1756, and signed John Wesley.

The letter was written to expose what Wesley judged to be the extravagances of a false, mystic, so-called philosophy.

After paying a well-deserved tribute to Law's abilities, his pure motive, and the great value of some of his earlier writings, particularly the *Treatise on Christian Perfection* and the *Serious Call*—works " which must remain as long as England stands, almost unequalled standards of the strength and purity of our language, as well as of sound, practical divinity,"—he reminds Law of one of his sayings, " Religion is the most plain, simple thing in the world. It is only, *We love him because he first loved us.* So far as you add philosophy to religion, just so far you spoil it." He then accuses him of blending philosophy with religion more than any writer in England. Then the letter is occupied with extracts from two of Law's later books, *The Spirit of Prayer,* and *The Spirit of Love,* and with Wesley's replies to them.

Law had become a mystic through the writings of Behmen. " But Law himself, who has shaken so many intellects, sacrificed his own at last to the reveries and rhapsodies of Jacob Behmen."—Southey, *Life of Wesley.*

The letter has been severely condemned by many writers. Both it and Wesley's motive in writing it are very fairly judged by Canon Overton in his *Life of William Law.* " It was written, like everything that was written by that great and good man, from the purest motives ; nor is it difficult to see what those motives were. To do reasonable justice to Wesley we must remember that he was an eminently practical man. The question with him would be, Is such teaching likely to do my people practical harm ? And remembering that he had seen what had been the practical effect of the sort of diluted mysticism of the London Moravians upon his people, we can hardly wonder that he concluded that harm would be done. Hence this well-meant, if not very judicious attempt to counteract the evil." Law described it in a private letter as "a juvenile composition of emptiness and pertness, below the character of any man who had been serious in religion but half a month." Canon Overton thinks that, "regarding it purely as an intellectual performance, perhaps Law was not very far wrong." He judges that Wesley had but a very imperfect acquaintance with Behmenism. Law showed his true Christian feeling by refusing to reply, advising a friend, who censured the Methodists in this very matter, to " wish them well in all that is good."

The Letter has not been republished entire. An extract is given in the *Preservative Against Unsettled Notions in Religion,* (No. 191). This extract appears also in the *Works* (1830), ix. 466-509.

175. AN ADDRESS TO THE CLERGY. By John Wesley, M.A., late Fellow of Lincoln College, Oxford. London: Printed in the year 1756. 8vo., pp. 31.

Dated at the end Feb. 6, 1756, and signed John Wesley.

"Let it not be imputed to forwardness, vanity or presumption, that one who is of little esteem in the Church, takes upon him thus to address a body of people, to many of whom he owes the highest reverence." Wesley sat down to write this on the day of the great Fast, to be noticed hereafter. It is a very serious and searching address to clergymen of all denominations, to consider what manner of men they ought to be, and whether indeed they were such. He enumerates the natural and acquired gifts which he judges a minister ought to have. Amongst the former are a good understanding, some liveliness and readiness of thought. Of the latter, to a competent share of knowledge of his office he should add a knowledge of the Scriptures—"the literal meaning of every word, verse, and chapter, without which there can be no firm foundation on which the spiritual meaning can be built." He further needs an acquaintance with the original tongues, profane history, the sciences, especially logic, metaphysics, natural philosophy, and even geometry, "to give clearness of apprehension and the habit of thinking closely and connectedly." To all these must be added the knowledge of the Fathers, "the most authentic commentators on Scripture, chiefly those who wrote before the Council of Nice;" also "knowledge of the world;" "discernment of spirits, so far as it may be acquired by diligent observation; common sense; the courtesy of a gentleman, and a strong and clear voice." But above all these the minister needs the grace of God, which should animate his intentions, his affection, and his practice. A very tender appeal closes the whole.

It is an address that any Christian minister may read with profit. Though severe enough to humble him to the dust, it is hopeful enough to encourage him to effort.

Tyerman thinks Wesley had a two-fold object in view,—to awaken the zeal of the clergy, and so prevent the necessity for a separation; and to curb the ambition of his own preachers, by setting a very high standard of excellence before them, of which, in some respects, many fell immeasurably short. But Wesley's letter, written at the close of the Conference of that year, does not bear out the latter supposition, for he expressly affirms them not to be contemplated; and besides, he never spoke of them as clergy. Tyerman (ii. 269, 270) gives some rough words from a letter of William Law, and an account of two pamphlets occasioned by the address, one of them being very curious. Wesley's real purpose in writing the pamphlet is suggested in the *Life of Charles Wesley*, ii. 100.

The Address is included in Wesley's own edition of his collected Works.

176. AN EXTRACT FROM THE REVEREND MR. JOHN WESLEY'S JOURNAL, from July 20, 1749, to October 30, 1751. London: Printed in the year 1756. 12mo., pp. 107. [No. viii.]

An "Erratum in the title page of the last Journal" is noticed on page opposite to title-page. This number of the Journal contains an extended account of hard labour and much travelling, and of the severe, violent and cruel persecution to which the Methodists in Ireland were subject. It also makes special reference to the Moravians and to Kingswood School. Amongst the most painful records is one concerning "that wonderful self-deceiver and hypocrite, James Wheatley," which was published as a separate tract with the title:—

176A. EXTRACT OF THE REVEREND MR. JOHN WESLEY'S JOURNAL, FOR THE YEAR 1751. 12mo., pp. 4.

Half-page title; no date, or name of publisher. A copy of this is in the Didsbury College Library. There is no record as to the time when it was printed.

This extract, which is now very rarely met with, is taken from the Journal under date July 8, 1751. It is an account of the means adopted by Wesley and his brother with a view to reclaim James Wheatley, who "by his obstinate wickedness had brought a great scandal on the Gospel. And what a curse on his own head!" Charles had been importuned by one of the Society narrowly to inquire into Wheatley's behaviour, which he did, writing down the particulars and reading them over in Wheatley's presence. The latter was compelled to acknowledge their truthfulness in the main. After waiting some time and deeply pondering the matter, Wesley wrote a paper which he and his brother signed and put into Wheatley's hands. In it they declared they could in no wise any longer receive him as a fellow-labourer, unless he gave them clear proof of his "real and deep repentance." They then waited still longer, but as Wheatley gave no sign of penitence, the final step of separating him from them was taken; and Wesley appeals to any impartial judge to determine "whether they had shown too much severity: whether, indeed, they had not leaned to the other extreme, and shown too much lenity to so stubborn an offender:" see *Works*, ii. pp. 236-8.

For an account of Wheatley, the first minister expelled from the Methodist Connexion, see Tyerman's *Life of Wesley*, ii. pp. 121-7.

177. Short Account of the Death of Richard Moore. Printed in the year 1756. 12mo., pp. 11.

The above is inserted by Osborn, but not mentioned by Heylin. There is no name of printer, or place where printed, given. On the title-page is an imprint of one of Farley's woodcuts (an angel flying through clouds.) The pamphlet was obviously not written by Wesley, though it may have been edited by him. The preface speaks of the writer as a woman, probably Moore's wife to whom there is a reference at the end. The account is divided into numbered paragraphs, as Wesley's writings generally are; and the preface and the last two paragraphs, additions to the original account; are quite in Wesley's style. As it is not unlikely that it was edited, and portions of it written by him, it may be numbered amongst his publications, but with an expression of doubt. It is not found in Wesley's edition of his collected Works; nor is it in the catalogues.

It was evidently printed as a warning against "such as preach Christ so as to supersede holiness of heart and life; for by listening to these Mr. Moore lost his faith for some time and suffered much at last." He was daily visited by "Mr. W. (ah, how fallen since!) and Mr. Larwood." Were these James Wheatley and Samuel Larwood, two of Wesley's preachers who had left him?

178. The Good Soldier. Extracted from a Sermon preached to a Company of Voluntiers, Raised in Virginia, August 17, 1755. London: Printed in the year 1756. 12mo., pp. 15.

This anonymous tract is ascribed to Wesley, without hesitation, by Osborn and by Heylin. Tyerman says, "The publication was doubtless occasioned by the threatened invasion of England by the French, at the beginning of the year, when Wesley himself proposed to raise 'for His Majesty's service a body of at least two hundred volunteers.'"—*Life of Wesley*, ii. 265. But by whom the sermon was preached, and by whom the extract was made, are points not cleared up. As it is catalogued amongst Wesley's publications, it was in all probability extracted by him, though there is hardly a sentence in the whole pamphlet that can be confidently attributed to him. It may have been preached by one of the preachers in Virginia from whom he heard early in this year, and to whom he refers in his Journal under March 1, 1756.

179. A ROMAN CATECHISM, WITH A REPLY THERETO. Reprinted in the year 1756. 12mo., pp. 79.

There is apparently not a sentence of Wesley's in the whole of this pamphlet; but strange to say it is copied bodily into his own edition of his collected Works, without a note of any kind; as is the case also in the 1812 and 1830 editions. But what is more remarkable still, it was reprinted in 1825 in four separate parts, each bearing the title "A ROMAN CATECHISM, Faithfully drawn out of the allowed writings of the Church of Rome; with a Reply thereto: By Rev. John Wesley, A.M., sometime Fellow of Lincoln College, Oxford. Third edition:" London: Published and sold by J. Kershaw, 14, City Road, and 66, Paternoster Row. The original has been traced to a writer in the days of James II.

That it must be reckoned amongst Wesley's *publications*, is plain from the following. It having been suggested that the Methodists had some connection with Popery, and that Wesley had not repudiated it, he refers to several of his writings, and adds:—"Many things to the same purpose occur in the 'Journals' and the 'Appeals to Men of Reason and Religion,' over and above those whole treatises which I have published entirely upon the subject: 'A Word to a Protestant,' '*A Roman Catechism*,' and 'The Advantage of the Members of the Church of England over the Members of the Church of Rome.'"—*Journal*, Dec. 20, 1768. It is also inserted in his catalogues.

There is a very curious and unexplained fact in reference to all the publications of this year, with a single exception only,—No. 181. Not one of them has in it the name of the printer. Two have only the words "Printed in the year 1756;" and all the rest "London: printed in the year 1756." This applies also to several important reprints—the fifth edition of *Hymns and Sacred Poems*, 1739 (No. 15), and the third edition of *Hymns and Sacred Poems*, 1742 (No. 40), also the third edition of *Hymns for Times of Trouble and Persecution* (No. 59), the third edition of *Hymns Occasioned by the Earthquake* (No. 148), the sixth edition of *Psalms and Hymns* (No. 30), and the fourth edition of *Hymns and Spiritual Songs* (No. 165).

180. A WORD TO THOSE FREEMEN OF THE ESTABLISH'D CHURCH WHO MAKE THE SCRIPTURES THE ONE RULE OF THEIR FAITH AND PRACTICE. (Rom. xiv. 22). Printed in the year 1756. 12mo., pp. 15.

Osborn inserts this on internal evidence alone; and, therefore, with some hesitation. Heylin does not mention it. It is not in any edition of the collected Works, nor is it in the catalogues. Yet in all probability it is Wesley's. In the *Journal* for March 3rd of this year is the following entry:— "I found Bristol all in a flame; voters and non-voters being ready to tear each other in pieces. I had not recovered my voice, so as either to preach or speak to the whole Society. But I desired those members who were freemen to meet me by themselves, whom I mildly and lovingly informed how they ought to act in this hour of temptation. And I believe the far greater part of them received and profited by the advice." It is quite in Wesley's style, and has the same words on the title-page, which distinguish nearly all the publications of this year,—see note No. 179.

There is a copy in the Library of the Methodist Book Room, London.

181. HYMNS FOR THE YEAR 1756, particularly for the Fast Day, February 6. Bristol: Printed by E. Farley at Shakspear's-Head in Small-Street. 1756. 12mo., pp. 24.

Second edition, simply "Hymns for the Fast Day." Bristol, Farley, n. d. An Edition not numbered, Dublin, S. Powell, 1756; another, "Hymns for the year 1756," Second Edition, Bristol; Fourth, London, Hawes, 1780.

This is the only new publication issued by the Wesleys this year that bore the name of the printer. C. W. was in Bristol in the early part of the year; J. W. in London.

There are seventeen hymns in this tract; three of them are included in the large Hymn Book, being Nos. 60, 61, and 62, "Righteous God whose vengeful phials," "Stand the omnipotent decree," and "How happy are the little flock." Some of them Jackson thinks are equal "in sublimity and force to any compositions that had ever proceeded from Charles Wesley's pen."

The political condition of the country at this time was greatly disturbed from several causes, the most prominent being the very unsettled state of Ireland and America, the attitude of France and her threat of the invasion of England. Much fear was felt by many. A national fast was proclaimed to be held on the 6th of February. Concerning it Wesley says, "The Fast Day was a glorious day; such as London has scarce seen since the Restoration. Every church in the city was more than full; and a solemn seriousness sat on every face. Surely God heareth the prayer; and there will yet be a lengthening of our tranquillity. Even the Jews observed this day with a peculiar solemnity."—*Journal*, Feb. 6, 1756.

"The publication of this admirable tract was not the only service which Mr. Charles Wesley rendered to the cause of religion and of the nation in this season of distress. He also reprinted, with enlargements, the *Hymns for Times of Trouble and Persecution*, [No. 59], which he had composed during the rebellion of 1745, as being applicable to the present state of the country, menaced as in the former instance by papal intolerance. At the same time he put to press another edition of his *Hymns on the Earthquake of 1750*, [No. 148], with three additions: one, a prayer for the English in America; another on the destruction of Lisbon; and a third for 1756."—*Life of C. Wesley*, ii. 102.

1757.

182. THE DOCTRINE OF ORIGINAL SIN: ACCORDING TO SCRIPTURE, REASON, AND EXPERIENCE. By John Wesley. Bristol: Printed by E. Farley in Small Street. 1757. 8vo., pp. 522.

One page of *errata*. Price, bound and lettered, six shillings. Re-published, London: Kershaw, 1825, 12mo.

This was written in reply to "*The Scripture Doctrine of Original Sin proposed to free and candid examination*. In three parts. By [Dr.] John Taylor [of Norwich]. The Third edition, with large additions. To which is added a supplement, &c., containing remarks upon two books, viz., *The Vindication of the Doctrine of Original Sin*, and *The Ruin and Recovery of Mankind*, &c.:" London: Waugh, 1750, pp. 268 and 227. This work was brought under Wesley's notice some years before. He then read it carefully, and partly transcribed it; and many times afterwards "diligently considered" it. He waited long, hoping that someone of position and competent ability would answer it. Being impressed by the importance of the subject and the subtle, dangerous power of Dr. Taylor's "smooth, decent" writing, and observing the prevalence of what he judged to be erroneous views on the subject, he could wait no longer. "Being now in the very midst of Mr. Taylor's disciples, I enlarged much more than I am accustomed to do on the doctrine of Original Sin; and determined, if God should give me a few years' life, publicly to answer his [Dr. Taylor's] new gospel."—*Journal*, April 10, 1751.

The work is divided into four parts, the first three corresponding with the divisions in Taylor's book; and, like them, each has a date appended to it. In the first part, dated January 18, 1757, Wesley inquires into the moral state of mankind in all ages; and then proceeds to account for it, dealing severally with those Scriptures which Taylor had cited in the first part of his book. To the first part of Taylor's book, dated Norwich, November 20, 1735, an answer had already appeared by Dr. Jennings, from which Wesley quotes largely. The second part of Taylor's treatise is dated December 31, 1735. In it are examined the texts cited by the Westminster Assembly of Divines in their Larger Catechism. Wesley pursues the same course as in the first part, considering passage by passage, and quoting Dr. Jennings and Hervey's *Theron and Aspasio*. This portion is dated Lewisham, January 21.

He then deals with the third part of Taylor's work (dated February 5, 1735-6), in which objections and queries are answered, and the connexion of the doctrine of Original Sin with other parts of religion considered. Here, again, Wesley proceeds to examine Taylor's views point by point. This completes the second part of Wesley's work; it is dated Lewisham, January 25, 1757.

Taylor wrote a considerable *Supplement* to *The Scripture Doctrine of Original Sin*, as an answer to Jennings and Watts. It is divided into eight sections. To this Watts replied; and Taylor followed with a rejoinder of "Remarks;" both are included in the edition of Taylor's book used by Wesley. They are not dated. Wesley considers the *Supplement* and *Remarks* in the third part of his work. It is curious to observe that Wesley, following the example of Taylor, does not append the date to this part.

The fourth part of Wesley's book, dated Lewisham, March 23, 1757, is made up of extracts from Watts's *Ruin and Recovery*, the work attacked by Taylor; from some scarce tracts by the Rev. Samuel Hebden, of Wrentham, in Suffolk; and from Boston's *Fourfold State of Man*. He had purposely refrained from reading Dr. Watts's work until he had written his own answer to Taylor, but when he had read it he was so surprised at the imperfect view given of it by Taylor that "to do justice to that great and good man, as well as to his argument," he felt constrained to select and publish these very copious extracts.

He adds, "I have now gone thro', as my leisure would permit, this whole complicated question;" and avers that were it not on a point of so deep importance he would no more enter the lists with Dr. Taylor than lift his hand against a giant. He then makes a fervent appeal, extending over four pages, to Dr. Taylor, on account of his great abilities and possible widespread usefulness and the dangerous character of the views held by him, "to review his whole cause and that from the very foundation." This appeal is dated Lewisham, March 24, 1757. In the same spirit he wrote his earnest and very interesting letter to Taylor, from Hartlepool, in 1759, (*Journal*, July 3), which Jackson includes in his edition of the Works, as though it had been published separately, which is very doubtful. To the appeal he adds one more extract, taken from Boston's *Four-fold State of Man*, and dated Bristol, August 17, 1757. These extracts, given without note or comment, occupy more than two-fifths of the whole volume.

This is judged by some to be Wesley's greatest work; but it lacks the unity of design, the close concatenated reasoning, and the brilliancy that mark the *Appeals*. It suffers from its plan, from its too fragmentary character, and from its having been written at intervals, and in contradiction to the views of others, and not as a positive and original treatise on its great subject.

"It has been said that Dr. Taylor always spoke of Mr. Wesley with the highest respect; and that when he first heard of his intention, he cried out, 'What is that servant of God going to write against me?'"—Moore's *Life of Wesley*, ii. 409. The controversy was at no time bitter.

The whole of this book was inserted in each edition of the collected Works, with a change in the number of parts from four to seven, the last part of the original work being divided into four.

183. A SUFFICIENT ANSWER TO LETTERS TO THE AUTHOR OF THERON AND ASPASIO; in a Letter to the Author. By John Wesley, M.A. Bristol: Printed by E. Farley in Small-Street. 1757. (Price One Penny.) 12mo., pp. 12.

Dated at the beginning Bristol, November 1, 1757; but not signed.

The writing of this pamphlet was provoked by a work of considerable size (some 500 pages), published anonymously, probably by John Glass or Robert Sandeman, of Sandemanian notoriety, under the pseudonym of *Palæmon*. Wesley writes,—" It is not very material who you are. If Mr. Glass is alive, I suppose you are he. If not, you are at least one of his humble admirers." Wesley in strong and bitter words accuses the writer of being "a gross, wilful slanderer," of not knowing what faith is, of self-contradiction, of want of charity, &c. What his object was in penning this caustic tract does not very clearly appear. There is but little defence of Hervey; and if it was designed to guard against false notions of faith (the chief error of Sandemanian teaching), it is too sarcastic for so serious a purpose. For although, in the three pages devoted to it, Wesley exposes the erroneousness of the views he attacks, yet it seems hardly to be worthy of him to do it in a manner which found its only justification in the style of the book he was assailing. It may be said that he held strong views of the evils of the teaching of both Glass and Sandeman. "Till now I imagined there had never appeared in the world such a book as the work of Machiavel. But Dr. Mandeville goes far beyond it. Surely Voltaire would hardly have said so much. And even Mr. Sandeman could not have said more."—*Journal*, April 14, 1756. About this time Wesley certainly wrote sharply and severely. Doubtless he had sufficient reason for so doing. He may have designed to arrest attention and fix his words where smooth ones would not stick.

In some catalogues it is called *A Defence of Theron and Aspasio*. It provoked a reply entitled *Remarks on the Rev. Mr. John Wesley's Sufficient Answer to the Letters on Theron and Aspasio*: By J. D., London, 1758, 8vo.

NOTE.—In this year was published a tract entitled *Reasons why the Electors of Bristol should vote for men that support the King; or Advice to the Electors, &c.* It is thought to have been written by either Wesley or Charles Perronet; but by which cannot be determined.

1758.

184. A LETTER TO A GENTLEMAN AT BRISTOL. Bristol: Printed by E. Farley, in Small-Street. 1758. [Price Twopence.] 12mo., pp. 19.

Dated at the beginning Bristol, January 6, 1758. Signed, John Wesley.

[1758.]   Nos. 185-186.

A paper had been addressed to the inhabitants of St. Stephen's Parish, Bristol, by a "Dr. T.," which called forth an answer entitled *A Seasonable Antidote Against Popery*. In both of them were some expressions and statements on which it was desired Wesley should give his opinion. He says, "At the request of several of my friends, I wrote *A Letter to a Gentleman of Bristol*, in order to guard them from seeking salvation by works on one hand and antinomianism on the other. From those who lean to either extreme, I shall have no thanks. But 'wisdom is justified of her children.'"—*Journal*, Jan. 3, 1758.

He explains that he had but little leisure and could not speak so fully as the importance of the subject required, and adds, "I can only just tell you wherein I do or do not agree with what is advanced" in the paper or its answer.

The tract is rare, and does not appear to have been reprinted separately; but it is included in Jackson's edition of the collected Works.

185. THE GREAT ASSIZE: A SERMON preached at the Assizes in St. Paul's Church, Bedford: on Friday, March 10, 1758. By John Wesley, M.A., late Fellow of Lincoln College, Oxford. London: Printed and sold by T. Trye, near Gray's-Inn-Gate, Holbourn; by G. Keith, in Gracechurch-street; by T. James, under the Royal-Exchange, and at the Foundery. n.d. 8vo., pp. ii. 36.

Second edition, same printers, n.d., 8vo., pp. 36, having the words on title-page, "Preached at the Assizes held before the Honourable Sir Edward Clive, Knight, one of the Judges of His Majesty's Court of Common Pleas, &c.," and "Published at the request of William Cole, Esq., High Sheriff of the County, and others." Another unnumbered, sm. 4to. pp. 36, n.d. (probably early); Third edition, London: Hawes, 1779, 12mo., pp. 23; Fourth, London: Paramore, 1787; Others, London, 1782, Paramore, "This sermon not to be sold but given away;" Another, 1783; London: Paramore, 1784; London: Storey, n.d.

"Having a sermon to write against the Assizes at Bedford, I retired for a few days to Lewisham."—*Journal*, Feb. 27, 1758. There this model sermon was carefully prepared. It is well-formed, plain, practical, earnest; the statements are all supported by apt Scriptures, and the truth faithfully applied to the conscience. It was preached when Wesley was in his strength, and to a congregation that was "very large and very attentive."

He had come down to Bedford on the Thursday, and found to his surprise that the sermon was not to be preached until the Friday, and he had engaged to be in Epworth on the Saturday; so that when the judge immediately after the sermon sent for him to dine with him, he was obliged to excuse himself, and setting out between one and two o'clock he rode thirty miles in face of snow, sleet, and hail. Renewing his journey between four and five the next morning, he accomplished the remaining ninety miles by night. Next day he preached two or three times in the church, and afterwards in the market-place, where, though the rain was heavy, it "neither lessened nor disturbed the congregation."

186. A LETTER TO THE REV. DR. FREE. By John Wesley, M.A. Bristol: Printed by E. Farley and Son, in Small-Street. 1758. 12mo., pp. 10.

Dated at beginning, Tullamore, May 2, 1758. Signed John Wesley.

Nos. 187-188. [1758.

187. A SECOND LETTER TO THE REVEREND DR. FREE. Bristol: Printed by E. Farley and Son. 1758. 12mo., pp. 16.

Dated at beginning, Fonmon Castle, August 24, 1758. Signed, at the end, John Wesley.

Dr. Free, vicar of East Crocker, Somerset, had written "a small tract," in which he vehemently, but falsely, accused the Methodists of holding and teaching doctrines, and of practices, such as no one in the slightest degree accurately informed of their views could possibly affirm of them. As he challenged Wesley to reply, he does so in a few but decisive words, nor does he fail to show that Dr. Free himself was far guiltier than the poor people whom he assails. Taking up the five points of Free's accusations, Wesley charges him with misrepresentation, and calls upon him for proof of his assertions. "I wrote a short answer to Dr. Free's weak, bitter, scurrilous invective against the people called Methodists. But I doubt whether I shall meddle with him any more; he is too dirty a writer for me to touch."—*Journal*, May 2, 1758. He was, however, compelled to "meddle" with him once more, for Dr. Free preached a sermon before the University at St. Mary's, Oxford, on *Rules for the Discovery of False Prophets; or, the Dangerous Impositions of the People called Methodists detected at the bar of Scripture and Reason*. It was published with a preface, and an appendix "containing authentic vouchers from the writings of the Methodists," &c.

In the preface he desires that if Wesley is not satisfied with the proofs of his assertions he will signify it by a private letter, when he is promised a more particular answer. But as Free had "appealed to the Archbishop, the University, the Nation," Wesley felt it was no more a matter between themselves; and as a serious charge had been brought against not only himself but a whole body of people, he must either let the case go by default or publicly reply. To this Wesley's second letter was directed, and, like the first, it exposes the utter want of foundation for the "many and heavy allegations" made against him and his people.

"I wrote a second letter to Dr. Free, the warmest opponent I have had for many years. I leave him now to laugh, and scold, and witticise, and call names just as he pleases; for I have done."—*Journal*, Aug. 24, 1758. Not so his opponent, for he follows up the strife with a pamphlet entitled, *Dr. Free's edition of Rev. Mr. John Wesley's First Penny Letter, &c., with Notes upon the Original Text, addressed to Mr. Wesley; and likewise a Dedication to the Reverend Author.* But Wesley was not to be drawn into further futile controversy.

188. A SHORT ACCOUNT OF THE LIFE AND DEATH OF NATHANAEL OTHEN, who was shot in Dover-Castle, October 26, 1757. Bristol: Printed by John Grabham in Wine Street; and sold at the New Room in the Horse-Fair; and at the Foundery, near Upper-Moor-Fields, London. n.d. 12mo., pp. 12.

Second edition, Bristol: printed by E. Farley & Son, n. d.; Third, Dublin: S. Powell, 1759; Another, London: G. Story, n. d.; Another, London, 1775; Another, 1795.

Another instance of a brand plucked from the burning. Othen, after an evil course, enlisted, deserted, passed through many adventures, was apprehended and condemned to death. He was removed to Dover Castle, where he was afterwards executed. Through the instrumentality of a godly drummer he was led to repentance, and found redemption through faith in Christ. The former part of the tract gives an account of his career as related by himself to someone not named who wrote it down, as he said, from his mouth. In addition to the visits of a pious clergyman and a number of Methodists, a "Mr. W——" frequently saw him and attended him to the scaffold. This could not be either Wesley, for John was in Bristol. Charles had retired from itinerating, and of his doings during this year we have no record. Jackson says, "Not a document in his handwriting bearing the date of 1757, when he is said to have become stationary, can be found; nor even the fragment of a letter, of the same period, addressed to him by his brother." His published Journal ceases at the end of the previous year.

The tract was published by Wesley in the following year, as he tells us, "I wrote the account of an extraordinary monument of divine mercy—Nathaniel Othen, who was shot for desertion at Dover Castle, in October, 1757."—*Journal*, Sept. 9, 1758. Both Osborn and Heylin assign it in error to 1757, doubtless misled by the date of the execution as it appears on the title-page.

189. A LETTER TO THE REV. MR. POTTER, by the Rev. Mr. Wesley. London: Printed and sold at the Foundery, Upper-Moorfields. 1758. 12mo., pp. 11.

Dated at the beginning, Norwich, Nov. 4, 1758; and at the end, Lakenheath, Nov. 7; and signed John Wesley. Wesley often dated his publications when he began them, although some time might elapse before they were finished.

This is of the same character as the letters to Dr. Free. Mr. Potter, of Rymerston, in Norfolk, had published a sermon on *The pretended inspiration of the Methodists* (Text, John iii. 5—Norwich, 1758, 8vo.) Wesley in this letter first corrects Potter's notions of the New Birth; and then at some length considers the chief accusation—the pretence of inspiration. He shows that what had been so vehemently declaimed against, and what the Methodists really pretended to, was in reality only that gracious illumination by the Divine Spirit which every true believer receives, and for which prayer is made in the service of the Church of England. Like Dr. Free, Mr. Potter had greatly misapprehended alike the teaching and the practice of the Methodists. Both of them received a very effective correction.

190. THE CASE OF THE UNHAPPY PEOPLE OF CUSTRIN. 12mo., pp. 7.

This is an anonymous tract. The title covers half the first page, and there is neither date nor name of writer or printer. At the end is a hymn of six stanzas, beginning "God of boundless pity, spare," which is inserted in the *Poetical Works of J. and C. Wesley*, xiii., p. 270, with this note appended, "Occasion and date unknown." The tract is a brief description of some of the barbarities practised by the Russian soldiery during the siege of New-Mark, Custrin, and other places in 1758. It is in Wesley's terse, compact, clear style. The hymn seems to have been written on the occasion.

191. A PRESERVATIVE AGAINST UNSETTLED NOTIONS IN RELIGION. By John Wesley, M.A. Bristol: Printed by E. Farley, in Small-Street. 1758. 12mo., pp. 246.

Another edition, 1770; Another, London: Mason, 1839.

No. 191. [1758.

Wesley found that many of the members of his societies had been shaken from their steadfastness by false teachers. Anxious to protect his flock, he, like a faithful shepherd, strove to make the defences round the fold more secure. With this end in view he collected together a number of pamphlets which he judged contained pithy and forcible arguments against the several seductive teachings that were producing such disastrous results. Some of these pamphlets were original, and had been already published; others were adapted from various writers; and all were now incorporated in a single volume.

His purpose is well stated in the brief preface. He says:—" My design in publishing the following tracts is not to reclaim, but to preserve; not to convince those who are already perverted, but to prevent the perversion of others. I do not therefore enter deep into the controversy even with *Deists, Socinians, Arians,* or *Papists;* much less with those who are not so dangerously mistaken, *Mystics, Quakers, Anabaptists, Presbyterians, Predestinarians,* or *Antinomians.* I only recite under each head a few plain arguments, which, by the grace of God, may farther confirm those who already know the truth as it is in Jesus."

There are thirteen tracts in all, of which those marked with an asterisk had been already published. It will be observed that they treat of the errors just named, and in the same order. They are:—

1. *An Extract of a Short and Easy Method with the Deists.*
Leslie's once well-known work is entitled *A Short and Easy Method with the Deists, wherein the Certainty of the Christian Religion is demonstrated by infallible proof from Four Rules, which are incompatible to any imposture that ever yet has been, or that can possibly be: In a Letter to a Friend.* It is not "short" enough for Wesley, who abridges it by omitting the *Preface against the Deists,* by reducing the twenty sections to nine, and by excising every sentence and even every word that he deems to be not essential to the strength of the argument. He does not append Leslie's *Letter to a Gentleman who had been converted by reading the Short and Easy Method with the Deists.*

2. *A Treatise concerning the Godhead of Jesus Christ. Translated from the French.*
It is divided into two sections, in which it is argued, "That if Jesus Christ is not the true God, of the same essence with the Father, (1) the Mahometan religion is preferable to the Christian, and Jesus Christ inferior to Mahomet," (this is treated in the first section); and (2) "The Sanhedrim did an act of Justice in putting Him to death." The second section is divided into five chapters in which the following propositions are maintained:—that Jesus Christ takes to Himself the name of God; that the apostles ascribe to Him the works and attributes which the prophets ascribe to God only; that they make Him equal with God; that He required and received adoration; and that those passages in the Old Testament which exhibit the characters of the Supreme God, are applied to Christ in the New Testament.

3. *The Advantage of the Members of the Church of England over those of the Church of Rome.*
This is an exact copy of No. 161. It is a brief but comprehensive tract in which the principal errors of the Church of Rome are stated and refuted in a clear and succinct manner, and as fully as the space will admit. Wesley has exerted his power of compression most effectively. It is a valuable little tract for the purpose for which it was designed.

4. *An Extract of a Letter to the Rev. Mr. Law; Occasioned by some of his late Writings.*
This, though called an extract, comprises almost the whole of the long letter which Wesley wrote to Mr. Law in 1755 and published the following year: see No. 174. No one can read this paper without seeing that Law laid himself open to severe animadversion, which Wesley was justified in making,

by the ill-effects Law's writings produced upon the societies Wesley was trying to form.

5. *A Letter to a Person lately joined with the people call'd Quakers. In Answer to a Letter wrote by him.* See No. 108.

6. *A Treatise on Baptism.*
This is a slight abridgement of *The Short Discourse of Baptism*, which appeared at the end of *The Pious Communicant Rightly Prepared; or a Discourse concerning the Blessed Sacrament: wherein the nature of it is described, our obligation to frequent communion enforced, and directions given for due preparation for it, behaviour at and after it. With Prayers and Hymns suited to the several parts of that Holy Office. To which is added, A Short Discourse of Baptism.* By Samuel Wesley, A.M., Chaplain to the Most Honourable John, Lord Marquis of Normanby, and Rector of Epworth, in the diocese of Lincoln. London: Printed for Charles Harper. 1700. The short treatise is divided into four parts, in which are considered, "What Baptism is; What benefits we receive by it; Whether our Saviour designed it always to remain in His church; and who are the proper subjects of it." Wesley has partially altered the wording of the discourse, but he has not changed its doctrinal teaching. He thus endorses his father's views of this Sacrament. But the whole of this little treatise must be read in the light of Wesley's own precise teaching in the Sermon on the New Birth: see *Works*, vi. 65-77. The Treatise is dated at the end Nov, 11, 1756, which is the date on which it was extracted.

7. *A Letter to the Rev. Mr. Toogood, of Exeter; Occasioned by his Dissent from the Church of England fully justified.* Dated at the end Bristol, Jan. 10, 1758. The Rev. Micaiah Towgood had written a work on Dissent from the Church of England. To this the Rev. John White, a clergyman, replied in three letters. This called forth a rejoinder from Towgood entitled *A Dissent from the Church of England fully justified: and proved the genuine and just consequence of the allegiance due to Christ, the only Law-giver in the Church. Being the Dissenting Gentleman's Three Letters and Postscript Compleat. In Answer to the Rev. John White's on that subject. To which is added a Letter to the Bishops, &c.* By Micajah Towgood. (Five editions at least of this were published.) This work attracted Wesley's attention and drew from him the letter named above. "I began a letter to Mr. Towgood, author of 'The Dissenting Gentleman's Reasons'"; I think the most saucy and virulent satire on the Church of England that ever my eyes beheld. How much rather would I write practically than controversially? But even this talent I dare not bury in the earth."—*Journal*, Jan. 9, 1758. See also *Life of C. W.*, ii. 77-8.

Heylin gives this as a separate publication, but it is extremely improbable that it was printed before it appeared (in the year in which it was written) in the *Preservative*. It is not named in any catalogue as a separate work.

8. *Serious thoughts concerning Godfathers and Godmothers.* See No. 157.

9. *The Scripture doctrine of Predestination, Election, and Reprobation.* See No. 27.

10. *An extract from a Short View of the Difference between the Moravian Brethren (so called) and the Rev. Mr. John and Charles Wesley.* See No. 68.
The following is prefixed:—"To the Reader. As those who are under the direction of Count Zinzendorf (vulgarly called Moravian Brethren) are the most plausible, and therefore far the most dangerous, of all the Antinomians now in England, I first endeavour to guard such as are simple of heart against being taken by those cunning hunters. Mr. Cudworth's writings (tho' less considerable) are likewise frequently cited in the Dialogue that follows."
The Cudworth referred to was once a follower of Whitefield, but left him and became the Minister of a small Independent Church in London. He published

No. 192. [1758.

a volume, to which Wesley refers, containing twelve tracts entitled *Christ alone Exalted:* Extracted and written by William Cudworth : London : J. Hart. 1747. To some of these tracts Wesley replied soon after their appearance, particularly in the *Dialogue between an Antinomian and his Friend*, Nos. 70 and 71. Cudworth's writings excited Wesley's severest indignation. Tyerman says truly, "If Wesley ever felt the least bitterness towards any of his opponents, it was towards Cudworth." In a letter to Mr. Harvey, he writes, "Give no countenance to that insolent, scurrilous, virulent libel, which bears the name of William Cudworth."—*Works*, xii. 145.

11. *An Extract from a Dialogue between an Antinomian and his Friend.* This is taken from the first of the Dialogues named above,—No. 70.

12. *A Letter to the Rev. Mr. ———.* This is a letter to Mr. Hervey on his work entitled *Theron and Aspasio.* It is dated at the beginning, Oct. 15, 1756, and signed J. W.

13. *Reasons against a Separation from the Church of England.* This is an extract made for this volume from a larger work on the same subject written by Wesley, but never printed. See an interesting account of it in Jackson's *Life of Charles Wesley*, ii. 84. "Wesley wrote at this time (1756) his *Twelve Reasons against a Separation from the Church of England*, though they were not published till 1758. They are a remarkable example of his terse style, his precise habit of thinking, and his large charity."—Stevens' *History of Methodism*, Bk. iv., c. iv.

"In the evening I retired to Lewisham, and spent the following days in finishing *A Preservative against Unsettled Notions in Religion ;* designed for the use of all who are under my care, but chiefly of the young preachers."—*Journal*, Dec. 11, 1757.

"This was an important work, comprising as it did, in a single volume, the opinions of Wesley on all the subjects which, at that time, excited the attention of the Methodists."—Jackson's *Life of Wesley*, ii. 320.

192. HYMNS OF INTERCESSION FOR ALL MANKIND. (i. Tim. ii. 1.) Bristol : Printed by E. Farley in Small-Street. 1758. 12mo., pp. 34.

An edition was printed in Dublin, by S. Powell, 1759 ; Another, London : Paramore, n.d.

This is a pamphlet of much interest. The hymns are truly "hymns of intercession"—the fervent breathings of a large, compassionate heart, to the throne of the heavenly grace, for "all sorts and conditions of men." There are forty hymns in all, thirty-four being in the majestic 6-8s metre, which seems to have been so great a favourite with Charles Wesley. Opening with a hymn "for all Mankind," from which the tract takes its name, it contains Prayers for Peace, for the Church, for Ministers, for the King, the Prince of Wales, the King of Prussia, for the Nation, for the Magistrates, the Nobility, the Parliament, the Fleet, the Army, the Universities, for All that travel by land or water, and for the other classes named in the Litany, for Jews, Turks, Heathens, for Arians, Socinians, &c. It closes with five hymns on "Thy kingdom come," the last three of which are of one metre, and are indeed parts of one continuous hymn. The tract derives special interest from the fact that the second portion of these three is the hymn commencing, "Lo ! He comes with clouds descending," the authorship of which created a considerable controversy. For a century it was attributed to Madan. Olivers also was affirmed to be the author. But to use the words of Mr. C. D. Hardcastle, who himself took part in the debate, "Nothing that has ever been said can deprive Charles Wesley of the authorship of this hymn." See an interesting account of the hymn in Julian's *Dictionary of Hymnology*, p. 681.

1759.

193. A SHORT EXPOSITION OF THE TEN COMMANDMENTS, extracted from Bishop Hopkins. London: Printed and sold at the Foundery, Upper-Moorfields; by W. Flexney, under Gray's-Inn Gate; E. Cabe, Avemary-lane; and G. Keith, Gracechurch-street, London; at the New-Room, Bristol; by W. Watkinson, Linen-draper, Leeds; and at the Orphan-house, Newcastle upon Tyne. 1759. 12mo., pp. iv. 96.

Preface dated June 21, 1759, and signed John Wesley.

Another edition, London: 1784; Another, London: Whitfield, 1799.

Wesley felt it to be his duty not only to guard unwary readers against dangerous errors, but also to apprise the reading public (the number of which he did so much to increase) where to find unadulterated truth. This tract is a fair example of the great work of this kind that he did so fully in the *Christian Library*, already noticed. In a brief preface he points to the supreme importance of keeping the commandments of God; but complains that many writers who speak highly of the commands and the duty of observing them, do so in a "dry and superficial manner; and that even those who penetrate deeper yet speak of faith and love, the soul of all the commandments, slightly and as it were by the by," or as standing in the same rank with the rest. Approving of Bishop Ken, "who has so beautifully resolved every commandment into Love," he yet judges him to be less explicit than might be desired on Faith. But in Bishop Hopkins he sees this defect fully supplied, and therefore heartily commends his exposition to all.

Persons familiar with Bishop Hopkins' work will be able to appreciate the amount of careful reading, close thought, and painstaking labour required to reduce it to these small dimensions.

194. AN EXTRACT OF THE REV. MR. JOHN WESLEY'S JOURNAL, from July xx, 1750, to October xxviii, 1754. London: Printed and sold at the Foundery, Upper-Moorfields; by J. Robinson, Ludgate-Street; and by T. James, under the Royal-Exchange. 1759. 12mo., pp. 90. [No. ix.]

By a strange inadvertence, the wrong date is inserted on the title, the extract actually commencing with November 2, 1751.

Almost exclusively a record of hard labour in travelling and preaching. During the time embraced by this extract Wesley had a serious illness. "Not knowing how it might please God to dispose of" him, and "to prevent vile panegyric," he wrote the following epitaph, giving orders that this, if any, inscription should be upon his tombstone: "Here lieth the body of John Wesley, a brand plucked out of the burning: who died of a consumption in the fifty-first year of his age, not leaving after his debts are paid ten pounds behind him; praying, God be merciful to me, an unprofitable servant."

Nos. 195-196. [1759.

195. A LETTER TO THE REVEREND MR. DOWNES, Rector of St. Michael, Wood-Street; Occasioned by his late Tract intitled, *Methodism Examined and Exposed*. By John Wesley, M.A. London: Printed and sold at the Foundery, Upper Moor-Fields; by W. Flexney, under Gray's-Inn-Gate; F. Cabe, Avemary-lane; and G. Keith, Grace-church-street; at the New-room, Bristol; by W. Watkinson, Linen-draper, Leeds; and at the Orphan-house, Newcastle upon Tyne. 1759. [Price Twopence.] 12mo., pp. 24.

Dated at the end, London, Nov. 17, 1759, and signed John Wesley.

Downes wrote an 8vo. pamphlet of 106 pages, entitled "*Methodism examined and exposed*; or *The Clergy's duty of guarding their flocks against false teachers*. A discourse lately delivered in four parts. By Rev. Mr. Downes, Rector of St. Michael, Wood-Street, and Lecturer of St. Mary-Le-Bow." The discourse is founded on Acts xx. 28-30. The character of this performance may be judged by an extract or two. "It is about twenty-five years ago that two bold, though beardless, divines, or (to speak in St. Paul's language) *Novices in Divinity*, being lifted up with spiritual pride, were presumptuous enough, in the very novitiate of their ministry, to become founders of the sect called Methodists." . . . "Long, very long, hath our Church been infested with those grievous Wolves, which though no more than two when they first entered in among us (and they so young they might rather be called wolflings), have yet been so prolific as to spread their ravenous kind through every part of this kingdom." It will easily be believed that he made the most ridiculous, unfounded, and extravagant charges against "this rude, refractory tribe," the "frightful monster called Methodism."

Wesley answers the fool according to his folly, exposing his errors, un-charitableness and untruth; and declares, "If you can prove upon me, John Wesley, any one of the charges which you have advanced, call me not only a *wolf*, but an *otter* if you please."

196. A SERMON ON ORIGINAL SIN. By John Wesley, M.A., Late Fellow of Lincoln-College, Oxford. Bristol: Printed by John Grabham, in Wine-Street; and sold at the New Room in the Horse-Fair; and at the Foundery, near Upper-Moor-Fields, London. 1759. [Price Twopence.] 12mo., pp. 21.

Second edition, Bristol: W. Pine, n.d.

This appears as the first sermon in *Sermons on Several Occasions*, vol. iv. (No. 200), published in the following year, and was evidently printed from the same type.

We have no information as to when, or under what circumstances, this Sermon was written. Probably as there was no sermon professedly on the subject in the three volumes of sermons already published, it was composed in view of the forthcoming volume, to give completeness to the theological views represented in the sermons. He had already published an elaborate treatise on Original Sin, (No. 182). This sermon, which is not elaborate in any sense, is simply an affirmation of the doctrine as deduced from the condition of men before the flood, and their condition now, together with a few inferences. It is a condensation of the argument as illustrated in part i. of the Treatise.

197. FUNERAL HYMNS. London: Printed in the year 1759. 12mo., pp. 70. [Second Series.]
No name of either writer or printer is given.
Another edition, Bristol: W. Pine, 1769. 12mo., pp. 70.

This is not, as Jackson describes it, "a fourth edition of the former pamphlet of the same name (No. 96), greatly enlarged," but an entirely new work, containing forty-three hymns, now published for the first time. They were written at different times, some of them in this year. All but the first three were written in memory of persons whose names are prefixed. Several of them are of great interest, others of much beauty. Of the former are those in memory of *Mr. John Meriton*, a clergyman who was present at the first Conference in 1744; of *James Hervey*, written before the unfortunate publication of the eleven letters (see No. 227); of *Thomas Walsh*,
<blockquote>A zealous instrument of good,
A vessel fit for use Divine,</blockquote>
of whom Wesley speaks so often in his letters, and whom he describes as "the best Hebræan I ever knew," adding, "I never asked him the meaning of a Hebrew word but he would immediately tell me how often it occurred in the Bible, and what it meant in each place,"—the man who at the early age of twenty-eight years burnt out his life by excessive labours; of *Lampe*, "the brother of my choice;" of *Mrs. Lefevre*, whose letters Wesley afterwards published,
<blockquote>A spotless soul, a sinless saint,
In perfect love renewed;</blockquote>
and of his own *firstborn son*, for whom he mourned in forty-five verses in strains of tender pathos. Beauteous indeed are the three well-known hymns which are the first in the book—
<blockquote>Come let us join our friends above;
How happy every child of grace;
And let this feeble body fail.</blockquote>
"Many of Charles Wesley's elegies have an unearthly power, a sadness of the grave pervaded by the rapture of heaven. On the death of nearly every Methodist preacher, from Thomas Beard, the martyr, who was the first that died, till, with an elegiac verse on his lips, he lay down himself to die, he wrote not one only, but usually two or three of these affecting and beautiful memorials. His *Funeral Hymns*, occasioned, with hardly an exception, by actual deaths, constitute the most perfect part of the Methodist Psalmody, and for a hundred years and more these testimonials of the dying triumphs of their early brethren have been sung at the deathbeds and funerals of Methodists throughout the world."—Stevens' *Hist. of Methodism*, Bk. iv, chap. ii.

198. HYMNS ON THE EXPECTED INVASION. 1759. 12mo., pp. 12.
Half-title; no name or place mentioned. Eight hymns.
Another edition, 1779.

The fear of an invasion by the French had thrown the country into a state of great excitement and alarm. Charles Wesley writes in a letter to his wife, "I continued instant in prayer for near half an hour after the Sacrament. We wrestled for our Israel, and all the Reformed Churches. I could not help praying in a particular manner for the brave Admiral who is gone to sacrifice his life, if need be, for his King and country. . . . Neither Mr. Carty nor I can guess what I ought to do, if the French were landed. It will be shown me in that day. My brother is alarmed by false intelligence, that we have only eleven thousand soldiers in all England. My oracle, the Colonel, reckons upon seventeen thousand. But the matter will not be determined by numbers. If the French land, and the Lord of Hosts is with us, they will make more haste back than they came with. I do not know why it is I do not fear them more. I usually am most afraid before the danger. Perhaps the dread and the evil may now come together. However, we shall keep them off by prayer as long as we can. Mr. Galatin just now informs me that yesterday's 'Express' has thrown the Council into the utmost alarm and hurry. The Colonel could not learn particulars. Even the Lords of the Bedchamber are ignorant of the secret. It is supposed that news is come of the embarkation of the French. At present the wind is against them ; and if God is against them too, what signify all their designs and threatenings."—*Life*, ii. 162.

"No power less than that which defeated the Spanish Armada will rescue England now. You will see my thoughts (but not mine only), in a penny Hymn Book I shall publish against the fast."—Let. July 5, 1759, C. W. to Mrs. C. W., *Life*, ii. 164. He was greatly excited with fear for the safety of the nation, though he "verily believed God's people will either be delivered *from* the danger or *in* it."

It was with these feelings that he wrote his twelve-paged tract of eight hymns, as Jackson says, "to assist the devotions of the praying remnant in this crisis, as he had done upon former occasions." One of the hymns is well-known and has been much sung since those days, and with a wider application. It begins,

Come, Thou Conqueror of the Nations ;

and is the only one of the number that has found a permanent place in the hymnals of the Church.

But the cloud passed away, a signal victory was gained by Admiral Hawke on November 20, 1759, and the threatened and feared invasion did not take place. A day of national thanksgiving was appointed, for which another hymn-tract containing fifteen hymns was prepared, by the pen of this ready-writer. The spirit of the whole is shown in one verse :—

Thy single arm the victories gave,
And shewed Thou art not bound to save
By many or by few :
Number and strength of hosts is vain ;
Weakness itself, if Thou ordain,
Shall earth and hell subdue.

The second pamphlet was entitled :—

199. Hymns to be used on the Thanksgiving Day, Nov. 29, 1759, and after it. 12mo., pp. 24.

Half-title ; no name or place mentioned ; paging continued from the former, but the fifteen hymns numbered afresh.

No title appears to any of the hymns except the eleventh, which is, " The Song of Moses, sung by Great Britain and Ireland, for the victory given them over the French Fleet, Nov. the 20th, 1759."

An interesting account of the fears that throbbed in the breasts of Charles Wesley's friends, and the faith that triumphed in his own, may be found in Jackson's *Life of C. Wesley*, ii. 160-7.

1760.

200. Sermons on Several Occasions. By John Wesley, M.A. late Fellow of Lincoln College, Oxford. Bristol: Printed by J. Grabham and W. Pine in Wine-Street ;

and sold at the New-Room in the Horse-Fair; and at the Foundery, near Upper-Moorfields, London. 1760. [Vol. iv.] 12mo., pp. 324.

There were two editions, but not so named, issued by Grabham in the same year, one omitting the name of W. Pine from the title-page; and although almost all the letter-press is the same in both, page for page, yet there are some slight variations, and the head and tail pieces are different. The volumes, of which this is the fourth, were afterwards published together.

Fourth edition, London: Paramore, 1787; Fifth, with some additions, London: Whitfield, 1796.

This volume contains seven sermons. "All my leisure time, during my stay at Bristol, I employed in finishing the fourth volume of 'Discourses;' probably the last which I shall publish."—*Journal*, Oct. 1, 1759. The discourses occupy one-half of the volume. Then follow six tracts.

I. The *first* is entitled *Advice to the people called Methodists, with regard to Dress*. It consists of seventeen pages of close and earnest counsel, with strict rules and strong reasons for great plainness in dress. A sermon was afterwards published on the same subject, see No. 397 (vii. 167). Wesley was rigid in keeping, and in requiring others to keep, these rules. In the second and each subsequent edition of the *Large Minutes*, the preachers are instructed to read in every Society the *Thoughts concerning Dress*.

2. The *second* tract is on *The Duties of Husbands and Wives*. It is extracted from Whateley's pamphlet on the same subject, (see No. 163). A single paragraph is prefixed commending the extract.

3 and 4. The *third and fourth* are short papers entitled, *Directions to Children* and *Directions to Servants*. They were probably written by Wesley. Some of the paragraphs in the last were extracted in part from Gouge on *Domestic Duties*.

5. The *fifth* is entitled *Thoughts on Christian Perfection*, the preface to which is dated Bristol: Oct. 16, 1759. It was afterwards embodied in *The Plain Account of Christian Perfection* (No. 238).

"At the Conference in the year 1759, perceiving some danger that a diversity of sentiments should insensibly steal in among us, we again largely considered this doctrine; and, soon after, I published *Thoughts on Christian Perfection.*" —*Works*, xi. 394.

Osborn, Heylin, and Tyerman mention this as a separate publication under date 1759, the year in which it was written; but it is exceedingly doubtful if it was printed previously to its appearing in this volume. The descriptions given of it by these writers agree with its appearance in the volume; not anyone gives printer's name or place of printing, or seems to have seen a copy.

6. The *sixth* and last paper in the volume is entitled *Christian Instructions extracted from a late French Author*. It consists of 336 numbered sentences, each being a Christian apophthegm, or an assertion of a moral principle. It afterwards appeared slightly altered in the collected Works, vol. xxiv. 1773. There the title is changed to *Christian Reflections*. Osborn so entered it under that date; but he was afterwards led to believe that it was not published separately.

201. REASONS AGAINST A SEPARATION FROM THE CHURCH OF ENGLAND. By John Wesley, A.M. Printed in the year 1758. With Hymns for the Preachers among the Methodists (so called). By Charles Wesley, A.M.

No. 202.   [1760.

London: Printed by W. Strahan, and Sold at the Foundery in Upper-Moorfields. 1760. 12mo., pp. 22.

The hymns were reprinted by G. J. Stevenson. London: 1868.

This tract is, as we have seen, included in the *Preservative against Unsettled Notions in Religion*, 1758, (No. 191). To this reference is made on the title-page. It now appeared for the first time as a separate tract, but with the following changes. It has been re-edited and a few verbal alterations made. The original portion is signed, John Wesley. After this two paragraphs are added by Charles Wesley and signed by him, in which he joins his testimony to his brother's; and he appends seven hymns "for the lay-preachers; still further to secure this end, to cut off all jealousy and suspicion from our friends, or hope from our enemies of our having any design of ever separating from the Church."

The hymns are entitled, *Hymns for the use of the Methodist Preachers*. Six of them, 38 stanzas in all, are of one metre (6.8s). The seventh is entitled *The Preacher's Prayer for the Flock*. It is of ten verses. None of them are in the large Hymn Book.

Very great interest was created by the publication of this pamphlet. It was a time of grave importance in the history of Methodism. The question of separation was freely discussed. Both the brothers did their utmost to prevent it; but Charles was the more eager. The circulation of the *Reasons* with the appended hymns was one means employed by him. He read them to the Societies; he freely distributed them, and persuaded others to do likewise. "I walked to Spitalfields Chapel, still under my burden. I read the *Reasons* against leaving the Church, enforcing each; then my hymns; and then prayed *after* God. A spirit of unanimity breathed in all, or most of, our hearts. Great confidence I felt, that they will be none otherwise minded than myself; that they are determined to live and die in their calling. I told them my brother and I had agreed that I should warn them after this manner, and reprint his *Reasons* for each of our children's preservation. I bestowed another hour on the preachers, who *seem* (for I cannot see their hearts) like-minded."—Letter to his wife in *Journal*, ii. 229. Writing to Mr. Grimshaw he says, "I have read the *Reasons* to the Society here; and their hearts are as the heart of one man. Will you not join hand and heart with us in confirming the souls of the disciples?" To which Grimshaw replies, "I will circulate, you may depend upon it, as many as I can of the *Reasons against Separation*. Send me a hundred of them." See an account of the whole movement and of the larger manuscript treatise, from which this is an extract, in Jackson's *Life of C. Wesley*, vol. ii. 178-197. See also Tyerman's *Life of Wesley*, ii. 380-9.

The subject of Wesley's Churchmanship in his earlier and later years, and of the position of Wesleyan Methodism in regard to the Church of England since the death of Wesley is clearly set forth in *The Churchmanship of John Wesley, and the Relations of Wesleyan Methodism to the Church of England*: By James H. Rigg, D.D., London: Wes. Conf. Office, 1878.

202.   THE DESIDERATUM; OR, ELECTRICITY MADE PLAIN AND USEFUL. By a Lover of Mankind and of Common Sense. London: Printed and sold by W. Flexney, under Gray's-Inn Gate, Holbourn; E. Cabe, Avemary-Lane; George Clark, in Little Carter Lane; George Keith, Gracechurch Street; T. Smith, under the Change; and at the Foundery, in Moorfields. 1760. 12mo., pp. vii. 72.

Third edition, London; Fourth edition, London: Hawes, 1778: precisely the same as the First edition; Another, London: Baillière, Tindall, and Cox, 1781.

The preface is dated Nov. 1, 1759, but not signed. "Wednesday and Thursday I spent in revising and perfecting a treatise on Electricity."—*Journal*, Oct. 31, 1759.

Wesley says, in a characteristic preface, "In the following tract I have endeavoured to comprize the sum of what has been hitherto published on this curious and important subject by Mr. Franklin, Dr. Hoadly, Mr. Wilson, Watson, Lovett, Freke, Martin, Watkins, and in the monthly Magazines. But I am chiefly indebted to Mr. Franklin for the speculative part, and to Mr. Lovett for the practical, though I cannot in everything subscribe to the sentiments either of one or the other."

One half of the book is occupied with an account of various experiments in electricity, and with theories (some of them curious ones) of the nature of the newly-discovered power. The other portion gives a number of cases of relief from various ailments effected by the application of electricity.

The publication of this book was another endeavour on Wesley's part to alleviate human suffering. He had strong faith in the efficacy of electricity as a curative agent. He had tried it very extensively at his dispensaries; and so convinced was he of its utility that he purchased four electrical machines (one of which is still preserved in the Museum at the Wesleyan Mission House), and placed them in different parts of London for the benefit of the thousands who flocked "to try the virtue of this surprising medicine. So part were electrified in Southwark, part at the Foundery, others near St. Paul's, and the rest near the Seven Dials."—*Works*, ii. 388.

"Q. 9. 'Why did you meddle with electricity?' For the same reason as I published the 'Primitive Physic'—to do as much good as I can."—*Works*, xiii. 354.

Notes.—In this year the following were published:—

A.—A Concordance to the Holy Scriptures: with the Significations and Applications of the Words contained therein, &c., By John Fisher, *Philadelphus*. London: Printed for the author, and sold at the Foundery, Upper-Moorfields. 1760. 12mo. Unpaged—10 sheets.

Second edition, London: 1786.

This was not a work by Wesley, though issued from the Foundery. It is mentioned as a curiosity, very rarely met with. It is simple and compact in arrangement, and worthy of its place amongst the Foundery duodecimos. Fisher was one of the early preachers.

B.—Original Letters between the Rev. Mr. John Wesley and Mr. Richard Thompson, Respecting the Doctrine of Assurance. London: L. Davies. 1760. 8vo., pp. 52.

This was not published by Wesley, but with his permission.

No. 203. **[1761.**

C.—MONTANUS REDIVIVUS: OR, MONTANISM REVIVED, IN THE PRINCIPLES AND DISCIPLINE OF THE METHODISTS (COMMONLY CALLED SWADLERS): Being the substance of a Sermon upon 1 John iv. 1, preached in the Parish Church of Hollymount, in the Diocese of Tuam, in the year 1756. To which are added several letters which passed between Rev. John Wesley and the Author. Also an appendix. By the Rev. Mr. James Clark, a Presbyter of the Diocese of Tuam. Dublin: Saunders. 1760. 8vo., pp. 143.

Though this contains two letters by Wesley he had no hand in its publication.

The work is dedicated to the Lord Bishop of Clonfert and Killmacduagh, to whom the author appeals in defence of the Divine, or (which he takes to be the same in effect) the Apostolical Right of Episcopacy, "which," he says, "is none of the least questions controverted between me and Mr. Wesley in the following Letters." The Methodists are described as "a set of enthusiastic Pharisees in practice, but perfect Latitudinarians in principle, who at their setting out laid it down as a principle that orthodoxy, or right and sound belief, was but a slender, if it may be deemed any part at all of religion." He also accuses them of being "quite indifferent as to any form of Church government." The Letters form the greater part of the volume. There are three lengthy ones by Clark, and two by Wesley, in which he writes more at large than usually. The application of the name Swaddlers to the Methodists of Ireland is explained under No. 133. "I rode to Hollymount, and preached in the churchyard. I then visited my antagonist, Mr. Clark, who was lying extremely ill."—*Journal*, June 2, 1758. The correspondence took place in the year 1756.

D.—A LETTER TO MR. T. H., ALIAS PHILODEMAS, ALIAS SOMEBODY, ALIAS STEPHEN CHURCH, ALIAS R. W., dated December 12, 1760, and signed John Wesley. This appeared in the *London Magazine* for this year, p. 651. It is a curious defence of himself against many unjust and ludicrous aspersions. It is reprinted in the third edition of the *Works*, xiii. 350-5.

1761.

203. AN EXTRACT OF THE REV. MR. JOHN WESLEY'S JOURNAL, from February 16, 1755, to June 16, 1758. Bristol: Printed by William Pine, in Narrow-Wine Street. 12 mo., pp. 146. [No. x.]

Another edition, Bristol: W. Pine, 1768, pp. 150.

Heylin and Osborn date the first edition 1761: I have not seen a copy earlier than 1768.

A record of ceaseless labour. Riding, walking, preaching, reading, observing natural and spiritual phenomena, penning reflections on books, on men and public affairs and on matters affecting the struggling Methodist Societies, are the oft-recurring features of this interesting portion of the great autobiography.

204. Hymns for those to whom Christ is All in All. London: Printed in the year 1761. 12mo., pp. iv. iv. 144.

Another edition, Bristol: Wm. Pine, 1765; Third edition, London: 1768.

On the first page described as *Select Hymns*. But this volume must not be confounded with one published in the same year, entitled *Select Hymns with Tunes Annext* (No. 205), or with *Select Hymns for Christians of all Denominations* (No. 208), issued afterwards.

The hymns in this volume, 134 in number, are taken from the following books, already noticed: *Hymns and Sacred Poems* (No. 40), *Redemption Hymns* (No. 105), *Hymns on the Lord's Supper* (No. 83), and *Moral and Sacred Poems*, Vol. 3, (No. 58). There is nothing new in the volume but the "Advertisement" prefixed, which shows the purpose of the compilation in these words:—"The following hymns, it will be easily discerned, are peculiarly designed for the use of those, to whom Jesus Christ is made of God wisdom and righteousness and sanctification, and who enjoy in their hearts the earnest of their compleat and eternal redemption."

It was probably intended for private use by the persons referred to in the preface, or for the Classes and Band Meetings. It contains some of the best of the hymns written by the Wesleys. They are entirely without titles; they are not distributed into sections, or grouped under common heads, as is usually the case; nor are any tunes suggested. The hymns are simply numbered consecutively; and the head lines contain only the numbers of the pages. There is an index of first lines, and also about a dozen short foot-notes. There is neither author's nor printer's name.

205. Select Hymns: With Tunes Annext: Designed Chiefly for the Use of the People called Methodists. London: Printed in the year 1761. 12mo., pp. 139, iv. xii. 104, vi.

Second edition, corrected and enlarged, London: Printed in the year 1765, 12mo., pp. iv. 153, v. xii. 112, vii.; Third, Bristol: Pine, 1770. In all respects the same as the second edition.

In the first edition there are 132 hymns, according to the numbering, but actually 133, for the number 77 is given to two hymns. They are all selected from previous publications. They are headed on p. 5, "Select Hymns." At the end of the hymns is an "Index" of first lines, followed by twelve pages of instructions in music, commencing with the words, "The Gamut, or Scale of Music," in large type. These twelve pages are printed from engraved plates and are numbered consecutively. The tunes follow. They are 102 in number on 104 pages, also printed from engraved plates. The first of these is numbered 5, showing that probably something is omitted. At the end of the tunes is an index to them on five pages, likewise from engraved plates, followed by one page of type-printed Directions for singing, which the reader is exhorted

No. 206. [1761.

carefully to observe, in order that "this part of Divine Worship may be the more acceptable to God, as well as the more profitable to himself and others." The directions, seven in number, are in Wesley's most concise and practical style of writing.

In the second edition some changes are made. Seventeen hymns are added and one omitted, making the total 149. Twelve tunes are also added, total 114. Instead of the musical instructions beginning with the words "The Gamut or Scale of Music," which appeared in the first edition, a pamphlet of the same extent entitled *The Grounds of Vocal Music* (No. 207) is inserted. The index to the tunes is engraved afresh, and the Directions for singing are on a separate leaf. In some copies this is placed at the end, in others in the middle of the book.

There were probably only three editions of the combined work published. Some copies of the second edition of the "Hymns" have a different title-page, the words "with Tunes annext" being omitted. This may have been with the design of publishing the hymns without the tunes: see No. 208. The "Tunes annext" are entitled:—

206. SACRED MELODY: OR A CHOICE COLLECTION OF PSALM AND HYMN TUNES, WITH A SHORT INTRODUCTION. 12mo., pp. 112, vii.

The title-page is an ornamental one, showing musical instruments, two lines of music, and an open music book within a scroll border. This is found in the second and third editions, and was probably in the first also, but as the first four pages of this edition are wanting in all the copies I have seen, I am unable to determine. The title and the subsequent pages including the Index are printed from engraved plates. Neither date, nor name of author, editor or publisher is given. The name of the engraver only ("Bland: Sculp.") appears on the title-page. The tunes do not appear to have been published separately, though the hymns were: see No. 208.

In the second and third editions of the *Melody*, the same engraved plates are used as in the first edition, with the exception of two or three pages, which have been freshly engraved. The pages are differently numbered throughout. The "measure" where given in the first edition, is afterwards omitted; and a few other small changes are made. In every edition the treble only of the tune is given, and a single verse of a hymn is engraved between the lines. In the first edition the tunes of the same metre are placed together without reference to subject. In the second edition the additional hymns of various metres are all placed at the end.

The following extract from the Preface will explain the nature of the work: "I want the people called Methodists to sing true, the tunes which are in common use among them. At the same time I want them to have in one volume the best hymns which we have printed; and that in a small and portable volume, and one of an easy price. But I have been endeavouring for more than twenty years to procure such a book as this. But in vain: masters of music were above following any direction but their own. And I was determined whoever compiled this should follow *my* direction; not *mending* our tunes, but setting them down, neither better nor worse than they were. At length I have prevailed. The following Collection contains all the tunes which are in *common use* among us. They are pricked *true*, exactly as I desire all our congregations may sing them; and here is prefixed to them a collection of those hymns which are (I think) some of *the best* we have published. The *volume* likewise is *small* as well as the *price*. This, therefore, I recommend preferable to all others. John Wesley."

207. THE GROUNDS OF VOCAL MUSIC. 12mo., pp. 12.

Printed from engraved plates. Neither date nor name given. Two editions at least were published. Towards the close are seven "Lessons for exercising the voice." The whole was published separately at a cost of 3d., as appears from the catalogues. It also appears bound up with the second and third editions of No. 205, sometimes with, sometimes without the other twelve pages of musical instructions there named.

208. SELECT HYMNS FOR THE USE OF CHRISTIANS OF ALL DENOMINATIONS. The Fourth Edition, corrected. Bristol: Printed by William Pine. 1773. 12mo., pp. 153, v.

Sixth edition, London: R. Hawes, 1776; Seventh, London: Hawes, 1778; Eighth, London: Paramore, 1780; Ninth, London: Paramore, 1783; Tenth, London: Paramore, 1787.

This is the usual title of the hymn-book just named (205), when published without the tunes. The preface also is omitted. Osborn mentions a fourth edition of *Hymns with Tunes Annext*, Bristol: 1773. But probably it was this volume he was describing,—the first issue of the separate publication, and called the fourth edition as following the third of the combined work. It will be seen that the dates are the same. Heylin gives 1753 as the date of the first edition. In this he is mistaken: he probably confused it with *Hymns and Spiritual Songs intended for the Use of Real Christians of all Denominations*, (No. 165), which was first published in that year. He gives 149 hymns, which is not, however, the number in the first edition, but in the later ones only.

The hymns in this volume are the same as those of the second edition of *Hymns with Tunes Annext*. Although this did not appear as a separate publication with this title until the year 1773, it is placed here because of its connexion with the volumes just named. Reference will be made to it under the last date.

NOTE.—Osborn assigns another Tune-book, entitled *Sacred Harmony*, to this year. It was, however, probably not published until twenty years later: see No. 358.

1762.

209. A LETTER TO THE REV. MR. HORNE: occasioned by his late Sermon preached before the University of Oxford. London: Printed and sold by W. Flexney, near Gray's-Inn Gate, Holbourn; by G. Keith, in Gracechurch-Street; by T. James, under the Royal Exchange. n.d. 8vo., pp. 22.

Signed John Wesley. Horne's Sermon (on James ii. 24) was preached before the University, June 7, 1761. Wesley says the sermon was preached about 1762.—*Works*, 1st edit., xvii. 55.

Nos. 210-211. [1762.

"I retired to Lewisham to answer Dr. Horne's ingenious 'Sermon on Justification by Works.' O that I might dispute with no man! But if I must dispute, let it be with men of sense."—*Journal*, March 5, 1762. The Hutchinsonian Mr., afterwards Bishop, Horne, is happily better known by his *Commentary on the Book of Psalms* than by his sermons. "Here I met with Dr. Horne's 'Commentary on the Psalms.' I suppose the best that ever was wrote."—*Journal*, May 27, 1783.

Mr. Horne had spoken of "the new lights at the Tabernacle and the Foundery" in connection with "heresies making their periodical revolutions," and of "antinomianism being rampant." Wesley accuses him of not knowing his teaching, and proceeds to give considerable extracts from *The Appeals to Men of Reason and Religion* (Nos. 63, 64). He then quotes from the Scriptures, and from the Articles and Homilies of the Church of England, to show that his views entirely agreed with them. He further shows in what particulars Mr. Horne's teaching on justification by works differed from his own, and from the teachings of the Scriptures and the Church.

210. THE DIGNITY OF HUMAN NATURE. "Laborant quum ventum ad verum est : etc."—hor. Printed in the year 1762. 12mo., pp. 66.

No place or printer's name, or name of author given.

Another edition, London : Paramore, 1786; Another, Dublin : 1802.

This title is given in sarcasm. The pamphlet opens with the words, "In order to place this point [the dignity of human nature] in the clearest light, to the satisfaction of all impartial men, we have only to inquire, What is the real state, with regard to knowledge and virtue, wherein mankind have been from the earliest times? And what state are they in at this day?" Then follows a reprint, word for word, of Part I. (87 pages) of the work on *Original Sin* (No. 182), in which Wesley gives so sad and deplorable an account of the condition of the mental and moral state of mankind, both in past and present times. The pamphlet closes with, "Such (if we can believe our *eyes*, *ears* or *experience*) is the present *Dignity of Human Nature*." I cannot determine under what circumstances it was published.

211. THOUGHTS ON THE IMPUTED RIGHTEOUSNESS OF CHRIST. By John Wesley, M.A. Dublin : Printed by S. Powell, in Crane-Lane. 1762. 12mo., pp. 11.

Dated at end, Dublin, April 5, 1762.

Second edition, London : Printed by W. Strahan, 1762 ; London : Story, 1805 ; Another, London ; Kershaw, n.d.

This was written to counteract the effect of a tract on *The Imputed Righteousness of Christ*, that had recently been circulated in Wesley's name. It was composed of extracts from the ninth and tenth volumes of the *Christian Library*. "Eight pages of I know not what, which a shameless man has picked out of that work, tacked together in the manner he thought good, and then published in my name."—Letter of Wesley to the *London Chronicle*, quoted in Tyerman's *Life of Wesley*, ii. 470.

Wesley declares that he dare not insist upon the expression, "the imputing the righteousness of Christ," because he could not find it in Scripture, and because it had been " so frequently and so dreadfully abused, and because the

120

Antinomians use it at this day to justify the grossest abominations." He points out its evil tendency, and closes with a suitable quotation from Hervey's *Theron and Aspasio*.

212. A BLOW AT THE ROOT; or, Christ stabbed in the House of His Friends. (Luke xxii. 46.) Bristol: Printed by William Pine. 1762. 12mo., pp. 11.

Second edition, London: W. Strahan, 1762; Third, London, 1780; another Third, York: Ward, 1763; Fourth, London: Whitfield, 1798; London: Cordeux, 1817.

Written against a specious Antinomian teaching of the time, which declared, "That Christ had *done*, as well as suffered, *all*: that His righteousness being imputed to us we need none of our own: that seeing there was so much righteousness and holiness in Him there needs no more in us: that to think we have any or to seek to have any, is to renounce Christ: that from the beginning to the end of salvation all is in Christ, nothing in man; and that those who teach otherwise are legal preachers, and know nothing of the Gospel." "This," Wesley rightly affirms, "is indeed a blow at the root, the root of all holiness. Hereby Christ is stabbed in the house of His Friends, of those who make the largest professions of loving and honouring Him. The whole design of His death—namely, to destroy the works of the devil, being overthrown at a stroke. For wherever this doctrine is cordially received it leaves no place for holiness" (p. 6). There are several references in the *Journal*, towards the beginning and end of the year, to one or more of these enthusiasts.

213. CAUTIONS AND DIRECTIONS GIVEN TO THE GREATEST PROFESSORS IN THE METHODIST SOCIETIES. "Set the false witnesses aside, Yet hold the Truth for ever fast."—Rev. Mr. C. Wesley's Scrip. Hymns. London: Printed in the year 1762. [Price One Penny.] 12mo., pp. 12.

The *Cautions and Directions* are given against the following six perils:—1. Pride. 2. That daughter of Pride, Enthusiasm. 3. Antinomianism. 4. Sins of Omission. 5. Desiring anything but God. 6. Schism. It is a practical homily on the dangers to which Wesley's people were exposed, rendered necessary, he says, because there were persons amongst them—1. Who believe they shall never die. 2. Who go from house to house to persuade people to believe they are perfect when God hath not persuaded them. 3. Who believe they have the gift of discerning spirits. 4. That they cannot err. 5. That it is impossible for them to sin and fall; and 6. Because "the Methodist preachers who cannot subscribe the above nostrums are represented as being in the dark, and leading the people in the dark these twenty years." The tract was incorporated in the *Plain Account of Christian Perfection*, (No. 238).

The *Journal* for this year shows that Wesley was much hampered and troubled by false teachers around and even within his societies—George Bell being one of them—by whom a spirit of fanaticism was engendered. Many of the members declared themselves to be wholly sanctified, whose lives did not accord with their profession. It was a year of great unrest. At the close of it he wrote, "I now stood and looked back on the past year; a year of uncommon trials and uncommon blessings. . . . I have had more care and trouble in six months, than in several years preceding." The three pamphlets just noticed seem to have been called for by this state of things.

214. SHORT HYMNS ON SELECT PASSAGES OF THE HOLY SCRIPTURES. By Charles Wesley, M.A., and Presbyter of the Church of England. In Two Volumes. Bristol: Printed by E. Farley, in Small-Street. 1762. 12mo., pp. 392, 432.

Vol. I. has 1,160 hymns; Vol. II., 870.

Second edition, London: Paramore, vol. i. 1794; ii. 1796. Some of the hymns in the first edition are removed, and the numbers reduced to 1,064 and 817. Some copies appear without the name of place, author, or printer, and without signature to the preface.

The author says, "God, having graciously laid His hand upon my body, and disabled me for the principal work of the ministry, has thereby given me an unexpected occasion of writing the following hymns. Many of the thoughts are borrowed from Mr. Henry's Comment, Dr. Gill on the Pentateuch, and Bengelius on the New Testament. Several of the hymns are intended to prove, and several to guard, the doctrine of Christian Perfection. I durst not publish one without the other. In the latter sort I use some severity, not against particular persons, but against Enthusiasts and Antinomians."—*Preface.*

"In more than one instance in the course of these volumes the poet has for the moment superseded the theologian. It is therefore not suprising that, notwithstanding his intense admiration of his brother, John Wesley found it needful to caution some of the Society against being 'hurt by what they might find in these volumes contrary to the doctrine they had long received.'"— Osborn, *Meth. Bib.*

See an extended account of these volumes, and the sentiments here referred to, in Jackson's *Life of Charles Wesley,* ii. 199-212.

1763.

215. THE LIFE AND DEATH OF MR. THOMAS WALSH. COMPOSED IN GREAT PART FROM THE ACCOUNTS LEFT BY HIMSELF. By James Morgan, a member of the Church of England. (Psalm cxii. 6, Heb. xiii. 7.) "Heaven waits not the last moment," &c.—*Night Thoughts.* London: Printed by H. Cock, and sold by G. Keith, in Gracechurch-Street; and by W. Wyatt, in High-Holborn; at the Foundery, near Upper-Moorfields; E. Englefield, in West-Street, Seven-Dials; and at the New-Room, in the Horse-Fair, Bristol. 1762. 12mo., pp. xvi. 270.

Engraved portrait. Preface dated Canterbury, July, 1762.
Inserted by Wesley in his edition of his Works, 1771.

The following note is prefixed: "I have carefully read the following Account, and believe it to be strictly true. I think it will need no other recommendation to the children of God. Jan. 20, 1763. John Wesley." This is all that Wesley contributed to the book, and his date shows the time of issue.

James Morgan, though "a member of the Church of England," was one of Wesley's preachers from 1755 to 1774.

"I knew a young man about twenty years ago, who was so thoroughly acquainted with the Bible, that if he was questioned concerning any Hebrew word in the Old, or any Greek word in the New Testament, he would tell after a little pause, not only how often the one or the other occurred in the Bible, but also what it meant in every place. His name was Thomas Walsh. Such a master of Biblical knowledge I never saw before, and never expect to see again."—Wesley, *Works*, vii. 54. Yet he died in the 28th year of his age !

The memoir would be much improved if less weighted with the editor's reflections, and if more of the precious journal, which was in his hands, had been inserted. It might have been one of the most spiritual and exalted memoirs that we possess. It is included, with an appendix, in Jackson's *Lives of the Early Methodist Preachers*. Charles Wesley wrote three fine hymns on the occasion of Walsh's death.

216. A LETTER TO THE RIGHT REVEREND THE LORD BISHOP OF GLOUCESTER, OCCASIONED BY HIS TRACT ON THE OFFICE AND OPERATIONS OF THE HOLY SPIRIT. By John Wesley, M.A., late Fellow of Lincoln College, Oxford. London, printed : And sold at the Foundery, near Moorfields. 1763. 12mo., pp. 114.

Dated at end, Nov. 26, 1762, and signed John Wesley.

Second edition, Bristol: W. Pine, 1763 ; Dublin, 1763.

The Bishop (Warburton) in an octavo volume of 250 pages (afterwards published in two vols., small 12mo.) had accused "the famed Leader of the Methodists, Mr. John Wesley," of "laying claim to almost every apostolic gift, in as full and ample a manner as they were possessed of old ;" and he had also expressed views on the office and work of the Holy Spirit, which Wesley could not but contradict. To these two points Wesley gives full consideration, refuting the former charge mainly by appeals to his writings, and the latter by the Scriptures and authoritative writings of the Church of England, quoting largely from his second letter to Mr. Church, (No. 87). It is a calm and careful piece of writing, and a seemly counterpoise to the jaunty style adopted by the Bishop, who was reproved gently and respectfully by Wesley when he urged his lordship, if he thought it worth while to spend any more words upon him, "to be more serious;" adding, "It cannot injure your lordship's character or your cause." It appears that the Bishop forwarded his manuscript to Wesley before it was printed, with a request that he would notice its errors. "After correcting the false readings, improper glosses and other errors, I returned it." Writing to his brother, he says, "I was a little surprised to find Bishop Warburton so entirely unacquainted with the New Testament ; and notwithstanding all his parade of learning, I believe he is no critic in Greek :" see references in Tyerman's *Life of Wesley*, ii. 492. Warburton's book called forth many replies.

" From Monday 22 to Friday 26, I was employed in answering the Bishop of Gloucester's book. Monday 29—I retired to transcribe my answer to Bishop Warburton."—*Journal*, Nov. 1762.

217. A SERMON PREACHED BEFORE THE SOCIETY FOR REFORMATION OF MANNERS, on Sunday, January 30, 1763, at the Chappel. in West-Street, Seven-Dials. By John Wesley, M.A., Late Fellow of Lincoln College, Oxford. London : Printed and sold by William Flexney, near Gray's-Inn-Gate, Holbourn ; by Geo. Keith, in Grace-

Church-street; by John Danson, the corner of Gutter-lane, Cheapside; by M. Englefield, at the Bible in West-street, Seven-Dials, and at the Foundery, Upper More-fields. [Price Six-pence.] 8vo., pp. 31.

More than once reprinted in 12mo.

"I rode to Lewisham, and wrote my sermon to be preached before the Society for Reformation of Manners."—*Journal*, Jan. 17, 1763.

Towards the close of the previous century a few persons in London, oppressed by the abounding and open ungodliness of the nation, and especially of the metropolis, formed themselves into a "Society for Reformation of Manners." This Society continued in existence about forty years, and by its activities accomplished much good; but it had died out. In the year 1757 an attempt was successfully made to renew the good work; and the Society before which Wesley preached was formed. Sixty-five years before he preached this sermon (namely on Feb. 13, 1698) his father, the Rev. Samuel Wesley, M.A., preached before the earlier Society; and, by a singular coincidence, from the same text. They were both earnest, practical discourses, each having its own marked characteristics. See also *Journal*, Feb. 2nd, 1766.

218. A DISCOURSE ON SIN IN BELIEVERS. By John Wesley, M.A. London: Printed and sold at the Foundery, Upper Moor-fields. 1763. Price twopence. 12mo., pp. 23. [Text, 2 Cor. v. 17.]

Second edition, Bristol: W. Pine, n.d.; Fourth, London: The New Chapel, City Road, 1789; Fifth, London: Paramore, 1791.

"I retired to Lewisham, and wrote the sermon on 'Sin in Believers,' in order to remove a mistake which some were labouring to propagate, that there is no sin in any that are justified."—*Journal*, March 28, 1763. This sermon appears in Vol. i. of the collected Works (1771), and to the previous sermon, on "The Witness of our own Spirit," the following note is appended: "It may easily be observed, that the preceding discourse describes the experience of those that are strong in faith. But hereby those that are weak in faith may be discouraged; to prevent which, the following discourse may be of use."

It is mentioned by Heylin, but not by Osborn.

219. FARTHER THOUGHTS UPON CHRISTIAN PERFECTION. London: Printed in the year 1763. 12mo., pp. 39.

Without name of printer, and without signature: not reprinted separately.

In 1759 Wesley wrote on this subject a short tract entitled, *Thoughts on Christian Perfection*. It was included in the fourth volume of *Sermons*, published the next year, (No. 200). Referring to it, he says, "Two or three years ago, I published a few Thoughts which then occurred to me concerning Christian Perfection. In most particulars I think now as I did then: in some, I do not." And he declares himself to be "still open to further conviction, and willing to be taught of God, by whatever instrument he shall chuse." "Christian Perfection" was so prominent a topic in Wesley's teaching that it is desirable to trace the development of his views on this subject in the various works that he published upon it.

The tract entitled, *Cautions and Directions given to the greatest Professors in the Methodist Societies* (No. 213), is embodied, in a revised and expanded form, in the latter part of this pamphlet; and the whole, somewhat abridged, is incorporated in the *Plain Account of Christian Perfection* to be noticed hereafter: see No. 238.

The greater part of the present pamphlet is written in the form of question and answer; and the advices are enforced by a series of Reflections, which are recommended to the reader's "deep and frequent consideration, next to the Holy Scriptures."

"The next year, the number of those who believed they were saved from sin, still increasing, I judged it needful to publish chiefly for their use, 'Farther Thoughts on Christian Perfection.'"—*Works*, xi. 414. He afterwards wrote *Brief Thoughts on Christian Perfection*, and two letters on the same subject addressed to Dr. Dodd: see *Works*, xi. 446-454.

220. A SURVEY OF THE WISDOM OF GOD IN THE CREATION: or a Compendium of Natural Philosophy. In Two Volumes. Vol. 1. "These are thy glorious works. Parent of good," &c.—Milton. Bristol: Printed by William Pine. 1763. 12mo., pp. 286, 256, xxx.

Contents and Tables of principal matters, at the end of the second volume. One page of *errata* appended to each volume. Preface in first volume signed John Wesley, but not dated.

For some time he had been gathering materials for this work. So early as Dec. 11, 1758, he wrote, "Most of this week I spent in preparing materials for a 'Survey of the Wisdom of God in Creation;' or a full, plain, and correct system of Natural Philosophy."

Nothing could be more explicit than his description of the character of the book he had long desired to see, for which he had waited, and which he undertook to write only when others failed to do so. He wanted to provide a Compendium of Natural Philosophy not too diffuse, but comprised within a moderate compass, so as not to require any large expense either of time or money; containing "the heads of whatever was known with regard to the earth or the heavens," and written in the plainest language possible, "particularly free from all the jargon of Mathematics, which is mere heathen Greek to common readers." At the same time he wished "this short, full, plain account of the visible creation, directed to its right end; not barely to entertain an idle, barren curiosity, but to display the invisible things of God, His power, wisdom, and goodness."

The work is divided into text and notes. The former is mainly translated from the Latin of Buddæus, Professor of Philosophy at Jena; but he found occasion "to retrench, inlarge or alter every chapter, and almost every section." The notes are taken from many writers. He distinguishes the work as a descriptive one, and not an attempt "to account for things," as undertaking "barely to set down what *appears* in Nature, not the *cause* of those appearances."

The book is not to be judged in the light of our present knowledge, but in that of the time in which it was written. It was a most worthy effort to put a knowledge of the ascertained facts of nature within the reach of the great body of the community. The work is well printed, and appears to have been carefully carried through the press. It was afterwards expanded to three, and finally to five volumes, which will be noticed under their dates.

That this work and *Paradise Lost* (No. 222) should be issued in the same year shows both the activity of this tireless worker, and the wide range of his sympathies.

"At ten (and so every morning) I met the preachers that were in town, and read over with them the 'Survey of the Wisdom of God in Creation.'"— *Journal*, Nov. 8, 1764.

221. MINUTES OF SEVERAL CONVERSATIONS BETWEEN THE REV. MR. JOHN AND CHARLES WESLEY, AND OTHERS. London : Printed in the year 1763. 12mo., pp. 30.

This is the second edition of the so-called *Large Minutes*, the first of which appeared in 1753 (see No. 164). It is expanded from 16 to 30 pages, mainly by matters relating to Kingswood School, to the form of Deed for the settlement of the chapels, and to the best methods of establishing and extending the work of Methodism. Many additional advices are given to the preachers, some of which are of great practical value. In this number appear for the first time the words :—" Q. What may we reasonably believe to be God's design in raising up the preachers called Methodists ? A. To reform the nation, and, in particular, the Church : to spread Scriptural holiness over the land." (p. 2).

This pamphlet is distinguished by the fact that in it Wesley for the first time published his Indenture, or Model Deed, for the settlement of his chapels, in which Deed he named and determined the doctrinal standards of Methodism, which he declared to be his Notes on the New Testament (No. 172) and the four volumes of Sermons which he had already published (Nos. 88, 107, 139, and 200).

222. AN EXTRACT FROM MILTON'S PARADISE LOST. With Notes. London : Printed by Henry Fenwick. 1763. 18mo., pp. 322.

Preface "To the Reader," dated London, January 1, 1763, but not signed.

Second edition, 24mo., London : 1791.

Wesley declares that impartial judges gave the preference to this before all the poems of any age or nation. But the amount of learning crowded into it put it beyond the comprehension of many. His sympathies were with the multitude, and he laboured to bring "this inimitable work" within the reach of all. This he strove to do by omitting all those lines which he despaired of explaining without the use of "abundance of words," by adding short and easy notes of explanation, and by indicating those passages which he judged to be "peculiarly excellent." Thus he endeavours to make "the main of this excellent poem clear and intelligible to any uneducated person of a tolerable good understanding." He not unfrequently in his writings quoted from Milton, showing that what he commended to others was familiar to himself.

Brief explanatory notes are appended to each chapter.

223. HYMNS FOR CHILDREN. Bristol : Printed by E. Farley, in Small-Street. 1763. 12mo., pp. 84.

Re-printed, with the addition to the title of the words, "And others of Riper Years," London: 1766 ; Another, Bristol : 1767 ; Second edition, Bristol : W. Pine, 1768 ; Third, London : 1778 ; Fourth, London : Paramore, 1784.

The number of hymns is 100, but some are divided into parts, making the whole 105. About one-fourth have titles prefixed. The first 30 of the hymns are paraphrases of the *Instructions for Children* (No. 62). It was afterwards abridged (the number of hymns being reduced to 44), and published with a characteristic preface by John Wesley: see No. 414.

This little volume, without preface or name of author, contains some hymns of priceless worth; some suitable to more than children; and some that children might find it hard to sing. One, divided into three parts, entitled "Hymns for Girls," would better befit the reflections of seniors than of children. Boys "before, or in their work" are taught to say:—

    Let heathenish boys
    In their pastimes rejoice,
    And be foolishly happy at play;
    Overstocked if *they* are,
    We have nothing to spare,
    Not a moment to trifle away.

Twenty-four are "for the youngest," the first of these commencing,

    Gentle Jesus, meek and mild,
    Look upon a little child.

This hymn associated with the happy infancy of tens of thousands was first published in *Hymns and Sacred Poems*, 1742, (No. 40).

"It would perhaps be difficult to mention any uninspired book that, in the same compass, contains so much evangelical sentiment. The hymns are full of instruction, yet thoroughly devotional in their character. There is nothing puerile in them, either with respect to thought or expression. The language is simple, yet terse, pure, and strong."—*Life of C. Wesley*, ii. 230.

NOTE.—A small tract, published this year, and entitled *Jesus altogether Lovely: Illustrated in a Letter to some of the Single Women in the Methodist Society*, has by many been attributed to Wesley. Tyerman hesitates, but inclines to the same opinion (ii. 551). It is dated Hoxton, March 10, 1763. On that day Wesley was in Norwich.

It was written by Miss Bosanquet, afterwards Mrs. Fletcher, who at the time named lived in Hoxton, and on the 24th of the same month removed to Leytonstone. The character of the tract points to the position which she held in the Methodist Society at Hoxton. It is a parting address to the young women of the Society (of whom she seems to have had charge), on Chastity, Poverty and Obedience. It is worthy of the saintly woman, who wrote it. I have seen it attributed, in an old catalogue, to Mrs. Fletcher.

1764.

224. AN EXTRACT OF THE REV. MR. JOHN WESLEY'S JOURNAL, from June 17, 1758, to May 5, 1760. Bristol: Printed by William Pine, in Narrow Wine-Street. 1764. 12mo., pp. 106. [No. xi.]

Another portion of this most interesting record. It contains graphic accounts of the successful preaching of the Gospel, together with many instances of the revival of religion in different parts of the country, particularly in Everton under the ministry of the Rev. Mr. Berridge. It also contains an impressive letter to Dr. Taylor, of Norwich, respecting his work on Original Sin, in reply to which Wesley wrote No. 182. It does not appear to have been re-published separately.

225. LETTERS WROTE BY JANE COOPER : To which is prefixt Some Account of her Life and Death. London: Printed in the year 1764. 12mo. pp. 62.

Second edition, Bristol : Pine, 1764, pp. 40, smaller type ; Another, printed in the year 1764, pp. 38 ; Another, London : 1764 ; Third, Bristol : Pine, 1770 ; Third, London : Hawes, 1778.

The Preface, written by Wesley, but not signed or dated, occupies three pages, the Account twelve, the Letters forty-four. The whole seems to have been edited by Wesley. His estimate of the character of this young woman and of her writing was very high. "The sentiments are all just and noble ; the result of a fine natural understanding, cultivated by conversation, thinking, reading, and true Christian experience." Fragments only of her writing remained, but "' Though they're little, they are golden sands.'" The style is "simple and artless in the highest degree, but likewise clear, lively, proper ; every phrase, every word being so well chosen, yea and so well placed, that it is not easy to mend it." Such is the opinion formed by this keen critic of the Letters, "the almost inimitable Letters," of Jane Cooper,—a servant maid ! "I buried the remains of Jane Cooper, a pattern of all holiness, and of the wisdom which is from above, who was snatched hence before she had lived five-and-twenty years."—*Journal*, Nov. 26, 1762. He introduces one of her letters and a short account of her death into the *Plain Account of Christian Perfection* (No. 238), designating her "that burning and shining light, Jane Cooper." Years afterwards he speaks of her as "that lovely saint Jane Cooper."

NOTE.—A LETTER TO THE REV. MR. JOHN WESLEY, BY A GENTLEWOMAN. London : Sold at the Foundery, in Upper Moorfields ; and at Mrs. Englefield's, at the Bible, in West-Street, near the Seven Dials. 1764. 12mo., pp. 23.

Dated Laton-Stone, Nov. 8, 1764. Signed M. B. [Mary Bosanquet]. Inserted by Wesley in his Works, and Catalogues.

A statement of circumstances which led to her work in Laton-Stone (Leytonstone), with interesting particulars of the work itself. For a fuller account of that work, see Moore's *Life of Mrs. Mary Fletcher*, vol. ii., part i. pp. 41-82.

As this was only published, not written or even edited by Wesley, it is inserted on account of its interest, but not numbered.

1765.

226. A TREATISE ON JNSTIFICATION : Extracted from Mr. John Goodwin. By John Wesley. With a Preface, wherein all that is material in LETTERS just published, under the

Name of the REV. MR. HERVEY is answered. Bristol: Printed by William Pine, in Wine-Street. 1765. 12mo., pp. 46, 207, viii.

Wesley had long been urged, especially by several of the preachers, to abridge and publish Goodwin's work on Justification. He would have further delayed, having many things on hand, but a tract appeared entitled *The Scriptural Doctrine of Imputed Righteousness Defended*, by James Hervey. He then felt it incumbent upon him to publish *the real Scripture-doctrine*. And he did not think he could do it better than he found it done already to his hand in the able and closely reasoned treatise, which with great pains he carefully abridged. This he trusted would " stop the mouths of gainsayers concerning imputed righteousness, and teach them (at least the most candid) to speak as the oracles of God."—Letter in *Works*, xii. 305.

Goodwin's treatise is a close, argumentative, forcible piece of writing. Wesley held it in high esteem, and urged his preachers to distribute it widely, asking them to give it careful and close attention, "for," says he, "it can hardly be understood by a slight and cursory reading. And let whoever has read it declare, whether he (the author) has not proved every article he asserts, not only by plain express Scripture, but by the authority of the most eminent reformers."—*Works*, x. 349.

227. AN ANSWER TO ALL THAT IS MATERIAL IN LETTERS JUST PUBLISHED, UNDER THE NAME OF THE REVEREND MR. HERVEY. By John Wesley. Bristol: Printed by William Pine, in Wine-Street. 1765. 12mo., pp. 46.

Dated at the end, Hoxton Square, Nov. 16, 1764.

"I retired to Hoxton to answer what was personal in the letters ascribed to Mr. Hervey."—*Journal*, Nov. 12, 1764.

This is the preface to the preceding work, altered on the first page only: all the rest seems to have been printed from the same type. It was published separately.

Part of the *Answer* consists of a letter addressed by Wesley to the Rev. James Hervey (see No. 191, §12), containing criticisms on Hervey's *Theron and Aspasio*, published in 1755. In reply to this letter Hervey wrote eleven letters, but did not live to publish them; nor did he desire them to be published after his death, as only about half of them had been transcribed for the press. They were, however, published under the title of *Eleven Letters from the late Rev. Mr. Hervey, to the Rev. Mr. John Wesley; containing an Answer to that Gentleman's Remarks on 'Theron and Aspasio'; Published from the Author's Manuscript, left in the possession of his brother, W. Hervey: With a Preface showing the reason of their being now printed:* 1765, 12mo., pp. 297. It was in reply to these letters that Wesley re-published his own letter, with additions. See an extended account in Tyerman's *Life of Wesley*, ii. 526-532.

228. THOUGHTS ON A SINGLE LIFE. By John Wesley, A.M. London: Printed and sold at the Foundery. 1765. 12mo., pp. 11.

Bristol: W. Pine, 1770; London: 1784.

In the year 1743 Wesley published a small pamphlet under the title of *Thoughts on Marriage and a Single Life* (No. 42), the principal sentiments of which are embodied in this tract.

"My scraps of time this week I employed in setting down my present thoughts upon a single life, which, indeed, are just the same they have been these thirty years: and the same they must be, unless I give up my Bible."— *Journal*, Nov. 5, 1764; see also Feb. 2 and 6, 1751.

The advantages of a single life are carefully and delicately stated in Wesley's terse, brief way. His experience of married life may have added keenness to his convictions. To the " happy few " he gives some very shrewd advice.

Tyerman calls it a "queer tract," and names another *Jesus Altogether Lovely: Illustrated in a Letter to some of the Single Women of the Methodist Society*. He intimates that "it is far from certain that Wesley was its author; though it is not unlikely the one was connected with the other." But see Note, p. 127.

229. A SHORT HISTORY OF METHODISM. London: Printed; and sold at the Foundery. 1765. 12mo., pp. 11.

Second edition, London, 1765; Also, London, 1774; 1789; 1795.

Heylin and Tyerman assign this pamphlet to 1764; but on what ground does not appear. It is a mere tract, in which Wesley seeks to distinguish between his people and the various parties, whose views he entirely condemned, but who were often confounded with them. "Men lump together under this general name many who have no manner of connexion with each other, and then whatever any of these speaks or does is of course imputed to all." This *Short History* was written to " prevent persons of a calm and candid disposition from doing this." It was "not designed for a defence of the Methodists (so called) or any part of them," but to be "a bare relation of a series of naked facts, which alone may remove abundance of misunderstandings." See No. 355.

230. THE SCRIPTURE-WAY OF SALVATION. A Sermon on Ephes. ii. 8. By John Wesley. London: Printed and sold at the Foundery. 1765. 12mo., pp. 22.

There is said to have been another edition, but I have not seen it.

Although this sermon is from the same text as No. 8, *Salvation by Faith*, published in 1738, yet it is quite another sermon. It does not appear in the four volumes of sermons published previously to this date; but it is in Vol. iii. of the collected Works, 1771. It was written to correct the strange and fanatical teaching on the subject of entire sanctification, which Thomas Maxfield and George Bell had diffused through the Methodist Societies.

231. THE CHRISTIAN'S POCKET COMPANION: Consisting of Select Texts of the New Testament, with suitable observations in prose and verse, for every day in the Year. By John Barnes. (Job vxiii. [xxiii.] 12.) Carmarthen; Printed and sold by the Author, at Pembroke; Mr. Edmonds, at the Coventry-Cross, Holborn; and at the Foundery, in Moorfields, London. 1765. Small oblong (about 4 inches by 5), pp. vi. 372.

Preface dated Pembroke, July 30, 1764, and signed John Wesley.

Wesley reached Pembroke on Friday, July 27, before he was expected, so he "rested that night." On Sunday the minister invited him to preach in the church, but the Mayor forbade him. The people, being incensed and not to be disappointed, came in crowds to hear him elsewhere in the evening. The minister was probably Mr. Barnes, the author of this book, who was a clergyman at Pembroke. He was already so far friendly to the Methodists that he had written a pamphlet in their defence entitled, *Twenty charges against the Methodists, answered by the Word of God, for their Encouragement, and Conviction of their Enemies*. Wesley was very favourably impressed with the *Pocket Companion*, judging the reflections in it to be "abundantly deeper" than those of the useful *Golden Treasury*, dealing not only with the first principles of religion, but with the "whole work of God in the soul"; hence his commendatory preface, and the admission of the book among the Foundery publications.

232. MINUTES OF SOME LATE CONVERSATIONS, between the Rev. Mr. Wesleys and Others. Bristol: Printed by William Pine, in Narrow-Wine-Street. 1765. 12mo., pp. 12.

Dated on p. 3, after half-title, Manchester, August 20th, 1765.
Since the publication of the first *Minutes of Conference* in 1749 (Nos. 135, 136), two editions of what are called the *Large Minutes* had been issued (Nos. 164, 221). But up to the present date no *Annual* Minutes had been published. Very brief notes only of the intervening Conferences are recorded in Wesley's Journal. With the present pamphlet of 12 pages, commenced the series which has been continued to the present time, the volumes gradually expanding as Methodism has increased or its organisation become more complicated. The volume for the current year contains 594 pages. In this little tract the Stations, or appointments of the preachers, occupy about one page and a-half. All is entered in the form of questions and answers; and the short, sharp sentences declare plainly who prepared the *Minutes* for the press. There are some very interesting entries in this first issue. It was reprinted verbatim in the 8vo. edition, Vol i., 1812, and afterwards in the Revised Edition, 1862. As the *Minutes* for several years were sold for one penny each, they became known as "the Penny-Minutes."

233. A SHORT GREEK GRAMMAR. London: Printed by W. B. [William Bowyer.] And Sold at the Foundery, near Upper-Moorfields, and at the New-Room, in the Horse-Fair, Bristol. 1765. 12mo., pp. 80.

Without preface, or note, or name. The book was prepared for use at the School in Kingswood.
Wesley spent a week in Bristol in the early part of the year, but there is no record of how the time was occupied. He was probably engaged with his publications. He was there again nearly three weeks in the autumn when he spent some time at the school. This Grammar was in all likelihood prepared then.

234. EXPLANATORY NOTES UPON THE OLD TESTAMENT. By John Wesley, M.A., Late Fellow of Lincoln College, Oxford. Vol. I. Bristol: Printed by William Pine, in Wine-Street. 1765. 4to., pp. ix. 852.

No. 234. [1765.

Three volumes, pp. 2613, paged continuously throughout. The paging 1715-16 is duplicated.

In the first volume a portrait, engraved by Bland, from a painting by N. Hone, represents Wesley preaching in the fields.

These notes were written in response to many earnest entreaties, which for several years Wesley resisted. To begin such a work when he was entering upon his sixty-third year seemed to him to be a dream. Knowing he could not *compose* a commentary, his only alternative was to *abridge* the work of another, if there was "any exposition worth abridging." He selected two—each having its own good qualities—Matthew Henry's *Exposition* and Poole's *Annotations*. The former, however, was pervaded with "absolute, irrespective, unconditional predestination;" all of which he, of course, omitted, and, indeed, nineteen parts out of twenty of the whole work. This he must needs have done if he desired a cheap and portable commentary, for Henry's extended to "six folios, each containing seven or eight hundred pages," and the whole costing six guineas. Besides, of Henry he could write, "it seems to be his aim to say as much as he can, mine to say as little." He changed hard words into easy ones, and long sentences into short, not, however, altering any sentiment that he extracted. He added largely from Poole, whose writing was more to his taste. He says it was his constant method, "after reading the text, first to read and weigh what Mr. Poole observed upon every verse, and afterwards to consult Mr. Henry's exposition of the whole paragraph." His design was "to give the direct literal meaning of every verse, every sentence," and, as far as he was able, "of every word in the oracles of God."

The dates of publication are somewhat confusing. Tyerman reprints, from *Lloyd's Evening Post* for June 5, 1765, the following advertisement: "On Thursday, the 1st of August, will be published, price 6d., Number I. of Explanatory Notes upon the Old Testament. By John Wesley, M.A., late Fellow of Lincoln College, Oxford. Conditions: 1. That this work will be printed in quarto, on a superfine paper. 2. That it will be comprised in about sixty numbers (as near as can be computed), making two handsome volumes. 3. That each number will contain three sheets of letterpress, printed on a new type," &c. The work was to be delivered weekly to the subscribers.

From the above statement and from the notation at the foot of the pages, it was obviously intended to bind the whole work in two volumes, the second beginning with the Book of Ezra. But though prepared for two, it was generally (yet not always) bound in three; Vol. II. beginning at Judges xv. and ending with Psalm lxii. The weekly numbers, or parts, are indicated at the foot of the pages. There are 110, generally of twenty-four pages each. If the rate of publication was one number per week, it would occupy two years in its issue. To this the dates given fairly agree. The first, April 25, 1765, is at the end of the preface, written before the body of the work, according to Wesley's practice. The other, at the end of the work, giving the time of the completion of the manuscript, is Dec. 24, 1766. The later parts of the book would therefore not be issued until far into the year 1767. The title pages in the first and second volumes (but not in the third) were apparently printed from the same type. They all bear the same date. It is probable the division into three volumes was an afterthought, as the two volumes were found to be very bulky.

"The Notes on the Old Testament are allowed on all hands to be meagre and unsatisfactory; this is owing to a circumstance with which few are acquainted. Mr. Pine, the printer, having set up and printed off several sheets in a type much larger than was intended, it was found impossible to get the work within the prescribed limits of *four volumes*, without retrenching the notes, or cancelling what was already printed. The former measure was unfortunately adopted, and the work fell far short of the expectation of the public. This account I had from the excellent author himself."—Dr. Adam Clarke, *Gen. Pref. to Commentary*.

There are but one or two references to the work in the Journal:—"May 13 (1765) and the following days, I had leisure to go on with the Notes on the Old Testament." This was written in Ireland, the preface in Edinburgh. Sun., Feb. 23, 1766—"In the evening I went to Lewisham, and finished the Notes on the Book of Job." The Notes were composed wherever he could put down the ponderous tomes which must have accompanied him in his widespread journeys. For a view of his extraordinary labours from the Conference of 1765 to that of 1766, see Smith's *Hist. of Meth.*, Vol. I., Appendix D. The Notes have not been reprinted. "Q.—26. What shall be done with the remaining copies of the Notes on the Old Testament? A.—Let them be sold weekly at 3d. a number."—*Min. Conf.* 1781. From an inventory of the books in stock in the Methodist Book-room, taken immediately after Wesley's death in 1791, it appears that there were 750 copies of each volume still unsold.

1766.

235. THE LORD OUR RIGHTEOUSNESS: A Sermon preached at the Chapel in West-Street, Seven-Dials, on Sunday, Nov. 24, 1765. By John Wesley. London: Printed for the Benefit of the Poor, and sold by J. Fletcher, at the Oxford Theatre, St. Paul's Church-Yard; G. Keith, at the Bible, Grace-Church-Street; E. Cabe, Ave-Mary-Lane, and M. Englefield, at the Bible, West-Street, Seven-Dials. 1766. 8vo., pp. 36.

Another, Bristol: Pine, 1766, 12mo., pp. 23, smaller type; Fourth, Newcastle, 1766; another, London: 1766; Fourth, London, 1770; another, 1770; Sixth, London, 1789; London: Jones, 1809.

The sermon relates to a subject of dispute at the time, the imputation of the Righteousness of Christ. It is divided into two parts; in the first is considered, What is the Righteousness of Christ; in the second, When, and in what sense, it is imputed to us.

"Sunday, November 24, I preached in London on those words in the lesson for the day, 'The Lord our Righteousness.' I said not one thing which I have not said, at least, fifty times within this twelvemonth. Yet it appeared to many entirely new, who much importuned me to print my sermon, supposing it would stop the mouths of all gainsayers. Alas, for their simplicity! In spite of all I can print, say, or do, will not those who seek occasion find occasion?"—*Works*, xiii. 328.

"The controversy respecting Hervey's notions of imputed righteousness had attracted great attention. Wesley was misrepresented, and misunderstood; and the object of the sermon is to correct the errors in circulation concerning him."—Tyerman's *Life of Wesley*, ii. 551, which see for particulars respecting this sermon and also the last named, *The Scripture-Way of Salvation*. (No. 230).

It called forth a severe philippic from some unknown writer, in *A Letter to the Rev. Mr. John Wesley, concerning his inconsistency with himself, occasioned by the publication of his sermon entitled 'The Lord our Righteousness.'*

236. SOME REMARKS ON A DEFENCE OF THE PREFACE TO THE EDINBURGH EDITION OF ASPASIO VINDICATED. By

Nos. 237-238.   [1766.

John Wesley. Edinburgh: Printed by Auld and Smellie; Morocco's Close, Lawn-Market. 1766. [mdcclxvi.] 12mo., pp. 24.

On page 13, a postscript begins, in which Wesley rebuts an accusation made by Dr. Erskine, against a letter he had written, by inserting the letter in full. It extends beyond three pages, and is dated Edinburgh, April 24, 1765. Following this, two tracts, *Remember the Sabbath Day* (No. 79), and *A Word to a Drunkard* (No. 77), are reprinted.

Reference has been made to the Eleven Letters published in the name of Mr. Hervey, and to Wesley's reply (No. 227). Matters might have rested where they were, had these letters not been imprudently reprinted in Scotland. "I preached at Dunbar about noon, and in the evening at Edinburgh. My coming was quite seasonable (though unexpected), as those bad letters, published in the name of Mr. Hervey, and reprinted here by Mr. John Erskine, had made a great deal of noise."—*Journal*, April 23, 1765. Dr. Erskine had taken occasion in the preface to make some severe attacks upon Wesley; who was defended by James Kershaw "in an honest, amicable, and affectionate reply." Erskine issued a *Defence* of his "preface," and more violently attacked Wesley, whose reply is severe, but calm and dignified.

This is Wesley's reply; in which he says, "I have neither time nor inclination to write a formal answer to the Reverend Dr. Erskine's tract. My hope of convincing him is lost; he has drunk in all the spirit of the book he has published. But I owe it to God and His children to say something for myself, when I am attacked in so violent a manner, if haply some may take knowledge, that I also endeavour to 'live honestly and to serve God.'"

Not republished in Wesley's edition of his Works; but it appears in the 1812 edition, where it is dated at the head, Edinburgh, May, 1766.

237. MINUTES OF SOME LATE CONVERSATIONS BETWEEN THE REVEREND MR. WESLEY AND OTHERS. 1766. 12mo., pp. 23.

Half-title dated Leeds, Aug. 12, &c., 1766; and at end, London, August 22, 1766.

This is extended to twice the usual size of the ordinary (the "penny") *Minutes*. It partakes of the character of the first Minutes for 1744-9 (Nos. 135, 136). In it Wesley explains at some length the origin and growth of what was called his "power;" and many practical questions relating to the people and to the duties of the preachers are considered. It is the second of the Annual Minutes.

238. A PLAIN ACCOUNT OF CHRISTIAN PERFECTION as believed and taught by the Rev. Mr. John Wesley, from the Year 1725 to the Year 1765. Bristol: Printed by William Pine. 1766. 12mo., pp. 162.

Second edition, Bristol: Pine, 1766, pp. 92; Third, 1770, smaller type; Fourth, London: Hawes, 1777. Title altered to "as believed, &c., from the year 1725 to the year 1777." Fifth, London: Paramore, 1785; Sixth, London: 1789; Seventh, London: Paramore, 1794; Eighth, London: Story, 1801; Ninth, 1809; Seventeenth, London: Mason, 1840.

This tract underwent several revisions and enlargements, one of which appears in Vol. xxiv. of the collected Works, 1773. In every successive edition the date of the most recent revision was specified. The last revision appears to have been made in the year 1777; and since that period, this date has been generally continued on the title-page of the several editions,—see *Works*, xi. 366, Note. But there are only slight verbal differences between the first edition, 1766, and the fourth, 1777.

This is the plainest, fullest, and most exact account Wesley has given of his views on Christian Perfection. In it he traces historically, "from the beginning" —the year 1725, when he met with Bp. Taylor's *Rule and Exercise of Holy Living and Dying*—the steps by which he was "led during a course of many years to embrace the doctrine of Christian Perfection"; and he gives, in the order of their publication, an account of the several works which he and his brother had written on the subject, including Hymns, and Conversations held at the Conferences. From all these he makes extensive extracts. This volume, therefore, contains a precise and authoritative statement of his views on this sacred question. This causes a special interest to attach to the work. It was written mainly in defence of his teaching. Many false and garbled statements had been made by one and another. He had been charged with teaching the very contrary of that which it was his joy to proclaim; and the plainest words he or his brother had written were contradicted or misrepresented by factious persons. He takes the opportunity of clearly expounding while earnestly defending his views; and he specially aims at showing that he had preserved a consistency in his teaching from the beginning. With the exception of a few sentences, which he here corrects by foot-notes, he held and taught precisely the same doctrines for 40 years. Even the professors, "the greatest professors amongst the Methodists," of the attainment of this high Christian privilege gave occasion to him to be very explicit. Many of them became wild enthusiasts, and called forth the severe rebukes which appear at the end of the book.

NOTE.—A SHORT ACCOUNT OF THE BARBAROUS MURDER COMMITTED ON BOARD THE BRIG EARL OF SANDWICH. By P. MacKinlie, G. Gidley, A. Zekerman, and R. St. Quinten, with a particular Account of Richard St. Quinten, taken from his own Mouth in Newgate, the Evening before his Execution. (Rev. xv. 3.) Dublin: Printed: London, reprinted in the year 1766. 12mo., pp. 12.

Another, London : Hawes, n.d.

Osborn *(Wes. Bibliography)* gives the above under this year, but there is no evidence that it was written by Wesley. The writing is not like his. The preface is dated Dublin, March 6, 1766, at which time Wesley was in London. It is not in the collected Works; though it appears in some of the later catalogues, and was therefore sold at the Foundry.

1767.

239. A WORD TO A SMUGGLER. Bristol: Printed by William Pine. 1767. 12mo., pp. 11.

Dated at the end, London, Jan. 30, 1767.

No. 240. [1767.

Another, London: Hawes, 1775; Another, n.d., "This tract not to be sold, but given away."

"Q. 30.—How may we put a stop to smuggling? A. 1. Speak tenderly and frequently of it in every Society near the coasts. 2. Carefully disperse the 'Word to a Smuggler.' 3. Expel all who will not leave it off. 4. Silence every local preacher that defends it."—*Min. Conf.*, 1767.

This was one of the crying sins of the age. Wesley set himself most resolutely to oppose it, and called every preacher to his help. He denounced it in no measured terms. "A smuggler (and in proportion every seller or buyer of uncustomed goods) is a thief of the first order, a highwayman or pickpocket of the worst sort. Let not anyone of those prate about reason or religion. It is an amazing instance of human folly that every Government in Europe does not drive these vermin into lands not inhabited."—*Works*, ix. 226.

He searched it out wherever it existed amongst his people. Finding it in the Society at St. Ives, he told them plainly, either they must put this abomination away or they would see his face no more. At Sunderland he declared he would no more suffer it than robbing on the highway. A few would not promise to refrain, so he cut them off from the Society. Two years afterwards he found "most of the robbers, commonly called smugglers," had left, but more than twice their number had come in their place. "Extirpate smuggling, buying or selling uncustomed goods, out of every Society. Let none remain with us who will not abstain from every kind and degree of it."—*Works*, viii. 308.

240. AN EXTRACT OF THE REV. MR. JOHN WESLEY'S JOURNAL, from May 6, 1760, to Oct. 28, 1762. Bristol: Printed by William Pine. 1767. 12mo., pp. 141. [No. xii.]

In a short preface, addressed "To the Reader," and dated London, Jan. 31, 1767, he writes, "I am sensible there are many particulars in the ensuing Journal which some serious people will not believe and which others will turn to ridicule. But this I cannot help, unless by concealing those things, which I believe it my bounden duty to declare. I cannot do otherwise while I am persuaded that this was a real Work of God." He refers to the accounts of a very remarkable work of grace in different parts of the country, and especially to the many testimonies to the attainment of "a full salvation." At the end he quotes his brother's frequent declaration, "Your day of Pentecost is not fully come. But I doubt not, it will; and you will then hear of persons sanctified as frequently as you do now of persons justified;" and he adds, "Any unprejudiced reader may observe that it was now fully come."

In the earlier part of the pamphlet are copies of several letters which Wesley wrote to different public journals in defence or explanation of his work. One of them, addressed to the editor of the *London Chronicle*, is in reply to Mr. Law, who, in a recent publication entitled *A Collection of Letters*, had passed some severe strictures on Wesley's *Letter to Mr. Law* (No. 174), and his *Address to the Clergy* (No. 175). Another was sent to *Lloyd's Evening Post* in reply to a letter that had appeared in that Journal "from a very angry gentleman, who personates a clergyman," and who is "very warm against the people, vulgarly called Methodists;" and another to the editor of the same paper, in which he says, "Just as I had finished the letter published in your last Friday's paper, four tracts came into my hands; one wrote, or procured to be wrote, by Mrs. Downes; one by a clergyman in the County of Durham; the third by a gentleman of Cambridge; and the fourth by a member (I suppose dignitary) of the church of Rome. How gladly would I leave all these to themselves, and let them say just what they please! as my day is far spent, and my taste for controversy is utterly lost and gone. But this would not be doing justice to the world, who might take silence for a proof of guilt." He answers the salient points in each. A further letter was addressed to the editor of *Lloyd's Evening Post*; another to the editor of the *London Chronicle*; and yet another to the editor of the *Westminster Journal*. Finally a long letter was sent to the editor of the *London Chronicle* in answer to a tract entitled *A Caveat against the Methodists*. These letters illustrate the nature and measure of the opposition directed through the Press against Wesley and his work, and throw into relief his patient and determined perseverance.

241. CHRISTIAN LETTERS. By Mr. Joseph Alleine. London: Printed in the year 1767. 12mo., pp. 88.

Preface addressed "To the Reader," dated London, March 7, 1767, and signed John Wesley.

Second edition, Bristol: Pine, 1767; Third, London: Hawes, 1778; Fourth, London: Paramore, 1795.

These beautiful spiritual letters are commended to the reader in the brief preface, in which the relative value of Mr. Samuel Rutherford's letters and these is stated. Wesley does not scruple to give the preference to these, because he thinks that "in love Mr. Alleine has the pre-eminence." The letters have an exquisite tenderness and grace. Such heavenly words come only from heavenly souls. Most of them were written in the year 1663, and are addressed in endearing terms to his beloved people, from "the common gaol at Juelchester" (Ivelchester, Ilchester), where he was incarcerated after the passing of the Act of Uniformity. Together with a brief record of his life, they would make a very valuable devotional manual. Wesley did good service to his people in reprinting them and sending them forth with his commendation. If the old Methodists fed on such spiritual meat as this, no wonder they were strong and lusty.

242. THE WITNESS OF THE SPIRIT. A Sermon on Romans viii. 16. By John Wesley, M.A. Bristol: Printed by William Pine, in Wine-Street. 1767. 12mo., pp. 16.

Dated at end Newry, April 4, 1767.

Another Edition, Bristol: W. Pine, 1769.

A sermon on the same text is in the first volume of Sermons, published in 1746 (No. 88.) This is quite a different sermon. It appears in the collected *Works*, 1771, Vol. I, as *Discourse II., on The Witness of the Spirit*. It also appears in the 5th edition of the "first four volumes of Sermons" (1796-9). It is in the 5th vol. of Wesley's *Works*, ed. 1829.

It was apparently written as an exposition, and also to meet objections and to guard against fanatical misconceptions of what Wesley believed to be a very important truth, revealed in Scripture, " not once only, not obscurely, not incidentally; but frequently, and that in express terms; but solemnly and of set purpose, as denoting one of the peculiar privileges of the children of God."

243. THOUGHTS ON THE SIN OF ONAN. Chiefly extracted from a late Writer. London: Printed in the year 1767. 12mo., pp. 20.

Second edition, 1774; Another, Bristol: 1779.

In his desire to do good to the souls and bodies of his fellow-men, Wesley sought suitable advice on this important but delicate subject. He went the length of wading through one volume written by Dr. Tissot, which Wesley describes as a "most fulsome and shocking performance;" and another, a French tract then lately translated, some parts of which, he says, "most of the London street-walkers would be ashamed to read aloud." He extracted from these, chiefly from the former, what he judged to be useful, adding both delicate advices and burning words of warning.

A faulty and imperfect copy of this tract was published in Bristol in 1779, entitled *A Word to whom it may Concern*. In it is this note, "Much of this Treatise is extracted from Dr. Tissot."

244. MINUTES OF SOME LATE CONVERSATIONS BETWEEN REV. MR. WESLEY AND OTHERS. London: Printed in the year 1767. 12mo., pp. 8.

Dated at beginning August 18, &c., 1767; and at end, August 20, 1767.

In this year's *Minutes*, though brief, will be found some important and practical resolutions relating to the "preaching-houses," the term of ministerial service, the distribution of literature, ("Q. 27. How may the books be spread more? A. Let every Assistant give them away prudently; and beg money of the rich to buy books for the poor,") the revival of "the work," the prevention of smuggling and bribery, and the attendance of preachers at the Conference.

245. HYMNS FOR THE USE OF FAMILIES, and on Various Occasions. By Charles Wesley, M.A., late Student of Christ-Church. Bristol: Printed by William Pine. 1767. 12mo., pp. 176.

Neither preface nor index.

Another, "By Charles Wesley, A.M.," London: Hawes, 1776; Another, London: 1825, "second edition" on title-page.

There are 166 hymns: all following the 44th are distinguished as *Occasional Hymns*, to many of which titles are prefixed.

Lampe, a friend of the Wesleys, was allowed to use 24 of their hymns, and to publish them with original tunes under the title of *Hymns for the Great Festivals* (see No. 94). In the *Hymns for the Use of Families*; in *Hymns of Intercession* (No. 192); and in *Hymns and Prayers to the Trinity*, at the end of *Hymns on the Trinity* (No. 246),—the first twenty-four hymns in each, and the *Graces before and at Meat* (No. 98) are of the same metres as the hymns in Lampe's book; in the *Family Hymns* and *Hymns on the Trinity* they are in the same order, and in the others nearly so. Prefixed to each hymn in these several books, and following the word "To," is the first line of a hymn from Lampe's collection, indicating the particular tune to which the hymn is to be sung. In this way attention was also called by the Wesleys to their friend's production.

"Mr. Charles Wesley's Family Hymn-Book consists to a great extent of hymns which he had written under circumstances of peculiar excitement, affecting him as a husband, a father, and the head of a family. Others of them were composed for the use of his pious friends in seasons of especial anxiety, sorrow and joy. It is not probable that one of them was written with reference to an imaginary case which possibly might occur. They are all the genuine effusions of his heart: a heart eminently tender, sympathetic, generous, and deeply imbued with Christian feeling—not one of the hymns containing a stanza that is either trite or mean. The most common concerns of life are dignified by Christian sentiment, expressed in language of almost unrivalled force and beauty."—*Life of C. W.*, ii. 236.

"Numberless examples might be given of the genius and taste of the Rev. Charles Wesley. But however unfashionable it may appear, I cannot but give the palm to his Family Hymn Book. Such accumulated strength and beauty of expression, in presenting the daily wants, pains, trials, and embarrassments of a family to the God of the families of the whole earth, surely never before was presented to the suffering children of men. We expect a man of real genius to be great where the subject is inspiring; but to be great in the privacies of common life, to be a true poet (while the man of God equally appears) in those littlenesses, so called, of daily occurrence, shows an elevation and spirituality of mind that has been rarely, if ever, equalled."—*Life of Rev. John Wesley*, by H. Moore, ii. 371.

246. HYMNS ON THE TRINITY. Bristol: Printed by William Pine. 1767. 12mo., pp. 132.

Without Preface or Index, or name of writer.

A valuable work had been published entitled *The Catholic Doctrine of a Trinity proved by above an hundred short and clear arguments, expressed in the terms of Holy Scripture, compared after a manner entirely new, and digested under the four following Titles: 1. The Divinity of Christ; 2. The Divinity of the Holy Ghost; 3. The Plurality of Persons; 4. The Trinity in Unity: with a few reflections, &c.: By William Jones, M.A., F.R.S., Rector of Paston, &c.* This work passed through many editions. A recent one was edited by Rev. John L. F. Russell, M.A.: London, Rivingtons, 1866. In this work a large number of passages of Scripture are arranged in 119 sections of two or three passages each, collected together under the four heads named above.

Charles Wesley, following the order given, but interspersing other passages, raised the number of sections to 136. For each of these he composed a hymn expressive of the principal sentiment of the section. These 136 hymns, with the passages of Scripture prefixed and consecutively numbered, form the first part of the book. A second portion is composed of 52 hymns, having a fresh enumeration, and entitled *Hymns and Prayers to the Trinity*. The first twenty-four are of the same metres as the hymns in *Hymns for the Great Festivals* (No. 94), and the Tunes in that book are named at the head of these hymns: (see No. 245.)

In his *Life of Bishop Horne*, Mr. Jones complains somewhat severely of the use made of his book. He accuses John Wesley of selling the work, "as if it had been an original work, partly copied and partly put into English verse, without asking the consent of, or making a word of acknowledgment in the title or preface to the author." Had Charles Wesley written a preface, or had John edited the volume, reference would doubtless have been made to the work from which the orderly grouping of the passages of Scripture was borrowed. (For full account and for defence of C. W., see *Life*, ii. 232-4.) It will have been observed, how comparatively careless Charles Wesley was in editing his own hymn-books.

"There is not in the English language a volume that, in so small a compass, shows more clearly the Scriptural doctrine on the subject, with its practical importance; and it has this peculiar advantage, that it proposes the subject, not as a matter of controversy, but of faith and adoration, of prayer, thanksgiving, and praise."—*Life of C. W.*, ii. 235.

"In some respects he has excelled his original. He repeatedly asserts the doctrine of our Lord's Divine Sonship, by his omission of which Mr. Jones has much impaired his claim to be considered as teaching the *Catholic Doctrine* of the Trinity. And he has never lost sight of the experimental and practical bearings of that doctrine. Mr. Jones has an excellent paragraph at the conclusion of his argument, warning his readers that a sound belief without a holy life will not profit them. But our poet, true to the mission of Methodism, makes experience the connecting link between knowledge and practice, and devotes an entire section of his work to 'Hymns and Prayers to the Trinity,' in which the doctrine is presented in most intimate connection with his own spiritual interests, and those of his reader."—*Poetical Works*, vii. 204.

"Mr. Jones's book on the Trinity is both more clear and more strong than any I ever saw on that subject. If anything is wanting it is the application, lest it should appear to be a mere speculative doctrine, which has no influence on our hearts or lives; but this is abundantly supplied by my brother's Hymns."—*Wesley's Works*, xiii. 30.

NOTE.—EXTRACTS FROM THE LETTERS OF MR. SAMUEL RUTHERFORD. By the Rev. John Wesley, M.A., sometime Fellow of Lincoln College, Oxford. 12mo.

This is thus given by Jackson in the third edition of *Wesley's Works*, xiv. 268. He is followed by Osborn and Heylin; but there is not the least probability that Wesley ever published these letters in a separate volume. He had inserted them fourteen years before in the *Christian Library*, vol. xxviii. (No. 131). There is no mention of any such volume in any catalogue from that date to 1825, when they were republished in a small 12mo. vol. (London: Kershaw). Jackson would doubtless have this volume before him, the title of which he has copied, altering the name from Rutherfoord, as Wesley wrote it, to Rutherford. He gives neither date of publication, nor number of pages, nor name of publisher. Osborn evidently copied the title from him, and he may have put it under this date as Wesley mentions the Letters in the preface to *Alleine's Letters*, which were published in this year. There are no words by Wesley in the volume. The letters were extracted from "*Joshua Redivivus: or Three Hundred and Fifty-Two Religious Letters*, by the late eminently pious Mr. Samuel Rutherfoord, Professor of Divinity at St. Andrew's. Divided into three parts:" 19th edition, Glasgow: John Bryce, 1765.

1768.

247. AN EXTRACT OF THE REV. MR. JOHN WESLEY'S JOURNAL, from October 29, 1762, to May 25, 1765. Bristol: Printed by William Pine, in Wine Street. 1768. 12mo., pp. 124. [No. xiii.]

Wrongly marked xii. on title.

The special features of this number of the Journal are an account of the separation of George Bell and his party, who had caused Wesley so much trouble and the Societies grievous injury by their wild fanaticism; and of Wesley's second appeal to the clergy, exhorting them to union in the great work of saving souls, but though he wrote to forty or fifty only three of them replied. In addition to the record of some ghostly occurrences, it contains a letter of much value on the duty of joining the Society, which might now appropriately be reprinted and widely circulated; also an interesting conversation between his grandfather, John Wesley, and the then Bishop of Bristol; and, over and above all, the details of dauntless, unwearied labour during the whole time.

248. THE REPENTANCE OF BELIEVERS. A Sermon on Mark i. 15. By John Wesley, M.A. London : Printed in the year 1768. 12mo., pp. 19.

Dated at the end, Londonderry, April 24, 1767.

This Sermon was written after he had "employed Monday, Tuesday, and part of Wednesday in speaking severally to the members of the Society" at Londonderry. It is a clear, plain, practical sermon, written with evident care. He speaks of " a Repentance and Faith which are necessary at the beginning of the Christian life—a Repentance which is a conviction of our utter sinfulness, and guiltiness, and helplessness, and which precedes our receiving the Kingdom of God, which is within us. But notwithstanding this, there is also a Repentance and a Faith (taking the words in another sense, a sense not quite the same and yet not entirely different) which are requisite after we have believed the Gospel: yea, and in every subsequent stage of our Christian course." The sermon was designed to show "the mischievousness of that opinion, that we are wholly sanctified when we are justified, and that our hearts are then cleansed from all sin." Wesley had already treated of this subject in his Sermon on *The Scriptural Way of Salvation* (No. 230), and in one on *Sin in Believers* (No. 218), written "in order to remove a mistake which some were labouring to propagate,—that there is no sin in any that are justified." In the re-awakening of the religious life of the country many extravagances were manifested, which called for much patience and labour in the endeavour to correct them. This sermon was a contribution to the effort.

The sermon appeared afterwards in the first volume of the collected *Works*.

249. A LETTER TO THE REVEREND DR. RUTHERFORTH. By John Wesley, M.A., late Fellow of Lincoln College, Oxford, and Chaplain to the Right Honourable the Countess Dowager of Buchan. Bristol : Printed by William Pine, in Wine-Street. 1767, [should be 1768]. 12mo., pp. 23.

Dated at beginning, March 24, 1768, and signed John Wesley.

This letter was occasioned by the publication in 1763 of *Four Charges to the Clergy of the Archdeaconry of Essex, by T. Rutherforth, D.D., F.R.S., Archdeacon, &c.* The first three of the charges are directed against the Methodists, accusing them of ignorance and of despising all learning, and inquiring into their doctrines " concerning inward feelings" and "assurances."

Although the charges had been published four or five years before Wesley saw them, he instantly hastened to reply to them when they were brought under his notice. This he does in his usual careful, logical, and precise way, and so as to convince every unbiassed mind that he and his " helpers " had been grievously misrepresented. He then turns round upon the Archdeacon, and inquires if he had " nothing more important wherewith to entertain the stewards of the mysteries of God than the mistakes, if there had been such, of the Methodists, so-called," reading him a very severe lesson on neglecting much more weighty and pressing matters, which he enumerates, and stooping to deal with what was not merely trifling and insignificant, but even mischievous, destructive, and fatal.

Nos. 250-251-252. [1768.

250. AN EXTRACT OF MISS MARY GILBERT'S JOURNAL. (*Immodicis brevis est Ætas, et rara Voluptas, &c.*—MART.) Chester: Printed by J. Harvie. 1768. 12mo., pp. 94.

Preface "To the Reader" dated Liverpool, April 7th, 1768, and signed John Wesley.

Second edition, London: Henry Cock, 1768, pp. 72; London printed: Philadelphia reprinted, 1769; Another, 1772; Third, London: Hawes, 1779; Fourth, London: Paramore, 1787; Fifth, London: Whitfield, 1799.

A Short Account of Miss Mary Gilbert, extending to eight pages, precedes the extract from the Journal. By whom this was written is not stated. It was probably by her father. Wesley says of her reflections, which are very freely interspersed through the Journal, they "are always just, frequently strong and affecting, particularly those on death, or the shortness of life, especially from the mouth of a child. And the language wherein they are expressed, although plain and altogether unstudied, is yet pure and terse in the highest degree—yea, frequently elegant; such as the most polite either of our lawyers or divines would not easily alter for the better. Such language I hardly know where to find unless in the almost inimitable Letters of Jane Cooper" (No. 225). And yet this young person died before she had completed her seventeenth year.

"While I stayed here (St. Martin's Ash, Chester) I corrected Miss Gilbert's Journal—a masterpiece in its kind. What a prodigy of a child! Soon ripe and soon gone!"—*Journal*, April 4, 1768.

251. THE GOOD STEWARD: A SERMON. By John Wesley, M.A., Chaplain to the Right Hon. the Countess Dowager of Buchan. Newcastle upon Tyne: Printed by J. White and T. Saint. 1768. 12mo., pp. 24.

Dated at end, Edinburgh, May 14, 1768.

Another, London: Printed in the year 1768; also Leeds: J. Bowling, 1768; and Bristol: William Pine, 1768; Another, London, 1769.

Re-printed in the 4th vol. of the collected *Works*.

This sermon, founded on Luke xvi. 2, was probably preached, as it was obviously written, in Edinburgh. The first edition, therefore, would be that printed in Newcastle, whither Wesley went, passing through "poor, dead Berwick," where he found, however, "a few living souls." He remained in Newcastle and the neighbourhood for some time.

The sermon deals with "the relation which man bears to God," as expressed in the word steward. The nature of the stewardship, its duration, the account to be given of it, and the solemn lessons such considerations afford, are the topics discussed. The subject is viewed in particular reference to the future, concerning which there are many speculative inquiries, a departure from Wesley's habit. But by far the greater part of the sermon is strictly and forcibly practical.

252. AN EXTRACT FROM THE REV. MR. LAW'S LATER WORKS. [Two volumes.] Vol. i. Bristol: Printed by William Pine, in Wine-Street. 1768. 12mo., pp. 251. Vol. ii., pp. 204.

1768.] **No. 253.**

These volumes contain Extracts from (1) *The Case of Reason, or Natural Religion, fairly and fully stated, in answer to a book entitled Christianity as Old as the Creation*; (2) *Law's Serious Answer to Dr. Trapp's Four Sermons on The Sin, Folly, and Danger of being righteous overmuch* (already published: see No. 118); (3) *Animadversions upon Dr. Trapp's late Reply;* (4) *Confutation of Bishop Warburton's projected Defence* (as he calls it) *of Christianity, in his Divine Legation of Moses*; (5) *The Spirit of Prayer*, Parts i. and ii.; (6) *The Spirit of Love*, Parts i., ii. and iii.; (7) Mr. Law's *Letters;* and (8) *Address to the Clergy*.

There is neither preface nor index. The Extracts are included in vols. vi. and vii. of the collected *Works* (1772) without any note.

That Wesley had a very high regard for some of Mr. Law's earlier writings is well known, and is particularly shown in his republishing the greater portion of his two chief works, *A Serious Call to a Holy Life* (No. 48), and *A Treatise on Christian Perfection* (No. 45), to the value of which and his indebtedness to them he bears repeated witness; and his re-printing two volumes of extracts from Law's later works shows that he likewise thought highly of them. But from the beginning he found occasion to differ largely from some of Law's views. "Meeting now with Mr. Law's *Christian Perfection* and *Serious Call*, although I was much offended at many parts of both, yet they convinced me more than ever of the exceeding height and breadth and depth of the Law of God."—*Works*, i. 99.

"I had been eight years at Oxford before I read any of Mr. Law's writings; and when I did, I was so far from making them my creed, that I had objections to almost every page."—*Works*, viii. 366. And even of the later writings, he is compelled to say to one of his correspondents, "You are more liable to receive hurt from his late writings than from any others which I know."—*ib.* xii. 182. Wesley well knew the dangers of Behmenism, which so deeply tinctured Law's writings. "I think the rock on which I had the nearest made shipwreck of the faith was the writings of the Mystics." By publishing these Extracts, Wesley designed to separate the wheat from the chaff. On Wesley's relation to Law, see Rigg's *Living Wesley*, Part iii. ch. i.

253. AN EXTRACT OF THE LIFE OF THE LATE REV. MR. DAVID BRAINERD, Missionary to the Indians. By John Wesley, M.A. Bristol: Printed by William Pine, in Wine-Street. 1768. 12mo., pp. 274.

Second edition, Bristol: Pine, 1771; Third, London: Paramore, 1793; Fourth, London: Whitfield, 1800.

This is really an autobiography, prepared for publication by Mr. Jonathan Edwards, Minister of Northampton, in New-England. It was first published in this country in Edinburgh, 8vo., 1765. It is mainly in Brainerd's own words taken from his diary, certain portions, in which the editor summarises the account, being placed in brackets. Wesley does not appear to have inserted a single sentence, except the "advertisement," which is prefixed, and possibly one or two of the foot notes. He much prized this memoir, though he found occasion to grieve over some parts, when he read it many years before. "I read the surprising *Extract of Mr. Brainerd's Journal*. Surely then God hath once more 'given to the Gentiles repentance unto life!' Yet amidst so great matter of joy I could not but grieve at this: that even so good a man as Mr. Brainerd should be 'wise above that which is written,' in condemning what the Scripture nowhere condemns; in prescribing to God the way wherein He should work," &c.—*Journal*, Dec. 9, 1749. When commending him to one of the members of the Society as a pattern of self-devotion and deadness to the world, he adds, "But how much of his sorrow and pain had been prevented if he had understood the doctrine of Christian perfection ! How many tears did he shed because it was impossible to be freed from sin !"—*Works*, xii. 268.

In the fifth edition of the *Large Minutes* (1780) it is inquired, " Q. 57. What can be done to revive the work of God where it is destroyed ?" And the answer is : " 1. Let every preacher read carefully over the *Life of David Brainerd*. Let us be followers of him as he was of Christ, in absolute self-devotion, in total deadness to the world, and in fervent love to God and man. Let us but secure this point, and the world and the devil must fall under our feet," &c.—*Min. Con.* i. 579.

" Find preachers of David Brainerd's spirit, and nothing can stand before them."—*Works*, iii. 294.

The Memoir is inserted in a slightly abridged form in the collected Works, occupying nearly the whole of vol. xii. The Letters, Reflections, and Observations are in vol. xiii. Wesley there indicates by asterisks those portions of the memoir which he especially commends.

254. MINUTES OF SOME LATE CONVERSATIONS BETWEEN THE REV. MR. WESLEY AND OTHERS. Bristol : Printed by William Pine, in Wine-Street. 1768. 12mo., pp. 15.

Dated at beginning, Bristol, Tuesday, August 16, &c., 1768.

Two questions were seriously considered this year. The first, " Should itinerant preachers follow trades ?" It was concluded that by the succeeding Conference all who had been " concerned therein " could " give up all and attend to the one business." The other question received full attention. It is thus stated, "In many places the work of God seems to stand still. What can be done to revive and enlarge it ?" The answer embraces several highly practical and useful regulations, that even now ought not to be forgotten. Wesley's exclamation is, " O what can we do for more labourers? We can only cry to ' the Lord of the harvest.'"

NOTE.—THE DEVIL OF MASCON : or, a True Relation of the Chief Things which an Unclean Spirit did and said at Mascon in Burgundy, in the House of one Mr. Francis Pereaud, Minister of the Reformed Church in the same Town. Translated from the French. The Sixth edition. London : Printed in the year 1768. 12mo., pp. 34.

It was translated from Pereaud's book by Dr. Peter du Moulin, at the request of Robert Boyle, whose letter to the translator is prefixed, in which he says that the conversation he had with the author at Geneva, where he had opportunity to inquire both into his character and into the meaning of some passages in his book, overcame all his "settled indisposedness to believe strange things." Du Moulin's reply to Boyle is also inserted.

Osborn, in his *Outlines of Wesleyan Bibliography*, under this date, gives the above as one of Wesley's publications, and appends this note : " Inserted in sale Catalogues ; and afterwards published in part in the *Arminian Magazine*." He is not followed by Heylin ; nor by Smith, *Hist. of Wes. Meth.*, i. appendix N. ; nor by Tyerman.

It is very questionable if it should find a place here. It was revised and abridged by Wesley, and inserted in the *Arminian Magazine* for 1782 ; but it does not appear to have been published by him previously to that date. The edition of 1768 cannot on any ground be attributed to him, even if he allowed its sale at the Book-Room.

The whole story is very remarkable. Of those who would not question the veracity of the narrator, few would accept his explanation of the strange things which he records. Wesley's preface to the account, as published in the *Magazine*, is worthy of reproduction: "With my latest breath will I bear my testimony against giving up to infidels one great proof of the invisible world. I mean that of witchcraft and apparitions, confirmed by the testimony of all ages. I do not think any unprejudiced men can doubt of the truth of the following narrative. The truth of it was in the last century acknowledged by all Europe: against which the unaccountableness of it is no objection to those who are convinced of the littleness of their own knowledge."—*Arminian Magazine*, 1782, p. 366.

1769.

255. ADVICES WITH RESPECT TO HEALTH. Extracted from a late Author [Dr. Tissot]. Bristol: Printed by W. Pine, in Wine-Street. 1769. 12mo., pp. 218.

Third edition, London: Hawes, 1766; Fourth, London: New Chapel, 1789: These are precisely as the First edition. Fifth, corrected, London: Paramore, 1793, *Extracted from Dr. Tissot*, added on title-page: Titles of medicines at the end: also Index; Seventh, London: Story, 1801; Eighth, London: Cordeux, 1810, Title-page altered to *The Family Physician; or, Advice with Respect to Health: Including directions for the prevention and cure of acute diseases*. Index slightly altered: in all other respects as Fifth edition. It was sometimes sold bound up with the *Primitive Physic*.

The preface, which is Wesley's, is neither dated nor signed. In it he describes Dr. Tissot's book as "one of the most useful books of the kind which has appeared in the present century." He thinks it "speaks a person of strong understanding, extensive knowledge, and deep experience." He praises his humanity, his tender sense of the sufferings of his fellow creatures, and his desire to prevent or lessen them. His descriptions of disease he thinks are truly admirable, and so clearly stated that even common people of tolerable sense may readily distinguish them: his medicines are few, most of them quite simple, and both safe and cheap. He commends the stress laid upon regimen and the avoidance of large quantities of medicine, the repeated cautions against spirituous remedies, the insistence on fresh air, and a fearless exposure of so many vulgar errors. These characteristics were sure to approve themselves to the man who was ever searching for means to alleviate human suffering. But on the other hand, he condemns the frequent recommendation of bleeding; nor does he hesitate to express his disapproval of some of the remedies which were in favour at the time. His reference to medical writings shows how widely he had read upon the subject, and a comparison of the book with Tissot's work indicates with how much care he had prepared this abridgement. He says, "The following pages contain the most useful parts of Dr. Tissot's book: I believe the substance of all that will stand the test of sound reason and experience. I have added little thereto, but have judged it would be of use to retrench a great deal." He adds "(what it would not be so fashionable for a physician to believe, much less to mention), that as God is the sovereign disposer of all things, particularly of life and death, I earnestly advise everyone, together with all the other medicines, to use that medicine of medicines, *Prayer*."

Nos. 256-257. [1769.

256. AN EXTRACT FROM THE JOURNAL OF ELIZABETH HARPER.
London: Printed in the year 1769. 12mo., pp. 47.

Another edition, same date. The preface "To the Reader" occupies six pages; it is by Wesley, but not signed.

This is the journal of an unlettered woman, who set down in a plain way the feelings of her heart. Wesley taught the doctrine of Christian perfection as contained in the Scriptures and in the practical writings of godly divines, and as exhibited in the lives of many who adorned the doctrine of God their Saviour. He tells us that in order to place in the clearest and fullest light the truth that Christian perfection does not imply a freedom from human mistakes and infirmities, he had "published the following Extract from the artless journal of a plain woman, wrote merely for her own use." It was his painful duty to have to defend his teaching against every kind of objection. In several instances he used the journals of simple folk to rebut error as well as to illustrate the truth. This particular journal was published to show that "giving God all our heart and loving Him with all our heart, and our neighbours as ourselves," which he uses as a definition of Christian perfection, "is well consistent with a thousand infirmities which belong to every soul while in the body."

257. AN EXTRACT OF LETTERS BY MRS. L * * *. Bristol: Printed by William Pine, in Wine-Street. 1769. 12mo., pp. 111.

Brief preface " To the Reader," signed "J. W.," and the whole inserted in the collected Works.

Another, Bristol: W. Pine, 1773; London: G. Paramore, 1792; Bristol: W. Pine and Son, 1796; London: Story, 1804; Dublin: 1808.

These letters were written by Mrs. Lefevre, one of the early London Methodists. They were originally published in the year 1757. The editor, apologizing for the inaccuracies which some might find, stated that they were "not recommended as patterns of polite epistolary correspondence. Their merit," he adds, "is of another kind. It consists neither in the fineness of the language, nor in the elegance of the manner." Wesley thinks it does, and says he is not ashamed to recommend them "as patterns of truly polite epistolary correspondence, expressing the noblest sentiments in the most elegant manner, in the purest, yea, and finest language. Yet undoubtedly even the beauty of the language is nothing compared to the spirit which breathes throughout. Happy they who both taste her spirit and are partakers of it."—Preface.

John Fletcher's estimate of Mrs. Lefevre and her letters was very high. He speaks of her as "a Christian and an eminent Christian, not to say one of the brightest lights that God has raised since the late revival of godliness. The reproach of Christ was her crown of rejoicing, His cross her continual support, His followers her nearest companions, His example the pattern of her conversation. She lived a saint and died an angel. Each one of her letters may be a pattern for Christian correspondents, by the simplicity, edification, and love they breathe in every line. O when shall I write as she did ! When my heart be as full of God as hers was !"—*Letter to Mrs. Glynne, of Shrewsbury,* in *Works,* i. 39.

258. MINUTES OF SOME LATE CONVERSATIONS BETWEEN THE REV. MR. WESLEY AND OTHERS. Leeds : Printed by James Bowling, on the Bridge. 1769. 12mo., pp. 16.

Dated, Leeds, Tuesday, Aug. 1, &c., 1769.

Matters of special interest in this year's *Minutes* are : 1. The appointment of Boardman and Pilmoor as the first Missionaries to America, sent by the Methodist Conference in response to the "pressing call" from New York. 2. Arrangements for the more ample provision for the wives of the preachers. 3. An interesting paper read by Wesley to the Conference respecting his fruitless appeal to fifty or sixty of the clergy who believed and preached justification by faith, of whom only three vouchsafed an answer. 4. The adoption of measures for continuing "a firm union" between the travelling preachers in the Connexion, in the event of Wesley's death ; a matter which was brought up again and acted upon in 1773.

1770.

259. A SHORT ACCOUNT OF THE DEATH OF MARY LANGSON, OF TAXALL, IN CHESHIRE; who died January the 29th, 1769. (Psalm lxvi. 16, 1 Cor. xv. 55, 56, 57.) Printed in the year 1770. 12mo., pp. 12.

One of Charles Wesley's Hymns is appended, "Happy soul, thy days are ended," and a second hymn, "O Thou God of my salvation."

Another edition, also printed in the year 1770, not having the passages of Scripture on the title page, or the second hymn appended ; another, printed in the year 1771, (two passages and both hymns) in which the date of the death is erroneously stated on the title-page as January 29, 1771 ; another, Bristol : 1772 ; London : R. Hawes, 1775 ; London : Paramore, 1795.

The tract was probably written by Thomas Olivers—one of Wesley's early preachers, and author of the hymn, "The God of Abraham praise," he being in the Cheshire Circuit at the time of Mary Langson's last illness and death, to which mainly the account refers. The second hymn, "O Thou God of my salvation," is also attributed to him on the circumstantial evidence that it first appeared in this tract. It is quite in his style and in one of his favourite metres : see *Hymns by Thomas Olivers with Biographical Sketch*, by Rev. John Kirk : London, Sedgwick, 1868.

The original, revised and slightly abridged by Wesley, was inserted in his collected Works, vol. xiii. 1772. Perhaps that should therefore be regarded as the first edition published by him ; but this must remain uncertain, for there is nothing to show by whom or where the first edition was published. Wesley may have met with the account, or heard of it, and urged its publication when he went on his way "slowly through Staffordshire and Cheshire to Manchester" in March, 1770 : see *Journal*. For an interesting account of Olivers and a list of his writings, see *The Lives of Early Methodist Preachers*, by Thomas Jackson, vol. ii., in which a *Descriptive and Plaintive Elegy on the Death of the Rev. John Wesley*, of eighty-two stanzas, is inserted.

260. THE QUESTION, WHAT IS AN ARMINIAN? ANSWERED. By a Lover of Free Grace. Bristol : Printed by W. Pine. 1770. 12mo., pp. 8.

Nos. 261-262. [1770.

London: Printed in the year 1770; London: G. Whitfield, 1798; London: Cordeux, 1817.

This little tract was written to explain the meaning of the word Arminian, and to point out the difference between Arminianism and Calvinism. The occasion for it is thus stated, "To say, 'This man is an Arminian,' has the same effect on many hearers as to say, 'This is a mad dog.' It puts them into a fright at once; they run away from him with all speed and diligence; and will hardly stop, unless it be to throw a stone at the dreadful, mischievous animal. The more unintelligible the word is, the better it answers the purpose. Those on whom it is fixt, know not what to do; not understanding what it means, they cannot tell what defence to make, or how to clear themselves from the charge. And it is not easy to remove the prejudice which others have imbibed, who know no more of it than that it is 'something *very* bad,' if not '*all* that is bad.'"

It shows, as clearly as so few words can, the origin of the use of the term, and the doctrinal difference between those who hold the views it is intended to represent, and those who are distinguished by the term Calvinist. It was written by Wesley to guard himself and his people from imputations that were made by ignorant or malicious persons, who mis-applied this and other terms.

261. THE DOCTRINE OF ABSOLUTE PREDESTINATION STATED AND ASSERTED. By the Reverend Mr. A—— T——. London: Printed in the year 1770. 12mo., pp. 12.

Another edition, Bristol: Printed by W. Pine, 1770.

In the previous year Toplady had published a pamphlet entitled *The Doctrine of Absolute Predestination Stated and Asserted; with a preliminary discourse on the Divine attributes: Translated in great measure from the Latin of Jerom Zanchius*. Of this the above is an abridgement. "An honest and faithful abridgement of Toplady's pretended translation; but the truth is, by divesting the work of Toplady of its cloudy verbiage, the Calvinistic theory was presented in a form enough to horrify every man of reason and religion."—Tyerman. The only words of Wesley in the pamphlet are the first and last paragraphs. At the beginning is this "Advertisement.—It is granted that the ensuing tract is in good measure a translation. Nevertheless, considering the unparalleled modesty and self-diffidence of the young translator, and the tenderness wherewith he treats his opponents, it may well pass for an original." The closing words are, "The sum of all is this. One in twenty (suppose) of mankind is elected; nineteen in twenty are reprobated. The elect shall be saved do what they will; the reprobate shall be damned do what they can. Reader, believe this or be damned. Witness my hand, A—— T——." This was sure to evoke reprisals; but Toplady's rejoinder in a *Letter to the Rev. Mr. John Wesley*, relative to his pretended abridgement of Zanchius on Predestination, is a scurrilous and undignified performance.

It is one of the many pamphlets which Wesley felt himself called upon to write in opposition to views which he had good reason to believe greatly hampered his work, led astray many of his followers, and were productive of a wild Antinomianism, than which nothing so excited his indignation.

262. SOME ACCOUNT OF THE EXPERIENCE OF E. J. London: Printed by J. and W. Oliver, in Bartholomew-Close, near West-Smithfield. 12mo., pp. 11.

Bristol: Printed by William Pine, in Wine-Street, 1770; London: Hawes, n.d.; London: Hawes, n.d.; London: Paramore, 1792.

A simple, unequivocal testimony to the possibility of attaining and retaining "Christian perfection." In the course of it is this statement : "For these ten years I have enjoyed this haven of rest. It has been to me as a day without a cloud. I never have had a tedious moment, nor a murmuring thought. I have been tempted in all things; yet nothing obscures my light, or obstructs my way: but still I 'rejoice evermore, pray without ceasing, and in everything give thanks.'" Tyerman suggests that it may be an account of a Mr. Edward Jackson. But it is more likely to be that which Wesley mentions in writing to Miss Bosanquet in this very year,—"The experience of Eliz. Jackson has animated many. It is the very marrow of Christianity; and if it be diligently spread among our believers, it may be of unspeakable use."—*Works*, xii. 386. The whole was evidently revised and prepared for the press by Wesley. It is inserted in the collected Works, vol. xiv.

263. A SHORT ACCOUNT OF ANN ROGERS. By John Johnson. London : Printed by J. and W. Oliver, in Bartholomew-Close, near West-Smithfield. 1770. 12mo., pp. 12.

Bristol: Printed by William Pine, in Wine-Street, 1770; London: Paramore, 1786; London: G. Whitfield, 1798.

This is another testimony similar to that of "E. J." (No. 262), communicated to Wesley, and by him published in confirmation of the truth which he taught on the possible attainments of the Christian life. Ann Rogers was a member of the Methodist Society in Dublin; John Johnson was one of the preachers living there. The former part of the account is a narrative of his visits to her during the last two days of her life, and is dated at the beginning, Saturday, April 8, 1769; the latter part contains extracts from her private diary. Wesley was in Ireland at the time. It is not possible to determine in reference to this pamphlet or the next preceding, which of the two earlier editions was printed first. The order given is probably the right one.

264. FREE THOUGHTS ON THE PRESENT STATE OF PUBLIC AFFAIRS. In a Letter to a Friend. (*Periculosœ plenum opus aleœ, &c.*—Hor.) London : Printed by J. and W. Oliver, in Bartholomew-Close. 1770. 8vo. pp. 47.

Another, same date and publishers, smaller type, 12mo., pp. 24.

This is a patriotic pamphlet, written in response to an urgent request from a friend who desired him freely to express his views on the state of the nation. Excusing himself as being no politician—"politics lie quite out of my province"—he proceeds to set down his "naked thoughts, and that without any art or colouring." Remarking upon the impossibility of the general public knowing with any accuracy the facts of which they form and express their judgment, or the springs of action which give rise to those actions and on which, more than on the bare actions themselves, the characters of the actors depend, he ridicules the idea of every Englishman being a politician, "able to reform the nation, point out every blunder of this and that Minister, tell every step they ought to take, and be the arbiters of all Europe." "I grant," he adds, "every Cobbler, Tinker, Porter and Hackney-Coachman can do this. But I am not so deep-learned : while they are sure of everything, I am sure of nothing, except of that very little which I see with my own eyes, or hear with my own ears" He defends the King, the Ministers of State, and the Parliament; and points to hidden causes of the unrest of the nation that lie outside of politics—covetousness, ambition, pride, envy, resentment and other moral delinquencies in the national character, and from these he judges the nation has more to fear than from the faults and errors of its rulers. If Wesley were indeed no politician, he had a clear view of the state of public affairs and good common-sense and high principles of patriotism to guide him in giving the judgments on those affairs, which are contained in these pages. It is inserted in the first edition of the collected Works. In the third edition, it is stated that it was written in the year 1768 (vol. xi. 14), but Jackson gives no authorities.

265. A SURVEY OF THE WISDOM OF GOD IN THE CREATION: OR, A COMPENDIUM OF NATURAL PHILOSOPHY. In three volumes. The Second edition. Vol. i. "These are Thy glorious works, Parent of good," &c.—Milton. Bristol: Printed by William Pine. 1770. 12mo., pp. 286, xxx. 256, 242, x. iv.

The first two volumes are a reprint of No. 220, with no other change than the correction of the *errata*. Vol. iii. is entirely new, and forms an appendix to the several sections of the previous volumes, being a collection of philosophical experiments and observations, each of which is referred to its proper place in those volumes.

It appears that when Wesley published his original sketch of Natural Philosophy in 1763 (No. 220), he had no thought or design of ever going any further, or of making any additions to it. But it was so favourably received, far beyond his expectation, that he was encouraged, as he says, in his "leisure hours" (!) to look further into the subject, and to set down from time to time whatever appeared most worthy of observation, and in a second edition to expand the first. But on reflection he judged it would be more useful to the purchasers of the original edition to issue an Appendix to it. The Appendix, however, swelled into a volume, which is so prepared that it may be read either as a separate treatise, or together with the earlier volumes.

His wide range of reading is illustrated in the subjects embraced in the volume:—viz., the Structure of the Human Body; Descriptions and Habits of Beasts, Birds, Fishes, Reptiles and Insects; the Structure of Plants; the Nature of Metals, Minerals and Fossils; together with various phenomena of Earth, Water, Fire, Air and Vapours; and some account of the Solar System and other branches of Astronomy.

The work was afterwards expanded to five volumes: see No. 325.

"Mr. Wesley's *Survey of the Wisdom of God in the Creation* was not intended as a history of the present state of philosophy; nor as an introduction to the philosophical systems that have prevailed, or do now prevail, though he gives a little sketch of them; but as a general view of the most useful and remarkable things in natural history, and an illustration, for common use, of the wisdom and goodness of the Creator. Considered in this light, it is well entitled to public approbation: and the moral reflections it contains are as much distinguished by their justness and elegance, as by their utility. Upon the whole it is the most useful Christian compendium of philosophy in the English language."—*Life of Wesley* by John Whitehead, M.D., ii. 491.

266. A SERMON ON THE DEATH OF THE REV. MR. GEORGE WHITEFIELD. Preached at the Chapel in Tottenham-Court-Road, and at the Tabernacle, near Moorfields, on

Sunday, November 18, 1770. By John Wesley, M.A., late Fellow of Lincoln-College, Oxon ; and Chaplain to the Right Honourable the Countess Dowager of Buchan. (2 Sam. xii. 23.) London: Printed by J. and W. Oliver, in Bartholomew-Close. Sold by G. Keith, in Gracechurch-Street ; W. Harris, in St. Paul's Churchyard ; E. Cabe, in Ave-Mary-Lane ; P. Jones, in Tottenham-Court-Road; M. Englefield, in West-Street, Seven-Dials; and at the Foundery. 1770. [Price Sixpence.] 8vo., pp. 32.

Reprinted at Dublin, by S. Powell, 1770, in smaller type, pp. 36. Price threepence. Another hymn, "Glory, and thanks, and love," is added to "Servant of God, well done !" which occurs in the first.

Text: Numbers xxiii. 10. A hymn, "Servant of God, well done!" is appended. In the *Poetical Works* it is entitled "An Hymn on the Death of the Rev. Mr. Whitefield."—Vol. vi. p. 316. It was probably prepared for and sung for the first time at the funeral service.

At the back of the title-page is printed : "N.B.—This Sermon is entered in the Hall Book of the Company of Stationers."

After briefly tracing the principal incidents of Whitefield's life, Wesley sketches his character with the faithfulness of a friend, bears his utmost testimony to the many excellent qualities of this remarkable man, and gathers up the lessons which his useful life affords. He gives prominence not only to his unparalleled zeal and the greatness of his labours, but also to his tenderness to the afflicted and charity to the poor, his deep gratitude to all who were instruments of good to him, and his tender friendship which seemed "the distinguishing part of his character, and which, quick and penetrating as lightning, flew from heart to heart, which gave life to his sermons, his conversation, his letters." He speaks of his modesty, the frankness and openness of his conversation, his courage and intrepidity, his fearlessness of labour and pain, his steadfastness in pursuing whatever he undertook for his Master's sake. He is equally emphatic in his reference to "that torrent of eloquence which frequently bore down all before it ; and that astonishing force of persuasion which the most hardened sinners could not resist ;" and he affectionately refers to the great honour which "it pleased God to put upon his faithful servant, by allowing him to declare his everlasting Gospel in so many various countries, to such numbers of people, and with so great an effect on so many of their precious souls." "Have we read, or heard," he asks, "of any person since the Apostles, who testified the Gospel of the grace of God through so widely extended a space, through so large a part of the habitable world ? Have we read or heard of any person who called so many thousands, so many myriads of sinners to repentance ? Above all, have we read or heard of any who has been a blessed intrument in his hand of bringing so many sinners from darkness to light, and from the power of Satan unto God ?"

"I returned to London, and had the melancholy news of Mr. Whitefield's death confirmed by his executors, who desired me to preach his funeral sermon on Sunday, the 18th. In order to write this, I retired to Lewisham on Monday, and on Sunday following went to the chapel in Tottenham-Court-Road. An immense multitude was gathered together from all corners of the town. I was at first afraid that a great part of the congregation would not be able to hear ; but it pleased God so to strengthen my voice, that even those at the door heard distinctly. It was an awful season: all were as still as night : most appeared to be deeply affected ; and an impression was made on many, which one would hope will not speedily be effaced."—*Journal*, Nov. 18, 1770.

Charles Wesley poured out his sorrow in very fervent and affectionate strains in an Elegy to the memory of his friend: see No. 278.

267. MINUTES OF SOME LATE CONVERSATIONS BETWEEN THE REV. MR. WESLEY AND OTHERS. Bristol: Printed by W. Pine. 1770. 12mo., pp. 12.

In the *Minutes* of this Conference the question is asked,—" Q. 28. What can be done to revive the work of God where it is decayed ?" In the reply is the following.—"6. Take heed to your doctrine. We said in 1744, 'We have leaned too much toward Calvinism.' Wherein ?" To this an extended answer is given (see *Min. Conf.* i. 95-6), which was the occasion of a degree of excitement and ill-will, and of the issue of an amount of polemical literature, that are truly astonishing. The discussion extended over a period of six years. It is evident that Wesley judged the Calvinism of that day to be promotive of Antinomianism; and he laid stress in the "Minute" on the requirements of the moral law. To argue thus was affirmed by some leading Calvinists, notably the Countess of Huntingdon, and her cousin and chaplain, the Hon. and Rev. Walter Shirley, to favour the doctrine of justification by works. This Wesley utterly repudiated. It has been thought that the Minute which is drawn up in Wesley's usual terse and brief manner, might, as a whole, have been better guarded, and doubtless would have been, had he intended it for popular use and not solely for the benefit of his preachers. But our interest is with the bibliographical aspects of the controversy; and they are manifold, as will presently be seen.

In Appendix "A" to Tegg's edition of Stevens' *History of Methodism*, vol. ii., 1864, no less than forty-three publications are mentioned as growing out of the "Minute controversy," including Fletcher's "Checks," writings by Toplady, Sir Richard and Rev. Rowland Hill, and others. Dr. Stevens (*Hist. Meth.* bk. v. c. ii.) devotes an entire chapter to "The Controversy," to which readers are referred for an impartial and extended view of "this stormy battle-field." See also Jackson's *Life of Charles Wesley*, vol. ii., ch. 22. The Rev. John Fletcher resigned the presidency, and Mr. Benson was discharged by its founder, the Countess of Huntingdon, from the Mastership of Trevecca College, in consequence of the attitude assumed by them on the "Minute Controversy."—*Life of John Fletcher*, pp. 54-8.

268. MINUTES OF SEVERAL CONVERSATIONS BETWEEN THE REVEREND MESSIEURS JOHN AND CHARLES WESLEY AND OTHERS. London: Printed in the year 1770. 12mo., pp. 60.

The Third edition of the so-called *Large Minutes*.

The present number of the *Large Minutes* is an extension of the previous ones (Nos. 164, 221). The additional matter consists of regulations made at the intervening annual Conferences. They relate to better methods for promoting the spiritual welfare of the members of the Societies; to the following of trades by the "Helpers," which was to be abandoned; to the best means for increasing the personal holiness of the preachers; and to the definition of the work of the Assistants. Amongst financial questions, are methods for providing for the wants of the preachers and their families, and for removing the debts that had been incurred. Regulations are introduced respecting the order of procedure in the Conferences; and a deliverance is made on the accusation brought against Wesley of exerting undue power over the preachers and the people. The Minute which occasioned the controversy referred to in No. 267 is included. The edition embraces all the general regulations and resolutions of the Conference up to this date, including the important ones made this year. With the other editions it is republished in the revised *Minutes*, 8vo., 1862. It is a very interesting volume, showing the principles by which the early Methodists were guided in their great evangelistic work.

269. AN EXTRACT FROM DR. YOUNG'S NIGHT-THOUGHTS ON LIFE, DEATH, AND IMMORTALITY. Bristol: Printed by William Pine, in Wine-Street. 1770. 12mo., pp. 241.

Second edition (but not so called), London: Paramore, 1794. An unabridged edition of the *Night Thoughts*, with Wesley's notes, together with a *Poem on the Last Day*, by Dr. Young, and a Preface by Thomas Jackson, was published by Mason, London, 1840, 18mo., pp. 386; and a "New edition," 24mo., 1863.

The preface, signed John Wesley, occupies four pages. Wesley describes his design, in making this "extract," as:—(1) To leave out all the lines that contain childish conceits, that rise into the turgid, the false sublime, or are incurably obscure. (2) To explain words that are obscure to unlearned readers; and (3) To point out the sublimest strokes of poetry, and the most pathetic strokes of nature and passion. Brief explanatory notes are given at the end of each "Night."

"In the latter part of this month I took some pains in reading over Dr. Young's 'Night Thoughts,' leaving out the indifferent lines, correcting many of the rest, and explaining the hard words, in order to make that noble work more useful to all, and more intelligible to ordinary readers."—*Journal*, Dec., 1768.

Jackson, in his preface named above, says, "Mr. Wesley especially recommended the book on account of its intrinsic excellence, and beneficial tendency. He published copious extracts of it soon after its first appearance; and in the year 1770 he reprinted it in an abridged form, with short explanatory notes. These notes are here re-published; but the poem is given entire. Not a line has been omitted."—p. iv. The Extracts referred to are to be found in volume ii. of *Moral and Sacred Poems* (No. 58). They are from the first seven *Nights* of the *Complaint* (pp. 229-373). There are no notes appended, and the name of the author is not given.

1771.

270. AN EXTRACT OF THE REV. MR. JOHN WESLEY'S JOURNAL, from May 27, 1765, to May 18, 1768. London: Printed by J. and W. Oliver, in Bartholomew-Close. 1771. 12mo., pp. 128. [No. xiv.]

Another edition, London: Paramore, 1781.

One continuous record of steady, hard work. On preaching in the open-air he makes this reflection, "Surely this is the way to spread religion: to publish it in the face of the sun."—June 20, 1765.

The *Extract* contains a letter by Wesley published in *Lloyd's Evening Post*. It is in reply to an attack made upon him, in the *Christian Magazine*, in reference to some expressions in *The Character of a Methodist*, a publication issued by Wesley in 1742 (see No. 34). "Rusticulus, or Dr. Dodd," gives garbled extracts, and draws unwarranted conclusions from these expressions as to the pretensions of the Methodists. These Wesley in the letter corrects.

271. A Short Account of John Dillon. Bristol: Printed by W. Pine, in Wine-Street. 1771. 12mo., pp. 12.

Another, Bristol: Pine, 1772; *A Short Account of the Life and Death*, &c: London: Hawes, 1777; London: Story, 1805; London: Blanshard, 1817, having the words, "preacher of the Gospel, Written by Himself," added to the title-page.

Another simple story of the power of the Divine grace working in the heart of a reprobate, who becomes a happy witness of the full salvation of the Gospel. The whole account, excepting the last sentence, seems to have been written by Dillon himself towards the close of his life. It was probably edited by another hand. It is inserted in Wesley's edition of his works, vol. xxiii.

Dillon was one of Wesley's preachers, and laboured in Ireland with much zeal, and amidst many privations.

272. A Letter to the Reverend Mr. Fleury. (Psalm cxx. 7). Dublin: Printed in the year 1771. 12mo., pp. 16 (?).

Dated at the end, Limerick, May 18, 1771, and signed by John Wesley. I have not seen an original copy of this.

Wesley was in Waterford in June, 1769. He had no sooner left than he was attacked from the pulpit of the Cathedral by the Reverend Mr. Fleury. Being there again, and learning that he was to receive like favour, he went to hear; and he found the preacher to be as good as his word—" You drew the sword, and, in effect, threw away the scabbard. You made a furious attack on a large body of people, of whom you knew just nothing. Blind and bold, you laid about you without fear or wit, without any regard either to truth, justice, or mercy. And thus you entertained, both morning and evening, a large congregation who came to hear 'the words of eternal life.'"

Not having leisure himself to wait on his assailant, he sent one of his preachers the next morning, who proposed an interchange of letters. The reply was: "No; if anything can be said against my sermon, I expect it shall be printed. Let it be done in a public, not a private way." Wesley says, "I did not desire this; I had much rather it had been done privately. But since you will have it so, I submit." He then proceeds to examine the sermons, replying fully to their grossly inaccurate statements and false conclusions, and he begs his reverend brother, if he further designs to write about the Methodists, first to learn who and what they are. It is a severe and dignified reply.

Objections raised against lay-preaching, Wesley answers, "not by anything new,—that is utterly needless; but barely by repeating the answer which convinced a serious Clergyman many years ago." He then inserts the whole of one of his former publications, entitled *A Letter to a Clergyman* (No. 110).

273. A Defence of the Minute of Conference (1770) Relating to Calvinism. By John Wesley. Printed for private circulation. Dublin: 1771.

Dated July 10, 1771. Never republished.

I have not seen a copy of this. It is given on the authority of Heylin in the appendix to Tegg's edition of Stevens' *History of Methodism*, pp. 777-99, and of Smith's *History of Wesleyan Methodism*, bk. ii. chap. iii. Smith says, "Wesley was in Ireland from March 24th to July 22nd (1771), during which time he appears to have received the circular (Rev. Mr. Shirley's, see No. 267), for he then drew up and printed, at Dublin, under date July 10th, 1771, a clear and logical exposition of the 'Minutes' which had called forth so much opposition. A copy of this printed paper he probably sent to several of his preachers and friends, it would scarcely have been printed but with this object. The one before me has a manuscript note in Mr. Wesley's handwriting at the top of the first page, and is addressed to Miss Bishop, of Bath. In this note he requests her not to 'show it before Conference,' adding, If the Calvinists do not or will not understand me, I understand myself; and I do not contradict anything I have written these thirty years. Towards the conclusion are the words, ' Poor Mr. Sh.'s triumph will be short.'"

Wesley writes of "those eight terrible propositions which conclude the Minutes of our Conference. At the instance of some who were sadly frightened thereby, I have revised them over and over; I have considered them in every point of view; and truly, the more I consider them, the more I like them; the more fully I am convinced, not only that they are true, agreeable both to Scripture and to sound experience, but that they contain truths of the deepest importance, and such as ought to be continually inculcated by those who would be pure from the blood of all men."—Letter in *Works*, xiii. 21.

274. THE CONSEQUENCE PROVED. London: Printed in the year 1771. 12mo., pp. 11.

Toplady had lately published a pamphlet, an extract from which was issued by Wesley under the title of *The Doctrine of Absolute Predestination stated and asserted, by the Rev. Mr. A.——T.——*" (No. 261). It concludes with the words, "The sum of all this is—One in twenty, suppose, of mankind is elected; nineteen in twenty are reprobated. The elect shall be saved do what they will: the reprobate shall be damned do what they can." It was vehemently objected that no such consequence followed from the doctrine of absolute predestination. Wesley in the present pamphlet says, "I calmly affirm, it is a fair statement of the case: this consequence does naturally and necessarily follow from the doctrine of absolute predestination as here stated and defended." This he proceeds to show in a few syllogistic sentences containing extracts from Toplady's pamphlet. And he closes with the words, "I defy any man living, who asserts the unconditional decree of reprobation or preterition (just the same in effect), to reconcile this with the Scriptural doctrine of a future judgment. I say again, I defy any man on earth to show, how, on this scheme, God can judge the world in righteousness." It called forth a fierce reply entitled, *More Work for Mr. John Wesley; or, A Vindication of the Decrees and Providence of God from the defamations of a late printed paper entitled, 'The Consequence Proved.'* From this it appears that *The Consequence Proved* was issued in August, 1771.

275. MINUTES OF SOME LATE CONVERSATIONS BETWEEN THE REV. MR. WESLEY AND OTHERS. Bristol: Printed by W. Pine. 1771. 12mo., pp. 8.

Dated Bristol, Tuesday, August 6, 1771. Relates only to the stationing of the preachers and to finance.

No. 276. [1771.

Joseph Benson was admitted *on trial* at this Conference, having left the head mastership of Trevecca College, in consequence of his defending the "Minute" of 1770. For the first time *America* appears in the list of Stations, with the names Richard Boardman, Joseph Pilmoor, Francis Asbury, and Richard Wright, the last two having been appointed at this Conference out of five who were willing to go over and help the brethren who "call aloud for help." The number of members entered for America is 316.

Though the printed *Minutes* for this year are very brief, the Conference is also notable for the step taken by the Calvinistic party, to whom the Minutes of the preceding Conference had given so much umbrage (see No. 267). One portion of these Minutes had led the Calvinists to accuse Wesley of teaching "justification by works." That Wesley held such a doctrine no one familiar with his writings could suppose; but the Minutes on Calvinism were "not sufficiently guarded." Fletcher confesses that "at first they appeared to him to be unguarded if not erroneous." Wesley himself acknowledged the unguarded character of the writing; and to prevent future misconstruction a Declaration was drawn up which he and the members of the Conference, with one exception, signed. In this document it is affirmed that, the doctrinal points in the *Minutes* having been misunderstood to favour justification by works, the signatories declare they had no intention to convey such a meaning, and that they abhor the doctrine as a most perilous and abominable one.

Wesley did not include this in the printed Minutes of the Conference. It was first published in *A Narrative of the principal circumstances relative to the Rev. Mr. Wesley's late Conference, held at Bristol, August 9, 1771*: By the Rev. Mr. Shirley: Bath, 1771: 8vo. It was afterwards reprinted in *A Conversation between Richard Hill Esq., the Rev. Mr. Madan, &c., relative to some doctrinal Minutes, advanced by the Rev. Mr. Wesley and others, &c.* London: 1771, 12mo It may be found in Watson's *Life of John Wesley*, ch. xi.

276. THE WORKS OF THE REV. JOHN WESLEY, M.A., Late Fellow of Lincoln-College, Oxford. [Thirty-two vols.] Vol. I. Bristol: Printed by William Pine, in Wine Street. 1771. 12mo., pp. 350, v.

This is the first edition of Wesley's collected Works. It was issued in weekly numbers of 72 pages each, price six-pence; also in thirty-two volumes in this and the three following years.

Wesley informs us that for several years he had desired to print in one collection all his prose writings, except the *Notes on the Bible*, the *System of Philosophy*, the *Christian Library*, and the books which were designed for the use of Kingswood School; that he "desired to methodize the whole, to range them under proper heads, placing those together which were on similar subjects, and in such order that one might illustrate another." The reader, he judged, would "then readily observe that there is scarce any subject of importance, either in practical or controversial divinity, which is not treated of more or less, either professedly or occasionally." As far back as Dec. 1. 1763, he wrote, "All the leisure hours I had in this and the following months, during the time I was in London, I spent in reading over our Works with the Preachers, considering what objections had been made, and correcting whatever we judged wrong, either in the matter or expression."—*Journal*.

But there was a yet more necessary task: he found on carefully examining many of his previous publications, that the errors of the press were far greater than he had supposed. "These," he says, "in many places were such as not only obscured, but wholly destroyed the sense; frequently to such a degree, that it would have been impossible for anyone but me to restore it, neither could I do it myself in several places, without long consideration; the word inserted having little or no resemblance to that which I had used. . . . Accordingly, I have altered many words or sentences; many others I have omitted, and in various parts I have added more or less as I judged the subject required: so that in this edition I present to serious and candid men my last and maturest thoughts; agreeable, I hope, to Scripture, Reason and Christian Antiquity." One other thing he notices as "a little out of the common way"; he has marked with an asterisk those passages which he thought to be most worthy of the reader's notice. Unfortunately the edition was not printed with strict accuracy.

In this year the first five volumes were issued. In the first volume are an Address to the Reader, signed John Wesley, and dated March, 1771; the Preface to the first volume of *Sermons on Several Occasions*, published in 1746 (No. 88); the twelve sermons contained in that volume, together with four others, a table of Contents, and one page of *errata*. The four additional sermons are the following:—"The Witness of the Spirit," "Sin in Believers," "Repentance of Believers," and "The Great Assize." They had already been published separately; see Nos. 242, 218, 248, and 185.

Vol. ii. contains fourteen sermons (xvii.-xxx.) being the twelve that are in the second volume of *Sermons on Several Occasions*, published in the year 1748 (No. 107); one from the third volume, 1750 (No. 139); and one entitled "The Lord our Righteousness," already published separately in 1766 (No. 235).

Vol. iii. has in it seventeen sermons (xxxi.-xlvii.) being eleven taken from the third volume of *Sermons on Several Occasions*, published 1750 (No. 139); four from the fourth volume published 1760 (No. 200); one on "Wandering Thoughts," which first appeared in a second undated edition of No. 139; and one entitled "The Scripture Way of Salvation," published separately in 1765 (No. 230).

Vol. iv. contains six sermons (xlviii.-liii.) being the three remaining ones in the fourth volume of *Sermons on Several Occasions* (No. 200), and three others already in print, namely "The Good Steward," published 1768 (No. 251), "Reformation of Manners," 1763 (No. 217), and one on "The Death of the Rev. George Whitefield," 1770 (No. 266). There is thus a total of *fifty-three sermons* in these four volumes, and to these it is generally supposed that allusion is made in the Trust Deeds of the Methodist Chapels as constituting together with Wesley's *Notes on the New Testament* (No. 172), the Doctrinal Standards of Methodism, as laid down by Wesley in his original Model Deed or Indenture included in the second number of his "Large Minutes" published in 1763 (No. 221). The accuracy of this opinion has recently been questioned. In addition to the six sermons named above, there are in this fourth volume the following tracts:—*Advice to the People called Methodists, with regard to Dress; The Duties of Husbands and Wives; Directions to Children; Directions to Servants*, and *An Extract from Mr. Law's Treatise on Christian Perfection*. This extract extends to the end of the fifth chapter of No. 45, the remaining three chapters are in the following volume.

Vol. v. In addition to the three chapters just named, this volume contains also the first seventeen chapters of *An Extract from Mr. Law's Serious Call to a Holy Life*, already published, see No. 48. Both these works have undergone a further revision and slight abridgement; but they are not wholly free from press errors. In fact to each of the five volumes issued this year a page of *errata* is appended, which adds strength to the judgment formed of the entire series by Dr. Whitehead, Wesley's friend and biographer,—"Mr. Wesley's Works were printed together in 1774, in thirty-two volumes, *but very incorrectly*."—*Life of Wesley*, ii. 495.

277. AN EPISTLE TO THE REVEREND MR. GEORGE WHITE-
FIELD. Written in the year 1755. By Charles Wesley,
A.M., late Student of Christ-Church, Oxford. London:
Printed by J. and W. Oliver, No. 12, in Bartholomew-
Close. 1771. 8vo., pp. 8.

The recent death of Whitefield, which took place Sep. 30, 1770, may have led to the publication of this Epistle, written so long before. It is one of several similar poetical letters composed by Charles Wesley in the year 1755, of which one only, that addressed to his brother, was published at the time. The others were addressed to Howell Harris, Mr. Stonehouse, Vicar of Islington, and Count Zinzendorf. These, with another of earlier date, addressed to a Friend, were transcribed into a volume by the author, who gave it the title of *Epistles to Moravians, Presbyterians, and Methodists: By a Clergyman of the Church of England.* It bears the motto, "Other sheep I have which are not of this fold; them also must I bring, and they shall hear my voice; and there shall be one fold and one shepherd" (John x. 16). Jackson, who furnishes this information, thinks that Charles Wesley intended at some time to print the whole: but that design was not carried out. See *Life of Charles Wesley,* ii. 96-8. They are not all included in the *Poetical Works,* edited by Osborn.

This poetical Epistle is an exultation over the unity that had succeeded the sad estrangement between the Wesleys and their friend Whitefield. On Nov. 5, 1755, Wesley wrote, "Mr. Whitefield called upon me;—disputings are now no more: we love one another, and join hand in hand to promote the cause of our common Master."—*Journal.*

The Epistle begins—

    Come on my Whitefield! (since the strife is past,
    And friends at first are friends again at last),
    Our hands and hearts, and counsels let us join
    In mutual league, t' advance the work Divine:

and ends—

    His love the tie that binds us to His throne,
    His love the bond that perfects us in one;
    His love (let all the ground of friendship see),
    His only love constrained our hearts to agree,
    And gives the rivet of eternity.

278. AN ELEGY ON THE LATE REVEREND GEORGE WHITE-
FIELD, M.A., who died September 30, 1770, in the 56th
Year of his Age. By Charles Wesley, M.A., Presbyter of
the Church of England. Bristol: Printed by William
Pine. 1771. [Price sixpence]. 8vo., pp. 29.

Another, Dublin: Printed by W. Kidd, 1771. 8vo., pp. 23. Reprinted in Jackson's *Life of Charles Wesley,* vol. ii.; also in Charles Wesley's *Journals,* vol. ii.

The Elegy extends to 536 lines. It is a memoir in verse; a panegyric of a life spent in self-consuming service for mankind; a fervent outpouring of loving, brotherly appreciation of the character and the great labours of this mighty and honoured preacher. "Every line of it appears to have flowed from the writer's inmost soul. It describes, in pure and sterling English, the piety, zeal, talents, energy, and usefulness of the deceased ambassador of Christ, and glorifies God in him, as the sole author of all the good that he possessed and that he was a means of producing in others."—*Life of C. Wesley,* ii. 245.

Tyerman, after quoting the Elegy at some length, adds "Charles Wesley often wrote more polished poetry than this, but his loving lines truthfully portray some of the features of Whitefield's character, and likewise show the profound affection which he cherished for his brother George."—*Life of Whitefield*, ii. 612.

1772.

279. THOUGHTS UPON LIBERTY. By an Englishman. " I scorn to have my free-born toe Dragoon'd into a wooden shoe."—Prior. London : Printed in the year 1772. 12mo., pp. 21.

Dated at end, February 24, 1772.

Another edition, Bristol, printed in the year 1772, pp. 24, dated at end, March 10. This date is probably an error, as on the 9th Wesley set out for his north journey from Bristol, "after having spent a few comfortable days there." Another, Edinburgh : 1776.

A smartly-written patriotic tract in opposition to the foolish outcry for "liberty" raised by John Wilkes and the *Letters of Junius*. It asserts that real civil and religious freedom is enjoyed by every honest Englishman. "You see whence arose this outcry for liberty, and these dismal complaints that we are robbed of our liberty echoing through the land. It is plain to every unprejudiced man they have not the least foundation. We enjoy at this day throughout these kingdoms such liberty, civil and religious, as no other kingdom or commonwealth in Europe, or in the world, enjoys; and such as our ancestors never enjoyed from the Conquest to the Revolution. Let us be thankful for it to God and the King" (p. 20).

280. THOUGHTS CONCERNING THE ORIGIN OF POWER. Bristol: Printed by W. Pine, in Wine-Street. 1772. 12mo., pp. 12.

Neither signed nor dated. This and the tract on Liberty were inserted in the collected Works.

Political troubles were brewing from the spread of democracy. Wesley's position was that "*all power is of God*"—"the powers that be are ordained of God." The cry around was "the people are the source of power." He showed how, in the existing state of things, the *people* certainly did not confer power, nor make laws, even by their representatives, for not all men and no women had votes. "The supposition, then, that *the people* are the origin of power, is every way indefensible. It is absolutely overturned by the very principle on which it is supposed to stand—namely, that a right of choosing his governors belongs to every individual; consequently, not to freeholders alone, but to all men ; not to men only, but to women also ; not only to adult men and women, to those who have lived one and twenty years, but to those who have lived eighteen or twenty, as well as those who have lived threescore. But none did ever maintain this, nor probably ever will. Therefore this boasted principle falls to the ground, and the whole superstructure with it. So common sense brings us back to the grand truth, '*there is no power but of God.*'" As the case is thus stated it may not be difficult to detect a flaw in Wesley's logic.

This pamphlet and the former (No. 279) may have been published anonymously in order to avoid foolish prejudice against them.

281. PRAYERS FOR CHILDREN. Bristol: Printed by William Pine, in Wine-Street. 1772. 12mo., pp. 22.

London: Hawes, 1777; London: Cordeux, 1813; Another, London: Mason, 18mo.; Twelfth, London: Mason. n.d. 32mo.

Heylin erroneously assigns it to 1779.

In this pamphlet is given a brief prayer for the morning and evening of each of the seven days of the week, beginning with Monday; also a short prayer for relations, &c., "to be used after morning and evening prayer;" and two "Graces" for use before and after meals. A tender preface in plain and simple language is addressed to "My dear child." No signature follows. This little piece was not inserted in the first edition of the collected Works, which was being carried at this time through the press; but it appeared in the 1812 edition with the names of the days of the week prefixed and the preface signed John Wesley. The prayers were afterwards published "with suitable hymns (seven) annexed." The hymns were taken from *Hymns for Children* (No. 223). Subsequently the prayers for the Lord's Day were removed from the end to the beginning. Several editions with the hymns have since been published.

As we have already seen, Wesley paid very great attention to the preparation of books for the young, and in many ways sought to promote their best welfare. In the *Minutes of Conference* for 1768, amidst many advices given with a view "to revive and enlarge" the work of God, the following occurs, "But what can we do for the rising generation? Unless we can take care of these the present revival of religion will be *res unius ætatis*: it will only last the age of a man. Who will labour herein? Let him who is zealous for God and the souls of men begin now. 1. Spend an hour a week with the children in every large town; whether you like it or no. 2. Talk with them every time whenever you see them at home. 3. Pray in earnest for them. 4. Diligently instruct and vehemently exhort all parents at their own houses. 5. Preach expressly on this, particularly at Midsummer, when you speak of Kingswood."

That Wesley had carefully studied the requirements of little children is shown in his sermons on *Family Religion*, *The Education of Children*, and *On Obedience to Parents*: see *Works*, vii. 76-108.

282. MINUTES OF SOME LATE CONVERSATIONS BETWEEN THE REV. MR. WESLEY AND OTHERS. Leeds: Printed by J. Bowling, in Boar-Lane. 12mo., pp. 11.

Dated on p. 3, Leeds, Tuesday, Aug. 4, 1772.

Consists almost wholly of the stations of the preachers and the numbers of the members in the Societies in England, Ireland, and America. The total was 31,338, of whom there were only 316 in America. Details of finance complete the record. Four preachers only were after trial "admitted this year," of whom one was Joseph Benson.

283. SOME REMARKS ON MR. HILL'S REVIEW OF ALL THE DOCTRINES TAUGHT BY MR. JOHN WESLEY. (*Humanum est nescire et errare.* "Be calm," &c.—Herbert.) Bristol: Printed by W. Pine, in Wine-Street. 1772. 12mo., pp. 54.

Dated at end, Bristol, September 9, 1772.

This is one of the publications which grew out of the *Minute Controversy*, (see No. 267). Fletcher had written his *Second Check to Antinomianism*, which had called forth a pamphlet of 151 pages from Sir Richard Hill, entitled *A Review of all the doctrines taught by the Rev. Mr. John Wesley: Containing a full and particular answer to a book entitled 'A Second Check to Antinomianism.' In six Letters to the author of that book, &c., to which is added a Farrago of hot and cold medicines. By the Rev. Mr. John Wesley, Author of the 'Preservative Against Unsettled Notions in Religion.'* Extracted from his own publications. It is signed only "The Author of P. O." (*Pietas Oxoniensis*, a curious pamphlet relating to the expulsion of six students from Oxford.)

Hill accuses Wesley of inconsistency and self-contradiction, "Saying and unsaying is nothing new with Mr. W., who has only shown himself consistent by a regular series of inconsistencies" (page 10). "All his journals and tracts are replete with proofs of his having been tossed from one opinion and from one system to another, from the time of his ordination to the present moment." He cites 101 instances in which he affirms Wesley contradicts himself, as shown by passages from his writings arranged in parallel columns. Wesley deals with these passages one by one, explaining and defending his words throughout.

That the author of the *Review* wrote in a bitter, vituperative vein, and with rude extravagance of language, will not appear improbable when it is known that he charged John Fletcher with using a pen "dipt in gall," with having a "severe acrimonious spirit," and with being guilty of "sneer, sarcasm, and banter, yea notorious falsehoods, calumny, and gross perversions" (p. 2).

284. A SHORT ACCOUNT OF ANN JOHNSON, by John Johnson. See *Works*, xiii. 188.

This, though not written by Wesley, was probably edited by him; and he places it amongst his own published works. It does not appear to have been published separately.

285. PREPARATION FOR DEATH, IN SEVERAL HYMNS. London : Printed in the year 1772. 12mo., pp. 46.

No name of author, or publisher; nor either signature or date.

The hymns in this tract are mainly reflections in contemplation of death; some merge into supplication for grace to help in the final hour or for meetness for it. They represent the cry of the lowly, penitent, but trustful believer, conscious of unworthiness and of unfitness for the solemn change. There is an occasional outburst of rejoicing and hope; but none of the jubilant exultation of the *Funeral Hymns* already named (Nos. 96 and 197). They are all written as with death in view; and their general character is well represented in the closing verse :—

> This, this is all my heart's desire,
> When mercy doth my soul require,
> By Jesus found mature in grace,
> In full conformity divine,
> My spotless spirit to resign
> And see my Saviour face to face.

There are forty hymns of various metres, merely numbered; one only, the sixth, having any title (Isaiah xlvi. 4). Heylin says that there were forty other hymns on this subject left in manuscript; but in the *Poetical Works*

No. 285. [1772.

(see vol. vii. 394-421), only twenty-eight are added, three of which had appeared in the *Arminian Magazine*, Nos. lvii. and lviii. in the issue for 1780 (p. 397), and No. lv., under the title of *An Old Man's Prayer*, in that for 1781 (p. 228).

NOTE.—In this year appeared eleven volumes (vi.-xvi.) of the collected Works.

Vol. vi. In addition to the remaining two chapters of Law's *Serious Call to a Holy Life*, this volume contains extracts from his later works, including *An Extract from the Case of Reason, or Natural Religion, fairly and fully stated, In answer to a book entitled Christianity as old as the Creation; An Extract from A Serious Answer to Dr. Trapp's four Sermons on the Sin, Folly, and Danger of being Righteous overmuch; Some Animadversions upon Dr. Trapp's late Reply;* and *A Short but sufficient Confutation of Bp. Warburton's projected defence (as he calls it) of Christianity, in his Divine Legation of Moses, in a Letter to the Right Reverend the Lord Bishop of London.* These are taken from the first of two volumes published by Wesley in 1768, and entitled *An Extract from the Rev. Mr. Law's Later Works* (No. 252), the remaining portion of which volumes are inserted in

Vol. vii. The portions of Law's Works included in this volume are extracts from *The Spirit of Love;* from *Letters* to various persons; and from *An Address to the Clergy.* There does not appear to have been any revision of the former edition of these extracts from Law's writings. They are precisely reproduced in these two volumes, save that there are several *errata*, lists of which are given in these as in each volume of the collected edition. In many instances, the errors of the first issue are repeated. In this volume also is commenced *An Extract of the Christian's Pattern.* This is a slightly abridged reproduction of No. 26, but not verbally so accurate. To it is prefixed the preface from the small edition of *The Christian Pattern*, published by Wesley in 1735 (see No. 3).

Vol. viii. contains the remainder of the extract from *The Christian's Pattern* together with an extract from Norris's *Treatise on Christian Prudence*, one of Wesley's earliest publications (No. 2). It is here re-produced even with its errors. Then follows *Nicodemus: or a Treatise on the Fear of Man*, also an early publication of Wesley's (No. 12, 1739). It is re-printed without any alteration, except in the more moderate use of capital letters. The earlier edition, however, is more correct. The next piece is another extract from Mr. Norris's writings. It is entitled *Reflections upon the Conduct of Human Life with reference to Learning and Knowledge.* It is likewise an early publication, having been issued in 1741 (No. 25). The remarks made upon the relative correctness of the two preceding editions apply to these also, and to the last piece in this volume, first published in 1743, *The Life of God in the Soul of Man* (No. 51).

Vol. ix. contains the following reprints:—
    The Manners of the Ancient Christians. 1749. No. 123.
    The Doctrine of Salvation, Faith and Good Works; extracted from the Homilies of the Church of England. 1739. No. 9.
    An abridgement of *The Pilgrim's Progress.* 1743. No. 46.
    A Word of Advice to Saints and Sinners. 1746. No. 86.
    Christian Letters by Joseph Alleine. 1767. No. 241.
    A Word to a Sabbath-Breaker. 1745. No. 79.
    A Word to a Swearer. 1745. No. 78.
    A Word to a Drunkard. 1745. No. 77.
    A Word to an Unhappy Woman. 1745. No. 80.

A Word to a Smuggler. 1767. No. 239.
A Word to a Condemned Malefactor. 1745. No. 81.
A Word in Season : *or Advice to an Englishman.* 1745. No. 76.
A Word to a Protestant. 1745. No. 82.
A Word to a Freeholder. 1747. No. 104.
Advice to a Soldier. 1743. No. 44.

These are printed without abridgement, but there is the same lack of accuracy in printing that is observable in the previous volumes.

Vol. x. embraces ten pieces, all of which had been previously published. The first of them is entitled *Serious Thoughts Occasioned by the late Earthquake at Lisbon.* It was issued in 1755 (see No. 171). The "Postscript" there given is not inserted. The reprint is from the earlier editions. The second piece in the volume was first printed in 1733. It was Wesley's first publication, *A Collection of Forms of Prayer for every Day in the Week* : see No. 1, where an edition, the fifth, is described, which is exactly reproduced in this volume, except that the preface and a single foot-note at the end are omitted. After the title are the words, "First printed in the year 1733." This is followed by *A Collection of Prayers for Families* (No. 74). It has not undergone any alteration. *An Address to the Clergy* (No. 175), the next in order, is unchanged. The same is to be said of *A Short Account of the Death of Thomas Hitchens,* published in 1747 (No. 102); of *A Short Account of the Death of Samuel Hitchens,* published in 1746 (No. 89); of *A Short Account of the Life and Death of Nathanael Othen* (No. 188, 1758); and of *Some Account of the Life and Death of Matthew Lee,* issued in 1751 (No. 158). In this last case the Psalm and Hymn appended to the original edition are omitted. To these succeeds *An Extract of the Life and Death of Mr. John Janeway.* Wesley's first issue of the account of this estimable man under his own revision was in 1753 (see No. 159). It is here abridged, and a few sentences from an earlier account than Wesley's are added. The number of chapters is preserved. The remainder of the volume is occupied by the first two parts of *An Extract of the Life and Death of Mr. Thomas Haliburton* (No. 10). This was the first of the Extracts of lives of various persons which Wesley published. In this volume it is slightly abridged in the first part, and there are a few verbal changes elsewhere.

Vol. xi. Besides the remainder of the account of Mr. Haliburton, this volume contains *An Extract of the Life of Monsieur De Renty, A Late Nobleman of France.* It was first published in 1741 (see No. 21). It was the second abridged memoir that Wesley issued. It is reprinted here without change of any sort. Wesley greatly admired these men, and he circulated the Extracts far and near, urging both preachers and people to read them and frequently holding the subjects of them up as patterns of holiness and devotion. The remainder of the volume is occupied with *An Extract from the Life and Death of Thomas Walsh,* originally written by James Morgan, and published, with Wesley's brief recommendation, in 1763 (No. 215). Morgan's Preface is omitted, and his Introduction abridged. The whole work is judiciously curtailed by the omission of many of Morgan's notes and reflections and most of the poetical quotations. The text also has undergone considerable revision and abridgement. The order of the parts and chapters is preserved. The last chapter is given in the following volume.

Vol. xii. is mainly occupied with *An Extract of the Life of the late Rev. Mr. David Brainerd, Missionary to the Indians.* This is taken from Wesley's own *Extract of the Life of Brainerd* (No. 253), originally published by the Rev. Jonathan Edwards, Minister of Northampton, in New England. The work is substantially as Wesley first published it, though it has undergone revision and some abridgement. The Memoir is completed in this volume. Brainerd's letters and the Reflections and Observations are placed in the next volume.

No. 285. [1772.

Vol. xiii. In addition to the closing chapters of the above-named work there are several small pieces in this volume. The first is *An Extract of Miss Mary Gilbert's Journal*, which Wesley had published in 1768, and of which he spoke in highly commendatory terms in his preface (see No. 250). Of it this is an almost exact reprint, a few short sentences only in different parts of the Journal being omitted. This is followed by *An Extract from Elizabeth Harper's Journal*, first printed in 1769 (No. 256). Wesley's preface, containing remarks on Christian Perfection and some account of the life of Elizabeth Harper, is inserted. The Journal as originally printed is given without any alteration. The next is *A Short Account of Ann Johnson, By John Johnson*. This had not been previously published. Some brief references to it are made under No. 284. *A Short Account of Ann Rogers, By John Johnson*, succeeds. It is No. 263, and was originally published in 1770. It is reproduced without change. *A Short Account of the Death of Mary Langson* follows. This was originally written by Thomas Olivers. It was published in 1770 (see No. 259). In this volume it is abridged, a number of reflections which are dispersed through the account being omitted. Of the two hymns appended Charles Wesley's "Happy soul, thy days are ended" is given, but not the one attributed to Olivers. *A Short Account of the Death of Mrs. Hannah Richardson* is the next in order. It was written by Charles Wesley, and is the only one of his prose writings, except one sermon, that was published during his lifetime. It was issued in 1741 (No. 23). It is reprinted without any change. Although this is a comparatively short tract, it bears evidence of the clearness and force with which Charles Wesley could write. To this is added *A Letter to the Rev. Mr. John Wesley, By a Gentlewoman* [Miss Bosanquet, afterwards Mrs. John Fletcher]. It appeared in 1764 (see Note, p. 128), under which date an account of it is given. It will be seen that in these collected Works, Wesley has included several papers that are not from his own pen. The letter is printed as originally published, without any alteration. It gives particulars of her school and work at Leytonstone, of which Wesley wrote in his Journal, "I rode over to Leytonstone, and found one truly Christian family : that is, what that at Kingswood should be, and would, if it had such Governors " (Dec. 12, 1765) ; and again, "I preached at Leytonstone. O what an house of God is here ! not only for decency and order, but for the life and power of religion ! I am afraid there are very few such to be found in all the King's dominions" (Feb. 12, 1767). The remainder of the volume is occupied with *An Extract of Letters, By Mrs. L * * *.* [Mrs. Lefevre] : see No. 257. Wesley inserts his own preface as there given ; and nearly all the letters are re-produced in this volume just as they appeared in the earlier edition.

Vol. xiv. completes the *Letters of Mrs. L * * *.*, together with the small pieces found at the end of the original publication. To these are added *Letters written by Jane Cooper*, to which is prefixed *Some Account of her Life and Death*, with Wesley's preface (see No. 225). The whole is re-printed without change, as is the following, *Some Account of the Experience of E.J.* (No. 262). It will be seen that these very brief Extracts and Accounts are inserted without any regard to the order of their previous publication. Their being grouped together is in harmony with Wesley's plan as stated in his Preface. *An Earnest Appeal to Men of Reason and Religion* (No. 47), and *A Farther Appeal to Men of Reason and Religion*, Part i. (No. 63), complete the volume. At the conclusion of the former are the words, "Written in the year 1744," with a Hymn in two parts, of 30 stanzas altogether, entitled *Primitive Christianity*, which was appended to the second edition of the original work. In the *Farther Appeal* even the errors of the original edition are reproduced. The letter which is added in that edition is omitted, also one entire paragraph of the text.

Vol. xv. contains *A Farther Appeal to Men of Reason and Religion*, parts ii. and iii. (No. 64), which are re-printed entire ; also *A Plain Account of the*

People called Methodists (No. 126), first published in 1749. From this several portions are omitted. This is followed by *The Nature, Design, and General Rules of the United Societies* (No. 43), signed by John and Charles Wesley, and dated May 1, 1743, therefore taken from the second edition. Then follow *Minutes of some late Conversations between the Rev. Mr. Wesleys and others*. This is a reprint of the *Doctrinal Minutes* published in 1749 (No. 135), slightly abridged. To this succeeds not, as we might have expected, the companion volume to No. 135, the *Disciplinary Minutes* of 1749 (No. 136), but: MINUTES OF SEVERAL CONVERSATIONS BETWEEN THE REVEREND MESSIEURS JOHN AND CHARLES WESLEY, AND OTHERS. This is a fourth edition or reprint of the *Large Minutes*, and does not appear to have been published separately. It differs very slightly from the third edition, printed in 1770 (No. 268). The doctrinal principles of Methodism remained as at the beginning, without undergoing any change; but the methods of work, embodied in the successive editions of the *Large Minutes*, varied as necessity required. The remainder of the volume is occupied with two small reprints, both of which have undergone slight abridgement. They are *The Character of a Methodist* (No. 34), and *A Short History of Methodism* (No. 229). From the former, the hymn entitled *The whole Armour of God* is omitted.

Vol. xvi. contains eight reprints. The first, *Advice to the people called Methodists* (No. 73), is unaltered. *The Principles of a Methodist* (No. 35), was first published in 1742, but is here stated to have been "written in 1740," which must be an error, as the work it was designed to refute was not published till 1742. It is abridged by one considerable omission and by many minor ones. Many of the expressions also are varied. It is an important re-statement of some of Wesley's doctrinal views. It is badly printed, even the errors of the original being reproduced. The third piece is *An Answer to the Rev. Mr. Church's Remarks on the Rev. Mr. John Wesley's last Journal* (No. 65). It is followed by *The Principles of a Methodist farther Explained: Occasioned by the Rev. Mr. Church's Second Letter to Mr. Wesley, In a Second Letter to that Gentleman* (No. 87); *A Letter to the Right Rev. the Lord Bishop of London: Occasioned by his Lordship's late charge to the Clergy* (No. 103); *A Letter to a Clergyman* (No. 110); *A Letter to the Author of the Enthusiasm of the Methodists and Papists compared* (No. 140); and *A Second Letter to the Author of the Enthusiasm of Methodists and Papists compared* (No. 152). All these are reprinted without change, in many cases even the errors of the original reappearing.

1773.

286. THOUGHTS ON THE PRESENT SCARCITY OF PROVISIONS. London : Printed by R. Hawes, in Lamb-Street, facing Crispin-Street, near the Market in Spital-fields. 1773. 12mo., pp. 22.

Dated at end, Lewisham, Jan. 20, 1773. "Observed Friday, Jan. 8, as a day of fasting and prayer, on account of the general want of trade and scarcity of provisions."—*Journal*.

Food was dear and work was scarce ; the people therefore were starving. The eye of this ever-wakeful philanthropist was open to see all this. In a few plain words he states the causes of these evils, and propounds his remedies. "Bread-corn" was dear, he says, because such immense quantities were used in distilling—converting it thereby into deadly poison. Oats were dear because so many horses were kept. But the most terrible cause of all was luxury. Land was dear because, to increase their income and to meet the high cost of living, landlords raised their rents. Well nigh everything else was dear "because of the enormous taxes;" and the taxes were high because of the National Debt. "I have heard," says he, "that the national expense seventy years ago was in time of peace three millions; and now the bare interest of the public debt amounts yearly to above four millions!" He then names his remedies. His first advice is, Find the people work and "you'll find them meat;" then "procure vent for what is wrought" by sinking the price of provisions, "for then people would have money to buy other things too." Do this "by prohibiting for ever that bane of health, that destroyer of strength, of life and of virtue, *distilling;*" by reducing the number of horses, "laying a tax of ten pounds on every horse exported to France" and "an additional tax on gentlemen's carriages"; "by increasing the breed of sheep and horned cattle; by letting no farms of above an hundred pounds a year"; and especially "by restraining luxury, which is that grand and general source of want." He inquires whether this is to be done "by laws, by example, or by both—I had almost said by the Grace of God; but to mention this has long been out of fashion." Taxes are to be reduced by discharging half the National Debt, so saving the nation above two millions a year, and by abolishing all useless pensions," so saving "good part of a million more." Then, as in despair, he cries, "But will this ever be done? I fear not; at least we have no reason to hope for it shortly; for what good can we expect (suppose the Scriptures are true) for such a nation as this, where there is no fear of God; where there is such a deep, avowed, thorough contempt of all religion as I never saw, never heard or read of, in any other nation, whether Christian, Mahometan, or Pagan!"

287. SOME REMARKS ON MR. HILL'S FARRAGO DOUBLE-DISTILLED. By John Wesley. (Rom. xii. 18.) Bristol: Printed by William Pine. 1773. 12mo., pp. 44.

Dated at end, Bristol, March 14, 1773.

The issue of *Some Remarks on Mr. Hill's Review of all the Doctrines Taught by Mr. John Wesley*, published in the previous year (see No. 283), called forth a rejoinder from the author in a shilling pamphlet entitled *Logica Wesleiensis; or the Farrago Double-Distilled: With an Heroic Poem in Praise of Mr. John Wesley: By Richard Hill, Esquire;* London: E. and C. Dilly: 1773. To this Wesley here replies, in a tract of precisely the same character as the former—close, careful, logical, and vigorous. Tyerman says it is marked by his wonted keenness, courtesy, wit, and brevity. It was inserted this year in the collected Works, vol. xxiii.

As a sample of the kind of writing Wesley had here to reply to, the following may fitly be quoted. "'Poor Mr. Wesley,' says Mr. Hill, opening his cause with native eloquence, 'has published various tracts, out of which Mr. Hill collects above an hundred gross contradictions. At this Mr. W.'s temper is much ruffled;' (I believe not; I am not sensible of it;) 'he primes, cocks, and fires at Calvinism; and there is smoke and fire in plenty. But if you can bear the stench (which indeed is very nauseous) there is no danger of being wounded. He calls this last cannon, or pop-gun, *Remarks on my Review.* Men of sense say it is quite unfit for duty; men of grace compassionate the caster of it; men of pleasantry laugh heartily at it; but some good old women speak highly of it.' I give this passage at some length as a genuine specimen of Mr. Hill's manner of writing."—(pp. 3, 4). But the pamphlet after all, deals with important and solemn questions, and Wesley speedily adopts and maintains a dignity of address befitting them. One paragraph is written in a lighter vein.

In reference to the poem written in his praise, Wesley says: "Perhaps Mr. Hill may expect that I should make some return for the favour of his heroic poem. But

Certes I have for many days
Sent my poetic herd to graze.

And had I no:, I should have been utterly unable to present him with a parallel: yet, upon reflection, I believe I can, although, I own, it is rather of the lyric than the heroic kind. And because possibly he may be inclined to write notes on this too, I will tell him the origin of it. One Sunday immediately after sermon, my father's clerk said, with an audible voice, 'Let us sing to the praise and glory of God an hymn of mine own composing.' It was short and sweet, and ran thus:—

King William is come home, come home:
King William is come home;
Therefore let us together sing,
The hymn that's call'd Te D'um!"

He closes with several sound and searching appeals.

288. SOME ACCOUNT OF THE LIFE AND DEATH OF NICOLAS MOONEY. London: Printed by R. Hawes, in Lamb-Street, near the Market, in Spittle-Fields. 1773. 12mo., pp. 39.

Dated on p. 36, Newgate, April 23, 1752, and signed Nicolas Mooney, after which are "Some farther particulars relating to Nicolas Mooney."

Other editions, London: Hawes, 1776; London: Whitfield, 1796; London: Cordeux, 1810.

Not in Heylin, nor in the collected Works, but in the sale catalogues.

This is an abridgement of a pamphlet entitled *The Life of Nicolas Mooney, alias Jackson, Born at Regar, near Rathfarnham, in the County of Dublin: wherein is contained an account of his parentage and education, &c. The whole delivered by him to the Sheriff at the place of execution, and published at his own request*: Dublin: Golding, 1752. Second edition: Bristol, Felix Farley, and R. Raikes, Gloucester: n.d., 8vo,, pp. 48.

A most extraordinary account of human vileness ultimately cured by Divine grace. It was written at the poor creature's dictation when in a penitent state, and immediately printed. On the day of his death he gave a printed copy of it to the Sheriff, saying, "This was revised by me last night, and it contains nothing but the truth, and it is my desire it should be dispersed abroad as much as possible, to show my wickedness and God's goodness, who has forgiven me all my sins."

It is edited in Wesley's characteristic style, but there is not any apparent connexion of the story with the Methodists, though they may have been the persons who visited Mooney when in prison.

289. A SHORT ROMAN HISTORY. Bristol: Printed by William Pine. 1773. 12mo., pp. 155.

This must not be confounded with the *Short Roman History* mentioned in the *Journal*, Oct. 11, 1750,—"I prepared a short *History of England* for the use of the children; and on Friday and Saturday a short *Roman History*, as an introduction to the Latin Historians." It is clearly and instructively written, evidently with much care, and is in Wesley's most exact and succinct style. It forms a worthy addition to his numerous other school-books already noticed. It does not appear to have passed into a second edition.

It was taken from *The Roman History, from the building of Rome to the ruin of the Commonwealth*: By N. Hooke, Esq. A copy of the 4th ed. of this (London : Tonson, &c.), is in the Richmond College Library, with Wesley's abridgements marked throughout, as though he had prepared it for publication, or for use in Kingswood School: (see Note A on p. 71).

290. A Sermon on Romans viii. 29, 30. By John Wesley, M.A. London: Printed by R. Hawes, and Sold at the Foundry in Moorfields; and at the Rev. Mr. Wesley's Preaching-Houses, in Town and Country. 1776. 12mo., pp. 12.

Another, Bristol : W. Pine, 1776.

It is difficult to fix the time at which this sermon was first issued. It bears date Armagh (Saturday), June 5, 1773, and may have been published in Ireland first. It is given by Heylin (1773), but not by Osborn. I have not seen an earlier edition than the above.

The subject of the sermon is Predestination. It was re-published under that title in *Sermons on Several Occasions*, vol. v. p. 73 (No. 397). Wesley judges the passages of scripture relating to this subject to be of the things hard to be understood; especially is this evident, he thinks, "when we consider how men of the strongest understanding, improved by all the advantages of education, have continually differed in judgment concerning them. And this very consideration, that there is so wide a difference upon the head between men of the greatest learning, sense and piety, one might imagine would make all who now speak upon the subject exceedingly wary and self-diffident. But I know not how it is," he continues, "that just the reverse is observed, in every part of the Christian world. No writers upon earth appear more positive than those who write on this difficult subject. Nay, the same men, who writing on any other subject are remarkably modest and humble, on this alone lay aside all self-distrust,

And speak *ex cathedra* infallible.

This is peculiarly observable of almost all those who assert the absolute decrees." All that he pretends to offer, "not to the lovers of contention, but to men of piety and candour, are a few short hints, which perhaps may cast some light on the text." He then proceeds to expound in order each phrase of the text, and concludes, "What is it then that we learn from this whole account? It is this and no more. 1. God knows all believers. 2. Wills that they should be saved from sin. 3. To that end justifies them, 4. Sanctifies, and 5. Takes them to glory."

291. Minutes of some late Conversations between the Rev. Mr. Wesley and Others. London : Printed by Robert Hawes, (No. 34) Lamb Street, near Spital-Square. 12mo., pp. 12.

Dated at the beginning, London, Tuesday, Aug. 3, 1773.

These brief *Minutes* are distinguished by the following question and answer. " Q. 17.—Can anything be done now in order to lay a foundation for the future Union? Would it not be well, for any that are willing, to sign some articles of agreement before God calls me hence? A.—We will do it. Accordingly the following paper was written and signed: We whose names are underwritten, being thoroughly convinced of the necessity of a close Union between those whom God is pleased to use as instruments in this glorious work, in order to preserve this Union between ourselves, are resolved, God being our helper: 1. To devote ourselves to God: denying ourselves, taking up our cross daily, steadily aiming at one thing, to save our own souls, and them that hear us. 2. To preach the old Methodist Doctrines, and no other, contained in the Minutes of the Conferences. 3. To observe and enforce the whole Methodist Discipline laid down in the said Minutes." Then follow forty-nine signatures, among them being many of those who became prominent amongst the early Methodist preachers.

This brief declaration had already been brought forward at the Conference of 1769, from the Minutes of which we learn that it was originally designed as a means of preserving the preachers together as a united body after the death of Wesley (see *Revised Minutes*, 8vo. ed. pp. 88,89). It was brought forward again in subsequent years, and finally superseded by the Deed of Declaration. Stevens suggests that it is worthy of notice, as a proof of Wesley's growing conviction that Methodism would be compelled, sooner or later, to take an independent and permanent form.—*Hist. Meth.* Bk. iv. ch. vi.

"After the Societies began to increase there was nothing Mr. Wesley had so much at heart, as that the preachers and people should remain united after his death."—Myles, *Chronological History of the People called Methodists*, p. 128.

292. A Short Account of the Life and Death of Miss Alice Gilbert, who died August the 27th, 1772, in the nineteenth Year of her Age. London: Printed by R. Hawes, in Lamb-Street, facing Crispin-Street, near the Market, in Spital-fields. 1773. 12mo., pp. 25.

London: Hawes, 1776; an ed. 1790; London: G. Whitfield, 1798: On title-page, "Daughter of Nathaniel Gilbert, Esq., of the Island of Antigua."

This was probably written by Mr. Gilbert. It may have been revised by Wesley. It has not, however, even a brief preface, or recommendation by him, nor is his name attached to it, nor is it in the collected Works. It was sold at the Foundery, and was catalogued amongst Wesley's publications.

293. An Extract of Two Discourses on the Conflagration and Renovation of the World. Written by James Knight, D.D., late Vicar of St. Sepulchre, London. 1773. 12mo., pp. 31.

This is thus given by Heylin. Osborn inserts it under the same date and names Bristol as the place of publication. But he was afterwards led to believe that it was not published separately. The number of pages given by Heylin indicates that he must have referred to the pamphlet as it appeared in the collected Works. There is no evidence that it was ever published as a separate pamphlet by Wesley. It appeared only in the Works, vol. xx.

The discourses are founded on 2 Peter iii. 10, 11. They discuss (1) The extent and cause, the end and time of the general burning and destruction of all things. (2) The extent and cause, the end and time of the renovation. Wesley has not added any remarks.

294. AN EXTRACT FROM A TREATISE CONCERNING RELIGIOUS AFFECTIONS: In three parts. Part I. Concerning the nature of the affections, and their importance in religion. Part II. Showing what are no certain signs that religious affections are gracious, or that they are not. Part III. Showing what are distinguishing signs of truly gracious and holy affections. By the late Rev. Jonathan Edwards, A.M. and President of the College of New Jersey.

Preface by Wesley, dated Bristol, Sept. 1, 1773.

An edition, London: Conference Office, G. Story, 1801. Several editions of the original work issued in this country by different publishers, one of the most recent being a well printed one by the Religious Tract Society: n.d. 12mo., pp. xv. 500.

Heylin gives 12mo., pp. 69, which Osborn follows; but neither gives publisher's name. The figures are doubtless taken from a late edition. It does not seem to have been published by Wesley before it appeared in vol. xxiii. of the collected Works. It is not inserted in the catalogues until late in the century. The 1801 edition is the earliest separate one I have seen.

Edwards, Wesley tells us in his preface, had given, in three preceding publications, an account of a glorious work in New England, when "abundance of sinners of every sort and degree were converted to God," though in time many fell away. Wesley says the plain inference is "that a true believer may make shipwreck of faith." But Edwards was a Calvinist and declared that their falling away showed they were no believers at all. In order to prove this "he heaps together so many curious, subtle, metaphysical distinctions, as are sufficient to puzzle the brain and confound the intellects of all the plain men and women in the universe." It is out of this "dangerous heap wherein much wholesome food is mixed with much deadly poison," that Wesley selects what he thinks may be "of great use to the children of God." He does not insert Edwards's preface, and he greatly reduces the body of the work. "Edwards's works will live as long as powerful reasoning, genuine religion and the science of the human mind continue to be objects of respect."—Orme.

295. CHRISTIAN REFLECTIONS. Translated from the French.

There are 336 brief reflections, all numbered, each containing some good, practical, and elevated sentiment on the conduct of human life.

Again Osborn follows Heylin, who gives this under date, 1773, 12 mo., pp. 60. But Osborn, at least, was led to believe it had not been published separately, or previously to its appearance in the Works (Vol. xxiv.).

Appended is a short tract entitled :—

296. INSTRUCTIONS FOR MEMBERS OF RELIGIOUS SOCIETIES. Translated from the French.

The latter part is entitled *Directions to Preserve Fervency of Spirit.* At the end is the date, London, Feb. 26, 1768, on which date Wesley says in his Journal, "I translated from the French one of the most useful tracts I ever saw, for those who desire to be 'fervent in spirit.' How little does God regard men's opinions! What a multitude of wrong opinions are embraced by all the members of the Church of Rome! Yet how highly favoured have many of them been!"

These both appear for the first time in vol. xxiv. of the collected Works, published this year. Together with *Instructions for Children*, No. 62, also reprinted in vol. xxiv. of the Works, they were afterwards issued together under the title of *Instructions for Christians*. Many editions were published. One, a beautiful 32mo., 14th edition, London : Mason, 1836, is still kept on sale. *Instructions for Christians* is named frequently in the catalogues; *Christian Reflections* and *Instructions for Members of Religious Societies* do not appear in any, and were probably never printed separately.

297. SELECT PARTS OF MR. HERBERT'S SACRED POEMS. London : Printed by R. Hawes, in Lamb-Street, facing Crispin-Street, near the Market in Spitalfields. 1773. 12mo., pp. 32.

Neither preface nor signature.

The pamphlet contains about one-sixth of *The Temple*; but on what principle the selection was made does not readily appear. That the poems of " good Mr. Herbert," whom he held to be both "a wise and good man," were pleasing to Wesley is shown by his frequent quotations from them. Osborn is reported to have said, " It is a wonder Mr. Wesley did not abridge the Gospel according to St. John,"—a remark which one who was so familiar with Wesley's many abridgements, including the *Pilgrim's Progress* and *Herbert's Sacred Poems*, might well be led to make.

It does not appear in the catalogues, and was not reprinted.

NOTE A.—ADVICES WITH RESPECT TO HEALTH. Extracted from a late Author. 1773. 12mo., pp. 30.

This is thus given by Osborn, but it presents many difficulties. It is not mentioned in any of the catalogues of the time, or subsequently; nor is it named in any edition of the Works, or by Heylin, or Tyerman. Nor is it entered in the Inventory of the books on sale at the death of Wesley. The only approach to such a pamphlet that is known is in vol. xxv. of the collected Works, published *this year*, in which is contained, *Advices with Respect to Health* (previously published separately—see No. 255), the first thirty pages of which are, in some sense, preliminary—being general advices ; no specific disease is mentioned until after them. It is possible that a few copies of these were printed separately, the numbering of the pages being altered; or, as is more probable, the same mistake is made with this as with others in the same year, that of entering as separate publications what appeared for the first, or only, time in a volume.

NOTE B.—In this year, nine volumes (xvii.-xxv.) of the collected Works were published.

Vol. xvii. contains *A Second Letter to the Lord Bishop of Exeter in Answer to his Lordship's late Letter* (No. 154) ; *A Letter to the Rev. Mr. Potter* (No. 189) ; *A Letter to the Rev. Dr. Free* (No. 186—the former of the two letters addressed to Dr. Free in 1758 : the second letter is not included in the collected Works) ; and *A Letter to the Rev. Mr. Downes, occasioned by his late Tract*

No. 297. [1773.

intitled Methodism Examined and Exposed (No. 195). None of these have undergone any change. *A Letter to the Reverend Dr. Horne, occasioned by his late Sermon preached before the University of Oxford* comes next, with the words added "about 1762." Perhaps this is because the original letter had no date either on the title-page or at its close. More than ten pages of quotations from the *Appeal* are omitted. It is No. 209, and is followed by *Some Remarks on a Defence of the Preface to the Edinburgh edition of Aspasio vindicated* (No. 236). This is omitted from the table of contents at the end of the volume. It is dated at the beginning (but not in the original), Edinburgh, May, 1766. Some slight corrections are made, but there are many errors in the numbering of the paragraphs. *A Letter to the Rev. Dr. Rutherforth* (No. 249) comes next. This is dated differently from the original. It is slightly abridged, and there are a few corrections. Then follows *A Narrative of the Work of God at and near Northampton in New-England, Extracted from Mr. Edwards's Letter to Dr. Coleman*. This was first published by Wesley in 1744 (see No. 54). A few slight omissions are made; otherwise the original is reproduced without change. The volume also comprises *The Distinguishing Marks of a Work of the Spirit of God* (No. 49), and *Thoughts concerning the present Revival of Religion in New-England* (No. 66). Both of these were originally extracted from the writings of the Rev. Jonathan Edwards, Minister of Northampton, in New-England. The original extracts have been entirely revised, and considerably abridged.

Vol. xviii. opens with *A Brief Account of a Trial at the Assizes held at Glocester, the 3d of March, 1743*, extracted from Mr. Whitefield's Letter (No. 52). In this no change is made in the body of the work; Wesley's preface is given; but the hymn entitled *A Prayer for His Majesty King George*, appended to the original, is omitted. *Modern Christianity, Exemplified at Wednesbury and other adjacent places in Staffordshire* (No. 72) comes next. The last four pages of this are omitted. They contain Wesley's own account of his treatment at Wednesbury. It is given, almost in the same words, in his *Journal*, Oct. 19-21, 1743. There follow *The Case of John Nelson* (No. 56, revised and partially abridged); *A Letter to the Rev. Mr. Baily of Cork, in answer to a letter to the Rev. John Wesley* (No. 143, unchanged); and *A Letter to the Reverend Doctor Conyers Middleton, occasioned by his late Free Inquiry* (No. 121). This also has undergone no alteration. At the end of it is the piece entitled *A Plain Account of Genuine Christianity*, which was published as a separate pamphlet (see No. 122). The last piece in the volume is *A Letter to the Reverend the Lord Bishop of Gloucester, Occasioned by his tract on the Office and Operations of the Holy Spirit* (No. 216). This is inserted entire and without change.

Vol. xix. contains *A Letter to a Roman Catholic* (No. 134), originally published in 1749. It is inserted without alteration; as are also *A Roman Catechism: With a Reply thereto*, issued in 1756 (No. 179), and the following paper, entitled *A Short Method of converting all the Roman Catholics in the Kingdom of Ireland, humbly proposed to the Bishops and Clergy of that Kingdom* (No. 156), which is not included in the table of contents. The remainder of the volume is taken up with the following: i. *An Extract of a Short and Easy Method with the Deists*; ii. *A Treatise concerning the Godhead of Jesus Christ*; iii. *The Advantage of the Members of the Church of England over those of the Church of Rome*; iv. *An Extract of a letter to the Reverend Mr. Law, occasioned by some of his late writings*; v. *A Letter to a person lately joined with the people called Quakers, in answer to a letter wrote by him*; vi. *A Treatise on Baptism*; vii. *A Letter to the Reverend Mr. Toogood, of Exeter, occasioned by his dissent from the Church of England fully justified*. These form part of *A Preservative against Unsettled Notions in Religion* (No. 191), from which they are taken without revision or change. Following them is a paper (not from that volume), entitled *Thoughts upon Infant-Baptism, extracted from a late writer*. It is No. 149, and is reprinted without any variation.

Serious thoughts concerning Godfathers and Godmothers closes the volume. It is taken without alteration from the *Preservative*, as are the first three papers in the following volume.

Vol. xx. At the commencement of this volume are the following: *The Scripture Doctrine of Predestination, Election, and Reprobation; An Extract from a Short View of the difference between the Moravian Brethren (so called) and the Rev. Mr. John and Charles Wesley;* and *An Extract from a Dialogue between an Antinomian and his Friend,* all taken without variation from No. 191. At the close are the words, "The End of the Preservative." This means the end of the extracts from the *Preservative,* for in that work there are two other pieces, one of which, *A Letter to the Rev. Mr.*———[Hervey], is not inserted in the collected Works, whilst the other, *Reasons against a Separation from the Church of England,* is in a subsequent volume. The volume contains besides these the following: *A Dialogue between a Predestinarian and his Friend* (No. 24), inserted without change, and *Free Grace, a Sermon preached at Bristol.* This sermon was preached and published in 1739 (No. 11). Wesley did not include it in any of the collections of his sermons published by him, probably because it was the occasion of the painful separation of Whitefield. In the preface to the original edition he says that nothing but the strongest conviction, not only that what is here advanced is the truth as it is in Jesus, but that he was indispensably obliged to declare this truth to the world, would have induced him openly to oppose the sentiments of those whom he highly esteemed for their work's sake. The preface is not given in this volume. The sermon is inserted as it was at first published, together with the long hymn entitled *Universal Redemption.* It is followed by *Serious considerations concerning the Doctrines of Election and Reprobation, extracted from a late Author* (No. 16). It is reproduced with slight verbal alterations only. *Serious Considerations on absolute Predestination* (No. 22, unchanged), follows together with *Serious Thoughts on the Perseverance of the Saints* (No. 153, also unchanged); *Predestination calmly considered* (No. 155, unaltered, save that one entire section is omitted, being wholly a quotation from another writer); *The Consequence Proved* (No. 274, also unchanged); *Thoughts on the Imputed Righteousness of Christ* (No. 211); *A Blow at the Root: or Christ stabbed in the House of his Friends* (No. 212); and *A Sufficient Answer to Letters to the Author of Theron and Aspasio; in a letter to the Author* (No. 183). *An Extract of two Discourses on the Conflagration and Renovation of the World,* by James Knight, D.D., late vicar of St. Sepulchre, London, is published here for the first time (see No. 293). This completes the volume.

Vol. xxi. is a reprint of the work entitled *The Doctrine of Original Sin: According to Scripture, Reason, and Experience,* published in the year 1757 (No. 182). Only a slight revision of the earlier edition has been made, very few of the sentences being altered, and that but partially: even the dates at which the several sections of the book were written are inserted, as in the original. The latter portion is divided into parts, which is not done in the earlier edition, the many *errata* of which however are almost all corrected in this. The work requires a carefully prepared synopsis. This edition is reproduced in the third edition of the collected Works, 1829-31.

Vol. xxii. contains an exact reprint of No. 264, *Free Thoughts on the Present State of Public Affairs, In a Letter to a Friend;* of *Thoughts upon Liberty by an Englishman* (No. 279), to which is added a single foot-note; and of *Thoughts concerning the Origin of Power* (No. 280). These are the earliest of Wesley's political tracts. The first was published in 1770; the last two in 1772. These are followed by *Some Remarks on Mr. Hill's Review of all the Doctrines taught by John Wesley* (No. 283). It is unchanged in any particular; as is *An Extract of Mr. Baxter's Aphorisms of Justification,* where however the propositions, 33rd. to the 45th., are wrongly numbered. This was first published in 1745. It is No. 67. Nearly one-half of the volume is occupied with the first part of *A Treatise on Justification, Extracted from Mr.*

173

No. 297. [1773.

John Goodwin (No. 226). The *Preface*, "Wherein all that is personal in Letters just published, under the name of the Rev. Mr. Hervey, is answered," is given in full; but the extract from Goodwin's closely reasoned *Treatise* is much abridged, one whole chapter being omitted, with portions of several paragraphs. Unnecessary words and phrases have been eliminated, and the whole has been re-edited with care, though it is not accurately printed, one of the chapters is not numbered and another is wrongly numbered, and there are many other errors.

Vol. xxiii. commences with the second part of Goodwin's *Treatise on Justification*, continued from the previous volume. The number of chapters is preserved, but the same number is given to two of them, which with many other instances of the same kind shows the carelessness with which these volumes were printed. This part is abridged and revised similarly to the former. The synopsis of the whole, which appears at the end of Wesley's original work, is entirely omitted. There follows next *Reasons against a Separation from the Church of England*, first published in the *Preservative against Unsettled Notions in Religion* (No. 191). It was afterwards expanded by the addition of Charles Wesley's words of approval, and by an appendix of seven *Hymns for the use of the Methodist Preachers* (see No. 201). The next reprint is *The Christian Sacrament and Sacrifice: Extracted from a late author*, Dr. Brevint. Wesley issued this in 1745 as a preface to a volume entitled *Hymns on the Lord's Supper* (No. 83). It has undergone no change. This is followed by *An Extract from a Treatise concerning Religious Affections*, by the late Rev. Jonathan Edwards, A.M., President of the College of New Jersey, (see No. 294); and by *Some Remarks on Mr. Hill's Farrago Double-distilled*. The former first appeared in this volume, and the latter was published for the first time in this year, (see No. 287). It is inserted without any change. The last piece is *A Short Account of John Dillon* (No. 271). It is unaltered.

Vol. xxiv. begins with *A Plain Account of Christian Perfection as believed and taught by the Rev. Mr. John Wesley, From the year 1725 to the year 1773*. This was first published in 1766 (see No. 238). In this volume it has undergone the following changes,—The extract from the *Journal of Jane Cooper* (No. 225), extending to six pages (92-7), is omitted, also that portion of section No. 25 that follows the answer to question No. 38, (pp. 141-54), in which is a series of reflections, numbered 1 to 8. This is followed by *Instructions for Christians*, a re-publication of No. 62, published in 1745, and then entitled *Instructions for Children*. These *Instructions* are literally translated from *Les Principes solides de la religion et de la vie Chrétienne appliqués à l' éducation des enfants*, by M. Pierre Poiret, a Protestant mystic writer, the editor of Madame Guyon's Works, &c. The next two, *Christian Reflections*, and *Instructions for Members of Religious Societies*, are both translated from the French (see Nos. 295 and 296). After them appear *Thoughts on a Single Life* (No. 228, unabridged), and *A Letter to a friend concerning Tea* (No. 119), which is unaltered. This is followed by *The Desideratum: or Electricity made Plain and Useful, By a Lover of Mankind and of Common Sense* (No. 202). It is a verbatim copy of the first edition, published in 1760.

Vol. xxv. is devoted to *Primitive Physic: or An Easy and Natural Method of curing most Diseases*. It was originally published in the year 1747 (No. 101), and at the date of the issue of this volume it had passed through fourteen editions. The sixteenth was published in the following year. The prefaces, dated London, June 11, 1747, Bristol, Oct. 16, 1755, and London, Nov. 10, 1760, are given. The whole of the work has undergone revision. The number of ailments treated is increased from 274 as in the thirteenth edition, to 291; but the number of remedies is reduced from 939 to 925. A short additional preface is prefixed, dated Aug. 10, 1773. The remainder of the volume is occupied with the larger work entitled *Advices with respect to Health, Extracted from a late Author*. It is a reprint of No. 255, without any change whatever, even errors being reproduced.

1774.

298. THOUGHTS UPON SLAVERY. By John Wesley, A.M. London: Printed by R. Hawes, (No. 34) in Lamb-Street, near Spital-Square. 1774. 8vo., pp. 53.

Second edition, London: Hawes, n.d., pp. 28, smaller type; Third, London: Hawes, 1774; Another, Philadelphia, 1774.

The evils of slavery are sufficiently appalling to stir a slow pen and to move a cold heart to its denunciation. But Wesley had not a cold heart; nor did he wield an unready pen. Into these few pages are crowded as thorough a condemnation of this villainy as could well be put within such limits. To a brief account of the early history particularly of West Indian slavery, begun by the Spaniards and Portuguese in the sixteenth century, is added a description of the countries lying along the African coast for three or four thousand miles, showing the happy, peaceful, and prosperous condition of the industrious, law-abiding inhabitants, before the ravages of slave-hunting and trading began. The origin and the progress of the vile traffic are traced, as far as the space will allow, its horrid barbarity is described, and every attempt at the justification of its unmitigated wickedness is treated with scorn. The brutal cruelties practised in procuring, and transporting the poor creatures, and in their after treatment are fearlessly denounced; and the perpetrators of them are threatened with condign punishment from the righteous Judge of all. The whole is closed by appeals, exhortations, and entreaties to men, at all risks of loss, to abandon the iniquitous traffic, and to cry for mercy to Him who will not fail to avenge His suffering ones. Wesley was one of the first to denounce the evils of slavery.

See an interesting letter on slavery written by Wesley a few days before his death, and a note relating to this tract in the third edition of the Works, xiii. 128; also a letter in *The Arminian Magazine*, 1787, p. 44.

299. A SERMON, preached at the opening of the New Meeting-House, at Wakefield, on the 28th of April, 1774, by the Rev. John Wesley. Taken down in shorthand, at the time of delivery, by Mr. Williamson, a Teacher of that Art; and published at the request of many of the hearers. Leeds: Printed and sold by all the booksellers. [Price threepence.] 12mo., pp. 12.

The text is 1 Cor. i. 23, 24.

This was not published by Wesley. As the title-page indicates it was taken down in shorthand at the time of delivery; it has consequently its own special interest as a specimen of what may have been Wesley's method of *extempore* address. The style is very different from that of the written sermons.

"On Thursday I opened the new House at Wakefield. What a change is here, since our friend was afraid to let me preach in his house, lest the mob should pull it down! So I preached in the main street: and then was sown the first seed, which has since borne so plentiful a harvest."—*Journal*, April 28, 1774.

300. THOUGHTS UPON NECESSITY. By John Wesley, A.M. London: Printed by R. Hawes, (No. 34) Lamb-Street, near Spital-Square. 1774. 12mo., pp. 33.

Nos. 301-302. [1774.

Dated at the end, Glasgow, May 14th, 1774.

Second Edition, London : Hawes, 1775.

In a brief address to the reader, which is prefixed, Wesley tells us that he had finished what he had designed to say on this subject, when there fell into his hands an *Essay on Liberty and Necessity*, published some years before—"a most elaborate piece, touched and retouched with all possible care." This occasioned a considerable enlargement of the *Thoughts*. Wesley could not, he tells us, believe "the noblest creature in the visible world to be only a fine piece of clockwork."

He contends for the freedom of the human will against the old Manichæan and Stoical notions, against the Calvinistic views involved in the teachings of the Westminster Assembly of Divines concerning God's decrees, "whereby, from all eternity, He hath, for His own glory, unchangeably fore-ordained whatsoever comes to pass in time," and against the same views as developed by President Edwards. The last, carried to their logical issues, would, in Wesley's opinion, destroy all morality, in any true sense of the word, making man a mere machine, and leaving no room for judgment on human conduct, or for either its reward or punishment.

The theme is thus introduced :—"Is man a free-agent or is he not? Are his actions free or necessary? Is he self-determined in acting ; or is he determined by some other being? Is the principle which determines him to act, in himself or in another? This is the question which I want to consider. And is it not an important one? Surely there is not one of greater importance in the whole nature of things."

301. AN EXTRACT OF THE REV. MR. JOHN WESLEY'S JOURNAL, from May 14th, 1768, to September 1st, 1770. London: Printed by R. Hawes, (No. 34) in Lamb-Street, near Spital-Square; and sold at the Foundery, near Moorfields. 1774. 12mo., pp. 112. [No. xv.]

Second Edition, London : Hawes, 1775.

This extract of the Journal contains a most interesting record of indefatigable labours in travelling, visiting, and preaching in all parts of the country, and for some considerable time in Ireland; also of great diligence in reading in many departments of literature, together with the usual fruitful reflections on books, and men, and events. There is also an entry of a number of strange occurrences, real or imaginary, such as a "Spiritualist" would exult over, given at some length, concerning one of which Wesley says, "I proceed to as remarkable a narrative as any that has fallen under my notice. The reader may believe it if he pleases ; or may disbelieve it, without any offence to me. Meantime let him not be offended if I believe it, till I see better reason to the contrary."

302. MINUTES OF SOME LATE CONVERSATIONS BETWEEN THE REVEREND MR. WESLEY AND OTHERS. Bristol : Printed by W. Pine, in Wine-Street. 1774. 12mo., pp. 14.

Dated, Bristol, Tuesday, August 9th, 1774.

To the usual entries are added some practical suggestions, one being "Q.24. What can be done where we have no good leader? A. Let the preacher constantly meet the Society as a class." With a view "to lay a foundation for future union," a paper, similar to the one presented to the last Conference, was signed by the preachers.

303. An Extract from Dr. Cadogan's Dissertation on the Gout and all Chronic Diseases. 1774. 12mo., pp. 49.

So given by Heylin. Osborn also enters it under this date, but evidently, by his precise reference to the Works, with a doubt as to its separate publication. Subsequent inquiry justified this. There is not the slightest probability that Wesley issued it separately. It was prepared for his own edition of his collected Works, which was now in course of publication (*vide infra*).

"I read over Dr. Cadogan's ingenious treatise on Chronical Distempers. It is certainly true that 'very few of them are properly hereditary,' that most of them spring from indolence, or intemperance, or irregular passions. But why should he condemn wine *toto genere*, which is one of the noblest cordials in nature? Yet stranger, why should he condemn bread? Great whims belong to great men."—*Journal*, Sep. 9, 1771. "But there is another sort of intemperance, of which I think Dr. Cadogan does not take the least notice, and yet it is the source of more nervous disorders than even intemperance in food; I mean, intemperance in sleep; the sleeping longer than nature requires."—*Thoughts on Nervous Disorders* (see *Works*, xi. 511).

304. The First Part of an Equal Check to Pharisaism and Antinomianism; containing i. An Historical Essay on the danger of parting Faith and Works. ii. Salvation by the Covenant of Grace. A Discourse preached in the Parish Church of Madeley, April 18, and May 9, 1773. iii. A Scriptural Essay on the rewardableness of works, according to the Covenant of Grace. iv. An Essay on Truth, or a Rational Vindication of the doctrine of Salvation by Faith. (2 Cor. vi. 7). By the author of the *Checks to Antinomianism*. The Second Edition. Bristol: Printed by W. Pine, in Wine-Street, 1774. (Price One Shilling and Sixpence.) 12 mo., pp vi. 181.

Preface dated, Madeley, May 21, 1774.
This must be inserted amongst the many examples of Wesley's skilful use of the pruning-knife. The original work is comprised in 269 pages, 8vo. The following note at the end of the preface reveals his otherwise hidden hand and demands for the book its place amidst the numerous extracts and abridgements in the preparation of which so much of his time and labour was expended.—
"N.B.—I have considerably shortened the following tracts; and marked the most useful of them with a *.—J. W."

Note.—In this year the remaining seven volumes (xxvi.-xxxii.) of the collected Works were issued.

The first of these, vol. xxvi., commences with *An Extract from Dr. Cadogan's Dissertation on the Gout, and all chronic Diseases*. In a brief "Advertisement" Wesley informs his readers that a "few things in this excellent tract have been censured with some reason;" but that "they are omitted or altered in the following extract," which he therefore recommends "to men of understanding, as the most masterly piece upon the subject, which has yet appeared in the English language." This advertisement is followed by an address "To the Reader," in which he dissents from Dr. Cadogan's exaggerated condemnation of all smoked and salted meats, and pickles; also from the assertion that gout is not "an hereditary distemper," but is the product only of intemperance, indolence or violent passions. For, says he, "I am a living witness to the contrary. Those who know me do not charge me with intemperance in meat or drink. I am not indolent. I never travel much less than five thousand miles in a year, and I bless God I have no violent passions. Yet I have within these thirty years had the gout (of which my father was frequently ill and my mother died) nine or ten times." Neither can he subscribe to the "condemning of wine in general," for Dr. Hoffman shows at large that several sorts "are so far from being unwholesome, that they are some of the most powerful medicines yet known in some very dangerous diseases." And he himself was ordered by Dr. Cheyne, "not the warmest advocate for liquors," to take a small quantity every day, which contributed much to the recovery of his strength. "But," he goes on to say, "it seems we are to make a pretty large allowance for what the Doctor says on this head; seeing he grants it will do you little or no harm to take 'a plentiful cup now and then.' Enough, enough! Then it will certainly do you no harm, if instead of drinking that cup in one day (suppose once a week) you divide into seven, and drink one of them every day. I cannot but think if your wine is good in kind, suited to your constitution, and taken in small quantities, it is full as wholesome as any liquor in the world, except water; yet the grievous abuse of it which almost universally prevails might easily prejudice a benevolent man against it and make him endeavour to prevent the abuse by forbidding the use of it."

He equally condemns Dr. Cadogan's strong "prejudice against so harmless a thing as bread," and what he says "concerning the unwholesomeness of *flesh throughly* roasted or boiled." "But," he adds, "allowing the Doctor is not infallible, allowing him to be mistaken in these and a few other particulars, his general plan is truly excellent. No reasonable man who looks round about him can doubt, but ninety-nine chronical distempers in an hundred are occasioned by one or other of the causes, which he has so judiciously assigned. He cannot doubt but ninety-nine in a hundred of those distempers which are supposed to be hereditary, are really owing to one of these three causes, intemperance, indolence, or irregular passions." On each of these he makes a few comments, and closes by inquiring for "the cure for either lingering or impetuous passions, that either furiously overturn this house of earth, or sap the foundations of health and life, by sure though slow approaches." Here "the whole *materia medica* is of no avail." This is "a sickness drugs cannot cure. What can cure it but the peace of God? No other medicine under heaven. What but that love of God, that sovereign balm for the body as the mind?" Thus he finds opportunity even here for preaching the gospel of peace.

It is not a little interesting to observe this man of letters, the head of a great religious movement, finding time to condense a treatise on one of the evils that afflict a comparatively small number of mankind. It is another instance, added to the many that have already presented themselves, of the breadth of Wesley's sympathies and of his thorough devotion to the best interests, bodily and spiritual, of his fellow men. This is my apology for so lengthy a notice of this treatise.

The work of which Wesley has here presented an abridgement is entitled, *A Dissertation on the Gout, and all Chronic Diseases, jointly considered, as proceeding from the same causes; What those causes are: and a rational and natural method of Cure proposed: Addressed to all Invalids*: By William Cadogan, Fellow of the College of Physicians: The ninth Edition, London: J. Dodsley: 1771, 8vo. Wesley's extract is taken from this edition, part of the preface to which, dated Nov. 20, 1771, is given. Wesley has adopted his usual method of abbreviation, omitting whatever he thought to be superfluous, whether paragraph, sentence, or word; leaving only the plain argument of the writer. This volume also contains *A Short English Grammar*, an exact re-print of No. 113. One sentence only is added, at the end, "I cannot but subscribe to the remark of a late eminent writer, that in the simplicity of its structure the English far exceeds all modern tongues, and I verily believe all ancient too; at least all that I have any acquaintance with, Greek and Latin in particular." It is followed by *Directions concerning Pronunciation and Gesture*, first published in 1749 (No. 125). This is unaltered. The remainder of the volume is occupied with *An Extract of the Rev. Mr. John Wesley's Journal*, from his embarking for Georgia, to his return to London: Number i. first published in 1739 (No. 13). To this succeeds extract Number ii. extending from February 1, 1737-8, to Wesley's return from Germany (No. 18). These are exact reprints of the original extracts from the Journal.

Vol. xxvii. contains *Extracts from the Journal*, Number iii. from August 12, 1738, to November 1, 1739 (No. 37), and Number iv., November 1, 1739, to September 3, 1741 (No. 53). These are exact reprints, with the sole exception that in Number iv. the hymns entitled *The Means of Grace* and *The bloody issue*, which are appended to the original *Extracts*, are omitted.

Vol. xxviii. also contains two numbers of the *Extracts of the Journal*, v. and vi., the former extending from September 3rd, 1741, to October 27th, 1743 (No. 120), and the latter (No. 160) from October 27th, 1743, to November 17th, 1746. They are without change.

Vol. xxix. contains *Extract* Number vii., from November 25, 1746, to July 20, 1749, wrongly printed in table of contents, "From November 25, 1756, to July 20, 1751." It is No. 166, which see. From the end of this nearly eight papers are omitted. They begin, "I had now an opportunity of inquiring into the real state of the late transactions at Corke; an account of which is subjoined, being the extracts of some papers, which were about this time put into my hands." The pages omitted do not, therefore, relate to Wesley's personal history. *Extract* Number viii. follows, from July 20, 1751, to October 28, 1754. It is so stated on p. 184, but Number viii. is wholly omitted, the extract given being Number ix., extending from November 2, 1751, to October 28, 1754 (No. 194)—a striking instance of the carelessness with which these volumes are printed. Two long lists of *errata* occupy a page at the end of this volume.

Vol. xxx. This contains two numbers of the *Extracts*, Nos. 203 and 224. The first extends from February 16, 1755, to June 16, 1758. It is Number x., though here printed ix. The second is called Number x., but is in reality Number xi. It includes from June 17, 1758, to May 5, 1760. They are unabridged.

Vol. xxxi. contains Numbers xii. and xiii. (Nos. 240, 247), though called xi. and xii. The first is preceded by Wesley's Address to the Reader, dated London, Jan. 31, 1767. The *Extract* begins with May 6, 1760, and ends with Oct. 28, 1762. The second begins with Oct. 29, 1762, and extends to May 20, 1765. They are without abridgement. The *errata* are very numerous.

Vol. xxxii., the last volume, completes the *Extracts from the Journal* up to Sep. 1, 1770. It contains two numbers, xiv. and xv. (Nos. 270 and 301), wrongly numbered xiii. and xiv. They are unchanged. The errors are very numerous. There follows next *An Explanation of the Latin Sentences* (pp. viii). All the Latin quotations in the several volumes are given, with an English translation beneath each one. These are followed by a compact *Index* to each volume in order (pp. xxii).

It will be seen that although this collection of Wesley's prose Works contains nearly all the original works he had published, it also embraces several volumes, about a third of the whole, of extracts he had made from the writings of others. All the school books, both Latin and English, the *Grammars* and the Dictionary, the *Notes on the Old and New Testament*, the *Minutes of the Conference*, the *Large Minutes*, with two exceptions only, and the *Survey*, and other pieces, are all omitted. It cannot, therefore, be called a complete collection of Wesley's Works. It is greatly to be regretted that Wesley had not the opportunity of correcting for the Press, whilst the work was being printed. The mistakes are very numerous. To every volume is appended a list of *errata* larger or smaller.

A second collection of his Works, in 17 vols., 8vo. (of which the last two are bound together, vol. xvii. of 107 pages containing only indexes, though having a separate title-page), was published in the years 1809-1813, under the editorship of the Rev. Joseph Benson; and a third in fourteen volumes in the years 1829-1831. This was compiled by the Rev. Thomas Jackson, who had exceptional opportunities for producing a correct edition. It is beautifully and accurately printed.

1775.

305. A CALM ADDRESS TO OUR AMERICAN COLONIES. By John Wesley, M.A. "*Ne, pueri, ne tanta animis,*" &c.— Virgil. Bristol: Printed by Bonner and Middleton, in Castle-Green. 1775. 12mo., pp. 24.

Other editions, London: Hawes, n.d.; Bristol: W. Pine, 1775, "A new edition corrected and enlarged," pp. 16 and 8. In this edition a Preface "to the Reader" and *A Calm Address to Americanus, by a Native of America*, are added, and the twelve sections of the earlier editions are extended to fourteen, the seventh being enlarged and divided into three. Stevenson says the first edition of this pamphlet was published in four pages 4to., and that it was sold for a penny.—(MS. Note).

An agitation amongst the American colonists had thrown the nation into great excitement. The "grand question" debated was, "Has the English Parliament power to tax the American colonies?" Dr. Johnson had written a pamphlet entitled *Taxation no Tyranny: An Answer to the Resolutions and Address of the American Congress*. Wesley tells us that the reading of this pamphlet had entirely changed his views; and that as soon as he had received more light himself he judged it his duty to impart it to others. He therefore extracted the chief arguments, and added an application "to those whom it most concerns." And he says, "I was well aware of the treatment this would bring upon myself; but let it be, so I may in any degree serve my king and country."—Preface to the so-called new edition. "I made some additions to the *Calm Address to our American Colonies*. Need anyone ask from what motive this was wrote? Let him look round: England is in a flame! a flame of malice and rage against the King and almost all that are in authority under him. I labour to put out this flame. Ought not every true patriot to do the same? If hireling writers on either side judge of me by themselves, that I cannot help."—*Journal*, Nov. 11, 1775.

"About a year and an half ago, being exceedingly pained at what I saw or heard continually, I wrote a little tract entitled 'A Calm Address to our American Colonies.' But the ports being just then shut up by the Americans I could not send it abroad as I designed. However, it was not lost; within a few months, fifty, or perhaps an hundred thousand copies, in newspapers and otherwise, were dispersed throughout Great Britain and Ireland."—*A Calm Address to the Inhabitants of England*" (No. 316).

"Such, indeed, was the temper of the Americans, that a friend to the Methodists got possession of all the copies of the *Calm Address* which were sent to New York, and destroyed them, foreseeing the imminent danger to which the preachers would be exposed if a pamphlet so unpopular in its doctrines should get abroad. But the part which Wesley had taken could not be kept secret; the Methodists in consequence became objects of suspicion, and the personal safety of the preachers was often endangered."—Southey's *Life of Wesley*, ch. xxxvii., which see for extended notice of Wesley's political writings.

"Another fact which Dr. Clarke told me he received from Mr. Wesley was this: that when he published his *Calm Address to the American Colonies*, exhorting them to submission, he sent a private letter to Lord North, then at the head of the Government in England, pressing upon him the necessity of moderate counsels, assuring his Lordship, from what he knew of the Americans, that if matters were driven to an extremity, and war actually began, the Americans would assuredly gain their independence, and Great Britain lose some of her most valued colonies. The advice which Mr. Wesley voluntarily tendered was not taken, and the results of which he gave warning all ensued."
—Jackson's *Recollections of My Own Life and Times*, p. 246. The letter is given in Smith's *History of Methodism*, vol. 1, appendix E.

This pamphlet called forth a number of publications of various kinds. Amongst them were the following: *A Letter to the Rev. Mr. John Wesley occasioned by his 'Calm Address to the American Colonies,'* signed "Americanus." To this Wesley appended a reply in the enlarged edition:—*A Calm Address to Americanus, by a Native of America*. A second publication was called, *A Cool Reply to a Calm Address, Lately published by Mr. John Wesley:* By T.S. Toplady wrote his unworthy piece entitled, *An Old Fox Tarr'd and Feather'd: By An Hanoverian*. Mr. Fletcher entered the lists in defence of his friend, and published a pamphlet of 130 pages having the title, *A Vindication of the Rev. Mr. Wesley's Calm Address to our American Colonies, in some letters to Mr. Caleb Evans*. This was followed by a rejoinder of 103 pages by Evans; to which Fletcher replied in *American Patriotism further confronted with Reason, Scripture, and the Constitution*. For an extended account of the controversy which this address occasioned see Stevens' *History of Methodism*, Bk. v., ch. v.; Tyerman, iii. 185-201; Smith's *History of Methodism*, Bk. ii., ch. iii.

306. A SERMON ON 1ST JOHN V. 7. By John Wesley, M.A. Dublin: printed by William Kidd, for William Whitestone, Bookseller and Stationer, No. 33, Skinner Row. 1775. 8vo., pp. 31.

Another, London: R. Hawes, 1776, 12mo, pp. 23; Another, London, Paramore, 1782; also 1784. On both the latter are the words, "This sermon is not to be sold, but given away." Both entitled *On the Trinity;* inserted in *Sermons on Several Occasions*, vol. v. (No. 397).

In the first two editions appears an "Advertisement," dated Cork, May 8, 1775, prefixed to the sermon. In this Wesley tells us that he had been desired to preach on the text; that on the previous day he had done so, and was pressed to write down and print the sermon if possible before leaving Cork. He says: "I have wrote it this morning; but I must beg the reader to make allowance for the disadvantages I am under; as I have not here any books to consult, nor indeed any time to consult them."

307. MINUTES OF SOME LATE CONVERSATIONS BETWEEN THE REVEREND MR. WESLEY AND OTHERS. Leeds: Printed by J. Bowling. 1775. 12mo., pp. 12.

Nos. 308-309. [1775.

Dated August 1, 1775.
The following curious provision for supplying the places of deceased Trustees occurs:—
" *Q.* 20. Are not many of the Trustees for the preaching-houses dead? And are not others out of the Society? *A.* Let the remaining Trustees for each House meet as soon as possible, and indorse their deed thus (having affixt to it three new stamps :) *We the remaining Trustees for the Methodist preaching-House in* ——— *have this day, according to the power lodged in us by this Deed, chosen and named* ——— *to be* ——— *Trustees for the preaching-House aforesaid, in the room of* ———. *Witness* : *A. B., &c.*"
The classes which contain above thirty members are ordered to be divided. The names of eighty-one preachers are given, who "signed the agreement to adhere to each other, and to the old Methodist doctrine and discipline" (see Nos. 291, 302). The following words are appended : "N.B. We all deny that there is, or can be, any *merit* (properly speaking) in man."

308. THE IMPORTANT QUESTION : A SERMON PREACHED IN TAUNTON, SOMERSETSHIRE, on Monday, Sep. 12 [should be 11], 1775. By John Wesley, M.A. Published at the request of many of the Hearers, for the Benefit of a Public Charity. London : Printed by J. Moore and Co. 1775. 12mo., pp. 23.

Dated at end, Bristol, Sep. 30, 1775, when probably it was written out for the press. Text, Matthew xvi. 26.

Another, London : R. Hawes, 1776, pp. 23 ; another, 1785, "*not to be sold but given away.*"

Monday, Sep. 11 : "I preached again in the new meeting at Taunton, to such a congregation as I suppose was never there before. I was desired to preach on the same text as at Wellington, and it was attended with the same blessing."—*Journal.* The entry for the previous day was, "Sunday, 10. I came to Wellington [Somerset] in an acceptable time, for Mr. Jesse was ill in bed ; so that if I had not come, there could have been no service, either morning or evening. The church was moderately filled in the morning. In the afternoon it was crowded in every corner, and a solemn awe fell on the whole congregation, while I pressed that important question, 'What is a man profited, if he should gain the whole world, and lose his own soul?'" For an interesting incident connected with this sermon see *Methodist Magazine*, 1824, p. 568.

I have not seen a copy of the first edition.

309. A SERMON PREACHED AT ST. MATTHEW'S BETHNAL-GREEN, ON SUNDAY, NOV. 12, 1775. By John Wesley, M.A. For the Benefit of the Widows and Orphans of the Soldiers who lately fell near Boston, in New England. London : Printed by R. Hawes, (No. 40), the corner of Dorset-Street, Crispin-Street, Spitalfields. [Price Sixpence]. 8vo., pp. 33.

Dated at the end, Nov. 7, 1775. Evidently therefore written before delivery. Text, 2 Samuel xxiv. 17.

Another, London, 1784 ; New Edition, 1813.

"I was desired to preach in Bethnal-Green Church a charity sermon for the widows and orphans of the soldiers that were killed in America. Knowing how many would seek occasion of offence, I wrote down my sermon."—*Journal*, Nov. 12, 1775.

In this sermon, as in many of his writings at this time, Wesley, in strong terms, denounces the sinfulness of the nation, in the calamities of which he sees the righteous judgment of God.

In the third edition of the collected Works it is entitled *National Sins and Miseries*; but whether by the editor or by Wesley does not appear.

1776.

310. SOME OBSERVATIONS ON LIBERTY: Occasioned by a late Tract. By John Wesley, M.A. Edinburgh: Printed in the year 1776. 12mo., pp. 36.

Another, London: Printed by R. Hawes, and sold at the Foundry, in Moorfields, and at the Rev. Mr. Wesley's Preaching-Houses in Town and Country, 1776: 12mo., pp. 36.

The Edinburgh edition is probably the first, as Wesley wrote the tract when on his long journey, and he went through Edinburgh before returning to London; and further the nine *errata* of the Edinburgh edition are corrected in the London one.

The tract which "occasioned" the issue of this pamphlet was written by Dr. Price, a Unitarian minister. It was entitled *Observations on the Nature of Civil Liberty, the Principles of Government, and the Justice and Policy of the War with America*. Wesley contends that the liberty desired is not mere liberty but independence. "They claim to be independent of England; no longer to own the English supremacy." Against this claim Wesley argues with his usual keenness and ability. Dr. Price's tract was highly estimated. It is said to have been considered the ablest work in exposition of the injurious policy pursued by England towards America that had hitherto appeared. In approbation of it the London Common Council presented the author with the freedom of the city in a golden box.

"I began an answer to that dangerous Tract, Dr. Price's 'Observations upon Liberty;' which, if practised, would overturn all government, and bring in universal anarchy."—*Journal*, April 4, 1776. In travelling through the country Wesley tells us he diligently made two inquiries—the first concerning the increase or decrease of the people; the second concerning the increase or decrease of trade. In the former there had been "a very large and swift increase;" the latter had "amazingly increased." His reflection is, "Such is the fruit of the entire civil and religious liberty which all England now enjoys."—*Journal*, May 1, 1776.

"In his *Observations on Liberty* addressed to Dr. Price, in answer to a pamphlet of the Doctor's, which did its share of mischief in its day, he (Wesley) contradicted on his own sure observation the Doctor's absurd assertion, that the population of the country had greatly decreased; he commented upon the encouragement which was held out to the Americans in that pamphlet, and upon the accusations which were there advanced, that the British Government had secured to the Canadians the enjoyment of their own laws and their own religion, for the purpose of bringing up from thence an army of French Papists—for Dr. Price had not been ashamed to bring this charge against his country! In opposition to the Doctor's position, that liberty is more or less complete, according as the people have more or less share in the government, he contended, and appealed to history for the fact, that the greater share the people have in the government, the less liberty, either civil or religious, does the nation in general enjoy. 'Accordingly,' said he, 'there is most liberty of all, civil and religious, under a limited monarchy, there is usually less under an aristocracy, and least of all under a democracy.'"— Southey's *Life of Wesley*, chap. xxvii.

311. A SEASONABLE ADDRESS TO THE MORE SERIOUS PART OF THE INHABITANTS OF GREAT BRITAIN, RESPECTING THE UNHAPPY CONTEST BETWEEN US AND OUR AMERICAN BRETHREN: WITH AN OCCASIONAL WORD INTERSPERSED TO THOSE OF A DIFFERENT COMPLEXION. By a Lover of Peace (Luke xix. 41, Phil. iv. 5). Bristol: Printed and Sold by W. Pine. 1776. And sold by all the Booksellers in Town and Country. Price 2d., or 12s. per hund. to those who give them away. 12mo., pp. 18.

Second edition, Bristol: Pine, 1776, pp. 24.

An earnest and importunate address chiefly to the more serious, but also to the frivolous part of the nation, on the horrors of the fratricidal war in which the nation was engaged. Wesley strongly declaims against war as a means of settling this or any dispute; and he dwells at some length on the grievous suffering which must ensue from it. "A matter is in dispute relative to the mode of taxation. So these countrymen, children of the same parents, are to murder each other with all possible haste, to prove who is in the right. Now what an argument is this! What a method of proof! What an amazing way of deciding controversies! Now who that seriously considers this awful contest, can help lamenting the astonishing want of wisdom in our brethren to decide the matter without bloodshed! What, are there no wise men amongst us? None that are able to judge between brethren? But brother goeth to war against brother; and that in the very sight of the heathen. Surely, this is a sore evil amongst us! Oh! how are the mighty fallen. How is wisdom perished from the wise. What a flood of folly and madness has broke in upon us!" The causes of the war he finds in the conduct of the Government, but especially in the sinfulness, "the universal impiety," of the people, to whom he addresses fervent words of exhortation to repentance, that so the judgment of God, as he regards the horrors of the war to be, may be averted, and mercy may be showed to an evil nation. It is as the voice of one of the old prophets denouncing his people's wickedness, and threatening Divine punishments, unless, by timely contrition and the breaking off of the evil, punishment be escaped, and proffered mercy be accepted.

The pamphlet was written some months before its publication, unavoidable circumstances delaying its issue: and, "as things in general wore a worse aspect," a Postscript of six pages was added to the second edition, raising the total to 24 pp.

312. MINUTES OF SOME LATE CONVERSATIONS BETWEEN THE REV. MR. WESLEY AND OTHERS. London: Printed by R. Hawes, (No. 40), the corner of Dorset-Street, Crispin-Street, Spitalfields. 1776. 12mo., pp. 12.

Dated, London, Tuesday, August 6, 1776.

Statements having been made that some of the preachers were "utterly unqualified for the work, and that others did it negligently," they were "examined at large," and, as the result, one was excluded for inefficiency and two for misbehaviour. We learn that "Joseph Bradford travels with Mr. Wesley; John Atlay keeps his accounts; Thomas Olivers corrects the press." Regulations were made with a view to prevent (1) sluts from spoiling the houses; (2) the people from crowding into the preachers' homes, as into coffee-houses; and (3) the spread of Calvinism, "the grand hindrance of the work of God," which men "swallow greedily because it is so pleasing to flesh and blood, the doctrine of final perseverance in particular."

313. A Concise History of England. From the Earliest Times to the Death of George II. By John Wesley, A.M. In Four Volumes. Vol. 1. London: Printed by Robert Hawes, the corner of Dorset-Street, Crispin-Street, Spitalfields, and sold at the Foundry, Moorfields. n.d. 12mo., pp. ix. 335, 359, 348, 292, and Index 42.

Fourth Volume, only, dated 1776. Preface dated London, Aug. 10, 1775.

The principles on which Wesley compiled his History of England are sufficiently explained in the preface. He objects to the histories already written that they relate wholly unimportant incidents—"For instance: it no more concerns us to know nine parts in ten of what is contained in Rapin's History, than to know that on such a day 'a bird dropped a feather on one of the Pyrenæan Mountains'"—or they are too concise; or the historians lack judgment, or are biassed by partiality; or the histories suffer from a further defect, "there is nothing about God in them." These faults he tries to remedy. He makes use principally of Goldsmith, Rapin, and Smollett, "only with various corrections and additions." And "ten thousand dull passages are omitted; which could be inserted for no other purpose than to enlarge the volume, and consequently the price; to oblige the bookseller rather than the reader." He declares his wish to be "to habituate the readers of English History to see God pervading the moral as well as the natural world; to see Him in all civil events, as well as in all the phenomena of nature." "Let there be at least one History of England, which uniformly acknowledges this; let there be one Christian History of what is still called (tho' by a strong figure) a Christian country." It is a clear, concise record; and as full as the limits of four duodecimo volumes permitted. "At all my vacant hours in this and the following week I endeavoured to finish ' The Concise History of England.' I am sensible it must give offence, as in many parts I am quite singular; particularly with regard to those greatly injured characters, Richard III. and Mary Queen of Scots. But I must speak as I think; although still waiting for, and willing to receive, better information."—*Journal*, Jan. 27, 1776.

A personal friend of Wesley's thus writes:—"In historical compositions Mr. Wesley did not excel. His habit of generalising, and reducing to a few heads, every subject of which he treated, and the too great confidence he had in the authority of his own assertions, when he himself was convinced, in some degree indisposed him to enter into that detail of evidence from facts, so highly necessary to establish a general principle in history and biography. His works, therefore, of this kind have not the same merit as his other compositions."— John Whitehead, M.D., *Life of Wesley*, ii. 490.

An anecdote relating to this book, which is at least curious, rests on the authority of Mr. Thomas Olivers. It is to the effect that, finding he had made a profit of about £200 by the publication, Wesley gave it away in about a week. This is one part of Olivers' answer to Rowland Hill's scandalous assertion that Wesley "had an eye to profit :" (see *Rod for a Reviler*, p. 20).

314. AN EXTRACT OF THE LIFE OF MADAM GUION. By John Wesley, M.A. London : Printed by R. Hawes, and sold at the Foundry, in Moorfields, and at the Rev. Mr. Wesley's Preaching-Houses in Town and Country. 1776. 12mo., pp. 230.

Preface dated London, Nov. 9th, 1776, and signed John Wesley.

Madame Guyon's Memoirs, of which this is an extract, were written wholly by herself. Wesley, in his preface, very highly extols them, but though he judged them to contain abundance of uncommonly excellent things, there were, in his view, several utterly false and unscriptural. He endeavours to separate one from the other. "Such another Life," he says, "as that of the celebrated Madam Guion, I doubt whether the world ever saw. I am sure I never did." He believed her to be not only a good woman, but good in an eminent degree; deeply devoted to God, and often favoured with uncommon communications of His Spirit; but he thought her far from infallible, and all the more because she held herself to be incapable of being deceived. Her chief error lay in trusting to inward impressions, to inspirations as she called them, and in neglecting the plain guidance of the Word of God. In addition to a careful weeding out of what Wesley judged unscriptural, he placed notes at the foot of the page wherever it was necessary to contradict her opinion or condemn her practice. In these notes the reader is guarded against the errors which are common to most of the mystic writers : yet the Life is worthy of the high praise which Wesley accords it. It is the record of the most resolute struggles of a fervent soul intent upon attaining at all costs a perfect absorption in the will of God, and of the acutest sufferings of mind and body in so doing. "There are many excellent things in Madam Guion's Works; and there are many that are exceedingly dangerous. The more so because the good things make way for the bad ones. And it is not easy, unless for those of much experience, to distinguish the one from the other."—*Letter to Miss Ritchie* in Works, xiii. 41.

315. AN ACCOUNT OF THE EXTRAORDINARY DELIVERENCE OF THOMAS CROSS, one of the Bristol-Gazette Newsmen : who was overset in a small boat, crossing the New Passage, on the River Severn, on Sunday, Nov. 6, 1774, in company with seven other persons, who were all drowned. London : printed by R. Hawes, and sold at the Foundry, in Moorfields, and at the Rev. Mr. Wesley's Preaching-Houses in Town and Country. 1776. [Price one penny.] 12mo., pp. 12.

The account was written by Thomas Cross himself. It appears to have been edited by another, most likely Wesley, by whom also the "Advertisement" prefixed may have been written. It is named in the catalogues.

It was published at the earnest request of many persons, as "a caution to everyone who does not understand managing a boat, not to meddle with anything belonging to it on the water." So far it comes within the scope of

1777.] **No. 316.**

Wesley's benevolent work; but it cannot be said there is no doubt as to its having been prepared by him. His usual, though not invariable, plan of numbering the paragraphs is not observed.

NOTE.—THE SAINTS' EVERLASTING REST; or, a Treatise on the Blessed State of the Saints in their Enjoyment of God in Glory. Extracted from the Works of Mr. Baxter. London: printed by R. Hawes, and sold at the Foundry, in Moorfields, and at the Rev. Mr. Wesley's Preaching Houses in Town and Country. 1776. 12mo., pp. 442.

Another, 1780 (Osborn and Heylin), 12mo., pp. 335; another, London: Whitfield, 1798.

Other editions have always been on sale at the Methodist Book-Room. This book is a very interesting example of Wesley's method of bringing large works within the reach of ordinary readers. *The Saints' Rest* in its original form, is divided into four parts, containing forty-six chapters, and occupies 328 pages of double columns, folio; many of the pages being heavily laden with notes and long Latin extracts in smaller type. Wesley reduced the text to less than a fourth of its original size, omitting the whole of part ii., in which is a considerable digression from the subject of the work, also all the marginal notes and the extracts. The remaining thirty-six chapters are compressed to twenty-eight, and a table of contents is added.

To anyone who is wishful to understand how Wesley prepared his many handy *Extracts* of great books, and brought them within moderate dimensions without sacrificing any of their essential teaching, a better exercise could scarcely be suggested than the comparing this edition of the *Saints' Rest* with the original. It is only by some such examination that any correct idea can be formed of the extreme care, the patience and labour, which he expended upon the volumes.

Although this is mentioned here, being now for the first time issued in a separate form, yet it had been published twenty-two years before in the *Christian Library*, vol. xxxvii. (see p. 88). The only difference between the two is that in the earlier edition the table of contents is at the end, in the latter at the beginning. As it had been previously printed in another form, it is not numbered.

1777.

316. A CALM ADDRESS TO THE INHABITANTS OF ENGLAND. By John Wesley. London: Printed by J. Fry and Co., and sold at the Foundry, near Upper-Moorfields. 1777. 12mo., pp. 23.

Second edition, London: Hawes, 1777.

The reasons which led to the writing of this tract are thus stated:—" Hearing there was some disturbance at Bristol, occasioned by men whose tongues were set on fire against the Government, I went down in the diligence, and on Tuesday evening strongly enforced those solemn words, 'Put them in mind to be subject to principalities and powers, to speak evil of no man.' I believe God applied His word, and convinced many that they had been out of their way. Finding the repeated attempts to set fire to the city had occasioned a general consternation, on Wednesday I opened and applied those words to a crowded audience, 'Is there any evil in the city, and the Lord hath not done it?' On Thursday, I wrote 'A Calm Address to the Inhabitants of England.' May God bless this, as He did the former, to the quenching of that evil fire which is still among us."—*Journal*, Feb. 6, 1777.

The character of the pamphlet may be gathered from this extract. Wesley traces the course of recent events in America, and the rise of the rebellion there; contrasts the perfect liberty, civil and religious, enjoyed in this country with the absence of it there; and exhorts the people, and especially the religious portion, whether of the Church of England, Dissenters, or Methodists, to prize highly their privileges, and not to speak evil of dignities.

317. A SERMON ON NUMBERS xxiii. 23. Preached, Monday, April 21, 1777, on Laying the Foundation of the New Chappel, near the City Road, London. By John Wesley. London: Printed by J. Fry and Co., and sold at the Foundry, near Upper-Moorfields. 1777. 12mo., pp. 47.

Another, in smaller type. London: printed by R. Hawes. 1777. 12mo., pp. 24.

The words of the text, "What hath God wrought," are memorable to Methodists. Since their use on this interesting occasion, they have often been quoted as an acknowledgment of the divine interposition in the establishment and extension of Methodism, both at home and abroad.

In the sermon Wesley tells us that Bishop Gibson, of Gloucester, denied that there had been any extraordinary work wrought in England; and that Bengelius had placed the grand revival of religion in 1836, because, though "all the prophecies would incline him to place it a century sooner," yet he did not "know of any remarkable work of God wrought upon earth between the year 1730 and 1740." In the sermon Methodism is regarded as such a work; and is considered first in its rise and progress, and secondly in its nature.

The sermon is interesting from the circumstances under which it was preached, as well as from its own character. "Monday, 2, [21, this error is repeated in the subsequent editions of the Journal] was the day appointed for laying the foundation of the new chapel. The rain befriended us much by keeping away thousands who purposed to be there. But there were still such multitudes that it was with great difficulty I got through them to lay the first stone. Upon this was a plate of brass (covered with another stone), on which was engraved, 'This was laid by Mr. John Wesley on April 1, 1777.' Probably this will be seen no more by any human eye; but will remain there till the earth and the works thereof are burned up."—*Journal*.

The error in the date noted above, and in the date said to be engraved on the brass plate—April 1—are both corrected in Benson's edition of Wesley's Works (1809), and in Stevenson's *History of City-Road Chapel* (p. 67), to April 21, the date on which the foundation-stone was laid and the sermon preached, and the date which would appear on the stone. It is strange that Jackson in the third edition of the Works (1829) has repeated these errors.

"Although Mr. Wesley's intention seems to have been to defend his own position and Societies rather than to give offence to any, yet that sermon was made the source of a fierce controversy. It had not long been in print when the Rev. Rowland Hill, in defending Independency, published a furious attack on Mr. Wesley under the title of *Imposture Detected*. To this Thomas Olivers replied in a powerful and caustic pamphlet of sixty-four pages, entitled *A Rod for a Reviler*. Mr. Wesley also wrote and published *An Answer to Mr. Rowland Hill's Tract*" (No. 320).—Stevenson's *History of City Road Chapel*, p. 70.

318. An Extract of the Rev. Mr. John Wesley's Journal, from Sep. 2, 1770, to Sep. 12, 1773. London: Printed by R. Hawes, and sold at the Foundry, in Moorfields, and at the Rev. Mr. Wesley's Preaching-Houses in Town and Country. 1777. 12mo., pp. 119. [No. xvi.]

Another section of the story of this tireless evangelist's labours. It records the death of Whitefield, for whom Wesley thrice preached a funeral sermon, wishing "in every place to show all possible respect to the memory of that great and good man;" also a remarkable revival of the work of God in Wardale and Everton. It also contains Wesley's definition of the powers, the limited powers of the leaders, a definition rendered necessary by the state of the Society in Dublin.

319. Thoughts upon God's Sovereignty. By John Wesley, A.M. London: Printed by J. Fry and Co., and sold at the Foundry, near Upper-Moorfields. 1777. 12mo., pp. 11.

Third edition, London: Hawes, 1777; Fourth edition, London: Cordeux, 1817.

A brief tract, covering only eight pages of loosely printed matter. Wesley distinguishes between the two-fold character in which God reveals Himself—as a Creator and as a Governor. The purpose of the tract is shown in one sentence, "He will punish no man for doing anything which he could not possibly avoid, neither for omitting anything which he could not possibly do." Keeping this distinction in view, we shall "give God the full glory of His sovereign Grace, without impeaching His inviolable Justice." It was designed as a further defence against Calvinism. "On Saturday I wrote 'Thoughts upon God's Sovereignty.' To a cool man, I think the whole matter will appear to rest on a single point: As a Creator he could not but act on His own sovereign will; but as a Governor he acts, not as a mere Sovereign, but according to justice and mercy."—*Journal*, June 14, 1777.

320. An Answer to Mr. Rowland Hill's Tract entitled "Imposture Detected." By John Wesley, A.M. (Cant. viii. 6; Jude v. 9.) London: printed by R. Hawes, and sold at the Foundry in Moorfields; and at the Rev. Mr. Wesley's Preaching-Houses, in Town and Country. 1777. (Price one penny.) 12mo., pp. 12.

Dated at end, London, June 28, 1777.

Another, London: printed by J. Fry and Co. 1777. Three editions were published this year.

The pamphlet of forty pages 8vo. to which this is an answer is entitled, *Imposture Detected, and the Deed Vindicated, in a letter to a friend: Containing some gentle strictures on the false and libellous harangue lately delivered by Mr. John Wesley, upon his laying the first stone of his new Dissenting Meeting-House near the City Road:* By Rowland Hill, M.A. It bears date Wotton Underedge, May 15, 1777. A second edition is dated in the postscript Aug. 19, 1777: and announces that speedily will be published *A Full Refutation of Mr. John Wesley's pretended 'Answer' to the pamphlet entitled 'Imposture Detected.'*

"*Thur. 26.*—I read the truly wonderful performance of Mr. Rowland Hill. I stood amazed ! Compared to him, Mr. Toplady himself is a very civil, fair-spoken gentleman. *Friday, 27.*—I wrote an answer to it, 'not rendering railing for railing' (I have not so learnt Christ), but 'speaking the truth in love.'"—*Journal*, June, 1777. Wesley rightly complains that in the tract published by Mr. Hill there are several assertions which are not true, and that the whole pamphlet is written in an unchristian and ungentlemanly manner ; he justifies the one complaint and illustrates the other. Thomas Olivers, who wrote a reply entitled *A Rod for the Reviler*, told Mr. Hill that he might be mistaken for the chief of Billingsgate on account of his manner of attacking Wesley; and so anyone would think who cared to read Hill's unworthy words.

321. MINUTES OF SOME LATE CONFERENCES between the Rev. Mr. Wesleys and Others. Bristol : printed by William Pine. 1777. 12mo., pp. 10.

Very brief notes beyond the usual business. The Conference began on Tuesday, August 5, and ended on Friday, "as it had begun, in much love. But there was one jarring string ; John Hilton told us he must withdraw from our Connexion, because he saw the Methodists were a fallen people. Some would have reasoned with him, but it was lost labour ; so we let him go in peace."—*Journal*, August 8, 1777.

As the report had spread far and wide that the Methodist work was now decreasing, Wesley in the Conference particularly inquired into the matter. The uniform answer, he says, was, "If we must 'know them by their fruits,' there is no decay in the work of God among the people in general. The Societies are not dead to God : they are as much alive as they have been for many years. And we look on this report as a mere device of Satan, to make our hands hang down."—*ib.*

322. PROPOSALS FOR PRINTING BY SUBSCRIPTION THE ARMINIAN MAGAZINE : consisting of extracts and original treatises on Universal Redemption.

"I drew up proposals for the *Arminian Magazine*."—Journal, Aug. 14, 1777. See copy of the proposals in Tyerman's *Life of Wesley*, vol. iii. pp. 281-2.

323. A SHORT ACCOUNT OF THE DEATH OF ELIZABETH HINDMARSH, who died Sept. 6th, 1777, in the twenty-first Year of her Age. London : printed by R. Hawes, and sold at the Foundry, in Moorfields, and at the Rev. Mr. Wesley's Preaching-Houses, in Town and Country. 1777. 12mo., pp. 12.

Third edition, London : Hawes, 1778 ; Leeds : James Bowling, 1778.

This is another of the many examples of conversion, and of triumphant Christian death, which Wesley published. It seems probable that Miss Hindmarsh was a daughter of James Hindmarsh, one of Wesley's preachers, who was stationed in London at this time. The account may have been written by Mr. Bailey, one of the masters of Kingswood School, who very diligently visited her during the illness, in consequence of which she had gone to Kingswood, where Mr. Hindmarsh was once stationed, and where she died.

324. A Sermon Preached November 23, 1777, in Lewisham Church, before the Humane Society. By John Wesley, M.A. London : Printed by J. Fry and Co., and sold at the Foundery, Upper-Moorfields. 1777. [Price Twopence.] 12mo., pp. 24.

Text, Matthew xxv. 34. Dated at end, Nov. 21, 1777, probably the day on which Wesley finished writing it.

Entitled, in old catalogues, *Sermon before the Society for the Recovery of drowned Persons*. After making some reflections on good works in general, Wesley speaks at large of the special work done by this Society, and closes with a brief application. He appears to have written with ease, and with freedom from all restraint. He quotes six lines from Virgil in Latin, also from Herbert and other poets. He writes thus, "I preached in Lewisham Church for the benefit of the Humane Society, instituted for the sake of those who seem to be drowned, strangled, or killed by any sudden stroke. It is a glorious design, in consequence of which many have been recovered, that must otherwise have inevitably perished."—*Journal*, Nov. 23, 1777.

325. A Survey of the Wisdom of God in the Creation: or a Compendium of Natural Philosophy. In Five Volumes. The third edition, enlarged. By John Wesley, A.M. "These are Thy glorious works," &c.—Milton. London : Printed by J. Fry and Co., in Queen-Street, and sold at the Foundry, Upper-Moorfields, and by the Booksellers in Town and Country. 1777. 12mo., pp. 369, 335, 369, 348, 331.

Additional preface, dated March 25, 1775.

4th edition, London : Paramore, 1784 ; "A new edition, revised and corrected," 1809, 5 vols., London : Maxwell & Wilson ; 6th edition, Dublin : 1810, 4 vols. ; "A new edition, revised, corrected, and adapted to the present state of science," by Robert Mudie, was published in three volumes in "The Family Library series :" London, Tegg, 1835.

The first edition of this work in two vols. was published in 1763 (No. 220) ; the second in three vols. in 1770 (No. 265). The preparation of this enlarged edition must have involved much labour to one so engrossed as Wesley was. He tells us in the preface that he had finished the additions which he designed to make before seeing Dr. Goldsmith's *History of the Earth and Animated Nature*, the reading of which made him almost repent of having written anything on the subject, as the work had been done by one having both more time and more knowledge.

The third volume of the second edition consisted of notes on the several topics treated in the other volumes. These are now, with additional matter, incorporated in the work itself, and they occupy the first three volumes and a part of the fourth. The remaining portion of the fourth volume contains an abridgement of *The Contemplation of Nature*, by M. Bonnet, of Geneva. The

No. 326. [1778.

fifth volume comprises extracts from Duten's *Enquiry into the Origin of the Discoveries Attributed to the Moderns;* an Appendix on the Human Understanding written chiefly on the plan of Dr. Brown, late Bishop of Cork ; and a *Conclusion* mainly in the words of the Lord Chief Justice Hale. A brief note on p. 170 is dated London, Nov. 26, 1777. The Introduction and Conclusion are evidently Wesley's composition.

"I will beg you, with all possible diligence, to procure subscriptions for the *Philosophy.* Spare no pains. It will be the most complete thing of its kind of any in the English tongue. But it is well if I procure as many subscribers as will pay the expense of the edition."—Circular letter to the Assistants, in *Works,* xii. 449.

NOTE.—A PLAIN ACCOUNT OF CHRISTIAN PERFECTION, as believed and taught by the Rev. Mr. John Wesley, from the year 1725 to the year 1777. The Fourth Edition. London : Printed by R. Hawes, and sold at the Foundry in Moorfields, and at the Rev. Mr. Wesley's Preaching-Houses in Town and Country. 1777. 12mo.

Although this is called the fourth edition, an edition had been published since the third, and different from it, in vol. xxiv. of the collected Works, 1773 : see p. 174.

Fifth edition, London : Paramore, 1785 ; 6th, London : Printed and sold at the New Chapel, 1789; 8th, London: Story, 1801; 9th, London: John Jones, 1809; 17th, London: Mason, 1840.

This is not, in any sense, an additional work, nor is there anything to distinguish it from the first edition, 1766 (No. 238), except a few verbal alterations. It is the last of several revisions, and the title, as above, is used in all subsequent editions.

1778.

326. A LETTER TO THE REV. MR. THOMAS MAXFIELD, OCCASIONED BY A LATE PUBLICATION. By John Wesley, M.A. London : Printed by J. Fry and Co., Queen Street; and sold at the Foundery, near Upper-Moorfields, and at the Rev. Mr. Wesley's Preaching-Houses in town and country. 1778. [Price One Penny.] 12mo., pp. 11.

Dated at end, February 14, 1778. Signed John Wesley.

This was a year of trouble. "Never in his life," says Tyerman, "was Wesley the subject of more infamous press-persecution than in 1778." Many of these publications were of the foulest and filthiest description, and deserved only the silent contempt that Wesley gave them. Maxfield's publication differed wholly from these ; yet it contained several erroneous statements and grievous misrepresentations, and Wesley felt himself driven publicly to correct them. It must have been a painful sense of duty that compelled him to write as he did to one over whom he had both rejoiced and wept. Maxfield was his first laypreacher. Of him he could say, "Did you not eat of my bread and lodge in my house?" He had been Wesley's helper at the Foundry, rejoicing to serve him as a son in the Gospel. But he had come under the influence of men who wrought great mischief amongst the London Methodists, and who instilled false views into his mind. Wesley bore long and patiently with him, remonstrating, warning, intreating him, but all to no purpose. For more than fifteen years he was, as Wesley twice wrote, the head and fountain of the evil that afflicted the London Society. That Society he finally divided, drawing away numbers with him to a rival church which he established near Moorfields. Yet, notwithstanding his unparalleled ingratitude, Wesley visited him in his last illness, prayed with him, and even preached for him in his chapel. Tyerman has given an extended account of Maxfield's conduct and of Wesley's treatment of him (ii. 431-441). See also Wesley's *Journal* for the year 1763. It is in the light of these facts that Wesley's *Letter* must be read. It is a clear and firm reply, yet written in a calm and even tender tone to a once honoured, but now faithless friend.

327. A SERIOUS ADDRESS TO THE PEOPLE OF ENGLAND, WITH REGARD TO THE STATE OF THE NATION. By John Wesley, A.M. London: Printed by R. Hawes, and sold at the Foundery, in Moorfields; and at the Rev. Mr. Wesley's Preaching-Houses in town and country. 1778. 12mo., pp. 28.

It is addressed to "Friends and Countrymen," and is dated at the end, London, Feb. 20, 1778. A postscript occupies four pages.

The purpose for which this pamphlet was written is thus stated in the *Journal*, Feb. 17:—"I wrote 'A Serious Address to the Inhabitants of England,' with regard to the present state of the nation—so strangely misrepresented both by ignorant and designing men—to remove, if possible, the apprehensions which have been so diligently spread, as if it were on the brink of ruin." In pointing out the real, prosperous condition of the country he makes large use of a paper, written with the same intent, by the Dean of Gloucester; and he begs the people to be afraid of nothing but of the judgment of God.

328. A COMPASSIONATE ADDRESS TO THE INHABITANTS OF IRELAND. By John Wesley, M.A. Belfast: Printed by James Magee, at the Bible and Crown in Bridge-street. 1778. 12mo., pp. 11.

Written on Saturday, May 9, and dated at the beginning, Limerick, May 10, 1778. "I wrote a 'Compassionate Address to the Inhabitants of Ireland,' through which, as well as through England, the mock patriots had laboured to spread the alarm, as though we were on the very brink of destruction."--*Journal*.

He endeavours to rally the hearts of his "poor neighbours that they may not be frightened to death." He compares the armies of America and France with that of England to the great advantage of the latter.

329. A CALL TO BACKSLIDERS. A Sermon on Psalm 77: v. 7, 8. By John Wesley, M.A. Dublin: Printed in the year 1778. 12mo., pp. 23.

Dated at the end, Sligo, May 20, 1778.

Second edition, London: R. Hawes, 1778; 4th edition, London Hawes, 1778; Reprinted in *Sermons on Various Occasions*, vol. vii: 1788, but without the date.

It is difficult to determine why Wesley should at this time write a special sermon on this subject. He preached in Sligo on the 19th, and wrote, "Will God revive His work even in this sink of wickedness, and after so many deadly stumbling-blocks?" But he found, on inquiry, that there had been for some time a real revival of religion there, and that the congregations had increased and the Society nearly doubled. Possibly his attention had been called to the subject by his meeting on the 17th with "one eminent backslider, who had drunk in iniquity like water, who was utterly broken in pieces, and resolved to cut off the right hand at once, and to be altogether a Christian."—*Journal.*

It was written to encourage penitent backsliders not to cast away hope. It is a careful examination of those passages of Holy Scripture which such persons are apt to wrest to their grievous discouragement.

330. A BRIEF NARRATIVE OF THE REVIVAL OF RELIGION IN VIRGINIA. In a Letter to a Friend. (Psalm cxi. 2.) London: Printed by R. Hawes, and sold at the Foundery in Moorfields; and at the Rev. Mr. Wesley's Preaching-Houses in Town and Country. 1778. [Price Three-pence.] 12mo., pp. 35.

Third edition, London: 1786; 4th, 1779.

The chief portion of this narrative consists of a long letter addressed to Mr. Thomas Rankin, then one of the preachers in America, by the Rev. Devereux Jarratt, a clergyman of the English Church in Virginia, and giving an account of a very remarkable revival of religion in that part of the country. This bears date Sept. 10, 1776. The other part of the narrative is a further account by Mr. Rankin of his visit to Mr. Jarratt. It is addressed to Mr. Wesley, and dated June 24, 1778. It begins, "You have the narrative of the Rev. Mr. Jarratt: I send this as a supplement to it."

Dr. Bangs, who found Mr. Jarratt's account "inserted in Mr. Asbury's Journal," and republished it therefrom, speaks of Mr. Jarratt as "a minister of the English Church, who participated largely in that revival, and contributed by his labours to its advancement, by favouring the Methodist preachers, and administering the ordinances to such as desired them."—*Hist. Meth. Epis. Ch.* i. 90.

331. SOME ACCOUNT OF THE LATE WORK OF GOD IN NORTH AMERICA, in a Sermon on Ezekiel i. 16. By John Wesley, M.A. London: Printed by R. Hawes, and sold at the Foundery in Moorfields; and at the Rev. Mr. Wesley's Preaching-Houses, in Town and Country. 1778. [Price Two-pence.] 12mo., pp. 23.

Second edition, London: Hawes, 1778; 4th, London: Hawes, 1778; London: G. Story, 1788.

The words of the text are, "The appearance was, as it were, a wheel in the middle of a wheel." Wesley tells us his purpose was to deal with a few well known facts "relating to the late transactions in America." Starting with the year

1736, "when it pleased God to begin a work of grace in the newly-planted colony of Georgia," he traces that work for some time, until its arrest by the increase of wealth in the country, leading to pride, luxury, and other evils. This is one wheel; the other is the desire for independency, which he thinks is over-ruled "by the justice and mercy of God, first to punish those crying sins, and afterwards to heal them." Each "wheel" is first considered by itself, and then in its relation to the other; and the discourse closes with a promise of the time of blessing when the one wheel shall have counteracted the other. "Thus we have observed each of these wheels apart: On the one hand, trade, wealth, pride, luxury, sloth and wantonness spreading far and wide, through the American provinces. On the other the spirit of independency, diffusing itself from North to South. Let us now observe how each of these wheels relates to and answers the other: How the wise and gracious Providence of God uses one to check the course of the other, and even employs (if so strong an expression may be allowed) Satan to cast out Satan." However correct the thesis may be, the interpretation of the Scripture that is quoted is exceedingly fanciful, and not in harmony with Wesley's usual method. It is less a sermon than a record of events.

In the preface to an edition of Wesley's sermons, published in 2 vols, 1825, edited by T. Jackson, it is said that this sermon was re-printed with a few alterations about 20 years after it first appeared. The alterations are retained in the edition named. But in the 3rd edition of Wesley's Works, also edited by Jackson, it is restored to its original form. The alterations were confined to the last paragraph, and were left presumably by Wesley in MS. The sermon is not in the second edition of the *Works*.

332. MINUTES OF SOME LATE CONVERSATIONS BETWEEN THE REV. MR. WESLEY AND OTHERS. Leeds: Printed by James Bowling. 1778. 12mo., pp. 11.

Dated, Leeds, Tuesday, August 4, &c., 1778.
The following entries appear.—"Q. 19. Is it not advisable for us to visit all the jails we can? A. By all means. There cannot be a greater charity. . . . Q. 23. Why do so many of our preachers fall into nervous disorders? A. Because they do not sufficiently observe Dr. Cadogan's rules, to avoid indolence and intemperance. They do indeed use exercise. But many of them do not use enough: not near so much as they did before they were preachers. And sometimes they sit still a whole day. This can never consist with health. They are not intemperate in the vulgar sense: they are neither drunkards nor gluttons. But they take more food than nature requires; particularly in the evening. Q. 24. What advice do you give to those that are nervous? A. Advice is made for them that will take it. But who are they? One in ten, or twenty? Then I advise:—1. Touch no dram, tea, tobacco, or snuff. 2. Eat very light, if any, supper. 3. Breakfast on nettle, or orange-peel tea. 4. Lie down before ten;—rise before six. 5. Every day use as much exercise as you can bear;—or, 6. Murder yourself by inches."

332A. MINUTES OF THE CONFERENCE. Dublin: 12mo., pp. 6.

There is no title-page, or title of any kind; but only the date, Dublin, Tuesday, July 7, 1778, on the upper half of the first page.
This pamphlet is interesting as being the first printed *Minutes* of the Irish Conference. It was not generally known until recently that the Dublin *Minutes* for this year had been printed. The first mentioned by Osborn is for

the year 1783. A new edition of *Minutes of the Methodist Conferences in Ireland* (then for the first time published in a collected form) was printed in Dublin in 1864. It was "prepared under the direction of the Conference of 1863, by a committee to whom that duty was assigned." In it a short extract only is given from the English Minutes of the numbers in the Irish Societies; and the following note is inserted, "It is strange that the English Minutes for this year do not, as usual, give the Stations of the Preachers in Ireland. The reason of this omission cannot now be ascertained." The explanation is that the Irish Minutes for this year had been separately published. This seems to have escaped all observation, for on page 21 of the volume just quoted it is said, "The earliest Minutes of which any printed copies now remain are those of the following year [1783] which were published by Mr. Wesley, and from that date the publication has been continued with one exception [1791] to the present time." There is a copy of the Minutes for 1778 in one of two small volumes of Minutes, formerly in the possession of the late Rev. Samuel Bradburn, now in the Library of the Wesleyan College, Richmond.

One subject of great moment was discussed :—"Our little Conference began, at which about twenty Preachers were present. We heard one of our friends at large upon the duty of leaving the Church; but after a full discussion of the point, we all remained firm in our judgement—that it is our duty not to leave the Church, wherein God hath blessed us, and does bless us still."—*Journal*, July 7, 8, 1778.

"This summer [1778] Mr. Wesley held a Conference at Dublin. The Rev. Edward Smyth (who sometime before had been expelled from a Church in the North of Ireland, for preaching the truth) was now in connexion with the Methodists. He revived the controversy respecting the Church of England, and laboured, with all his might and with manifest uprightness of mind, to persuade Mr. Wesley and the brethren to separate from it. The debate ended by the Conference agreeing to the following propositions, which were afterwards adopted by the English Conference, and published in the [Irish] Minutes. Q. Is it not our duty to separate from the Church, considering the wickedness both of the clergy and of the people? A. We conceive not. 1. Because both the priests and the people were full as wicked in the Jewish Church, and yet God never commanded the holy Israelites to separate from them. 2. Neither did our Lord command His disciples to separate from them, He rather commanded the contrary. 3. Hence it is clear, *that* could not be the meaning of St. Paul's words, 'Come out from among them, and be ye separate.'"—*A Chronological History of the People called Methodists*, by William Myles, p. 141, 4th edition. This is nearly a verbatim extract from the *Minutes*. Myles at this time was a preacher in Ireland, and in all probability was present at the Conference of this year.

333. THE ARMINIAN MAGAZINE. Consisting of Extracts and Original Treatises on Universal Redemption. Vol. I. For the year 1778. London: printed by J. Fry & Co. in Queen-Street; and sold at the Foundery, near Upper-Moorfields, and by the Booksellers in Town and Country. 8vo., pp. viii. 600.

Three portraits. Preface dated London, Nov. 1, 1777.

"Having been many times desired, for near forty years, to publish a Magazine, I at length complied; and now begin to collect materials for it. If it once begin, I incline to think it will not end but with my life."—*Journal*, Nov. 24, 1777. See curious notice of the work taken from the cover of the first number, in Smith's *History of Wesleyan Methodism*, vol. i. Bk. ii. ch. iv. p. 411.

In his preface Wesley makes heavy charges both of erroneous teaching and of unbecoming methods, on the part of many persons whose widely-spread views it was his purpose to counteract by the publication of this Magazine. His aim was to maintain "that God willeth all men to be saved, by arguments drawn partly from Scripture, partly from reason: proposed in as inoffensive a manner as the nature of the thing will permit." To this end he designs to publish "some of the most remarkable tracts on the universal love of God, and on His willingness to *save all men* from *all sin*, which have been wrote in this and the last century."

Each number was to consist of four parts: "First, A defence of that grand Christian doctrine, 'God willeth all men to be saved, and to come to the knowledge of the truth.' Secondly, An extract from the life of some holy man, whether Lutheran, Church of England man, Calvinist or Arminian. Thirdly, Accounts and letters containing the experience of pious persons; and, Fourthly, Verses explaining or confirming the capital doctrines we have in view." In form it was similar to *The Gospel Magazine*, one of those publications whose spirit and teaching he so strongly and justly condemned. In this work Wesley's power of condensation is called largely into use in the many extracts made from voluminous writings, and brought within the compass of magazine articles. Each must be noted, as far as possible, for in this periodical he continued his former work of editing and abridging the writings of others for the benefit of the multitude. It is sometimes difficult to determine with precision which of the articles were thus prepared by him and from what works he took them. In this volume are the following:—

1. *A Sketch of the Life of Arminius*. Extracted from an Oration spoken at his Funeral.

The oration was delivered in the Hall of the University of Leyden, on the 22nd of October, 1609, by the Rev. Peter Bertius, Regent of the College of Divinity. It was placed at the beginning of the Dutch edition of the Works of Arminius. A translation may be found in Nichol's edition of *The Works of James Arminius, D.D.*, London: Longmans, 1825. Wesley passes over the eulogium and gives a brief outline of the Life of Arminius extracted and abridged from the Oration. It is an appropriate introduction, as the following and subsequent articles are appropriate contents of the first volume of the *Arminian Magazine*.

2. *An Account of the Synod of Dort*.

This is extracted from the third volume of *The History of the Reformation and other Ecclesiastical Transactions in and about the Low Countries. From the Beginning of the Eighth Century down to the Famous Synod of Dort*: By the Reverend and Learned Mr. George Brandt. Four vols., folio, London: John Nicks, 1722.

The extract is reduced from a long account contained in the first 312 pages of vol. iii., Bks. xxxiii.-xli. It must have involved considerable labour in its preparation.

From the same work were taken the portraits of several foreign personages that illustrate the early volumes of the Magazine, *e.g.*, Arminius (by G. Vertue).

3. *The Examination of Tilenus before the Triers*. "Wrote by one who was present at the Synod of Dort."

This is taken from Bp. Lawrence Womack's writings. Tilenus was professor of Divinity at Sedan. He was first opposed to Arminius, but was afterward convinced of the truth of the Arminian views, and threw in his lot with the Remonstrants.

4. *The Life of Martin Luther*. Written originally in German by John Daniel Hernnschmid. A succinct account of the life of the great Reformer, evidently extracted and edited with care by Wesley.

5. *An Account of Sebastian Castellio, and Michael Servetus.* This is taken from *The History of Persecution:* in four parts: by Samuel Chandler: London, 1736. It is an almost verbatim extract from book iv. sec. 2, pp. 312-322.

6. *A Discourse Concerning the Necessity and Contingency of Events in the World, in respect of God's Eternal Decrees:* By Thomas Goad, D.D. "Wrote about the year 1620." Dr. Goad was one of the Divines at the Synod of Dort. He was opposed to the Remonstrants, but afterwards changed his views. The Discourse appears appended to Bp. Womack's *The Result of False Principles,* 4to., London, 1761. It had also been republished in a Collection of Tracts concerning Predestination and Providence, Cambridge, 8vo., 1719.

7. *An Appeal to the Gospel for the true doctrine of Divine Predestination, concorded with the orthodox doctrine of God's Free Grace and Man's Free Will:* By John Plaifere, B.D. "Wrote about the year 1630." Plaifere was also a Remonstrant.

8. *The Life and Death of Bernard Gilpin.* Extracted from Bp. Carleton's Life of Gilpin. A Life was also written by Wm. Gilpin, A.M., Prebendary of Salisbury; second edition, with preface by Irving, Glasgow, 1830, evidently from the same source as Wesley's; but the latter is much abridged in Wesley's own style.

9. *God's Love to Mankind. Manifested by disproving his Absolute Decree for their Damnation.* "In a letter to ———." This is extracted from a very able work by Mr. Samuel Hoard, published anonymously, London: 4to., 1633, and subsequently.

10. *Thoughts on Absolute Predestination.* Extracted from Mr. Lesley.

11. *Bishop Patrick's Picture of an Antinomian.*

12. *The Life of Bishop Bedell.* Extracted from *Life of William Bedell, Bishop of Kilmore, Ireland:* London: Chiswell, 1638.

Several smaller extracts similarly prepared.

13. *Letter to the Rev. Mr. Hervey,* on the delicacy of sentiment necessary to preserve true friendship.

14. *Part of the 104th Psalm paraphrased.* Signed J. W. This is republished in the *Poetical Works,* Vol. viii. Some of the other pieces of poetry may be Wesley's; but they have not hitherto been distinguished. An entire page of *errata* shows the difficulties under which he laboured as editor, and his strenuous efforts to make his work accurate. Many original notes are interspersed throughout the volume.

Of the Magazine Dr. Stevens writes: "It was one of the first four religious magazines which sprang from the resuscitated religion of the age, and which began this species of periodical publications in the Protestant world. . . . Its importance to the history of Methodism is inestimable; that history never could have been written had not Wesley published this repertory of its early biographies and correspondence."—*History of Methodism,* Book vi. chap. v.

334. AN ANSWER TO SEVERAL OBJECTIONS AGAINST THIS WORK [The Arminian Magazine]. In a letter to a friend. Half-title, 8vo., pp. 4.

Dated Londonderry, June 5, 1778, and signed John Wesley.

It was written and published in reply to a long letter which Wesley had received from an anonymous correspondent, "wrote with a friendly design and in an excellent spirit," and containing a series of objections that "seem to be partly his own, and partly repeated from others." Wesley answers them *seriatim.* "The first is, 'It is too short: some magazines are almost as long again: there are not so many lines in a page by ten or twelve, as in the

Spiritual Magazine.' I answer by confessing the charge. It is undeniably true that it does not contain so many lines, either in prose or verse, as the *Spiritual Magazine.* And
'Tonson, who is himself a wit,
Weighs writers' merits by the sheet.'
So do thousands besides; but I do not write for these. I write for those who judge of books, not by the quantity but by the quality of them : who ask not how *long*, but how *good* they are? I spare both my readers' time and my own by couching my sense in as few words as I can, &c."

1779.

335. AN EXTRACT OF THE REV. MR. JOHN WESLEY'S JOURNAL, FROM SEPTEMBER 13TH, 1773, TO JANUARY 2ND, 1776. London : Printed by R. Hawes, and sold at the New Chapel in the City Road, and at the Rev. Mr. Wesley's Preaching Houses in Town and Country. 1779. 12mo., pp. 82. [No. xvii.]

This extract contains two letters published by Wesley, one in *Lloyd's Evening Post* respecting his motives in writing the *Calm Address to the American Colonies;* the other in reply to Mr. Caleb Evans in the *Gazetteer;* also an account of a very serious (and, as it seemed to his friends, probably fatal) illness, which he suffered in 1775, but from which he recovered in a very surprising manner ; and further an account of his incarceration in the Tolbooth, Edinburgh, on a false charge. The case was tried and the prosecutor fined a thousand pounds. It forms another portion of the record of Wesley's extraordinary labours, not a whit less interesting than any of the preceding portions.

336. POPERY CALMLY CONSIDERED. By John Wesley, A.M. London : Printed by R. Hawes, and sold at the New-Chapel, City-Road, and at the Rev. Mr. Wesley's Preaching Houses in Town and Country. 1779. 12mo., pp. 25.

The same in larger type, Dublin : Printed by W. and H. Whitestone, No. 29, Capel Street, 1779, pp. 35 ; Second edition, 1779, pp. 24 ; Third, 1779; Another, Edinburgh : 1779, pp. 26.

The brief preface, "To the Reader," explains the nature of this pamphlet : "In the following tract I propose, first, to lay down and examine the chief doctrines of the Church of Rome ; secondly, to show the natural tendency of a few of those doctrines, and that with all the plainness and all the calmness I can." In four sections, he treats of the Church and the Rule of Faith ; of Repentance and Obedience ; of Worship ; and of the Sacraments. These are followed by "a few considerations of a more general nature." Tyerman affirms this to be one of the most timely and valuable productions of Wesley's pen. Charles Wesley says he was told that some of the bitterest Calvinists were reconciled to his brother by the tract on Popery.—*Arm. Mag.*, 1789. The occasion of the writing of this pamphlet was probably his receiving information of the spread of Popery (see No. 339).

337. MINUTES OF SOME LATE CONVERSATIONS, &C., AT LONDON. Tuesday, August 3d, 1779. Printed by R. Hawes, (No. 40), the Corner of Dorset-Street, Spitalfields. 1779. 12mo., pp. 11.

A decrease in the numbers of the Society in twenty out of the sixty-one circuits led to the inquiry—"Q. 11. How can we account for the decrease in so many circuits this year? A. It may be owing partly to want of preaching abroad, and of trying new places; partly to prejudice against the King, and speaking evil of dignities; but chiefly to the increase of worldly-mindedness and conformity to the world. Q. 12. How can we stop this evil-speaking? A. Suffer none of those that speak evil of those in authority, or that prophesy evil to the nation, to preach with us. Let every assistant take care of this."

338. THE ARMINIAN MAGAZINE: For the year 1779. Consisting of Extracts and Original Treatises on Universal Redemption. Volume II. London: Printed by Frys, Couchman, and Collier, and sold at the New Chapel, near Upper-Moorfields, and by the Booksellers in Town and Country. 8vo., pp. viii. 664, vii.

Eleven portraits.
The original, or prepared, articles by Wesley are the following :—
1. *The Preface.* An address "to the Reader," dated January 1, 1779. It is a defence of the Magazine.
2. *An Appeal to the Gospel for the true Doctrine of Divine Predestination.* By John Plaifere, B.D. Concluded from the previous volume.
3. *God's Love to Mankind, Manifested by disproving his Absolute Decree for their Damnation.* By Mr. Samuel Hoard. Concluded.
4. *The Life of Bishop Bedell.* Concluded.
5. *The Scripture Doctrine Concerning Predestination, Election, and Reprobation.* Extracted from a late author. This is a reprint of a pamphlet published by Wesley in 1741 (No. 27).
6. *Thoughts on Salvation by Faith.*
7. *A Treatise concerning Election and Reprobation:* Extracted from a late author. To which the following paragraph is prefixed :—" To the Reader. It is impossible that the Predestinarians should, upon their own principle, have any occasion to blame me for the subsequent pages, since, if every action be the result of an irresistible fate (which it must be, or else their doctrine cannot stand), then an irresistible necessity rendered it impossible for me to do otherwise than I have done."
8. *An Account of Mrs. Sarah Ryan.* Written by herself, but evidently edited by Wesley.
9. *The Life of Dr. Donne.* Signed J. W.
10. *Predestination Calmly Considered.* A reprint of his own pamphlet published with the same title in 1752 (No. 155).
11. *The Life and Death of Archbishop Usher.* Published in a sermon at his funeral in the Abbey of Westminster, April 17, 1656. By Dr. Bernard.
12. *An Extract from the Minutes of a Conference, held at London, in August, 1779, between the Rev. John Wesley and others.*
To the above must be added the following letters :—
13. *Of Preaching Christ.* Dated London : Dec. 20, 1751.
14. *On Difficulties with regard to the Church.* To the Rev. Mr. Walker. Dated Bristol : September 24, 1755.

15. *On leaving the Church.* To the Rev. Mr. Thomas Adams. A reply. Dated Wintringham, October 31, 1755.
16. *On Christian Perfection.* Two letters to the Rev. Mr. Dodd. Dated February 5, 1756.
17. *Of a Catholic Spirit.* To the Rev. Mr. Clarke. Dated Castlebar, July 3, 1756.
18. To the Rev. Mr. Walker, in reply to one on *Advices concerning the Church.* Dated Kingswood, Sept. 3, 1756.
19. To Mr. N. on his charging Wesley with inconsistency and persecution.

There are many editorial notes interspersed. The accounts of different individuals, written by themselves at Wesley's request, were evidently carefully revised by him.

1780.

339. A LETTER TO THE PRINTER OF THE "PUBLIC ADVERTISER." Occasioned by the late Act passed in favour of Popery.

Dated City-Road, Jan. 21, 1780, and signed John Wesley.
This was afterwards published as a broadsheet, a copy of which is in the Conference Office Library, City-Road, London.

A pamphlet entitled *An Appeal from the Protestant Association* had been circulated. To it a "kind of reply" had also been published, a copy of which was put into Wesley's hands. This led him to write the letter named above, partly in defence of the *Appeal*, but mainly in consequence of the state of public feeling on the Catholic Disabilities Act, which at the time was exciting much attention. In the letter, Wesley asserts, "that no Government, not Roman Catholic, ought to tolerate men of the Roman Catholic persuasion." For, since the Council of Constance decreed that "no faith is to be kept with heretics," as also for other reasons stated, "no Roman Catholic can give security for his allegiance."

"Receiving more and more accounts of the increase of Popery, I believed it my duty to write a letter concerning it, which was afterwards inserted in the public papers. Many were grievously offended; but I cannot help it: I must follow my own conscience."—*Journal,* Jan. 18, 1780. Thus did he fulfil his determination to contribute his "mite to preserve our constitution both in Church and State."

The letter was afterwards reprinted in a pamphlet with two others: see No. 349. It evoked the unanimous thanks of the Protestant Association; and it was published in the organ of Wesley's bitterest antagonist, the *Gospel Magazine*, with an editorial note, that it had been almost universally approved of, and that it was a production of real merit.—See Tyerman's *Life of Wesley,* iii. 320.

340. AN ACCOUNT OF THE CONDUCT OF THE WAR IN THE MIDDLE COLONIES. EXTRACTED FROM A LATE AUTHOR. London: Printed in the year 1780. 12mo., pp. 55.

Also published under the title of *An Account of the Rise and Progress of the American War. Extracted from a late Author.* 12mo., pp. 56.

Second edition, London: 1780, smaller type, pp. 28; Fourth, London: 1780.

Nos. 341-342. [1780.

From the "Advertisement" prefixed we learn that the work, of which this is an extract, was written in order to contradict certain views of the war, which had been presented to the House of Commons, "to place the present national danger to the account of those to whose conduct alone it can be with justice imputed, and to expose to public view an attempt so inconsistent with the safety of the empire." It showed a strong bias in favour of retaining the American Colonies at all risks, which view Wesley shared, though he believed that end could have been attained by diplomacy without resort to arms. The Extract gives the writer's sentiments on the strength of the Middle Colonies, the general disposition of the people towards England, and the conduct of the war. He writes with obvious familiarity with the state of opinion in America, and with the scenes and circumstances of the war, which he describes with the clearness of an eye-witness. The work was written after his return to this country.

I have been unable to discover from what work this extract was taken.

341. REFLECTIONS ON THE RISE AND PROGRESS OF THE AMERICAN REBELLION. London : Printed by J. Paramore, at the Foundry, Moorfields. 1780. 12mo., pp. 96.

This is the largest and in some respects the ablest pamphlet written by Wesley on the American struggle, which he studied with so much interest. The measure with which he sympathised and which he strove here to advance was the establishment of a constitutional union in polity between Great Britain and the Colonies. He writes with a full knowledge not only of the opinions entertained in England and America, but of the history of the struggle, which he had watched with careful eye. The character of the pamphlet and its purpose may be gathered from its closing words : "I have briefly recited the causes of the present rebellion—the means by which it has grown to its present maturity—the state of American parties—the disposition of the colonists; to which I have added some general remarks on the incompetency of the measures proposed for reconciling the unfortunate dispute between the two countries, and on the prospect of success which other measures founded in the merits of the dispute must be attended with. If in doing this I shall have contributed to throw any light on the subject, or to point out those measures which will unite the two countries together, my purpose will be attained."

It is evident the writer wished not to be known, and there is no name of the author on the title-page; but it was not contrary to Wesley's practice sometimes to write anonymously. Some features of Wesley's style are wanting. But no doubt need be entertained as to its authorship. It was printed and sold at the Foundery, and announced in the catalogues.

The pamphlet, like several others, is not named in the collected Works, 1812 or 1829; nor is it referred to in the *Journals*, or, so far as is known, by any contemporary Methodist writer.

342. A LETTER TO MR. JOHN WHITTINGHAM. A broadsheet, dated, near London, July 13, 1780, and signed John Wesley. Printed by T. Luckman.

As a reply to Wesley's letter to the *Public Advertiser*, just mentioned (No. 339), a Mr. Whittingham issued a broadsheet in which he declared Wesley's statement that "the Council of Constance avows that no faith is to be kept with heretics," "a false assertion." He affirms, "No Council upon earth ever taught this." Wesley joins issue with him, and proceeds to prove his point.

Whittingham, in the course of his paper, made reference to some recent tumults in London, and implied that the Methodists were involved in them. Wesley declares that he "had nothing to do with them, being at the time two or three hundred miles from London;" nor were any of the Society concerned therein: both they and he totally condemned them. "Neither was it the Associators [members of the Protestant Association] who committed the outrages, but a mixt rabble of Protestants and Papists (some Papists were killed in the fact), who seized the opportunity, I fear, by the direction of wiser heads than their own." He concludes,—"If any man of sense has a desire to defend this bad cause, I am ready to give him an answer, but I have not time to answer every one that has a fancy to nibble at John Wesley."

A copy of the broadsheet is in the Allan Library. Whittingham's broadsheet drew forth another entitled *Popery Exposed and J. Wesley Vindicated*, signed *Philalethes*, and sold by T. Luckman. A copy is in the Wesleyan Conference Office, City Road, London.

343. MINUTES OF SOME LATE CONVERSATIONS BETWEEN THE REV. MR. JOHN AND CHARLES WESLEY AND OTHERS. Begun at Bristol, Tuesday, August 1, 1780. Bristol: Printed by William Pine, in Wine Street. 12mo., pp. 11.

There are no new regulations printed in this year's *Minutes*. The main business of the Conference, beyond its routine, was "to revise and inforce the Large Minutes of the Conference."

"Our Conference began. We have been always hitherto straitened for time. It was now resolved, 'For the future we will allow nine or ten days for each Conference, that everything relating to the carrying on of the work of God may be maturely considered.'"—*Journal*, Aug. 1, 1780.

344. MINUTES OF SEVERAL CONVERSATIONS BETWEEN THE REVEREND MR. JOHN AND CHARLES WESLEY AND OTHERS. From the year 1744 to the year 1780. London: Printed by J. Paramore, at the Foundry, Moorfields. 12mo., pp. 52.

This is the fifth edition of the *Large Minutes*.

In the first volume of the *Revised Minutes* (London: Mason, 1862) the several editions of the *Large Minutes* are printed at the end in parallel columns. On comparing these, it will be seen that the fifth edition varies considerably from the previous ones. In the ten years which intervened between the issuing of the third and of the fifth, no great legislative changes had been made. The alterations are mainly in the order in which the questions and answers are placed, the substitution of some new regulations for old ones, and the addition of a few others relating to health and preaching. The "Minute" against separating from the Church, passed at the Irish Conference in 1778 (see Note in that year No. 332A), is inserted. Special inquiries are instituted respecting "the decrease of the work of God" in some of the circuits; and the general advices as to what could be done to revive the work are expanded. The whole of the edition of 1772 is thoroughly revised, and in many parts abridged.

Nos. 345-346. [1780.

" "I began reading and explaining to the Society the Large Minutes of the Conference. I desire to do all things openly and above board. I would have all the world, and especially all of our Society, see not only all the steps we take, but the reasons why we take them."—*Journal*, Dec. 10, 1780.

345. DIRECTIONS FOR RENEWING OUR COVENANT WITH GOD. London : Printed by J. Paramore at the Foundry, Moorfields ; and sold at the New Chapel, in the City-Road ; and at the Rev. Mr. Wesley's Preaching-Houses in Town and Country. 1780. 12mo., pp. 23.

Second edition, London : 1781 ; Third, London : Paramore, 1784 ; Fourth, 1787. Many subsequently.

Wesley introduced the practice of renewing the Covenant in the year 1755. He says, "I mentioned to the congregation another means of increasing serious religion, which had been frequently practised by our forefathers, and attended with eminent blessing ; namely, the joining in a covenant to serve God with all our soul."—*Journal*, Aug. 6. The form in use was extracted from Richard Alleine's *Vindication of Godliness*, which Wesley had published two years before in the thirtieth volume of the *Christian Library* (No. 131). He does not appear to have published a separate form before the one now under notice.

Some of the preachers printed this or portions of it before a copy was issued from the Foundry Book-Room. One is entitled *Extract from the Thirtieth Volume of the Christian Library, published by Rev. Mr. Wesley*. Printed in the year 1779, 12mo., pp. 12. In a preface, dated Sheffield, Dec. 10, 1779, and signed Tho. Lee (the superintendent preacher), it is stated that this is what he read on New Year's Day at the renewal of the Covenant. And he goes on to say that at two o'clock in the afternoon they had preaching "in the principal places," and afterwards the Society remained, and after singing and prayer he read the extract, the people sitting, until he came to "the covenanting and prayer." Then they stood up or knelt down, and in a solemn manner renewed their covenant bonds, closing with prayer. He speaks of its having "always been an uncommon season" both to himself and the people. And he desires the practice should become uniform, even in little country places. The wish to promote the general good of souls was Lee's one motive in desiring that the form might be published. His extract ends at the close of the fifth Direction, and does not include the words of the Covenant.

Wesley's *Directions* continued in use without alteration for the greater part of a century. Some slight changes have been made in recent editions. It is still used in all the Methodist Societies.

346. THE ARMINIAN MAGAZINE, for the year 1780. Consisting of Extracts and Original Treatises on Universal Redemption. Volume III. London : Printed by J. Paramore, at the Foundry; and sold at the New Chapel, City-Road, and by all the Booksellers in Town and Country. 8vo., pp. 680, viii.

The following are either original articles by Wesley, or extracts made by him :—

1. *Address to the Reader:* dated Jan. 1, 1780.

In it he defends the character of the Magazine, and intimates that he has large stores of original and other writings already prepared for future issues. Referring to the chief object he had in view in commencing the Journal, he says, " In the last two years I have published some of the best tracts which I ever met with upon the Arminian controversy, such as I am fully persuaded never were and never will be answered."

2. *An Exposition of the ninth chapter of the Epistle to the Romans.* Extracted from John Goodwin.

This is a carefully prepared extract from Goodwin's well-known work, first published in 1653. It is abridged in Wesley's characteristic way.

3. *The Life of Armelle Nicholas.* The Life of Armelle was originally written in French by an intimate female friend, and published in two vols., 12mo. An extract was published in English, by S. Farley, Bristol, 1772, under the title of *Life of Armelle Nicholas, commonly called the Good Armelle; a poor maid-servant in France, who could not read a letter in a book, and yet a noble and happy servant of the King of Kings.* Wesley's is an extract from this translation.

4. *Fate and Destiny, inconsistent with Christianity: In eight Conferences between Epenetus and Eutychus.* Extracted from Mr. Edward Bird, by John Wesley, M.A.

5. *The Life of Gregory Lopez.* This is a further revision of the Life of Lopez prepared by Wesley, and first published by him in the fiftieth volume of the *Christian Library* (see Note, p. 95). One chapter is entirely omitted, apparently by accident.

6. *A Thought on Necessity.*

7. *An Extract from the Minutes of a Conference, held at Bristol in August, 1780, between Rev. John and Charles Wesley and others.*

8. *An Exposition of the Seventh Chapter of the Epistle to the Romans.* Extracted from a late author.

9. *Thoughts upon Taste.*

To these must be added the *Accounts* of Thomas Lee, Alexander Mather, John Haime, and Thomas Mitchell. They were written at Wesley's request by the men themselves; but they bear marks of his careful revision. At the end of Mr. Mather's *Account* is the following, " I earnestly desire that all our preachers should seriously consider the preceding *Account*. And let them not be content never to speak against *the Great Salvation*, either in public or private; and never to discourage either by word or deed any that think they have attained it. No: but prudently encourage them to hold fast whereunto they have attained. And strongly and explicitly exhort all believers to go on to perfection; yea, to expect full salvation from sin every moment, by mere grace, through simple faith." Dated City Road, London, Jan. 5, 1780, and signed John Wesley.

Two of the *Accounts* were published separately—John Haime's (No. 379) in 1785, with an account of his death by Mr. Story; and Thomas Mitchell's in 1781 (No. 350).

Seventeen original letters by Wesley, many of them of great interest, are inserted. There are also short hymns by Charles Wesley, and some probably by Wesley himself.

347. HYMNS WRITTEN IN THE TIME OF THE TUMULTS, JUNE, 1780. Bristol: Printed in the year 1780. 12mo., pp. 19.

No name of author or publisher. Thirteen hymns of various metres; to three only are distinctive titles prefixed. No. 7 is headed, *Upon notice sent one that his house was marked.* This is supposed to have been Charles Wesley's own house. No. 12, *For the Magistrates;* and No. 13, *Thanksgiving.*

The "Tumults" referred to were the Gordon Anti-Papal Riots. The third hymn was written on the memorable 8th of June, and six days after was enclosed by the author in a letter to his wife, with a brief extract from Virgil prefixed. In the letter, he says: "The roaring of the waves is ceased; but the agitation continues. If God had not rebuked the madness of the people at the very crisis, London had now been no more. No wonder your mother was terrified, when I was *proscribed* as a popish priest—for I never signed the petition, or ranked among the patriots."—*C. Wesley's Journal,* ii. 281.

For an interesting account of the circumstances amidst which these hymns were written, and which they so vividly portray, see *Life of Charles Wesley,* ii. 318-26.

348. A Collection of Hymns for the Use of the People called Methodists. London: Printed by J. Paramore, at the Foundry. 1780. [Price Three Shillings, sewed.] 12mo., pp. 504, xvi.

Preface dated London, Oct. 20, 1779, signed John Wesley.

Second edition, London, 1781; Third edition, corrected, London, 1782; Fourth, London: Paramore, 1784; Fifth, London, 1786; Sixth, London, 1788; Seventh, London, 1791.

In these editions were five hundred and twenty-five hymns; one by Herbert, seven by Dr. Watts, one by S. Wesley, sen., one by S. Wesley, jun., two by Dr. Henry More, twenty-seven by John Wesley, and four hundred and eighty-six by Charles Wesley. The Index was revised in the second edition, and Hymn No. 441 was slightly altered; after which the text remained unchanged during Wesley's life, up to and including the seventh edition.

The Methodists from an early period had been richly supplied with hymn-books for use in their various meetings. "It may be doubted," says Wesley, "whether any religious community in the world had a greater variety of them." But they were very numerous, and the poor people could not afford to purchase them all. A wide-spread desire at length prevailed for such a book as could be generally used in all the congregations in Great Britain and Ireland, one "not too large, that it may be cheap and portable, and not too small, that it may contain a sufficient variety of hymns for all ordinary occasions." Some selections from the various books had already been made, notably *Psalms and Hymns* (No. 30), *Hymns and Spiritual Songs* (No. 165), which was more used than any other in the public services, and also *Select Hymns with Tunes annext* (No. 205). But not one of these quite met the common want; and Wesley was at length persuaded to prepare this Collection, which he did with much care and labour. He says of it:—"It is not so large as to be either cumbersome or expensive: and it is large enough to contain such a variety of hymns as will not soon be worn threadbare. It is large enough to contain all the important truths of our most holy religion, whether speculative or practical; yea, to illustrate them all, and to prove them both by Scripture and reason; and this is done in a regular order. The hymns are not carelessly jumbled together, but carefully ranged under proper heads, according to the experience of real Christians. So that this book is in effect a little body of experimental and practical divinity."—Preface.

No other work published by Wesley was subject to so many vicissitudes as this *Collection of Hymns.* No sooner had Wesley passed away than alterations began to be made by the manager of the publishing house, G. Whitfield. The eighth edition, 1793, the first published after Wesley's death, was changed in several particulars. The alterations were continued in "a new edition," 1796. In another "new edition" in 1797, the changes were very great. Twenty-four hymns of Wesley's selection were omitted and sixty-five others inserted, two of them being hymns which Wesley himself had designated "doggerel double distill'd." Many other alterations were made. These changes were continued in another "new edition," 1797 ; in another, 1797, slightly altered ; and in another with all the previous faults, 1798." By this time the book was found to be so faulty that at the Conference of 1799 a committee was appointed "to reduce it to its primitive simplicity as published in the second edition." This was done " to some extent, by the Committee then appointed, and has been still further attempted by succeeding Editors, though not with entire success."—Osborn.

The third edition was really the book as it finally left Wesley's hands. To that it has never been precisely restored.

A new edition, with very slight emendations, appeared in 1800 ; another, 1801 ; another, 1803, in which the task of reducing it to "its primitive simplicity" really began. Many changes were made. In 1804 the 16th edition was issued with further changes ; the 18th, 1805 ; the 20th, 1808 ; another 20th, 1808 ; 21st, 1808 ; 22nd, 1809 ; new edition, 1809 ; 23rd, 1810 ; another, 1811 ; 24th, 1812 ; stereotyped edition, 1812 ; another, 1813 ; new edition, 1814 ; one not numbered, 1816 ; another, 1817, Index to the verses introduced ; another, 1819 ; another, 1820 ; another, 1821 ; also "a corrected edition," 1821 ; stereotyped, 1824 (with portrait, engraved by Fry) ; corrected edition, 1826. In the year 1831 further changes were made, and a " Supplement " was added. Several unauthorised supplements had previously appeared, and some may have been used in the country chapels. The last-named edition was published in many sizes, and continued in use in all the congregations and Societies until the year 1875. Osborn says of it," There is no doubt that the book is on the whole improved for the purposes of general usefulness by such variations from Wesley's text as are now permitted, and which principally consist in additions ; the total number of hymns, exclusive of the Additional Hymns and Supplement, being now five hundred and thirty-nine."—*Meth. Bib.*

Many unauthorized editions of the entire work also were published in different parts of the country, and at different dates previously to 1875, when the original book underwent revision and was published with "A New Supplement." At the same time a fresh copyright was obtained.

On the cover of the *Arminian Magazine* for September, 1779, there appeared the following " Proposals for printing (by subscription) a Collection of Hymns For the use of the people called Methodists. Intended to be used in all their congregations. Conditions : I. This Collection will contain about five hundred hymns, and upwards of four hundred pages. II. It is now ready for the press, and will be printed with all expedition. III. The price is three shillings ; half to be paid at the time of subscribing ; the other half at the delivery of the book, sewed. IV. Booksellers only, subscribing for six copies, shall have a seventh gratis."

1781.

349. A LETTER TO THE PRINTER OF THE "PUBLIC ADVERTISER," OCCASIONED BY THE LATE ACT PASSED IN FAVOUR OF POPERY. To which is added a Defence of it, in two letters to the Editors of the *Freeman's Journal*, Dublin. By John Wesley, M.A. London : Printed by J.

No. 350. [1781.

Paramore, at the Foundry, Moorfields; and sold at the New Chapel, in the City-Road; and at the Rev. Mr. Wesley's Preaching-Houses in Town and Country. 1781. 12mo., pp. 22.

This consists of (1) "A letter addressed to the printer of the *Public Advertiser*" (see No. 339). (2) An address "To the Reader," relating to remarks made on this letter in the *Freeman's Journal* by "Father O'Leary, a Capuchin-Friar, in Dublin," and to other publications by him. This is dated London, Dec. 29, 1780. (3) Two letters to the editors of the *Freeman's Journal*, dated respectively Manchester, March 23, 1780, and Chester, March 31, 1780, and both signed, John Wesley.

Wesley's first letter raised many adversaries; but O'Leary was the most conspicuous and the most violent. He wrote a series of six letters to the *Freeman's Journal* on Wesley's letter to the *Public Advertiser*; Wesley writing two in reply. O'Leary subsequently published his letters with the title *Mr. O'Leary's Remarks on the Rev. Mr. Wesley's Letters in Defence of the Protestant Associations in England, to which are prefixed Mr. Wesley's Letters:* Dublin, 1780.

In the Address to the Reader, mentioned above, Wesley asserts that he had not written "in defence of the Association," and charges O'Leary not only with this mis-statement, but with inserting a spurious letter [signed J. W.] and with omitting both those addressed by him to the *Freeman's Journal*. He therefore republishes them in this pamphlet together with his original letter to the *Advertiser*. O'Leary, in a second edition (Dublin, 1781), changed the title, but did not insert Wesley's letters or withdraw the spurious one. The whole of Wesley's pamphlets named above appeared in the *Arminian Magazine*, May, June, and July, 1781.

"Wesley had exposed the errors of the Romanists in some controversial writings, perspicuously and forcibly. One of those writings gave the Catholics an advantage, because it defended [or was supposed to defend] the Protestant Association of 1780; and the events which speedily followed were turned against him. But upon the great points in dispute he was clear and cogent; and the temper of this, as of his other controversial tracts, was such, that some years afterwards, when a common friend invited him to meet his antagonist, Father O'Leary, it was gratifying to both parties to meet upon terms of courtesy and mutual good will."—Southey, *Life of Wesley*, ch. xxx.

350. A SHORT ACCOUNT OF THE LIFE OF MR. THOMAS MITCHELL. London: Printed by J. Paramore, at the Foundry, Moorfields. 1781. 12mo., pp. 24.

This account, written by Mitchell himself probably at Wesley's request, as was the case in many similar instances, is a simple narrative of the earlier years, conversion, labours, and bitter persecutions of this good and zealous man. In his early life he was a soldier; but on his discharge he became one of Wesley's preachers, and continued so from 1748 to 1784. Wesley appears to have revised the account for the *Arminian Magazine* (1780), and again more carefully for this issue which is slightly longer than the former, extending to two years beyond it. Dr. Priestley, hearing Mitchell preach on one occasion, said, "This man must do good for he aims at nothing else." In the *Minutes of Conference* for 1785, in answer to the question, "Who have died this year?" is the simple reply, "Thomas Mitchell, an old soldier of Jesus Christ."

351. THE HISTORY OF HENRY, EARL OF MORELAND. [Two volumes.] Vol. I. London : Printed by J. Paramore, at the Foundry, Upper Moorfields. 1781. 12mo., pp. vi. 378, 423.

Preface, dated Bristol, March 4, 1780.

Second edition, London : Paramore, 1793, two vols.; Third, London: Whitfield, 1802; Fourth, London: Cordeux, 1813; Another, Manchester, 1840; Another, 1859, edited by the Rev. R. Sinclair Brooke, with a Biographical Preface by Charles Kingsley, "who considered that the reader, in spite of the defects of the book, would learn more from it of what was pure, sacred and eternal, than from any book since Spenser's *Faerie Queene.*"—Chambers's *Ency.*, Art., *Henry Brooke.*

This is an abridgement of *The Fool of Quality; or, the History of Henry, Earl of Moreland. In Four Volumes. By Mr. Brooke:* London, Johnston, Second edition, 1767-70. It was intended originally to publish in four vols., but "the matter grew so upon the writer" that he was obliged to occupy a fifth. Wesley retrenched "at least one-third of what was published in those five volumes, more to the satisfaction of the bookseller than of the judicious reader," omitting a number of uninteresting dialogues, most of the trifling and ludicrous incidents, the remarks upon the feudal government, and "great part of the mystic divinity, as it is more philosophical than Scriptural." He describes the book as "the most excellent in its kind of any he had seen either in English or any other language," its greatest excellence being that it "perpetually aims at inspiring and increasing every right affection, at the instilling gratitude to God, and benevolence to man."

"I would recommend very few novels to young persons for fear they should be too desirous of more. Mr. Brooke wrote one more (besides the 'Earl of Moreland'), 'The History of the Human Heart.' I think it well worth reading; though it is not equal to his former production. The want of novels may be supplied by well-chosen histories."—Wesley, let. to Miss Bishop, in *Works*, xiii. 137.

The Fool of Quality was written by Mr. Councillor Henry Brooke, whose nephew, Mr. Henry Brooke, artist, was a devoted Methodist in Dublin, a personal friend and correspondent of Wesley and Fletcher. He has sometimes been mistaken for the author. Jackson appears to have made this error— see Index to Wesley's Works.

Wesley does not mention the author's name either on the title-page or in the preface ; and he has been held to have committed an act of piracy in publishing the work without acknowledgement. But that he prepared the work with the full concurrence of the author is shown by the following extract from a letter addressed to Wesley by Mr. Henry Brooke, and inserted in the *Arminian Magazine*, 1787, pp. 160, 161. "My uncle is deeply sensible of your very kind offer, and most cordially embraces it. He desires me to express the warmth of his gratitude in the strongest terms, and says he most cheerfully yields the volumes you mention to your superior judgment, to prune, erase and alter as you please. He only wishes they could have had your eye before they appeared in public. But it is not yet too late. A second edition will appear with great advantage when they have undergone so kind a revisal. But he is apprehensive your time is so precious, that it may be too great an intrusion upon it, unless made a work of leisure and opportunity. Yet as you have proferred it, he will not give up the privilege, but hope leisure may be found for so friendly and generous a work."

Nos. 352-353. [1781.

352. AN EXTRACT FROM A REPLY TO THE OBSERVATIONS OF LIEUT. GEN. SIR WILLIAM HOWE, ON A PAMPHLET ENTITLED, LETTERS TO A NOBLEMAN. London: Printed by J. Paramore, Foundry, Upper-Moorfields ; and sold at the Rev. Mr. Wesley's New Chapel, in the City Road; and at all his Preaching-Houses in Town and Country. 1781. 12mo. pp., 104.

The *Reply* from which this *Extract* was taken was written by the author of *Letters to a Nobleman*, presumably Mr. Galloway. In his *Observations* on the *Letters*, Sir William defends himself, and, assuming Mr. Galloway to be the author of the letters, takes occasion to cast serious reflections upon him. The *Reply* is anonymous, as were the *Letters*. An Appendix (p. 91) contains a letter to Sir William defending Mr. Galloway, signed "The Author" (of the Reply) and dated November 10, 1780; also a letter from Samuel Kirk to Sir William and his reply ; and a letter from the "Committee of Congress" to the President. These relate to the war. Appended to the whole on two unnumbered pages is a letter "From the Rev. Mr. Wesley to a Friend, concerning a passage in a *Monthly Review*," re-published in *Works*, xiii. 349, 350. In this Wesley criticises the comments of the *Review* on Sir William's vindication in which it is stated that "Mr. Galloway's book is here answered paragraph by paragraph." To this and other assertions Wesley replies, affirming that not "any one paragraph of Mr. Galloway's book" has been answered in a satisfactory manner, and further defending Mr. Galloway's character. The letter is dated, City Road, Jan. 25, 1781, and signed John Wesley.

On page 82 of the *Extract*, the author of the *Reply* acquits the General from the charge of mercenary motives in procrastinating the war. A foot-note says, "The editor of this extract cannot. He fears the enjoying of his immense appointment was one motive of his delays." It is uncertain if the other notes, chiefly references, are by Wesley.

353. AN EXTRACT OF A LETTER TO THE RIGHT HONOURABLE LORD VISCOUNT H * * E ON HIS NAVAL CONDUCT IN THE AMERICAN WAR. London : Printed by J. Paramore, at the Foundry, Moorfields ; and sold at the Rev. Mr. Wesley's New Chapel, in the City Road, and at all his Preaching-Houses in Town and Country. 1781. 12mo., pp. 27.

Second edition, London : Paramore, 1781, precisely as the first.

The letter, of which this is an extract, is signed, "The Friend of your Country." It was evidently written by a person having full knowledge of the circumstances of the war, of that part of the country where it was carried on, and of the sentiments of the American people respecting it. It contains a heavy indictment of Lord Howe. The writer charges him with an indolence and inactivity that could not be justified. He declares that Lord Howe neglected both parts of his high commission,—neither seeking to settle amicably the matters in dispute between Great Britain and her Colonies, as he was charged to do, and for the success of which there were good grounds of hope ; nor attempting with his greatly superior force any naval expedition, not even blocking the ports, which the writer affirms could easily have been done with one sixth part of the means at Lord Howe's command. The *Letter* is very ably written: and though motives are fearlessly exposed, it is entirely free from rancour.

Very little is said by any of Wesley's biographers concerning his publications on the war. The great event of his ordination of ministers for the American Churches seems to have drawn all attention to itself.

354. MINUTES OF SOME LATE CONVERSATIONS BETWEEN THE REV. MR. JOHN WESLEY AND OTHERS. Leeds: Printed by James Bowling. 1781. 12mo., pp. 11.

Dated Leeds, Tuesday, August 7, &c., 1781.

"About 70 preachers were present, all expressly invited by Wesley *(Journal*, Aug. 7, 1781). Nine candidates were received on trial; fourteen probationers were admitted to membership; two preachers desisted from travelling; two had died since the preceding session; one hundred and seventy-eight received appointments, including Wesley and Fletcher, the name of the latter appearing for the first time on the roll, probably for the reason that Wesley was now hoping to secure the Madeley Vicar as his successor in the event of his own death."—Stevens, *Hist. Meth*. bk. v. ch. x.

The question of erecting a school for preachers' children in Yorkshire was considered and the brethren were instructed to think of a place and a master, and to send Mr. Wesley word. "Q. 25. Have not our preachers printed anything without my consent and correction? A. Several of them have (not at all to the honour of the Methodists) both in verse and prose. This has: 1. Brought a great reproach; 2. Much hindered the spreading of more profitable books. Therefore we all agree, 3. That no preacher print or reprint anything for the time to come, till it is corrected by Mr. W.; and, 4. That the profits thereof shall go into the common stock."

355. A CONCISE ECCLESIASTICAL HISTORY, from the Birth of Christ to the Beginning of the present Century. In Four Volumes. Vol. I. London: Printed by J. Paramore at the Foundry, Moorfields; and sold at the New Chapel in the City-Road; and at the Rev. Mr. Wesley's Preaching-Houses in Town and Country. 1781. 12mo., pp. 347, 316, 332, 358.

The first volume contains Preface and Introduction, and the fourth an Index to the whole, pp. 76.

We are informed in the Preface that the author for many years had been earnestly importuned to compile and publish an ecclesiastical history. For this, however, he had not time.

"Abridging," he says, "I might possibly have found time for; but I knew no History of the Church worth abridging, till a few years since, a worthy man presented me with one, published thirty or forty years ago, by Dr. John Lawrence Mosheim, Chancellor of the University of Göttingen. This I read at leisure with the greatest attention, and it partly answered my expectations. Much of what was wanting in Mr. Echard, his vast learning and unwearied industry supplied. And he is not a dull writer. Much of his History is as lively as the nature of the subject will bear. But what is all this to the English reader? Dr. Mosheim writes in Latin." A translation by Dr. A. Maclaine "performed some years since in an accurate manner, with the addition of many notes," cost thirty shillings. Neither of these perfectly met Wesley's wish. He objected that nine parts in ten relating to heresies were neither instructive nor entertaining, that the views given of the internal state of the Church were unsatisfactory, and that the style was verbose. He accuses both author and translator with not rendering justice either to the transactions which they relate, or to the characters of many truly good men.

The entire work is reduced to the compass of less than four volumes of duodecimo. It is therefore, necessarily, a mere sketch; but as far as it goes, it is clear and adequate. Each century is dealt with separately, and in two parts, the External and the Internal History. The whole is divided into four books, embracing four remarkable periods; the first, from the rise of the Church to the time of Constantine the Great; the second to the reign of Charlemagne; the third to the time of Luther; and the fourth to the Eighteenth Century. The history of the fourth period is written at greater length. Each book is divided into chapters, and each chapter into numbered paragraphs. A good index is added.

A Short History of the People called Methodists is appended, extending to 113 pages. It is mostly extracted from Wesley's *Journals*, as they appear in the collected Works, to the volumes and pages of which references are made in foot-notes. It is written in the first person, and is dated at the end, London, November 16, 1781, but not signed. It is not the same as *A Short History of Methodism*, already named: see No. 229. Wesley's name does not appear on the title-page, or at the end of the preface.

356. THE ARMINIAN MAGAZINE FOR THE YEAR 1781. Consisting of Extracts and Original Treatises on Universal Redemption. Volume IV. London: Printed by J. Paramore, at the Foundry, Moorfields; and sold at the New Chapel, City-Road, and by all the Booksellers in Town and Country. 8vo., pp. 680, viii.

The following are the original or extracted articles :—

1. *The Preface* is signed London, January 1, 1781. Speaking of his hope that the magazine may maintain its character, Wesley says, "There is no danger that I should write myself out, that I should ever exhaust my stock of materials, as I have still by me a large number of compositions both in verse and prose, the greatest part of which never yet saw the light, nor probably ever would have done had they not been brought out of obscurity by the present publication. Add to this that I have had for many years, and have at this day, a greater number of pious correspondents, than any person in England, or perhaps in Europe." He proposes to make a few changes in the contents; and confesses that many of the portraits are not such as he desired. In this opinion many persons will agree with him. But he promises, "I will have better or none at all."

2. *Of Predestination; translated from Sebastian Castellio, in dialogues, between Lewis and Frederic.* To this Wesley prefixes an "Advertisement," in which he says that amongst the numberless Treatises written in this and the preceding age on the subject of Predestination he had not seen any that showed more good sense and good humour than Castellio's *Dialogues;* but though published above two hundred years before, they had not yet appeared in English.

1781.]   No. 357.

3. *Original Sermons by the Rev. John Wesley, M.A.*, are commenced in this volume. The following appear: (i.) 1 Timothy vi. 9; (ii.) 1 John v. 20, dated at end London, Dec. 22, 1780; (iii.) 1 John v. 21, dated London, Jan. 5, 1781; (iv.) 1 John v. 8, dated Jan. 20, 1781; (v.) Galatians iv. 18, dated Haverford West, May 6, 1781; (vi.) 1 Corinthians xiv. 20, dated Langham-Row, July 6, 1781.

4. *An Extract from a Survey of the Wisdom of God in the Creation*, being a carefully executed series of extracts from his own work, published in five volumes, 1777 (No. 325).

5. *Thoughts on the power of Music.* Dated Inverness, June 9, 1779.

6. *Some Account of Mr. Richard Whatcoat.*

7. *Thoughts upon Baron Montesquieu's Spirit of Laws.*

8. *Thoughts upon Jacob Behmen*, dated Dec. 22, 1780.

9. *A Scheme of Self-Examination, used by the first Methodists in Oxford.*

10. *A Plain Account of Kingswood School, near Bristol.*

11. *An Extract from the "Minutes of a Conference held in August, 1781, between Rev. Mr. John Wesley and others."*

12. *A Short Account of the Death of Elizabeth Marsh and two others.* Signed J. W.

13. *Letters.*—To a friend concerning a passage in the *Monthly Review*, dated City Road, Jan. 25, 1781. In a postscript Wesley complains that he had been frequently attacked by the *Monthly Review*, but did not answer, because they were not on even ground. "But that difficulty is now over. Whatever they object in their *Monthly Review*, I can answer in my *Monthly Magazine*." To ——— on the preaching and gathering congregations by the Methodists, dated April 10, 1761. *To the printer of the Public Advertiser.* Three letters on Popery already published as a pamphlet (No. 349). *To the Rev. Mr. F*———. In this he writes, "I have entirely lost my taste for controversy. I have lost my readiness in disputing, and I take this to be a providential discharge from it." Dated St. Ives, Sept. 15, 1762.

This volume contains also many extracts and accounts with prefaces and annotations; anonymous hymns and poetical pieces; and a number of letters addressed to Wesley, concerning which he says, "I am persuaded the preceding Magazines contain such a collection of letters as never appeared before in the English tongue; I mean for depth of genuine Christian experience; but I conceive none of them exceed, and not many of them equal, the following."

357. THE PROTESTANT ASSOCIATION. Written in the midst of the Tumults, June, 1780. London: Printed by J. Paramore, at the Foundry, Moorfields; and sold at Mr. Atlay's, in the City Road. 1781. 12mo., pp. 34.

In the year 1780 as we have seen (Nos. 339, 342, 349), a Bill for the relief of Roman Catholic subjects from various humiliating and oppressive disabilities gave rise to a violent anti-papal agitation. A "Protestant Association" was formed, the leading object of which was to obtain the repeal of the obnoxious Acts, which were alleged to be dangerous to the Protestant religion. Of this Association, Lord George Gordon was the president. Neither of the Wesleys belonged to it. A petition for the repeal of the Acts was signed by 100,000 persons. Immense excitement was aroused; many grievous excesses were committed by the mob and much property destroyed. The "Gordon Riots" are matters of history.

Under the title of *The Protestant Association* Charles Wesley wrote this stinging satirical poem, in four cantos, ridiculing alike the foolish malice of the mob and the careless weakness of the magistracy. To it are added an *Address*

No. 358. [1781.

to the City; Advice to the City; and a *Second Address to the City*, all written in the same vein. It is a smart and skilful performance. Though "written in the midst of the tumults, June, 1780," it was not published till the following year. It appears to have been neither reprinted, nor inserted in the catalogues.

358. SACRED HARMONY: OR A CHOICE COLLECTION OF PSALMS AND HYMNS. SET TO MUSIC IN TWO AND THREE PARTS, FOR THE VOICE, HARPSICHORD AND ORGAN. n.d., 8vo., pp. vi. 349.

"Praise Him in His holiness," &c., set to music on ornamental title-page, (similar to *Sacred Melody*, No. 206).

Index to tunes, at the beginning, occupying five pages; to the hymns, at the end, five pages. The book is printed entirely from engraved plates. On page 349 (but not in all copies) are the words, "T. Bennett, Sculp., Holborn Hill," but whether he is the person referred to in Wesley's most characteristic preface to the *Select Hymns with Tunes Annext* (No. 205), we have no means of knowing.

There are 120 tunes (107 of them taken from *Sacred Melody*, No. 206), and 128 hymns. A verse of a hymn is interlined with each tune, other verses following; in a few cases additional hymns are given. The hymns are numbered but not the tunes, the names of which are given but not the metres. The price of the volume in sheets was 5s., bound 7s. 6d., and "a few copies bound and gilt in a very elegant manner, 9s."

The same work with slight alterations was afterwards published in a cheaper form and rather smaller size, having the same title, but with a different title-page. Two editions of the cheaper book were issued. On the title-page of one edition are the words, "Price 4s. bound in calf. Sold by G. Whitfield, City-Road, London; and at the Methodist Preaching-Houses in Town and Country," pp. 157, ii. In the other edition the title-page is printed apparently from the same plate, but it has only the words, "Price two shillings and sixpence," without name of publisher, pp. 157, iv. Both editions are without date. As Whitfield became Book-Steward in 1789, one of these, and probably the other, was not issued until after that date. These editions differ from the larger work also in the following particulars:—only one verse of a hymn is given with each tune; the order of the tunes is slightly altered; four of the tunes that are in the larger book are omitted, and six new ones are added, making the total number of tunes in the smaller books 122. The tunes are not numbered. At the end of the tunes are the words, "G: Maund Sculpt."

Subsequently the same book was published with the title, *Sacred Harmony: A Set of Tunes collected by the late Reverend John Wesley, M.A., for the use of the Congregations in his Connexion:* An edition carefully revised and corrected by his nephew, Charles Wesley, Esq., Organist to His Majesty. London: J. Mason, long 8vo. pp. xvi. 152. The preface is dated, London, Nov. 3, 1821.

For a long time the date of the publication of the *Harmony* was uncertain, if indeed it can now be confidently fixed. Osborn entered it under 1761; Heylin under 1770, but without assigning any reason, or giving any particulars. He names "an edition 354 pp. 12mo., 1781," as above. It contains Olivers' hymn, "The God of Abraham praise," which some think was not written till 1770 or 1772. The most careful inquiry has led to the belief that it was not published until 1781. The late Mr. Dobson, for many years a diligent collector of Methodist literature, and especially of Methodist hymns and tunes, after prolonged research assigned it to this date. This opinion was shared by the

214

late Mr. William Sugden, of the Westminster Training College, who gave much time to the inquiry; and Mr. C. D. Hardcastle, who, with Mr. Sugden, wrote an article in the *Wesleyan Methodist Magazine* for April, 1866, on the psalmody of early Methodism, gives the same date. It was announced, apparently for the first time, on the cover of the *Arminian Magazine* for 1781.

1782.

359. A New Concordance to the Holy Scriptures of the Old and New Testament, &c. By Thomas Taylor (John v. 39, 2 Tim. iii. 15). York: Printed by A. Ward, for R. Spence, Bookseller, &c. 1782. [Price four shillings and six-pence.] Thick square, small 12mo., pp. viii. 700.

To this Wesley wrote the following preface:—" Mr. Cruden's Concordance is undoubtedly the best which hath yet been published in the English tongue, but abundance of people, who want a Concordance, cannot go to the price of it. I am in hopes this small, cheap, and portable one may answer the same intention. I therefore recommend it to all lovers of the Bible.—JOHN WESLEY. Scarborough, May 21, 1782."

The Concordance is compiled from Cruden's third edition, the mistakes of which are corrected, and the whole reduced to a fourth the size and a sixth the price. Thomas Taylor, one of Wesley's preachers, was stationed in York in 1780 and 1781, and so came into contact with Mr. Spence, the Methodist bookseller of that city.

360. An Estimate of the Manners of the Present Times. London: Printed in the year 1782. 12mo., pp. 23.

Second edition, in smaller type, pp. 12.

A pamphlet having this same title had been published some time before. In it the author affirmed that sloth and luxury were the chief characteristics of English manners. To this description Wesley objects, for, though allowing that neither of these evils "ever abounded in England as they do at this day," yet they are not the universal, the constant, or the peculiar qualities of English society. He affirms an almost universal *ungodliness* to be the great national characteristic,—"a total ignorance of God, a total contempt of Him." This leads to many evils, of which he names the neglect of worship, perjury, and "the stupid, senseless, shameless ungodliness of taking the name of God in vain." The tract closes with earnest words of entreaty, warning, and fervent appeal. Wesley had better opportunities of knowing the state of public morals than perhaps any other man then living; and, rightly or wrongly, he here, and in many other instances, writes of English society as though he were under the influence of a painful discouragement, or a depressing pessimism.

361. An Extract from John Nelson's Journal. Being an Account of God's Dealing with him from his Youth to the Forty-Second Year of his Age.

Written by himself. (2 Cor. i. 3, 4.) "Lord, Thou hast led the blind by a way that he knew not." London: Printed by J. Paramore, at the Foundery, Upper Moorfields. And sold at the Rev. Mr. Wesley's New Chapel, in the City Road, and at all his Preaching-Houses in Town and Country. 1782. 12mo., pp. 144.

Nelson published his journal in 1767, sm. 8vo., Bristol: E. Farley and Co. An edition was also printed by T. Saint, in Newcastle, 1770.

The one printed by Paramore in 1782 is Wesley's careful revision. No considerable change is made; the title-page and preface are altered, and there are occasional verbal corrections in the body of the work. Otherwise the story remains entirely in the writer's own words. It is a simple, artless, unaffected record of the devoted, heroic, whole-hearted service, and great suffering of this brave soldier of Jesus Christ—the man of whom Southey said he had "as high a spirit and as brave a heart as ever Englishman was blessed with."

"Amid thousands of spectators, a procession nearly half a mile long, sobbing and singing, bore the remains of the heroic John Nelson through the town of Leeds, and along the highway to lay him to rest in his native village of Birstall, the place of his first ministrations and greatest triumphs."—Stevens' *Hist. Meth.*, bk. v., ch. iv.

362. AN ALARM TO UNCONVERTED SINNERS. BY JOSEPH ALLEINE. *This book is not to be sold, but given away.* London: Printed by J. Paramore, at the Foundery, Moorfields. 1782. 12mo., pp. 107.

Another edition, London: Paramore, 1783; Another, London: Paramore, 1785. In all respects the same as the first edition.

This is a skilfully prepared extract, embracing almost the whole of Alleine's invaluable little work, with Richard Baxter's prefatory "Epistle to the Unconverted Reader," and the shorter one by Alleine, as in the 1688 edition. The first six chapters, edited according to Wesley's method, are given. The "Soliloquy for an Unregenerate Sinner," the seventh chapter containing "Motives to Conversion," and the "Conclusion" are omitted.

The *Alarm* had already appeared in the *Christian Library*, vol. xxiv. (No. 131), but without the same abridgment and thorough revision that it has here undergone. The two prefatory epistles only were omitted.

"No book in the English tongue (the Bible excepted) can equal it for the number that hath been dispersed; for there have been 20,000 of them sold under the title of the 'Call'; or, Alarm to the Unconverted,' in 8vo. or 12mo.; and 50,000 of the same book have been sold under the title of the 'Sure Guide to Heaven,' 30,000 of which were at one impression."—*Account of the Ejected Ministers*, (ii. 577), quoted in Bohn's edition of Southey's *Life of Wesley*, p. 495.

363. A CALL TO THE UNCONVERTED. By Richard Baxter. *This book is not to be sold, but given away.* London: Printed by J. Paramore, at the Foundery, Moorfields. 1782. 12mo., pp. 76.

Another, London: Paramore, 1783; Another, 1785, apparently printed from the same type.

The *Call* appears in its completeness in the second volume of Baxter's Works, fol. 1707, where it is entitled, *A Call to the Unconverted to turn and live, and accept of mercy while mercy may be had, as ever they would find mercy in the day of their extremity.* To it are added some forms of prayer.

The Introduction, signed Richard Baxter, and dated December the 10th, 1657, together with the extended preface addressed "to all unsanctified persons that shall read this book, especially my hearers in the Parish of Kidderminster," and the forms of prayer, are all omitted from Wesley's edition. The *Call* is based on Ezek. xxxiii. 11. Wesley abridged it with the same minute care that he bestowed on so many other works.

NOTE.—In 1782 Wesley and Coke instituted a "Society for the Distribution of Religious Tracts among the Poor." The "plan" of the Society was appended to the *Arminian Magazine* for November, 1784; and was reprinted in the *Wesleyan Methodist Magazine* for 1847, p. 269.

A "List of Books already printed" was attached to the "plan." It contains thirty titles, many of them being sermons or *Words*, written by Wesley, and for the most part previously published. The list is appended below. It is the first Methodist tract catalogue. On these tracts were printed the words, *This book is not to be sold, but given away.*

1. *A Serious Call to a Holy Life.*—No. 48.
2. *Alleine's Alarm.*—No. 362.
3. *Baxter's Call.*—No. 363.
4. *The Nature and Design of Christianity.*—No. 17.
5. *A Sermon on Awake, Thou that Sleepest.*—No. 33.
6. *The Important Question.*—No. 308.
7. *The Heavenly Footman.*—By Fletcher.
8. *The Great Assize.*—No. 185.
9. *The Good Steward.*—No. 251.
10. *Sermon on the Trinity.*—No. 306.
11. *The New Birth.*—No. 88.
12. *The Way to the Kingdom.*—No. 88.
13. *The Almost Christian.*—No. 28.
14. *On Original Sin.*—No. 196.
15. *On Salvation by Faith.*—No. 8.
16. *The Spirit of Prayer.*—No. 252.
17. *Instructions for Children.*—No. 62.
18. *Token for Children.*—No. 124.
19. *A Hymn to the God of Abraham.*—By Olivers.
20. *A Word to a Freeholder.*—No. 104.
21. *Word to a Smuggler.*—No. 239.
22. *Word to a Soldier.*—No. 44.
23. *Word to a Sailor.*—No. 44.
24. *Word to a Swearer.*—No. 78.
25. *Word to a Sabbath-breaker.*—No. 79.
26. *Word to a Drunkard.*—No. 77.
27. *Word to a Prostitute.*—No. 80.
28. *Word to a Condemned Malefactor.*—No. 81.
29. *John Janeway's Life.*—No. 159.
30. *A Collection of Hymns.* 1d.

It will be seen that Nos. 362 and 363 appear in this list. Two others should be noted:—No. 16, *The Spirit of Prayer.* It was printed by R. Hawes, London: Dorset Square, Spitalfields, n.d. pp. 24. It is an exact reprint of

Nos. 364-365. [1782.

the same tract as it appeared in *An Extract of Mr. Law's Later Works*, 2 vols. 1768 (No. 252). The other is No. 30, *A Collection of Hymns*, 1d. This may have been the same as *A Small Collection of Hymns selected from various authors*: London: Printed by J. Paramore, at the Foundry, Moorfields, 1781, 12mo., pp. 36. By whom this collection was made cannot be determined.

364. MINUTES OF SOME LATE CONVERSATIONS BETWEEN THE REV. MR. J. WESLEY AND OTHERS. London: Printed by J. Paramore, at the Foundry, Moorfields. 1782. 12mo., pp. 15.

Dated London, Tuesday, August 6, 1782.
The special matters that occupied attention at this Conference were the case of the Birstal Preaching-House; the observance of the Sabbath-day, and the enforcement of several neglected rules, relating to the attendance of strangers at the Society-Meetings; the office and duty of a Helper; and behaviour in public worship. The following also appears:—"Q. 34. Should we insist on that rule, Sing no hymns of your own composing? A. Undoubtedly; and let those who will not promise this be excluded at the next Conference." Several of these matters are recorded in *Addenda* to the *Minutes*.

365. THE ARMINIAN MAGAZINE FOR THE YEAR 1782. Consisting of Extracts and Original Treatises on Universal Redemption. Volume V. London: Printed by J. Paramore, at the Foundery, Moorfields; and sold at the New Chapel, City Road, and by all the Booksellers in Town and Country. 8vo., pp. 680, viii.

In this volume are the following original or extracted pieces:—
1. *French Mercy, Exemplified in the case of Monsieur Isaac Lefevre*.
2. *Remarks upon Mr. Locke's essay on Human Understanding*.
3. *Some Thoughts upon an Important Question,—On hearing Ministers who oppose the truth*.
4. *Some Account of Sarah Peters*.
5. *On the Origin of the Soul*. To this the following is prefixed, "I was many years in doubt concerning this question, finding nothing satisfactory wrote upon it. But I am thoroughly satisfied with the following account, which I think will satisfy any candid enquirer." "I read and abridged an old treatise on 'The Origin of the Soul.' I never before saw anything on the subject so satisfactory. I think he proves to a demonstration that God has enabled man, as all other creatures, to propagate his whole species, consisting of soul and body."—*Journal*, Nov. 7, 1770. Wesley directed his attention closely to this subject, for "many necessary points in divinity" depended upon it. In addition to the passages quoted above, see *Works*, iii. 153-5, and the extracts on *The true Original of the Soul* in the *Arminian Magazine* for 1783 (No. 372).
6. *How far is it the Duty of a Christian Minister to preach politics?*
7. *A disavowal of persecuting Papists*.
8. *A specimen of the Divinity and Philosophy of the highly illuminated Jacob Behmen*.
9. *An answer to Mr. Dodd*.
10. *Remarks on the Count de Buffon's Natural History*.
11. *Thoughts on the character and writings of Mr. Prior*.

218

12. *Sermons.* (vii.) on Rom. viii. 19-22, entitled *Free Thoughts on the Brute Creation*, and dated November 30, 1781; (viii.) Ephesians v. 16, dated London, January 20th, 1782; (ix.) Gen. iii. 19; dated Bristol, March 13, 1782; (x.) Gen. i. 31; (xi.) Rom. v. 15; dated Birmingham, July 9, 1782; (xii.) Mark ix. 48, dated Newport, Isle of Wight, Oct. 10, 1782; also *A Discourse on Romans viii. 29, 30*, delivered several years before at Londonderry, and printed at the request of several of the clergy; but inserted here as it was little known in England: dated Armagh, June 5, 1773 (No. 290).

13. *Extract from Castellio's Dialogues on Election and Free Will*, concluded.

14. *An Account of the Passions, or Natural Affections*: extracted from Dr. Watts.

15. *Serious Considerations concerning the Doctrines of Election and Reprobation*: extracted from Dr. Watts. Already published (see No. 16), but much condensed.

16. *An Extract from the Journal of Mr. G—— C——*: preceded by an address "to the Reader," dated Macclesfield, April 1, 1782. In it Wesley writes, "I do not remember to have met with a more remarkable account than is contained in the following Journal." He has selected "only the most material parts."

17. *A true Relation of the chief things which an evil Spirit did and said at Mascon, in Burgundy*: condensed from a pamphlet entitled *The Devil of Mascon*, mentioned in Note, p. 144.

18. *Extract from the Minutes of a Conference*, 1782.

366. HYMNS FOR THE NATIONAL FAST, FEB. 8, 1782. London: Printed by J. Paramore, at the Foundery, Moorfields: and sold at the New Chapel in the City Road; and at the Rev. Mr. Wesley's Preaching-Houses in Town and Country. 12mo., pp. 24.

Fifteen Hymns of various metres. Hymn iv. headed "Habakkuk i."; Hymn vi. "Mal. iv. i."; Hymns xiv. and xv. "For Peace." Osborn says: "These are the same with those published on a similar occasion in 1756" (No. 181.)—*Meth. Bib.* p. 213. It is not easy to account for this mistake.

367. HYMNS FOR THE NATION IN 1782. Half title. 12mo., pp. 12. [Part I. but not so numbered.]

Nine hymns in all.
Hymn i., entitled "After the Defeat at the Chesapeak;" ii., "For the loyal Americans;" iii., "Amos viii. 2;" v., "For His Majesty King George;" vii., "For Concord;" viii., "A Prayer for the Congress;" ix., "Thy Kingdom come."

There were at least two editions of this published.

368. HYMNS FOR THE NATION IN 1782. Part II., half-title. 12mo., pp. 11.

Eight hymns, numbered onwards from the last Part: not so the paging.

No. 369. [1783.

Hymn xii., entitled "For the Conversion of the French;" xiii., "For Her Majesty;" xiv., "For the Royal Family;" xv., "Thanksgiving for the success of the Gospel in America;" the rest are without titles. The second Part was probably not re-printed separately; but after the first edition the two were published together without any distinction of parts. The full title-page was:—

HYMNS FOR THE NATION, IN 1782. London: Printed by J. Paramore, at the Foundery, Moorfields; and sold at the New Chapel in the City Road; and at the Rev. Mr. Wesley's Preaching-Houses in Town and Country. n.d., 12mo., pp. 24.

Another edition, London: Paramore, 1781 (obviously a mistake). The same as the former one, page for page, except in the distribution of the last hymn. Hymn No. xvi. is wrongly printed xxvi.

Another with the same title and by the same printer, n.d., pp. 36, contains twenty-five hymns; six being taken from No. 367, omitting Hymns 2, 3, and 8; six from No. 368, omitting 3 and 7; and thirteen from No. 366, omitting 4 and 5. There are no new titles to any of the hymns.

And yet another was published, having the same title and by the same printer, n.d., pp. 47, containing 32 hymns. This is divided into two parts: Part I. comprising all the hymns (17) in Nos. 367 and 368; and Part II. the hymns (15) in No. 366. All in the same order.

It is impossible now to explain this curious intermingling of these publications. It may indicate the great demand for the hymns.

1783.

369. AN EXTRACT FROM THE REV. MR. JOHN WESLEY'S JOURNAL. From January 1, 1776, to August 8, 1779. London: Printed by J. Paramore, at the Foundry, Moorfields; and sold at the New Chapel, City-Road; and at the Rev. Mr. Wesley's Preaching-Houses in Town and Country. 1783. 12mo., pp. 120. [No. xviii.]

Second edition, London: Paramore, 1788.

Another portion of this remarkable record. There is no abatement of the labour of this servant of God and of man. He travels as much as ever, reading many hours a day while doing so. He preaches as frequently, both "in the house and abroad." His Societies are as carefully watched as formerly, and he has but slightly lessened his literary work.

Referring several years before to his literary labours, he makes the following reflections,—"I was musing on what I heard a good man say long since,— 'Once in seven years I burn all my sermons; for it is a shame if I cannot write better sermons now than I could seven years ago.' Whatever others can do, I really cannot. I cannot write a better sermon on the Good Steward (No. 251) than I did seven years ago; I cannot write a better on the Great Assize (No. 185) than I did twenty years ago: I cannot write a better on the Use of Money than I did near thirty years ago. Nay, I know not that I can write a better on the Circumcision of the Heart than I did five and forty years ago. Perhaps, indeed, I may have read five or six hundred books more than I had then, and may know a little more History, or Natural Philosophy, than I did; but I am not sensible that this has made any essential addition to my knowledge in Divinity. Forty years ago I knew and preached every Christian doctrine which I preach now."—*Journal*, Sep. 1, 1778.

369A. THE CASE OF THE BIRSTAL HOUSE. Folio circular, pp. 4.
Dated Jan. 3, 1783, signed John Wesley.
Reprinted in the *Arminian Magazine*, 1788, vol. xi. p. 148, &c., also in *Works*, 3rd ed., xiii. 241-4, with date at end, " London, Reprinted, January 12, 1788," signed John Wesley.
This relates to the legal settlement of a preaching-house in Birstal, the original deed of which, executed at an early period of the Methodist history, gave the trustees the power, "not only of placing but of displacing the preachers at their pleasure;" contrarily to the "Methodist Plan" or Model-Deed, which lodged that power in the hands of the Conference. For particulars of the painful controversy, which gave occasion for the writing of the above circular, see Wesley's *Works*, iv. 259, 260, xii. 136-8, xiii. 99: also Tyerman's *Life of Wesley*, iii. 373-383.

370. MINUTES OF SOME LATE CONVERSATIONS BETWEEN THE REV. MR. WESLEY AND OTHERS. Dublin, Tuesday, April 29, 1783. 12mo., pp. 8.
In the reprint of the Irish Minutes, published in Dublin, at the Religious and General Book Co., 72, Grafton Street, in 1864, the *Minutes* for 1783 occupy only two pages, and the following note is appended,—" It is singular that the numbers in Society are omitted from these first published Minutes. They are given in the English Minutes." The reprint of these *Minutes* is a very interesting volume to all who care to inquire into the early history of Methodism in Ireland. See No. 332.

371. MINUTES OF SOME LATE CONVERSATIONS BETWEEN THE REV. MR. J. WESLEY AND OTHERS. Bristol: Printed by W. Pine, in Wine-Street. 1783. 12mo., pp. 12.
Dated Bristol, Tuesday, July 29, 1783.
Contains regulations for the improvement of Kingswood School, which had fallen much below its original condition. Many of the faults are mentioned and the inquiry is made, " How may these evils be remedied, and the school reduced to its original plan? It must be mended or ended, for no school is better than the present school." One objection was "They (the children) ought never to play; but they do every day, yea, even in school." Preachers were not to beg for new chapels outside their circuits. Dr. Coke was appointed to visit the Societies throughout England in order to settle the preaching-houses on "the Conference plan," i.e. the Indenture or Model Deed, which Wesley had revised in 1780.

372. THE ARMINIAN MAGAZINE FOR THE YEAR 1783. Consisting of Extracts and Original Treatises on Universal Redemption. Volume VI. London: Printed by J. Paramore, at the Foundry, Moorfields; and sold at the New Chapel, City-Road, and by all the Booksellers in Town and Country. 8vo., pp. 688, viii.

No. 373. [1784.

The following are by Wesley:—
1. *Original Sermons* (xiii.) on Hebrews i. 14; (xiv.) Ephesians vi. 12, dated January 7, 1783; (xv.) 2 Thessalonians ii. 7; (xvi.) Isaiah ix. 11 [xi. 9], dated Dublin, April 22, 1783; (xvii.) Joshua xxiv. 15, dated Nottingham, May 26, 1783; (xviii.) Proverbs xxii. 6, dated London, July 12, 1783.
2. *Extract from The Second Spira. A Narrative of the death of the Hon. Fr. N——t, Son to the late——*. But see Dr. Clarke's *Wesley Family*, i. 122-126.
3. *An Extract from a book entitled Free Thoughts on the Brute-Creation*, by John Hildrop, D.D. A short preface.
4. *A Letter*, dated March 30, 1782, inserted as a preface to *An Answer to Mr. Madan's Treatise on Polygamy and Marriage, in a series of letters by the Rev. Mr. Wesley, by Joseph Benson.*
5. *Extracts from Mr. Bryant's Analysis of Ancient Mythology.*
6. *An Extract from the Depositions of William Floyd, &c., in the Court of King's Bench.* To it Wesley has appended original remarks.
7. *An Extract from Mr. Baxter's Certainty of the World of Spirits fully evinced by unquestionable Histories of Apparitions and Witchcraft, &c.*
8. *Some Account of the late Dr. Dodd.*
9. *A Thought on the manner of Educating Children*, signed J.W.
10. *Thoughts on the Writings of Baron Swedenborg*, dated Wakefield, May 9, 1782.
11. *An Extract from the Minutes of a Conference held at Bristol, in July, 1783, between the Rev. Mr. John Wesley and others.*
12. *Letters* to various persons.

A marked feature of this volume is the number of extracts from several works, some of them continued, others concluded from the preceding volume. They are, *An Extract from the Journal of Mr. G. C.*; *An Extract from the Survey of the Wisdom of God, in the Creation*; *Extracts from Locke on Human Understanding, with Short Remarks*; *An Account of the Passions, Extracted from Dr. Watts.*

1784.

373. THE DOCTRINE OF ORIGINAL SIN. EXTRACTED FROM A LATE AUTHOR. London: Printed by J. Paramore, at the Foundry, Moorfields; and sold at the New Chapel, City-Road; and at the Rev. Mr. Wesley's Preaching-Houses in Town and Country. 1784. 12mo., pp. 40.

Another, London: Story, n.d.

This is reprinted verbatim from Wesley's larger work, entitled *The Doctrine of Original Sin: according to Scripture, Reason and Experience*, puplished in 1757 (No. 182). It is taken from the close of that work (pp. 463-522), and is entirely an extract from Boston's *Fourfold State of Man*. There is not a single note or additional remark Even the introductory sentence is omitted, in which Wesley assigns as his reason for appending this extract to his larger work, "the unspeakable importance of thoroughly understanding this grand foundation of all revealed religion." Boston divides this section of his work into three parts, in which he aims, first, to prove the doctrine of the entirely corrupted condition of man; secondly, to represent this corruption in its several parts; and thirdly, to show how man's nature came to be corrupt. The last part occupies only a single paragraph. A practical application of the doctrine is appended,

Peculiar spellings are corrected, and the inordinate use of capitals and italics which marks the earlier work is wholly set aside. Wesley's purpose in omitting his name from the title-page may have been, as in other cases, to avoid prejudice. He certainly was not ashamed either of his views or his works.

374. Minutes of some Late Conversations between the Rev. Thomas Coke, LL.D., and Others. Dublin: Printed in the year 1784. 12mo., pp. 8.

Headed on third page, *Minutes*, &c., Dublin, Tuesday, July 6, 1784.

"Q. 14. What shall we do with those who wilfully and repeatedly neglect to meet their class? A. 1. Let the Assistant or one of his helpers personally visit them, wherever it is practicable, and explain to them the consequence if they continue to neglect, viz., expulsion. 2. If they do not amend, let the Assistant exclude them in the Society, informing it, that they are laid aside for a breach of our Rules of Discipline, and not for immoral conduct."

"Q. 16. What further can be done to stop the excessive use of tobacco in snuff, or by smoking or chewing the same? A. Let every preacher engage with an audible voice, in the presence of God, and his brethren, that he will not snuff, smoak or chew tobacco." A similar pledge was to be given by every preacher that he would "to the utmost of his power preach every morning, where he could have a congregation, and as far as practicable at 5 o'clock." The Deed Poll, which it was proposed to enrol "for the specification and establishment of the Conference of the people called Methodists," was approved; and an anonymous appeal designed to prevent its adoption was condemned.

375. Minutes of some Late Conversations between the Rev. Mr. Wesley and Others. Leeds: Printed by J. Bowling in Boar Lane. 1784. 12mo., pp. 12.

Dated Leeds, Tuesday, July 27, &c., 1784.

The preachers' probation was extended to four years: no preacher who denied Original Sin was to be allowed to preach: no one to make, or attend a wake, or feast. "Q. 22. Is the making candles for our own use, without paying duty for them, contrary to law? A. Certainly it is. It is a species of smuggling, not to be practised by any honest man."

376. The Sunday Service of the Methodists in the United States of America. With other Occasional Services. 1784. 12mo., pp. 320.

Preface dated Bristol, Sept. 9, 1784, and signed John Wesley.

    Fourth edition, London: 1790.

Wesley's estimate of the English Liturgy is given in a single sentence in the preface: "I believe there is no liturgy in the world, either in ancient or modern language, which breathes more of a solid, Scriptural, rational piety than the Common-Prayer of the Church of England." Although he says "little alteration" is made in this edition of it, yet the difference between *The Sunday Service* and *The Book of Common Prayer* is considerable. Of the 32 parts into which the "Contents" of the latter are divided 19 are omitted entirely. In the Morning and Evening prayer the following changes are made :—*The Exhortation* is abridged ; *the Absolution* gives place to a collect ; the *Venite, Benedicite, Benedictus, Magnificat, Nunc Dimittis*, and also the *Prayer for the Royal Family* are omitted, and the repetition of the *Lord's Prayer*. The *Prayer for all sorts and conditions of men* and the *Thanksgiving* are inserted before the *Prayer of St. Chrysostom*. The *Prayers and Thanksgivings upon several occasions*, the *Creed of St. Athanasius* ; the *Collects, Epistles*, and *Gospels* for Saints' and Holy Days (except Christmas, Good Friday, and Ascension Day) are omitted. The *Order of the Administration of the Lord's Supper ;* the *Ministration of Baptism ;* the *Communion of the Sick*, the *Matrimony* and *Burial Services* are more or less changed. The *Form and Manner of Making, Ordaining and Consecrating of Bishops, Priests and Deacons* are considerably abridged and are respectively changed into *The Form and Manner of making Deacons, Elders, and Superintendents*. The thirty-nine *Articles of Religion* are reduced to twenty-five. Many psalms are left out and many parts of others, "as being highly improper for the mouths of a Christian congregation," and throughout verbal changes are made.

The book was prepared for the use of the Societies in America, and in the preface is recommended to them.

No entry of any appointments of Ministers to America appears in the *Minutes of Conference* after 1775, until this year. The great national struggle had intervened. The appointment for 1784 is "*America*,—Thomas Coke, Rich. Whatcoat, Thomas Vasey." It was while they were waiting at Bristol to embark, that the preface to *The Sunday Service* was signed and dated there.

"Dr. Coke, Mr. Whatcoat and Mr. Vasey came down from London, in order to embark for America. . . . Being now clear in my own mind, I took a step which I had long weighed in my mind, and appointed Mr. Whatcoat and Mr. Vasey to go and serve the desolate sheep in America. . . . I added to them three more, which I verily believe will be much to the glory of God." —*Journal*, Aug. 31, Sept. 1, 2, 1784.

In a letter written by Wesley, Sep. 10, 1784, and appended to the *Minutes* of the following year, he remarks, "I have prepared a Liturgy little differing from that of the Church of England (I think the best constituted church in the world) which I advise all the travelling-preachers to use on the Lord's Day in all the congregations, reading the Litany only on Wednesdays and Fridays, and praying *extempore* on all other days. I also advise the Elders to administer the Supper of the Lord on every Lord's Day."

377. THE ARMINIAN MAGAZINE for the year 1784. Consisting of Extracts and Original Treatises on Universal Redemption. Volume vii. London: Printed by J. Paramore, at the Foundry, Moorfields ; and sold at the New Chapel, City-Road, and by all the Booksellers in Town and Country. 8 vo., pp. iv., 676, vii.

The following are original papers by Wesley, or extracts made and revised by him :—

1. *The Preface*, dated London, January 1, 1784.
2. *Original Sermons*. (xix.) On 1 Corinthians vii. 35 ; (xx.) James i. 4 ; (xxi.) 1 Corinthians xiii. 10 [9], dated Bristol, March 5, 1784 ; (xxii.) Romans xi. 33, dated Glasgow, April 28, 1784 ; (xxiii.) Colossians iii. 20 ; (xxiv.) 2 Corinthians vi. 17, 18, dated Otley, July 17, 1784.
3. *An Account of the late work of God at Epworth*.
4. The *Extract from a Survey of the Wisdom of God in the Creation*, cont.

1785.] **Nos. 378-379.**

5. *An Account of a Revival of the Work of God at St. Just, in Cornwall.*
6. *Some Account of an Eminent Man*, Dr. Philip Verheyen, of the University of Louvain. Signed John Wesley.
7. *Extracts from Locke on Human Understanding; with Short Remarks*, concluded. These extracts are continued through 3 vols. They are dated at the beginning, Pembroke, April 28, 1781, and at the end, Whitehaven, May 28, 1781, and are signed John Wesley.
8. *An Account of the Disturbances in my Father's House.* Dated at the end, Hilton-Park, March 26, 1784, and signed John Wesley.
9. *Thoughts concerning Gospel Ministers.*
10. *A Providential Event.* Signed J.W.
11. *An Extract from the Minutes of a Conference held at Leeds*, July 27, &c., 1784.
12. *Extracts from Mr. Bryant's Analysis of Ancient Mythology.* Continued through two volumes. Dated at the end, Tiverton, Sept. 4, 1782. Besides these are several short extracts and papers, and two letters.

378. A COLLECTION OF PSALMS AND HYMNS FOR THE LORD'S DAY. Published by John Wesley, M.A., Late Fellow of Lincoln College, Oxford; and Charles Wesley, M.A., Late Student of Christ Church College, Oxford. London: Printed in the year 1784. 12mo., pp. 104, iv.

Several editions were published.

Divided into two Parts, containing 118 Psalms and Hymns. The hymns are not consecutively numbered, but each has a title prefixed; they are all selected from the 144 Psalms and Hymns in the enlarged edition of *A Collection of Psalms and Hymns* published in 1741 (No. 30). It was bound up with the *Sunday Service* (No. 376); but the paging was not continuous.

After Wesley's death this was enlarged by Dr. Coke, and used in London and elsewhere at the forenoon service where the Liturgy was in use. Hence it was called *The Morning Hymn Book.* In 1816 the Conference recommended it to the congregations generally. On the publication of the Supplement in 1831, its use was gradually abandoned.

1785.

379. A SHORT ACCOUNT OF GOD'S DEALINGS WITH MR. JOHN HAIME. London: Printed by J. Paramore, at the Foundry, Moorfields; and sold at the New Chapel, City-Road; and at the Rev. Mr. Wesley's Preaching-Houses in Town and Country. 1785. 12mo., pp. 46.

John Haime—for many years a zealous preaching dragoon. The "extraordinary scenes" in camp and field in which Haime was a principal actor are graphically described by Stevens, who says, "He was one of those remarkable men who, like Nelson, Bradburn, and Bramwell, were raised up by Methodism from humble life to eminent usefulness, and who characterised its early lay ministry by their own strongly marked traits."—*History of Methodism*, Book iii., Ch. i.

On his return from the war he became for a few years one of Wesley's preachers. After much persuasion, he was induced, probably by Wesley, to write an account of his life, which he did in a simple, artless manner. It was then apparently revised by Wesley and inserted by him in the *Arminian Magazine* for 1780. The present publication is a reprint with an account of Haime's death, communicated by Mr. G. Story, which latter also appeared in the *Magazine* for January, 1785.

380. MINUTES OF SOME LATE CONVERSATIONS BETWEEN THE REV. JOHN WESLEY, M.A., AND OTHERS. Dublin: Printed in the year 1785. 12mo., pp. 7.

Headed on third page, *Minutes*, &c., Dublin, Friday, July 1st, 1785.

Contains some curious regulations respecting the sale of books. In the answers to Question 17, "How may the assistants be more useful?" are the following, " 3. By informing all the stewards of two universal Methodist rules, the one, that a married preacher is to have eighteenpence a week for each child; the other, that every circuit steward is to bear the expense of their preachers to and from the Conference. Also by informing them that the stipend of each preacher is £12 English yearly. . . . . 5. By preaching in every large town, at five in the morning, during summer."

381. MINUTES OF SOME LATE CONVERSATIONS BETWEEN THE REV. MR. WESLEY AND OTHERS. London: Printed by J. Paramore, at the Foundry, Upper Moorfields. 1785. 12mo., pp. 22.

Dated London, July 26, 1785.

The American appointments appear with Thomas Coke and Francis Asbury as "Superintendents"; with the names of 85 Assistants, or Preachers, and 20 "Elders;" also the number of members in the American circuits, including Nova Scotia and Antigua. The total is stated to be 71,217.

Q. 20.—"What is the state of our Societies in North America? A.—It may best appear from the following letter." Then follows Wesley's important letter on his ordaining ministers for America. In it he describes the condition of the churches in America, showing that many of the Provinces had been "erected into Independent States," that " the English Government had no authority over them either civil or ecclesiastical"; that "no one either exercises or claims any ecclesiastical authority at all"; that there are no Bishops, "neither any parish Ministers, so that for some hundred miles together there is none either to baptize or to administer the Lord's Supper." He says he had long been convinced "that Bishops and Presbyters are of the same order and consequently have the same right to ordain"; that, "importuned from time to time to exercise this right," he had hitherto refused "not only for peace' sake," but because he "was determined as little as possible to violate the established order of the national Church" to which he belonged; but that now in the altered state of affairs and believing that he violated no order and invaded no man's right, he had "appointed Dr. Coke and Mr. Francis Asbury to be joint *Superintendents* over the brethren in North America; as also Richard Whatcoat and Thomas Vasey, to act as *Elders* among them by baptizing and administering the Lord's Supper." A note is added, "If anyone is minded to dispute concerning Diocesan Episcopacy, he may dispute. But I have better work." Wesley's procedure is calmly discussed from a Church point of view by Canon Overton in *John Wesley*, pp. 195-208 : see also Moore's *Life of Wesley*, ii. 317-347 ; Southey, *ib.* ch. xxvii.

A Declaration is appended to the Minutes to the effect "that Mr. Wesley was desired at the last Bristol Conference, without a dissentient voice, to draw up a deed which should give a legal specification of the phrase 'The Conference of the people called Methodists,' that the mode of doing it was left to his judgment and discretion;" and that the substance and design of the Deed which he had "accordingly executed and enrolled," had the approval of the signatories whose names (69 in number) are given. For particulars of this important document called the Deed of Declaration and sometimes the Deed Poll, see *The Constitution and Polity of Wesleyan Methodism*, by the Rev. H. W. Williams, D.D., pp. 14-19, and Appendix No. i.

382. A Sermon Preached on Occasion of the Death of the Rev. Mr. John Fletcher, Vicar of Madeley, Shropshire. By John Wesley, M.A. London: Printed by J. Paramore, at the Foundry. 1785. [Price Sixpence.] 8vo., pp. 32.

Address "To the Reader" prefixed, dated London, Nov. 9, 1785, and signed John Wesley. The Sermon dated at the end Norwich, Oct. 24, 1785. An epitaph is added.

Another edition, London : Paramore, 1786.

Fletcher died on the 14th of August, and Wesley preached a funeral sermon on Sunday, November 6th ; but he did not write it at the time, being checked by a consciousness of his inability "to describe in a worthy manner such a person as Mr. Fletcher," judging "only an Apelles was proper to paint an Alexander." Submitting however to importunity, he hastily put together these materials, intending when he had more leisure to prepare a fuller narrative. This he did in the following year. The sermon is almost wholly composed of an account of Mr. Fletcher's life and labours, the chief part being in the words of Mrs. Fletcher.

Wesley's estimate of this good man is very striking. He says : " Many exemplary men have I known, holy in heart and life, within fourscore years. But one equal to him I have not known ; one so inwardly and outwardly devoted to God. So unblamable a character in every respect I have not found either in Europe or America. Nor do I expect to find another such, on this side of eternity."

383. The Arminian Magazine for the Year 1785. Consisting chiefly of Extracts and Original Treatises on Universal Redemption. Volume VIII. London; Printed by J. Paramore, at the Foundry, Moorfields : and sold at the New Chapel, City-Road, and by all the Booksellers in Town and Country. 8vo., pp. 668, viii. vi.

No. 384. [1785.

The following are original articles or edited extracts :—
  1. *Sermons* (xxv.) on 1 Cor. xiii. 1, 2, 3, dated London, October 15, 1784; (xxvi.) Heb. vi. 1, dated Tunbridge Wells, Dec. 6, 1784; (xxvii.) Hebrews xiii. 17, dated Bristol, March 18, 1785; (xxviii.) John i. 47; (xxix.) Phil. ii. 12, 13; (xxx.) Rev. xxi. 5.
  2. *An Extract from Dr. Whitby's Discourses on the Five Points.* This is continued through each month of this and the four following years.
  3. *Of the Fore-knowledge of God.* Extracted from a late Author.
  4. *An Extract from a Sermon on God is Love.*
"The following is the most remarkable discourse I ever saw upon the subject; and gives a full answer to one of the capital objections frequently made against Christianity. J.W." The sermon is by President Edwards.
  5. *An Extract from a Journey from Aleppo to Jerusalem; At Easter, A.D. 1797.* By Henry Maundrell, M.A.
  6. *Some Remarks on Article X. of Mr. Maty's New Review, for December, 1784.* Dated City-Road, Jan. 11, 1785, and signed John Wesley.
  7. *An Account of the Drummer of Tedworth.* Signed J.W.
  8. *Thoughts upon some Late Occurrences.* Dated, Plymouth Dock,\March 3, 1785, and signed John Wesley. The *Thoughts* relate to the Deed of Declaration.
  9. *A Strange Account.* Dated, Newcastle-upon-Tyne, May 31, 1784, and signed J.W.
  10. *A Question concerning Dew on Coach-glasses.*
  11. *A Thought upon Marriage*, (Matt. vi. 22). Dated, Lisburn, June 11, 1785, and signed J.W.
  12. *An Extract from the Minutes of a Conference held in London, July, 1785, between the Rev. John Wesley and others.*
  13. *Thoughts upon Dissipation.* Dated Hilton Park, March 26, 1783, signed J.W.
The volume contains several other extracts and one original letter by Wesley, also an interesting *Account of the Sunday-Charity Schools, lately begun in various parts of England.* This is dated Gloucester, June 5, 1784, and signed R. Raikes.
At the end of the volume are six pages of *errata* occurring in the first eight volumes, and attributed by Wesley to his "absence from the press."

384. PRAYERS FOR CONDEMNED MALEFACTORS. (Psalm lxxix. 12. [11].) London: Printed by J. Paramore, at the Foundry, Upper Moorfields. 1785. 12mo., pp. 12.

A poetical tract containing ten hymns of various metres, by Charles Wesley (his last publication). On page 8 begins a reprint of the tract entitled *A Word to a Condemned Malefactor*, by John Wesley (No. 81).
The first three hymns are the Church's intercession,
  For the sad sons of woe
  Cut off by man, to death consign'd.
The four following ones are headed *To be used by the Malefactors;* and the last three are also for their use, and are headed, *Just before their being led out to Execution.* They are tender, pleading words, showing how fully the writer entered into the circumstances of those who were "justly by man condemned to die," and how he pitied, mourned, and hoped for them, providing not only words for the church to offer in prayer on their behalf, but words of confession, of entreaty, and of humble faith for themselves. They form an appropriate memorial of the great work done by the early Methodists in the prisons of our land. Charles Wesley left several other similar hymns in manuscript for the same class of persons; see *Poetical Works*, vol. viii. pp. 347-353.

Southey, however, says "that 'the Wesleys do not appear to have repeated their visits after their early exclusion from the prisons, and that the early Methodists generally abandoned such good works.' The intimation is utterly false; the Methodist writings of the times abound in records of such labours; the Conference of 1778, some months before the death of Silas Told, formally recognised it as a duty of the preachers to visit the prisons; Wesley preached at Newgate when above eighty years old, while nearly half a hundred men under the sentence of death (such was the hanging of that day) wept around him. Charles Wesley visited Newgate and other prisons, and his last publication was a pamphlet of poetical *Prayers for Malefactors*, which he said had been answered 'on nineteen malefactors, who all died penitent' at one time."—Stevens' *History of Methodism*, Bk. v., ch. iv. note. The entry in Charles Wesley's *Journal* is, "These prayers were answered, Thursday, April 28, 1785, on nineteen malefactors, who all died penitent. 'Not unto me, O Lord, not unto me!'"—Vol. ii. p. 465.

385. A POCKET HYMN-BOOK FOR THE USE OF CHRISTIANS OF ALL DENOMINATIONS. London: Printed by J. Paramore, at the Foundry; and sold at the New Chapel, City-Road. 1785. Small 12mo., pp. 208, viii.

Preface, *To The Reader*, dated London, October 1, 1784, and signed John Wesley.

We learn from the preface that although the large Hymn Book (No. 348) contained more hymns than was at first intended, yet many, in no way inferior to them, were excluded, and several were not inserted from fear that "they would not be understood by a common congregation." As a strong desire was expressed for their publication, and as many of the preachers wished a small pocket Hymn Book to be provided for use in the Societies, this most beautiful little volume was prepared. It contains 200 hymns, and is divided into parts and sections similar to those of the larger book, from which thirty-nine of the hymns are taken. Each of the hymns has a tune assigned to it, and many have titles prefixed. Only one edition was issued. Olivers' hymn, "The God of Abraham praise," appears for the first time in any Wesleyan hymn book in this volume. For a very interesting account of this hymn see Julian's *Dictionary of Hymnology*, p. 1149.

Another book of similar title (No. 396) was published two years afterwards, the circumstances connected with the preparation of which gave it considerable notoriety.

NOTE.—THE LIFE OF GREGORY LOPEZ, WRITTEN ORIGINALLY IN SPANISH.

The above is given by Osborn, *Meth. Bib.*, under date 1785. But it had been already published twice by Wesley, in the first instance, in 1755, in the *Christian Library*, Vol. L. (No. 131), and again, more carefully edited, in the *Arminian Magazine* for 1780. Several years afterwards it was published separately, as appears from the catalogues for 1829-1850, but it is not in the catalogues between 1789 and 1815. In an inventory of the books on sale at the time of Wesley's death (1791) no mention is made of it. It is therefore probable that the copy from which the above title was taken was one of later date. Osborn was afterwards led to think that Wesley did not publish this separately. Heylin gives, under 1784, "*The Life of Gregory Lopez, written originally in Spanish, abridged by John Wesley.* 63pp., 18mo. No date [from *Arminian Magazine*, 1780.]" But there is no indication that Heylin had seen a separate issue of so early a date.

The original work was entitled, *The Holy Life, Pilgrimage and Blessed Death of Gregory Lopez, a Spanish Hermit in the West Indies.* It was translated by Abraham Woodhead, 1675; Second edition, London: 1686.

Wesley's estimate of Lopez was very high. "For many years I despaired of finding any inhabitant of Great Britain that could stand in any degree of comparison with Gregory Lopez or Monsieur De Renty. But let any impartial person judge if Mr. Fletcher was at all inferior to them."—*Life of Fletcher*.

1786.

386. AN EXTRACT FROM THE REV. MR. JOHN WESLEY'S JOURNAL. From August 9, 1779, to August 26, 1782. London: Printed by J. Paramore, at the Foundry, Upper Moorfields. And sold at the New Chapel, City-Road, and at the Rev. Mr. Wesley's Preaching Houses in Town and Country. 1786, 12mo., pp. 92. [No. xix.]

Dated at the end, Newington, January 19, 1786.

Another, London: Whitfield, 1797.

There seems to be no decline either of interest or vigour in Wesley's great work. He is able to preach "to thousands upon thousands at Bradforth" in the north, and to "two or three and twenty thousand" at Gwennap in Cornwall; his observations of nature and of public events are as minute, and his reading and labour apparently as great as they had been for nearly 50 years, though the records in the Journal are somewhat briefer. The following occurs : "Fri., 28 (June, 1782) I entered into my eightieth year; but, blessed be God, my time is not *labour* and *sorrow;* I find no more pain or bodily infirmities than at five-and-twenty. This I still impute—1. To the power of God, fitting me for what He calls me to; 2. To my still travelling four or five thousand miles a year; 3. To my sleeping, night or day, whenever I want it; 4. To my rising at a set hour; and 5. To my constant preaching, particularly in the morning."

387. MINUTES OF SOME LATE CONVERSATIONS BETWEEN THE REV. THOMAS COKE, LL.D., AND OTHERS. Dublin: Printed in the year 1786. 12mo., pp. 8.

Headed *Minutes*, &c., Dublin, Friday, July 7, 1786.

The Conference suggested an alteration should be made in the "General Deed" [the Model Deed] for the settlement of the "preaching-houses." This alteration was adopted by the English Conference which was held in the latter part of the same month. The change was substantially made in the form of the Deed, as published in the sixth edition of the *Large Minutes:* see *Min. Conf.*, 8vo. ed., i. 609. Wesley was urged to appoint the General [Circuit] Steward of every circuit and all the stewards of the particular Societies annually in the course of his visitation; and the following recommendations were made, "in order still further to carry on the present glorious revival of the work of God :—

1. Let the preachers fervently urge the leaders, and even the private believers, to go into the houses of the ungodly, and, wherever they are suffered, to pray earnestly with them and for them, and the world will be set on fire.
2. Let the preachers meet the classes in the country places as often as the circumstances of things will admit of it.
3. Let the assistants in planning the duties of the Lord's-day consider only the numbers of the congregations and Societies, and not be anywise influenced by the preaching-houses; rather than which let the preaching-houses be given to the bats and the moles."

388. MINUTES OF SOME LATE CONVERSATIONS BETWEEN THE REV. MESSRS. WESLEY AND OTHERS. Bristol: Printed by Bulgin and Rosser, No. 15, Broad-Street. 1786. 12mo., pp. 23.

Dated at the beginning, Bristol, July 25, 1786.

An important paper entitled *Of Separation from the Church* is appended. It is dated, Camelford, August 30, 1785, and signed John Wesley. A postscript is added, followed by another paper on *Service in Church Hours*, dated Bristol, July 22, 1786. These are reprinted in the *Works*, vol. xiii. pp. 222-4. To them are subjoined "A few little Advices" to the Preachers, signed John Wesley, and dated August 1, 1786, the day on which the Conference ended.

"Tues. 25—Our Conference began : About eighty preachers attended. We met every day at six and nine in the morning, and at two in the afternoon. . . On Thursday in the afternoon we permitted any of the Society to be present, and weighed what was said about separating from the Church. But we all determined to continue therein, without one dissentient voice ; and I doubt not this determination will stand, at least till I am removed into a better world."— *Journal*.

389. A SHORT ACCOUNT OF THE LIFE AND DEATH OF THE REV. JOHN FLETCHER. By the Rev. John Wesley. *(Sequor non passibus æquis.)* London : Printed by J. Paramore, at the Foundry, Upper Moorfields: and sold at the New Chapel, City-Road, and at the Rev. Mr. Wesley's Preaching-Houses in Town and Country. 1786. 12mo., pp. 227.

With portrait, which unfortunately is not often found. The preface "To the Reader," dated Amsterdam, September 12, 1786. The epitaph, as prepared by his widow and engraved on his tomb, is printed on the last page.

Wesley had known Fletcher longer and more intimately than had any other man in England. He therefore felt "obliged by the strongest ties to pay this small tribute to his memory." He acknowledges that he is little more than a compiler, the greater part of the account having been communicated by friends. Many persons contributed to make it what it is—a faithful, graphic, though brief, account of one of the most saintly men of that or of any age. Wesley says of him, "I can never believe it was the will of God that such a burning and shining light should be hid under a bushel. No, instead of being confined to a country village, it ought to have shone in every corner of our land. . . . He was as much called to sound an alarm through all the nation as Mr. Whitefield himself; nay, abundantly more so, seeing he was far better qualified for that important work. He had a more striking person, equal good breeding, an equally winning address; together with a richer flow of fancy, a stronger understanding, a far greater treasure of learning, both in languages, philosophy, and divinity; and, above all (which I can speak with fuller assurance, because I had a thorough knowledge both of one and the other), a more deep and constant communion with the Father, and with the Son, Jesus Christ." And yet Wesley regarded Whitefield as "one of the most eminent ministers that had appeared in England, or perhaps the world, during the century."—*Works*, xi. 302.

"I now applied myself in earnest to the writing of Mr. Fletcher's Life, having procured the best materials I could. To this I dedicated all the time I could spare till November, from five in the morning till eight at night. These are my studying hours. I cannot write longer in a day without hurting my eyes."—*Journal*, Sep. 26, 1786.

For a complete life of Fletcher reference must be made to *Wesley's Designated Successor: The Life, Letters, and Literary Labours of the Rev. John William Fletcher*. By the Rev. L. Tyerman. London: 1882.

390. THE SUNDAY SERVICE OF THE METHODISTS IN HIS MAJESTY'S DOMINIONS. With other Occasional Services. London: Printed by Frys and Couchman, Worship-Street, Upper-Moorfields. 1786. 12mo., pp. 320.

Another edition, 1788; Fourth, 1792; many subsequently.

Appended is the *Collection of Psalms and Hymns for the Lord's Day* (No. 378).

This is substantially the same as the *Sunday Service of the Methodists in the United States* (No. 376), the following changes only occurring:—the *Prayer for the Royal Family* is restored to the Morning and the Evening Prayer; and the Petitions for the Queen and the Royal Family to the Litany. The sentence in the prayer for the Church Militant, which in the American book reads:—"We beseech Thee to save and defend all Christian Governors; and especially Thy servants the Rulers of these United States; that under them we may be godly and quietly governed,"—is, in this one, restored to its original form.

This was soon afterwards (1788) altered to *The Sunday Service of the Methodists with other Occasional Services*, and is so continued at the present time. It is generally called *Wesley's Abridgement*. It must be distinguished from *The Book of Public Prayers and Services for the use of the People called Methodists*, first published in 1883.

391. THE ARMINIAN MAGAZINE for the year 1786. Consisting chiefly of Extracts and Original Treatises on Universal Redemption. Volume IX. London: Printed by J. Paramore, at the Foundry, Moorfields; and sold at the New Chapel, City-Road, and by all the Booksellers in Town and Country. 8vo., pp. 688, viii.

1. *Original Sermons.* (xxxi.) on Ephesians iv. 1-6, dated Bristol, Sept. 28, 1785; (xxxii.) Luke xii. 7, dated Bristol, March 3, 1786; (xxxiii.) 1 Cor. xii. 25, dated Newcastle-under-Lyne, March 30, 1786; (xxxiv.) James iv. 4, dated Wakefield, May 1, 1786; (xxxv.) Matt. xxv. 36, dated Aberdeen, May 23, 1786; (xxxvi.) Psalm xc. 2, dated Epworth, June 28, 1786.
2. *An Extract from a Survey of the Wisdom of God in the Creation.* See No. 325.
3. *An Extract from Three Dialogues.* By a late author.
4. *On the Church: in a letter to the Rev.*——, dated Plymouth Dock, Aug. 19, 1785; and signed John Wesley.
5. *Thoughts on Nervous Disorders: particularly that which is usually termed lowness of spirits.* Dated Melvill-House, May 20, 1784.
6. *God's Eyes are over all the earth.* Signed John Wesley.
7. *A remarkable Providence.* Signed J. W.
8. *Thoughts on Creation;* extracted from a late author.
9. *An Extract from the Life of Mr. Thomas Firmin.* To this is prefixed the note :—" I was exceedingly struck at reading the following Life; having long settled it in my mind that the entertaining wrong notions concerning the Trinity was inconsistent with real piety. But I cannot argue against matter of fact. I dare not deny that Mr. Firmin was a pious man, although his notions of the Trinity were quite erroneous. J. W."
10. *French Liberty: or, an Account of the Prison of Bicetre in France.* The following precedes the extract, "Some years ago a book fell into my hands which I had never heard of before: 'A Series of Letters by Oliver Mac Allester, Esq.,' a gentleman who resided several years at Paris, and who gives an account, p. 169 & seq., which one would wish every Englishman to be acquainted with. J. Wesley."
11. *Some Thoughts on an Expression of St. Paul, in the First Epistle to the Thessalonians, chap. v. ver. 23.* Dated Congleton, March 31, 1786.
12. *An Extract from the Minutes of a Conference held in Bristol, July 25, &c., 1786, between the Rev. Messrs. Wesley and others;* containing a paper entitled, *Of Separation from the Church,* dated Camelford, August 30, 1785, and signed John Wesley, and another dated Bristol, July 22, 1786.

There are many Extracts in this and the other volumes that are undoubtedly Wesley's, some of which must have cost him considerable labour; but in several instances it is impossible to determine with certainty the authorship, or the works from which the abridgements were made.

The following are continued from the previous volume :—Whitby's *Discourses on the Five Points;* and Maundrell's *Journey from Aleppo to Jerusalem.*

1787.

392. CONJECTURES CONCERNING THE NATURE OF FUTURE HAPPINESS. Translated from the French of Mons. Bonnet, of Geneva. Dublin: Printed by B. Dugdale, No. 150, Capel-Street. 1787. [Price Twopence.] 12mo., pp. 24.

Another edition, London: Paramore, 1790; Another, London: Paramore, 1791; Another, 1792; a new edition, with preface on title-page, London: Stephens, 1827.

The following appears on the back of the title-page: "To the Reader. Dublin, April 7, 1787. I am happy in communicating to men of sense in this kingdom, and at a very low price, one of the most sensible tracts I ever read. John Wesley."

Most readers will probably endorse Wesley's judgment of this thoughtful pamphlet, though some of the views are highly speculative. It is divided into nine sections. There are several footnotes by Wesley corrective of some of the sentiments expressed.

On the date named above Wesley preached twice at least, in all likelihood three times. At the communion after one of the services there were between seven and eight hundred communicants. After the evening service he held a lovefeast "which I suppose might have continued till midnight, if all had spoken that were ready to speak." He probably translated the tract at his lodgings "at Arthur Keene's, about half a mile out of town, a pleasant, healthy spot, where were peace and love, and plenty of all things."—*Journal.*

393. MINUTES OF SOME LATE CONVERSATIONS BETWEEN THE REV. JOHN WESLEY, M.A., AND OTHERS. Dublin: Printed by B. Dugdale, No. 150, Capel-Street. 1787. 12mo., pp. 8.

Headed, *Minutes*, &c., Dublin, July 6th, 1787.

To prevent dispute "about a trifle," instructions were given on the sounds of the five English vowels.

To preserve the freedom of debate it was determined that if anyone divulged anything of importance mentioned in the Conference he should be put back upon trial for four years, if in full connexion; if on trial, he should be suspended for a year.

Wesley added a long list of advices to the preachers, and closed by promising to print the Text of the New Testament (his own revised version) alone. This was done in 1790 (see No. 411).

394. MINUTES OF SOME LATE CONVERSATIONS BETWEEN THE REV. J. WESLEY AND OTHERS. London: Printed by J. Paramore, at the Foundry, Upper-Moorfields. 1787. 12mo., pp. 20.

Dated at the beginning, Manchester, July 31, 1787. Only one Conference had hitherto been held in Manchester, in 1765.

The ordinary questions and answers occupy nearly the whole of the *Minutes.* The numbers in the Societies are as follow:—

Europe...	62,087
United States	25,347
British Dominions	2,890
Under the Dutch Government...	62
Total	90,386

"Q. 23. Are there any directions to be given concerning singing? A. Let no anthems be introduced into our chapels or preaching-houses for the time to come, because they cannot properly be called Joint Worship."

395. THE ARMINIAN MAGAZINE for the year 1787. Consisting chiefly of Extracts and Original Treatises on Universal Redemption. Volume X. London: Printed by J.

Paramore, at the Foundry, Moorfields; and sold at the New Chapel, City-Road, and by all the Booksellers in Town and Country. 8vo., pp. 672, viii.

1. *Original Sermons.* (xxxvii.) 1 Cor. x. 13, dated London, October 7, 1786; (xxxviii.) 1 Peter iii. 3, 4, dated North Green, December 30th, 1786; (xxxix.) Luke xxii. 19, dated Oxon, Feb. 19, 1732. It is preceded by this note,—"The following discourse was written above five and fifty years ago, for the use of my pupils at Oxford. I have added very little, but retrenched much; as I then used more words than I do now. But I thank God, I have not yet seen cause to alter my sentiments in any point which is therein delivered. J. W." (xl.) 1 Cor. xii. 31; (xli.) Romans xv. 2, dated Castlebar, May 22, 1787; (xlii.) Ecclesiastes vii. 10, dated Dublin, June 27, 1787.

2. *An Account of Mr. Silas Told, written by himself.* The account of Silas Told, written by himself, was published in 1785. It is here revised and considerably abridged by Wesley, who published a fuller account in 1790, to be noticed hereafter (No. 406). The account is continued through this and the following volume.

3. *An Extract from a discourse concerning the mercy of God in preserving us from evil angels.* Written by Lord Chief Justice Hale, at Cambridge, March 26, 1661, upon occasion of a trial of certain witches.

4. *Thoughts upon Methodism.* Dated London, August 4, 1786.

5. *Thoughts on the Misery of Man.* Extracted from a late author.

6. *An Extract from God's Revenge against Adultery and Murder.* In an Address to the Reader, Wesley expresses a wish that the author, T. W. Reynolds, had given the real names of the offenders, "and that he had been less verbose. The former defect," he says, "is now incurable; but the latter I have attempted to remedy, by retrenching generally half, sometimes two-thirds, or even three-fourths of the narrative." Dated Feb. 3, 1787, and signed J. W. This may be taken as a sample of the amount of work done by Wesley in making the many extracts, large and small, contained in this and the other volumes of the Magazine, and generally headed *From a Late Author.*

7. *Superstition and Religion,* By a Late Author. A note is appended signed J. W.

8. *An Extract from the Minutes of a Conference held at Manchester, July 31, &c., 1787, between the Rev. J. Wesley and others.*

The following Extracts are continued: from Dr. Whitby's *Discourses on the Five Points;* from Maundrell's *Journeys in the East;* from a *Survey of the Wisdom of God in the Creation;* and from *Three Dialogues* between Sophronius and Callistus. The Magazine now describes a large number of very strange occurrences, real or imaginary.

396. A POCKET HYMN BOOK, FOR THE USE OF CHRISTIANS OF ALL DENOMINATIONS. London: Printed by J. Paramore, at the Foundery; and sold at the New Chappel, City-Road. 1787. 24mo., pp. 240, xi.

Preface containing seven numbered sections is dated Highbury Place, Nov. 15, 1786.

Contains 250 hymns; divided into sections and sub-sections, numbered and entitled precisely as in the large Hymn-book (No. 348). To each hymn a tune is assigned. Titles prefixed only in two or three instances.

Second edition, London: 1788; 3rd, London: 1789; 4th, London, 1790; 6th, London, 1791; 7th, London, 1791; 9th, London, 1793; 10th, London, 1794; 11th, London, 1794; 13th, London, 1798; 14th,

No. 397.   [1788.

1799; 17th, London, 1809; a 4th, London: Paramore, 1793; 12th, Dublin, 1801; 18th, Dublin, 1810; others Doncaster, 1805, 1806. One 1806 has Spence's name on title-page, as agent for York. In some editions preliminary hymns are inserted.

In 1781, a Wesleyan bookseller in York (Robert Spence) published *A Collection of Hymns from various Authors; Designed for general use*. It contained 172 hymns, 137 of which were taken without permission or acknowledgment from the works of the Wesleys. It was afterwards revised and enlarged, and published in small 24 mo. with the title, *A Pocket Hymn Book, Designed as a Constant Companion for the Pious: Collected from various Authors*. This book, although it contained many objectionable hymns, had been largely introduced into the Wesleyan Societies, when Wesley published his *Pocket Hymn Book*, in 1785 (No. 385). He was then advised at the Conference to reprint the York Book. This he did, making the following changes. He expunged 37 of the hymns, "because 14 appeared very flat and dull; 14 mere prose tagged with rhyme, and 9 more to be grievous doggerel." He also added a considerable number of what he judged the best hymns he and his brother had ever published, and he arranged the whole in proper order. The above is the book so prepared. Wesley bitterly complained of the introduction of so many improper hymns into his Societies.

NOTE.—On the cover of the *Arminian Magazine* for November, 1787, appears the following advertisement, relating to the above-mentioned work: "London, Nov. 1, 1787. This day is published, Price 1s. (the same size as the York Hymn Book) A POCKET HYMN BOOK, *for the use of Christians of all Denominations*. London: Printed by J. Paramore, and sold at the New Chapel, City Road. Also A SMALL POCKET HYMN BOOK *for the use of Children*. Price 6d." (In January 1788 the price is 3d.)

There is considerable uncertainty respecting this smaller book. No collector appears to have met with it. Osborn does not name it. Heylin prints the advertisement, but adds, "I have not seen a copy." Smith names it, but gives no particulars, indicating thereby that he had not seen it. In the very carefully prepared list of hymn-books published by the Wesleys, compiled by Mr. C. D. Hardcastle and inserted in the *Keighley Visitor*, August, 1861, the following entry is made: "1788—*A Small Pocket Hymn Book for the use of Children*. This we have not seen." The advertisement named above may have been intended to announce another edition of *Hymns for Children* (No. 223) or, as is more probable, the smaller book having the same title, issued in 1790, the publication of which may have been delayed until the preface was written which specially distinguishes that volume.

1788.

397. SERMONS ON SEVERAL OCCASIONS. By John Wesley, M.A., Fellow of Lincoln-College, Oxford. [Four Volumes.] Vol. v. Printed and sold at the New Chapel, City-Road, and at the Rev. Mr. Wesley's Preaching-Houses in Town and Country. 1788. 12mo., pp. 252, 322, 315, 291.

Preface dated London, Jan. 1, 1788.

On the cover of the Magazine appeared the following :—" London, Jan. 1, 1788. This day is published, price 10s., a New Edition of Four Volumes of Sermons, by the Rev. J. Wesley, M.A. There are also in the press, and will shortly be published in Four Volumes, price 10s., all the Sermons in the Ten Volumes of the *Arminian Magazine*, with alterations and additions by the author." For the first edition of the former four, see Nos. 88, 107, 139, 200. The second four are those named above. They contain fifty-six sermons, fourteen in each volume. Only forty-two of these sermons had been published in the Magazine up to this date, but several others afterwards appeared.

Wesley was induced to republish these sermons by hearing that a clergyman was about to do so; but although revised by him, they were very incorrectly printed.

The sermons, written during a course of years without any order or connexion, are here arranged methodically. Those placed first "are intended to throw light on some important Christian doctrines; afterwards those which more directly relate to some branch of Christian practice; and all in such an order that one may illustrate and confirm the other."—Preface : see also H. Moore, *L. of J. Wesley*, ii. 405-6.

These volumes contain the sermons distinguished as the Second Series in recent editions. A ninth volume was added after Wesley's death; but the most complete editions are those which have appeared since 1829.

398. MINUTES OF SOME LATE CONVERSATIONS BETWEEN THE REV. THOMAS COKE, LL.D., AND OTHERS. Dublin: Printed by B. Dugdale, 150, Capel Street. 1788. 12mo., pp. 10.

Headed, Dublin, July 8, 1788.

As some "gross sinners" had sprung up in the Society and had been expelled, a day of fasting and humiliation was appointed, " to deprecate the judgments deserved through these and other evils, and to pray the God of all grace to carry on the great revival He has begun."

Strict regulations were instituted to prevent illicit distilling; and sundry financial arrangements were made.

399. MINUTES OF SOME LATE CONVERSATIONS BETWEEN THE REV. J. WESLEY AND OTHERS. London : Printed in the year 1788. 12mo., pp. 27.

Dated at the beginning, London, Tuesday, July 29, 1788.

In the answer to the question, "Who have died this year?" appears the name of " Mr. Charles Wesley," and the brief record is added, " who after spending four-score years with much sorrow and pain quietly retired into Abraham's bosom. He had no disease; but after a gradual decay of some months ' The weary wheels of life stood still at last.' His least praise was his talent for poetry; although Dr. Watts did not scruple to say that ' that single poem *Wrestling Jacob* was worth all the verses he himself had written.'"

" Q. 21.—What further directions may be given concerning the Prayers of the Church of England ? A. The Assistants shall have a discretionary power to read the Prayer Book in the Preaching-Houses on Sunday mornings, where they think it expedient, if the generality of the Society acquiesce with it, on condition that Divine service never be performed in the Church-hours on the Sundays, when the Sacrament is administered in the Parish Church where the Preaching-House is situated, and the people be strenuously exhorted to attend the Sacrament in the Parish Church on those Sundays.' Q. 23.—Many of our Preachers have been obliged to go from the house of one friend to another for all their meals, to the great loss of their time, and to the injury of the work of God. What can be done to prevent this evil in the future? A. Let every circuit provide a sufficient allowance for the Preachers, that they may in general eat their meals at their own lodgings."

"The Conference Plan," or Model-Deed for the legal settlement of the "Preaching-Houses" is inserted. It is substantially the same as the one included in the *Large Minutes* (No. 343). The death of Charles Wesley and the enrolment of the Deed of Declaration (see No. 381) required however slight alterations to be made in it. It is the fourth revision of the original Deed (see *Large Minutes*, No. 221), and the last made in Wesley's life-time. It is repeated in the sixth edition of the *Large Minutes* (No. 404) published in 1789, and in the revised *Minutes of Conference*, vol. i., pp. 606-9. Precise instructions are given to the "Assistants" to guide them in obtaining and enrolling the Deeds.

Five missionaries were appointed to the West Indies. A brief address to the Societies in England and Wales is appended, in which attention is called to the reasonableness of each circuit providing for the preachers and their families "food and raiment for those who give up all their time and strength and labour." It is signed by Wesley, and dated London, Aug. 2, 1788.

400. THE ARMINIAN MAGAZINE, for the year 1788. Consisting chiefly of Extracts and Original Treatises on Universal Redemption. Volume xi. London: Printed and sold at the New Chapel, City-Road, and by all the Booksellers in Town and Country. 8vo., pp. 672, vii.

Original articles and abridgements :—

1. *Sermons* (xliii.) on Lev. xix. 17, dated Manchester, July 28, 1787; (xliv.) Matt. xvi. 3, dated St. Hellier's, Isle of Jersey, Aug. 27, 1787; (xlv.) Psalm viii. 3, 4, dated Manchester, July 23, 1787; (xlvi.) 1 Samuel ii. 17, dated Bristol, Oct. 7, 1787; (xlvii.) 2 Cor. i. 12, dated Bristol, April 8, 1788; (xlviii.) Heb. xi. 6, dated Stockport, April 9, 1788.

2. *An Extract from a Treatise called the Refined Courtier.* Preceded by this note : "To the Reader. I read this tract above fifty years ago, and took an extract from it. But I have now made a larger extract; which I recommend to all those that are lovers of common sense. J. W."

3. *An Extract from a Volume entitled a Review of Dr. Priestley's Doctrine of Philosophical Necessity.*

4. *The surest and safest way of Thriving.* Extracted from a late author (Mr. Thomas Gouge).

5. *Thoughts on Genius.* Dated Lambeth, Nov. 8, 1787.

6. *Remarks on the Swiftness of Time.* Extracted from a late author.

7. *The Case of Birstal House.* Recommended to the serious consideration of the people called Methodists. Dated London, reprinted Jan. 12, 1788, Signed John Wesley. At first issued as a folio circular in 1783, see No. 369A. After its appearance in the *Magazine* it was reprinted as a pamphlet.

8. *On the Folly of mis-spending Time.* Extracted from a late author.

9. *An Answer to an Important Question.* Dated Armagh, June 18, 1787. Signed J. W. This is a letter in reply to the question, Why do the clergy refuse to receive assistance from the Methodist preachers?

10. *Thoughts upon Dress.* Signed J. W.
11. *Thoughts on the consecration of Churches and Burial-Grounds.* Dated Dumfries, May 14, 1788, and signed J. W.
12. *An Extract from the Minutes of a Conference held in London, July 29, &c., 1788, between the Rev. J. Wesley and others.*
A great part of the Magazine is made up of extended extracts from the following :— Dr. Whitby's *Discourses on the Five Points ; An Account of Mr. Silas Told ; A Survey of the Wisdom of God in the Creation ;* and *God's Revenge against Murder and Adultery ;* all continued from volume x.

1789.

401. AN EXTRACT OF THE REV. MR. JOHN WESLEY'S JOURNAL, from September 4, 1782, to June 28, 1786. London : Printed and sold at the New Chapel in the City Road ; and at the Rev. Mr. Wesley's Preaching-Houses in Town and Country. 1789. 12mo., pp. 134. [No. xx.]

Dated at the end, London, Jan. 20, 1789. Three lines of errata.

Another edition, " London : Printed for the Author, and sold at the New-Chapel," &c., 1789. Errata corrected, but p. 115 printed 215.

The record of nearly four years of the same steady round of uninterrupted labour ; wondrous in a man of Wesley's years—perhaps in any man. During part of the time he suffered from severe illness, but it little impaired his work. Being now clear in his mind, he says, he took a step which he had long weighed, and appointed Mr. Whatcoat, Mr. Vasey, and others to act as elders, Dr. Coke and Francis Asbury as superintendents in America (see No. 381). The superintendents were afterwards called Bishops, but not by Wesley. " How can you, how dare you, suffer yourself to be called Bishop ? I shudder, I start at the very thought ! Men may call me a knave, or a fool, a rascal, a scoundrel, and I am content : But they shall never by my consent call me *Bishop !*"—Let. to Francis Asbury dated Sep. 20, 1788, in *Works,* xiii. 58.

402. MINUTES OF SOME LATE CONVERSATIONS BETWEEN THE REV. JOHN WESLEY, M.A., AND OTHERS. Dublin : Printed by B. Dugdale, 150, Capel-street. 1789. 12mo., pp. 12.

Headed, *Minutes, &c.,* Dublin, July 3d, 1789.

Earnest words against coveteousness are introduced :—" These *money-lovers* are the pest of every Christian Society. They have been the main cause of destroying every revival of religion. They will destroy *us,* if we do not put them away, &c." A report having " run through Ireland " that the Methodists were going to separate from the Church it was replied, "Nothing can be more false." Wesley "thinks it needful to observe further, that the Methodists never will separate from the Church till God calls him hence." A brief address to the Society was appended, similar to the one addressed to the English Societies in the previous year. It was dated Dublin, July 3, 1789, and signed John Wesley.

" I had much satisfaction in this Conference ; in which, conversing with between forty and fifty travelling preachers, I found such a body of men as I hardly believed could have been found together in Ireland ; men of so sound experience, so deep piety, and so strong understanding. I am convinced they are no way inferior to the English Conference, except it be in number."—*Journal*, July 9, 1789. This was Wesley's last visit to Ireland. He spent three months there in active work, during this stay, though at the Conference he had entered his eighty-sixth year.

403. MINUTES OF SOME LATE CONVERSATIONS BETWEEN THE REV. Mr. WESLEY AND OTHERS. Leeds : Printed in the year 1789. 12mo., pp. 21.

Dated, Leeds, Tuesday, July 28, 1789.

The following regulation appears : " No books are to be published without Mr. Wesley's sanction ; and those which are approved of by him shall be printed in his press in London, and sold by his book-keeper."

As it had been affirmed that many of the preachers disapproved of "the plan for settling the preaching-houses," one hundred and fifteen of them signed a declaration affirming their entire approval of it. A list of subscriptions by the preachers towards the new Preaching-House at Dewsbury is inserted ; the amount was £206 6s.

"Tuesday.—The Conference began : about a hundred preachers were present, and never was our Master more eminently present with us. The case of separation from the Church was largely considered, and we were all unanimous against it. We considered the case of Dewsbury House, which the self-elected trustees have robbed us of. The point they contended for was this —that they should have a right of rejecting any preachers they disapproved of. But this we saw would destroy itinerancy. So they choose J. A ——— for a preacher, who adopted W. E ——— for his curate. Nothing remained but to build another Preaching-House, toward which we subscribed two hundred and six pounds on the spot."—*Journal*, July 28, 1789. See No. 403a.

403A. THE CASE OF DEWSBURY HOUSE. 4to. circular of one page.

Dated Bristol, Sept. 11, 1789, and signed John Wesley.

This was a similar case to that of the Birstal House, see No. 369a. Wesley says, "When about fifty years ago, one and another young men offered to serve me as sons in the Gospel, it was on these terms, 'That they would labour where I appointed', otherwise we should have stood in each other's way. Here began itinerant preaching with us." As the number of the preachers increased, the work of stationing them became more and more difficult, and Wesley's desire, often expressed, was to transfer this work to one or more of the preachers themselves ; but none were then willing to accept it. The preaching-houses were vested in Trustees, whose duty it was to see that only those persons preached in them who were sent by Wesley. He goes on to say that "a new preaching-house had been built at Dewsbury, which the Trustees seized, and though they had promised to the contrary, positively refused to settle it on the Methodist plan ; requiring that they should have a power of refusing any preacher whom they disliked." The alternative before him was "either to sue for this House, or to build another." He preferred the latter course, as "being the most friendly," and he issued this circular in which he appeals to all his people, for the love of their " old and well nigh worn out servant, and for the love of antient Methodism, which if Itinerancy is interrupted will speedily come to nothing," and as " perhaps the last labour of love " he might have occasion to recommend to them, to exert themselves to the utmost to provide the necessary funds. Himself and Dr. Coke each subscribed fifty pounds.

404. MINUTES OF SEVERAL CONVERSATIONS BETWEEN THE REV. MR. WESLEY AND OTHERS, FROM THE YEAR 1744 TO THE YEAR 1789. London : Printed for the Author, and sold at the New Chapel, City Road, and at the Rev. Mr. Wesley's Preaching-Houses in Town and Country. 1789. 12mo., pp. 51.

The sixth edition of the *Large Minutes* and the last published during the author's life. Several editions were issued after his death, but since 1835 it has not been reprinted separately.

This edition is substantially the same as the fifth, pub. 1780 (No. 344). Slight verbal and other alterations are made. The principal are: 1. In the answer to question 51, on "the method of receiving a new helper." 2. Regulations on matrimonal engagements. 3. The extension of the term of probation to four years. 4. The omission of question 59 and its answer, on measures for securing "the future union of the Methodists," because rendered unnecessary by the Deed of Declaration, which had been executed in the interval. The same Deed, as we have seen, made a change necessary in the Model Deed for settling the preaching-houses.

" In 1797 this important document was revised and published as a 'Collection of Rules, or Code of Laws.' But on the title-page there is a typographical error, arising from the inverting of two figures, the date being given as 1779."— Advt. in *Min. Meth. Con.*, 8vo. 1862. In the *Constitution and Polity of Wesleyan Methodism* by Rev. H. W. Williams, D.D., (London, Wes. Meth. Book-Room, 1882), this document is reprinted and the changes which have been made in it by recent legislation are to a large extent indicated : see Appendix ii. p. 268. It is there called, ' The Form of Discipline.'

405. THE ARMINIAN MAGAZINE, for the year 1789. Consisting chiefly of Extracts and Original Treatises on Universal Redemption. Volume XII. London : Printed for the Author : and sold at the New Chapel, City-Road, Moorfields, and at the Rev. Mr. Wesley's Preaching-Houses in Town and Country. 8vo., pp. 672, vii.

Contains the following original papers and abridged extracts :—

1. *Sermons*, (xlix.) on Isaiah v. 4, dated Witney, October 17, 1787 ; (l.) Matthew xix. 24, dated Rochdale, April 22, 1788 ; (li.) Psalm viii. 4, dated Bradforth, May 2, 1788 ; (lii.) Heb. xi. 1, dated Yarm, June 11, 1788 ; (liii.) Jeremiah xxiii. 24, dated Portsmouth, August 12, 1788 ; (liv.) Luke xvi. 31, dated Birmingham, March 25, 1788. The first two are in the second four volumes of sermons published in 1788 (No. 397).

2. *Thoughts on Separation from the Church.* Dated Bristol, Sept. 20, 1788 ; signed J. W.

3. *Thoughts upon a late Phenomenon*, dated Nottingham, July 13, 1788.

The phenomenon is thus described by Wesley—" This I say again is an utterly new phenomenon ! I never saw, heard, or read of anything like it. The Methodists will not separate from the Church, though continually reproached for doing it. Although it would free them from abundance of inconveniences, and make their path much smoother and easier : although many of their friends earnestly advise and their enemies provoke them to it, the clergy in particular, most of whom, far from thanking them for continuing in the Church, use all the means in their power, fair and unfair, to drive them out

No. 406. [1790.

of it. One circumstance more is quite peculiar to the people called Methodists: that is, the terms upon which any one may be admitted into their Society. They do not impose, in order to their admission, any opinions whatever. Let them hold Particular or General Redemption, Absolute or Conditional Decrees: let them be Churchmen or Dissenters, Presbyterians or Independents, it is no obstacle. Let them chuse one mode of worship or another, it is no bar to their admission. The Presbyterian may be a Presbyterian still: the Independent or Anabaptist use his own mode of worship. So may the Quaker: and none will contend with him about it. They think and let think."

4. *An Extract from a Course of Sermons upon Death, Judgment, Heaven and Hell.* By a Late Author.

5. *An Extract from the Rev. Mr. Easterbrook's Account of George Lukins.*

6. *A clear and concise demonstration of the Divine inspiration of the Holy Scriptures.*

7. *The sufferings of Thecla, which happened about the year 67: Translated from a Greek Fragment.* The preface, signed J. W., ends with the words: "I neither affirm nor deny the truth of the following relation ; but that it is ancient, I cannot doubt."

8. *The Origin of Image Worship among Christians.*

9. *On the Manners of the Times.*

10. *An Extract from the Minutes of a Conference, held in Leeds, July 28, &c., 1789, between the Rev. J. Wesley and others.*

11. The following is inserted:—" To the Reader. My brother has left several manuscript volumes of short hymns upon various passages of Scripture: particularly on the four Gospels and the Acts of the Apostles. Many of these are no ways inferior to those that have been already published. A specimen of them I purpose to publish in the ensuing Magazines. The whole will probably see the light in some future period. J. W." Several are included in this volume.

Also several extended Extracts from different writers, of which the following are concluded: *An Extract from Dr. Whitby's Discourses on the Five Points; The Surest and Safest way of Thriving;* and *The Refined Courtier.* These are continued,—*A Survey of the Wisdom of God in the Creation;* and Dr. Priestley's *Doctrine of Philosophical Necessity.*

1790.

406. THE LIFE OF MR. SILAS TOLD. Containing many instances of the interposition of Divine Providence in his favour, when at sea; and in his sufferings abroad. Together with an account of the conversion of several malefactors, through his instrumentality. Written by Himself. (Psalm cvii. 23, 24.) London: Paramore. 1790. 12mo., pp. 113.

Preface dated City-Road, Nov. 13, 1789, and signed John Wesley. (In the Works the date is given Nov. 8. This is an error, as on that day Wesley was not in London).

Second Edition, corrected. London: Printed by Sammells and Ritchie: Sold by Whitfield, &c., 1790 ; Third, London : Whitfield, 1796 ; an unabridged Edition was published by W. Cowdroy, Salford : 1807, with a curious frontispiece.

This is Wesley's abridged and revised edition of *An Account of the Life and Dealings of God with Silas Told, late preacher of the Gospel; wherein is set forth the wonderful display of Divine Providence towards him when at sea; his various sufferings abroad; together with many instances of the grace of God, in the conversion of several malefactors under sentence of death, who were greatly blessed under his ministry*: Written by Himself, (Psal. cvii. 23, 24; Dan. xii. 3). London: Printed and sold by Gilbert and Plummer, (No. 13) Cree-Church-Lane, Leadenhall-Street, and by T. Scollick, Bookseller, City-Road, 1785, 12mo., pp. 174. Preface dated July 27, 1786, and signed Samuel Smith.

"I buried what was mortal of Silas Told. For many years he attended the malefactors in Newgate, without fee or reward; and I suppose no man for this hundred years has been so successful in that melancholy office. God had given him peculiar talents for it, and he had amazing success therein. The greatest part of those whom he attended died in peace, and many of them in triumph of faith."—*Journal*, Dec. 20, 1778.

407. A SERMON, preached at Leeds, July 29th, 1789, before the Methodist Preachers (assembled in Conference) and a large body of the people in connection with them; and now published at the request of many of the hearers. By James Hamilton, M.D., Fellow of the Royal College of Physicians of Edinburgh. (Acts ii. 17, 18.) London: Printed for the author, and to be had at the Rev. Mr. Wesley's Preaching-Houses in Town and Country. 1790. 8vo., pp. 20.

Dated at the end, Dunbar, January 1, 1790. Text, Jeremiah vii. 4. A hymn by Charles Wesley, "Father of boundless grace," is appended.

This sermon, preached by a layman before the Conference, is preceded by this address, "To the Reader. The following Discourse will recommend itself to all impartial persons. It contains deep and weighty truths, particularly needful to be considered at this time, especially by the people called Methodists, that they may fully understand, and thankfully improve the invaluable privileges which they enjoy. John Wesley. London, City-Road, Feb. 28th, 1790."

408. A SHORT ACCOUNT OF THE LIFE AND DEATH OF JANE NEWLAND, of Dublin, who departed this Life, October 22, 1789. London: Printed in the year 1790. 12mo., pp. 12.

This is a brief account of the conversion and zealous career of a Christian woman who in health and in sickness showed a dauntless, charitable, and devout spirit, and who was a witness of the "full salvation," which Wesley proclaimed.

The account seems to have been written by someone who was familiar with its subject, and afterwards revised by Wesley.

409. MINUTES OF SOME LATE CONVERSATIONS BETWEEN THE REV. THOMAS COKE, LL.D., AND OTHERS. Dublin: Printed by B. Dugdale, No. 150, Capel-Street. 1790. 12mo., pp. 10.

Headed, "Minutes of Some late Conversations, &c." Dublin, Friday, July 2, 1790.

The number of members reported in the Society was 14,106; at the beginning of the decade it was 6,109; the number of preachers had increased from 34 to 67.

No *Minutes* were published in Ireland in the following year, 1791. This volume is inserted as a continuation of the Irish Minutes to Wesley's death.

410. MINUTES OF SOME LATE CONVERSATIONS BETWEEN THE REV. MR. WESLEY AND OTHERS. Bristol: Printed in the year M.DCC.LXC. [1790.] 12mo., pp. 28.

Dated Bristol, Tuesday, July 27, 1790.

A Committee "for the management of our affairs in the West Indies," was appointed; also a Building Committee for Great Britain and one for Ireland. "Addenda taken out of former Minutes" are appended. No preacher was to be allowed to preach "three times the same day to the same congregation," or "oftener than twice on a week-day, or oftener than three times on the Lord's-day;" or to leave the Conference before its close, "without consent publicly obtained in the Conference." "These were Mr. Wesley's last directions in Conference."—MS. Note, signed S. Bradburn.

This was the last Conference that Wesley attended. "Mr. Wesley appeared very feeble; his eyesight had failed so much that he could not see to give out the hymns; yet his voice was strong, his spirit remarkably lively, and the powers of his mind and his love towards his fellow-creatures were as bright and as ardent as ever."—C. Atmore, in *Meth Mag.* 1845, p. 123.

411. THE NEW TESTAMENT, with an Analysis of the several Books and Chapters. By the Rev. J. Wesley, M.A. London: Printed and sold at the New Chapel, City-Road; and at the Rev. J. Wesley's Preaching-Houses in Town and Country. 1790. 16mo., pp. 424.

It has not been reprinted.

At the close of the Minutes of the Conference held in Dublin, July 6, 1787, after numerous interesting advices, Wesley adds, "I will print the text of the New Testament alone."

This may be regarded as Wesley's last important publication. It is a worthy finish to his great endeavour to supply the best literature he could to the British public, and at the lowest cost, and so by this means, as by others, "to spread Scriptural holiness through the land." The book contains his revised translation, which, he informs the reader, is brought as near as possible to the original. This is not a mere reprint of a previous edition: the text of the last corrected edition has been again thoroughly revised, and although "the alterations are few and seemingly small," the very minuteness of them, undetected except by careful comparison, shows how patiently he strove to make the work perfect. "The analysis of each Book and Epistle is prefixt to it." The analyses are taken from *Explanatory Notes on the New Testament* (No. 172), excepting that of the Book of the Revelation, which is new. "The short view" of the contents which is appended to the last-named in the previous editions is omitted, together with the Index of Words.

"Though the old division of chapters is retained, for the more easy finding of any text : yet the whole is likewise divided, according to the sense, into distinct sections: a little circumstance which makes many passages more intelligible to the reader."—Preface.

"The text is a new translation, and is remarkable as having anticipated many of the improved readings of later critics—not a few of Dean Trench's happiest suggestions for a revision of the text were anticipated by Wesley."—Heylin's edition of Stevens' *Hist. of Meth.* p. 766.

412. THE ARMINIAN MAGAZINE. For the year 1790. Consisting chiefly of Extracts and Original Treatises on Universal Redemption. Volume XIII. London : Printed for the Author, and sold at the New Chapel, City-Road, Moorfields ; and at the Rev. Mr. Wesley's Preaching-Houses in Town and Country. 8vo., pp. iv. 672, iv.

The following are original, as far as can be made out :—

1. *Preface, To the Reader.* Dated, Taunton, August 12, 1789, signed J.W.
2. *Sermons.* (lv.) on 2 Cor. v. 7, dated London, Dec. 30, 1788 ; (lvi.) Mark xii. 33, [32], dated, Dublin, April 9, 1789; (lvii.) Heb. v. 4, dated, Cork, May 4, 1789 ; strangely omitted from Jackson's two volumes of Sermons, (London : Kershaw, 1825), which it was presumed, contained "all the Sermons that have ever been published in Mr. Wesley's name, either by himself, or by those persons who had access to his papers after his decease." It is known as the "Korah Sermon." (lviii.) Jer. viii. 22, dated, Dublin, July 2, 1789 ; (lix). 2 Cor. v. 16, dated, Plymouth Dock, Aug. 15, 1789 ; (lx.) Matt. vi. 22, 23, dated, Bristol, Sep. 25, 1789.

3. *The Case of Dewsbury House : recommended to the consideration of the People called Methodists.* Signed John Wesley. See No. 403a.

4. *Farther Thoughts on Separation from the Church.* Dated London, Dec. 11, 1789 ; signed John Wesley.

5. *Thoughts on Memory.* Dated Yarmouth, Oct. 21, 1789 ; signed J. W.

6. *A Word to Whom it may Concern.* Relates to Mr. Atlay and the Dewsbury House. It is dated London, City-Road, Feb. 25, 1790.

7. *An Extract from the Minutes of a Conference held in Bristol, July 27, &c., 1790, between the Rev. J. Wesley and others.*

8. *Thoughts on a Late Publication, An Account of the Pelew Islands.* Dated Peckham, Dec. 30, 1789 : signed J. W.

9. *Thoughts on Suicide.* Dated Liverpool, April 8, 1790 ; signed J. W.

10. The following extended Extracts are concluded in this volume—*A Review of Dr. Priestley's Doctrine of Philosophical Necessity ; The Two Covenants of God with Mankind*, by Thomas Taylor, A.M. ; and *A Course of Sermons upon Death, Judgment, Heaven and Hell*, by a late Author. Several smaller ones are inserted. *The Extract from a Survey of the Wisdom of God in the Creation* is continued.

413. THE RULES OF THE STRANGERS' FRIEND SOCIETY IN BRISTOL.

These are dated Bristol, March 12, 1790, and signed John Wesley. This I give on the authority of Myles. See *Chronological History of the People called Methodists*, 4th ed. p. 180. I have not seen a copy; and I have no further particulars of the publication. The Rules themselves are inserted by Myles; and of the origin and growth of the Society Tyerman gives some interesting particulars in his *Life of Wesley*, iii. 252-4.

"Sunday was a comfortable day. In the morning I met the Strangers' Friend Society, instituted wholly for the relief, not of our Society, but of poor, sick, friendless Strangers. I do not know that I ever heard or read of such an institution till within a few years ago. So this also is one of the fruits of Methodism."—*Journal*, Mar. 14, 1790. The reference here is to the Bristol Society. It was founded in the year 1786; a similar Society had been established in London two years previously.

414. HYMNS FOR CHILDREN. London: Printed and sold at the New Chapel, City-Road. 1790. 16mo., pp. 34.

Contains forty-four hymns—a judicious selection made by Wesley, in his extreme age, from his brother's book entitled, *Hymns for Children and Others of Riper Years* (No. 223). More than half are taken from the section, *Hymns for the Youngest*, and amongst these are some of Charles Wesley's sweetest verses. The following preface, dated March 27th, 1790, is from Wesley's pen. "There are two ways of writing or speaking to children: the one is, to let ourselves down to them; the other, to lift them up to us. Dr. Watts has wrote in the former way, and has succeeded admirably well, speaking to children as children, and leaving them as he found them. The following hymns are written on the other plan: they contain strong and manly sense; yet expressed in such plain and easy language as even children may understand. But when they do understand them, they will be children no longer, only in years and in stature."

The original work (No. 223) was subsequently published with this preface. I have not seen a reprint of the smaller book.

1791.

415. AN EXTRACT OF THE REV. MR. JOHN WESLEY'S JOURNAL, from June 29, 1786, to Oct. 24, 1790. London: Printed by J. Paramore, North-Green, Worship-Street; and sold by G. Whitfield, New Chapel, City-Road; and at the Methodist Preaching-Houses in Town and Country. 1791. 12mo., pp. 206. [No. xxi.]

Another, London: Paramore, 1794.

This is the last number of the *Extracts* from the most extraordinary journal of evangelistic labour ever published. In it occurs this statement,—"Monday, June 28, 1790. This day I enter into my eighty-eighth year. For above eighty-six years I found none of the infirmities of old age; my eyes did not wax dim, neither was my natural strength abated. But last August I found almost a sudden change, my eyes were so dim that no glasses would help me. My strength likewise now quite forsook me, and probably will not return in this world. But I feel no pain from head to foot, only it seems nature is exhausted, and, humanly speaking, will sink more and more, 'Till the weary springs of life stand still at last.'"

At the end is the following *nota bene*—" There are unavoidable chasms in this Journal, owing to some parts being mislaid : and it is probable that many of the proper names of persons and places are not properly spelt ; as the whole of the manuscript was so ill written as to be scarcely legible."

"Wesley's Journals are the most entertaining productions of his pen. They are the history of the man and his cause. . . . Besides their historical value, they are replete with curious incidents, criticisms of books, theological and philosophical speculations, and references to contemporary men and events. For more than half a century they keep us not only weekly, but almost daily in the company of the great man, in his travels, his studies, and his public labours."—Stevens' *History of Methodism*, Book vi. chap. 5.

In reading these *Journals* it must be borne in mind that they are but " extracts " from the original manuscript ; and there is reason to suppose that they are but "a very modest selection " (see Smith's *Hist. Wes. Meth.*, bk. iii. ch. 4).

416. MINUTES OF SEVERAL CONVERSATIONS BETWEEN THE PREACHERS LATE IN CONNECTION WITH THE REV. MR. WESLEY. Manchester: Printed by T. Harper, Smithy-Door. 1791. 12mo., pp. 28.

Dated Manchester, Tuesday, 26th of July, 1791, and signed at the end William Thompson, President ; Thomas Coke, Secretary.

Another edition, London : Paramore, 1791.

The Conference assembled as usual, but with one sole exception—Wesley was no longer at its head. The change in the description of the *Minutes* is observable. There had been amongst the preachers a fear that on the death of Wesley the Deed of Declaration would give the Conference (as there defined) a power over the rest of the preachers. This fear had found expression, and of it Wesley was not uninformed. Accordingly in the year 1785, a year after the Deed was enrolled, Wesley wrote a letter addressed to the Conference, and entrusted it to the care of his travelling companion, Joseph Bradford, with instructions to read it at the first meeting after Wesley's death. It bears date, Chester, April 7th, 1785. In it Wesley begs the members of "the Conference" not to assume any superiority over the rest, but to let all things go on just as when he was with them. After the letter was read, a resolution was adopted that "all the preachers in full connexion shall enjoy every privilege that the members of the Conference enjoy." It is added, pathetically, "It may be expected that the Conference make some observations on the death of Mr. Wesley ; but they find themselves utterly inadequate to express their ideas and feelings on this awful and affecting event. Their souls do truly mourn for their great loss ; and they trust they shall give the most substantial proofs of their veneration for the memory of their most esteemed father and friend, by endeavouring with great humility and diffidence to follow and imitate him in doctrine, discipline, and life."

In the *Minutes* appears the following:—"Q. 8. What regulations are necessary for the preservation of our whole economy as the Rev. Mr. Wesley left it ? A. Let the three Kingdoms be divided into Districts : England into nineteen; Scotland into two; and Ireland into six." The "Assistant" of each Circuit had authority in any critical case, to summon the preachers of his District, who should select their own chairman: and their decision was to be final until the next Conference. No preacher was to be stationed in any Circuit for more than two years successively, "unless God has been pleased to use him as the instrument of a remarkable revival." The total number of members of the Methodist Societies in Europe and America reported to the Conference was 136,662.

417. THE ARMINIAN MAGAZINE, FOR THE YEAR 1791. Consisting chiefly of Extracts and Original Treatises on Universal Redemption. Volume XIV. London: Printed for the Editor; and sold at the New Chapel, City-Road, Moorfields; and at the Rev. Mr. Wesley's Preaching-Houses in Town and Country. 8vo., pp. 652, iv.

1. *Sermons* (lxi.) on Luke xii. 20, dated Balam, Feb. 19, 1790; (lxii.) Matt. xxii. 12, dated Madeley, March 26, 1790; (lxiii.) Psalm lxxiii. 20. This sermon, as were all the others, was divided into two parts, appearing in successive months. The former part was printed before Wesley's last illness; and the latter part was being printed on the day when his body lay in the chapel in City-Road. (lxiv.) Heb. xi. 1, which is dated London, Jan. 17, 1791, was the last sermon Wesley wrote. There were sixty-four sermons by Wesley published in the *Magazine* to this date. They were numbered consecutively; but with one exception are without titles, contrarily to his custom. All but two, 46 and 50, appear in the four volumes published in 1788: see No. 397.

In addition to the above are the following extended *Extracts*:—

2. *An Essay on the Liberty of Moral Agents.* Extracted from a late author. Preceded by an earnest recommendation, dated May 3, 1790, and signed John Wesley.

3. *An Extract from an Account of the Pelew Islands, in the Pacific Ocean.* By Captain Henry Wilson. An address "To the Reader" precedes, dated, City-Road, Jan. 8, 1790, and signed John Wesley.

"I looked over the finest picture of atheistical religion that I ever saw, in the account that Captain Wilson gives of Thule, King of Pelew. But how utterly needless is the knowledge of God (consequently how idle a book is the Bible,) if a man be all-accomplished, that has no more knowledge of God than a horse, and no more of His grace than a sparrow."—*Journal*, Jan. 16, 1789.

Wesley died March 2nd of this year, but he seems to have provided several articles for the later months. At length his busy pen was laid aside.

The *Magazine* was still issued after Wesley's death with the same title until the year 1798, when it was changed to the *Methodist Magazine*. In 1822 the title was further changed to the *Wesleyan Methodist Magazine*. It continued to be published in octavo and with the same general character to the end of 1893, when a considerable alteration in size and other respects was made. The title is still retained.

ADDITIONAL NOTES.

68. A Short View of the Difference between the Moravian Brethren, lately in England and the Reverend Mr. John and Charles Wesley.

From trustworthy information which I have received, I am of opinion that the former part of this tract was published in the year 1741. The title was the same except that the word "Now" occupied the place of "Lately."

83. Hymns on the Lord's Supper.

"In 1856 when suggestions were made for a union between the Wesleyan Methodists and the Church, the Rev. W. Gresley republished this in a tract of 30 pp. to show that Wesley's views on the subject were identical with the teachings of the Church."—Heylin. In 1871 a volume was published entitled *The Eucharistic Manuals of John and Charles Wesley, Reprinted from the Original Editions of 1748-57-94*, edited, with an Introduction, by W. E. Dutton, (London : Bull, Simmons and Co., 1871. 12mo., pp. xxviii. 257). It contained *A Companion for the Altar* (No. 36); *Hymns on the Lord's Supper*, with the preface concerning *The Christian Sacrament and Sacrifice*, extracted from Dr. Brevint—a reprint of the 4th edition of No. 83. The object of the publication of these *Manuals* was to attempt to prove that Wesley held High Church doctrine on the Sacrament. Similar opinions are promulgated in *John Wesley and Modern Methodism*, by Frederick Hockin, M.A., (London: Rivington, 1887, post 8vo., pp. 218); also in *The Churchman's Life of Wesley*, by R. Denny Urlin, Barrister, F.S.A., (in the Home Library Series, London : Society for Promoting Christian Knowledge, 1880, post 8vo., pp. vii. 352). But see *The Churchmanship of John Wesley, and the Relations of Wesleyan Methodism to the Church of England*, by James H. Rigg, D.D., (London : Wes. Con. Office, post 8vo. pp. vii. 120).

99. Hymns for Children.

Whilst these pages have been passing through the press a copy of this pamphlet has come into my hands. It is an anonymous 12mo. tract of 12 pages, but without title-page, date, or even printer's name. The title, as above, is on the upper part of the first page. It consists of five hymns for children taken from *Hymns and Sacred Poems* (No. 40), together with one by Dr. Watts, commencing 'Thee we adore, eternal Name,' and entitled *Life and*

Eternity. It was slightly altered by Wesley and appeared in No. 7. Next comes a Hymn for Sunday—'The Lord of Sabbath, let us praise,' by S. Wesley, jun. It is found in the 3rd volume of No. 58. These are followed by 'Jesu, the all-restoring Word,' and 'An Evening Hymn,' both from *Hymns and Sacred Poems* (No. 19); by *An Exhortation for a Child; Directions for a Child; A Morning and an Evening Prayer for a Child*; also Graces before and after Meat.

I am compelled to think that this tract was not compiled by Wesley. At the close of the evening prayer is the following, for use "At lying down in bed":—
    I lay me down, hoping to sleep,
    I pray to God my soul to keep;
    But if I die before I wake,
    I pray to God my soul to take.
I think it highly improbable that Wesley would have put these words into the lips of a child "at lying down." Nor are others of the hymns in my judgment, in harmony with Wesley's style, especially when addressing a child.

147. HYMNS FOR NEW YEAR'S DAY, 1751. Bristol: Printed by Felix Farley. [Price One Penny.] 12mo., pp. 11.

A copy of this has just come into my possession. It is precisely the same as the others named in the text.

172. NOTES UPON THE NEW TESTAMENT.

It appears from the following extract that this work subsequently underwent revision by other hands than the author's. "I was called to conduct through the press an edition of Mr. Wesley's revised translation of the New Testament, with his Explanatory Notes, of which I endeavoured to furnish a pure and correct text, which could only be done by a careful collation of various editions, and by availing myself of the author's manuscript corrections, contained in a copy which he left in his own library. This edition was comprised in two volumes octavo."—*Recollections of my own Life and Times*, by Thomas Jackson (London Wes. Conf. Office, 1873), p. 237. The two volumes were issued as the 11th edition, "with the last corrections of the author," London: Mason, 1831.

205. SELECT HYMNS WITH TUNES ANNEXT.

I think it highly probable that the "twelve pages of instructions in music," mentioned on page 117, and commencing with the words, "The Gamut or Scale of Music," were prepared by the author of *Harmonia Sacra: or, A Choice Collection of Psalm and Hymn Tunes, &c., Collected from the most celebrated Masters, and made use of in the principal churches and chapels in London; particularly at the Foundling, Lock and Magdalen Hospitals, with an introduction to Psalmody and several new tunes never before published*, by Mr. Thomas Butts, (London: E. & C. Dibly, booksellers in the Poultry, near the Mansion House, pp. 229, ii.). "The Introduction to Psalmody" here named has some features in common with the pages referred to above; and in the preface to No. 205 Wesley directs attention to the *Harmonia Sacra*, as exceeding "beyond all degrees of comparison anything of the kind which has appeared in England before." I have seen three different books by Butts bearing this title; in all of them are many of Wesley's hymns, one of them containing few others. It is probably to this last one in particular, that Wesley refers in the quotation just given. Almost all the tunes in Wesley's book are taken from Butts.

214. SHORT HYMNS ON SELECT PASSAGES OF THE HOLY SCRIPTURES.

In the *Poetical Works of John and Charles Wesley*, published 1870, these Short Hymns occupy vols. ix. x. xi. xii. and half of xiii. The editor says of them, "They were evidently favourites with the Author, as he spent many of the later years of his life in revising and enlarging them, especially those on the New Testament." Referring to the second edition (above p. 122), he describes it as "somewhat abridged," and adds, "but in the present reprint nothing is omitted, while the Author's manuscripts have supplied more than a hundred additional hymns—several of them not properly entitled 'Short Hymns'—of the value of which it would be difficult to speak too highly,"—vol. ix. pp. viii. x. They were further revised by John Wesley, as the following extract from his Journal indicates :—

"Wednesday 10, and the following days, I corrected my brother's posthumous poems: being short psalms (some few excepted) on the four gospels, and the Acts of the Apostles. They make five volumes in quarto, containing eighteen or nineteen hundred pages. They were finished April 25, 1765.
The revisal finished, April 24, 1774.
A second revisal finished, Jan. 26, 1777.
A third revisal finished, Feb. 20, 1780.
A fourth revisal finished.
A fifth revisal finished.
A sixth revisal finished.
A seventh revisal finished.
The last revisal finished, May 1787.
Many of these are little, if any, inferior to his former poems, having the same justness of thought, with the same beauty of expression; yea the same keenness of wit, on proper occasions, as bright and piercing as ever."—*Journal*, Dec. 10, 1788.

262. SOME ACCOUNT OF THE EXPERIENCE OF E. J.

It has been suggested that the subject and author of this pamphlet was Mrs. Elizabeth Johnson, of Bristol; or that the pamphlet is an abridgement of a brief memoir witten of her by Miss Ritchie. But neither of these suppositions is correct. Mrs. Johnson died in Bristol in 1798, and Miss Ritchie's memoir was not written until 1799. The title of it is *An Account of Mrs. Elizabeth Johnson, well-known in the City of Bristol for more than half a century, for her eminent Piety and Benevolence: To which is added an Extract from her Diary*, (Bristol: W. Pine and Son, n.d., 12mo., pp. 86). The preface is dated Bristol, Feb. 27, 1799. There is a marked difference between the style of Mrs. Johnson's writing and that of "E. J." The opinion expressed in the text is doubtless the correct one.

281. PRAYERS FOR CHILDREN.

As a beautiful and interesting evidence of Wesley's regard for children, the following may be quoted :—"At Bolton he had, in his congregation, five hundred and fifty children, all scholars in the Methodist Sunday-School; and it was either now, or soon after, that he preached to them a sermon, from Psalm xxxiv. 11, in which he engaged to use no word of more than two syllables, and literally fulfilled his pledge." This was in 1786, when he was in the 83rd year of his age; see *Journal*, April 16. "Old as he was [he had now nearly completed his 87th year] Wesley set out next morning [from Darlington] at half-past three o'clock, for Newcastle, where he preached, in the evening, from Isaiah lvii. 1, 2. The following night (Friday) he preached again his remarkable sermon to the children of the Sunday-school, taking as his text Psalm xxxiv. 11; the sermon being literally composed and delivered in words of not more than two syllables."—Tyerman's *Life of Wesley*, iii. 472, 607. Unfortunately the sermon has not been preserved.

COLLECTED WORKS.

The following editions of Wesley's collected Works have been noticed :—
1. The first edition compiled by Wesley himself and published in thirty-two duodecimo volumes in the years 1771-4. These volumes are fully described in the notes, see pp. 156, 162, 171, 177.
2. The second edition prepared by direction of the Conference of 1808 by the Rev. Joseph Benson, and published in 17 vols. 8vo. (see p. 180) in the years 1809-13. "This edition," Osborn says, "though in many respects better than the former, is still faulty both in respect to contents and arrangement. It contains much that Wesley neither wrote nor published, while some of his undoubted publications appear to have escaped the notice of the editors."—*Meth. Bib.* p. 59.
3. The third edition in fourteen volumes octavo. This was compiled by the Rev. Thomas Jackson, and published in the years 1829-31. It was followed by the *Explanatory Notes on the New Testament* in two volumes octavo, uniform with the other volumes. This edition is far more correct and complete than either of the others, Jackson having the advantage of access to Wesley's own corrected copy of the first edition. The work is admirably printed. Its progress through the press was watched with the utmost attention.

A smaller edition of this in fifteen volumes duodecimo, with a Life of Wesley by the Rev. John Beecham, D.D., was issued by the Methodist Book-Room in 1856, the fifteenth volume being the Notes on the New Testament. The works have been frequently reprinted in these two sizes.

A collection of the Wesley poetical writings has been published in thirteen volumes post octavo, bearing the title,

> THE POETICAL WORKS OF JOHN AND CHARLES WESLEY: Reprinted from the Originals, with the last corrections of the Authors. Together with the Poems of Charles Wesley not before published. Collected and arranged by G. Osborn, D.D. London: Wesleyan Methodist Conference Office, 1872.

A few particulars respecting these volumes may be added. The following extract from the Advertisement in the first volume explains the principle upon which this reprint is based and gives some account of its contents.

"The poetical publications of John and Charles Wesley originally appeared at various intervals during a space of fifty-two or three years. The total number of them, as far as at present ascertained is fifty-seven; of which, seven bore the names of the two brothers, seven of John Wesley only, eight of Charles Wesley only; while the remaining thirty-five were anonymous, though some were afterwards owned, and all are capable of being certainly identified.

They admit of a further classification in regard to their respective contents. (1.) Four are entirely extracted from other authors. (2.) Six are partly original and partly selected. (3.) Nine are mostly selected from previous publications of their own, with a few from other authors intermixed. While (4.) thirty-eight are strictly and exclusively original.

This fourth and largest class constitutes the basis of the present edition, along with three volumes of the second class which it has been deemed advisable to reprint entire, because in the majority of instances the selected poems have been altered and adapted by the editors for a purpose of their own, and according to their own taste. The third class, like the first, it is obviously unnecessary to include.

With these reprints, there will be published in successive volumes a large number of poems left by Mr. Charles Wesley in MSS., and carefully revised for publication, but which for some reason or reasons unknown were not published by him ; together with such single poems, whether in print already or in manuscript, as may not before have been collected : the whole forming as complete a collection as circumstances will permit of the poetry of these wonderful and blessed men.".—pp. xiii. xiv.

It will be observed that the number of publications named above does not correspond with the number mentioned in the text of this work. It is to be regretted that an entire list of the poetical works known is not given in the volumes ; and that the several reprints are not inserted in their chronological order. Nor is it less to be regretted that so able and diligent a student of these writings as Dr. Osborn was so sparing in his annotations on them.

SUMMARY.

The following were not, in my opinion, either edited or published by Wesley, Nos. 94, 99, 299; but see pp. 47, 49, 249, 175.

There is also much uncertainty respecting the editorship of Nos. 106, 144, 177, 178, 180, 190, 259, 271, 288, 292, 315; nor can it be determined what part Wesley took in the editing or publishing of Nos. 231, 359, 374, 387, 398; but there is an obvious propriety in inserting them.

Of the prose writings the following are by Charles Wesley, Nos. 23, 33, 141, and, perhaps, 144. All the rest are by John Wesley. On the combined authorship of many of the poetical works see pp. 22, 253-4.

The total number of publications recorded in the preceding pages is 423, including those referred to in the duplicated sections. Of these, as stated above, three have been wrongly attributed to the Wesleys, and sixteen are of doubtful authorship.

Of the works to be assigned with confidence to the Wesleys, 326 are Prose, (the 50 volumes of the *Christian Library* and the 14 volumes of the *Arminian Magazine* being in each case counted but as one work), 61 are Verse and 14 are Musical, a total of 391. The whole may be classified as follows :—

    233 are original Works by John Wesley :
    100 ,, extracted or edited by him :
      8 ,, Works for which he wrote a preface or notes only :
     20 ,, original Works by Charles Wesley :
     30 ,, Works in which the brothers shared, or of which it cannot be decided whether they were prepared by John or by Charles.

INDEXES.

INDEX TO TITLES.

(The Numbers in this Index refer to the Sections.)

Abstract of Life and Death of Thomas Haliburton . 10
Absolute Predestination, Serious Considerations on . 22
Account of Conduct of War in Middle Colonies . . 340
   ,,   ,, Genuine Christianity . . . 122
   ,,   ,, Kingswood School 127
   ,,   ,, The People called Methodists . . 126
   ,,   ,, Trial at Gloucester 52
   ,,   ,, Work of God in America . . . 331
   ,,   ,, Cross, Thomas 315
   ,,   ,, Dillon, John 271
   ,,   ,, E. J. 262
   ,,   ,, Fletcher, Rev. John 389
   ,,   ,, Gilbert, Alice 292
   ,,   ,, Haime, John 379
   ,,   ,, Hindmarsh, Elizabeth . . . 323
   ,,   ,, Hitchens, Samuel 89
   ,,   ,, Hitchens, Thomas 102
   ,,   ,, Hogg, Thomas 144
   ,,   ,, Johnson, Ann 284
   ,,   ,, Langson, Mary 259
   ,,   ,, Lee, Matthew 158
   ,,   ,, Mitchell, Thomas 350
   ,,   ,, Mooney, Nicolas 288
   ,,   ,, Moore, Richard 177
   ,,   ,, Newland, Jane 408
   ,,   ,, Othen, Nathanael 188
   ,,   ,, Richardson, Mrs. Hannah . . 23
   ,,   ,, Rogers, Ann 263
Address to Inhabitants of England, A Calm . . 316
   ,, to Inhabitants of Ireland, A Compassionate . 328
   ,, to Inhabitants of Ireland, A Short . . 133
   ,, to People of England on State of Nation, A Short 327
   ,, to American Colonies, A Calm . . . 305
   ,, to the Clergy 175
   ,, to Inhabitants of Great Britain, A Seasonable . 311

INDEX

Advantage of Church of England over Church of Rome	161
Advice to an Englishman	76
„ to the People called Methodists	73
„ to a Soldier	44
„ to Saints and Sinners, A Word of	86
„ to a Young Clergyman	4
Advices with respect to Health	255
Affairs, Free Thoughts on Present State of Public	264
Alarm to Unconverted Sinners, Alleine's	362
Alleine's Alarm to Unconverted Sinners	362
„ Christian Letters	241
Almost Christian, A Sermon on the	28
Altar, A Companion for the	36
America, Account of Work of God in	331
„ Sunday Service for United States of	376
American Colonies, A Calm Address to	305
„ Rebellion, Reflections on	341
„ War, Extract of Letter to Lord H * * e on his Conduct in	353
Answer to Dr. Gill	167
„ to Dr. Trapp's Sermons	118
„ to Hervey's Letters	227
„ to Hill's *Imposture Detected*	320
„ to Letter in *Bath Journal*	132
„ to Letters to Author of *Theron and Aspasio*	183
„ to Mr. Church	65
„ to Objections to Arminian Magazine	334
Antient Christians, Manners of the	123
Antinomian and Friend, Dialogue between	70
„ „ „ „ A Second	71
Aphorisms of Justification (Baxter)	67
Appeal to Men of Reason and Religion	47
„ „ „ „ A Farther, Part i.	63
„ „ „ „ A Farther, Part ii.	64
Arminian Magazine—See Magazine.	
„ „ Proposals for	322
Arminian, What is an?	260
Ascension Day, Hymns for	91
Aspasio Vindicated, Remarks on Defence of Preface to	236
Assize, A Sermon on the Great	185
Association, The Protestant	357
Awake thou that Sleepest, A Sermon on, (C. W.)	33
Backsliders, A Call to—a Sermon	329
Baily, Letter to Mr.	143
Band Societies, Rules of	57

INDEX

Baptism, Thoughts upon Infant	149
Barnes, Two Treatises by Dr.	14
Bath Journal, Answer to Letter in	132
Baxter's Aphorisms, Extract of	67
,, Call to Unconverted	363
Believers, A Sermon on Repentance of	248
Birstal House, Case of	369A
Bishop of London, Letter to	103
Blow at the Root, A	212
Brainerd, David, Extract of Life of	253
Brethren, Hymns Composed for the Use of the	137
Bristol, Rules of Strangers' Friend Society in	413

Cadogan on Gout	303
Call to a Holy Life, Serious, (Law)	48
,, ,, Unconverted Sinners (Baxter)	363
Calm Address to Inhabitants of England	316
Calvinism, Defence of Minute on, (1770)	273
Case of Birstal House	369A
,, ,, Dewsbury House	403A
,, ,, John Nelson	56
,, ,, People of Custrin	190
Catechism, Roman, with Reply	179
Catholic Spirit, A Sermon on	170
Cause and Cure of Earthquakes	141
Cautions and Directions to Professors	213
Character of a Methodist	34
Check, Extract from Fletcher's Equal	304
Children, Hymns for	99, 223, 414
,, Instructions for	62
,, Lessons for, Part i.	85
,, ,, ,, Part ii.	100
,, ,, ,, Part iii.	111
,, ,, ,, Part iv.	168
,, Prayers for	281
,, Token for	124
Christ, Imitation of (à Kempis)	3
,, ,, ,, Extract of	26
,, is All in All, Hymns for those to whom	204
Christian Letters, (Alleine)	241
,, Library	131
,, Perfection, A Sermon on	29
,, ,, Farther Thoughts on	219
,, ,, Practical Treatise on (Law)	45
,, ,, Plain Account of	238
,, Prudence, A Treatise on, (Norris)	2

Christian Reflections	295
Christians, etc., Select Hymns for Use of . .	208
,, ,, . Manners of the Antient . . .	123
,, ,, A Pocket Hymn Book for the Use of	385, 396
Christian's Pattern, The	3
,, ,,. Extract of the . .	26
,, Pocket Companion	231
Christianity Exemplified at Wednesbury . . .	72
,, A Plain Account of Genuine . .	122
,, Nature and Design of . . .	17
Church, Mr., Answer to	65
,, ,, Second Letter to . . .	87
,, of England, Advantage of Members of . .	161
,, Reasons against Separation from the . .	201
City Road Chapel, A Sermon on laying Foundation Stone of	317
Clergy, Address to the	175
Clergyman, Letter to a	110
,,. Advice to a Young	4
Collection of Prayers for Every Day in the Week .	1
,, . ,, . ,, for Families . . .	74
,, . ,, Hymns (1742)	41
,, ,, Hymns for People called Methodists (1780)	348
,, ,, Moral and Sacred Poems . . .	58
,, ,, Psalms and Hymns (1737) . . .	6
,, ,, ,, ,, (1738) . . .	7
,, ,, ,, ,, (1741) . . .	30
,, ,, ,, ,, for Lord's Day . .	378
,, ,, ,, ,, (Sacred Harmony) .	358
,, ,, Receits for the Poor . . .	69
,, ,, Tunes Sung at the Foundery . .	38
Colonies, Address to the American . . .	305
,, Account of War in the Middle . . .	340
Commandments, Exposition of (Hopkins) . .	193
Companion, The Christian's Pocket . . .	231
,, for the Altar	36
Compendium of Logick	142
Concordance (Taylor)	359
Conference, or Conversations—see Minutes.	
Conflagration and Renovation of the World, Extract of Discourses on	293
Conjectures on Future Happiness (Bonnet) . .	392
Consequence Proved, The	274
Considerations on Election and Reprobation . .	16
,, on Predestination . . .	22
Cooper, Jane, Letters by	225
Covenant, Directions for Renewing . . .	345
Craftsman, Letter to Author of the . . .	75

INDEX   261

Creation, Survey of the Wisdom of God in	220, 265, 325
Cross, Thomas, Account of	315
Custrin, Case of People of	190
Death of Fletcher, Rev. John, Sermon on	382
,, ,, Hitchens, Samuel, Short Account of	89
,, ,, Hitchens, Thomas, Short Account of	102
,, ,, Hindmarsh, Elizabeth, Short Account of	323
,, ,, Jones, Robert, Elegy on	39
,, ,, Langson, Mary, Short Account of	259
,, ,, Moore, Richard, Short Account of	177
,, ,, Whitefield, Rev. George, Sermon on	266
,, Preparation for, in Several Hymns	285
Defence of Minute of Conference (1770)	273
Desideratum, The (Electricity)	202
Dewsbury House, Case of	403A
Dialogue between Antinomian and Friend	70
,, ,, ,, ,, A Second	71
,, ,, Predestinarian and Friend	24
Dictionary, An English	162
Difference between Moravians and J. & C.W., View of	68
Dignity of Human Nature	210
Dillon, John, Account of	271
Directions for Married Persons	163
,, ,, Pronunciation and Gesture	125
,, ,, Renewing Covenant	345
Discourse on Sin in Believers	218
Discourses on Conflagration, Renovation, etc.	293
,, Extract of Zinzendorf's	50
Doctrine of Absolute Predestination (A— T—)	261
,, Original Sin, Extract of	373
,, ,, (Treatise on)	182
,, Salvation, Faith, etc. (Homilies)	9
,, Scripture, of Predestination, Election, etc.	27
Doctrines taught by Wesley, Remarks on Hill's Review of	283
Downes, Rev. Mr., Letter to	195
Drunkard, A Word to a	77
Earl of Moreland, History of Henry	351
Earthquake at Lisbon, Serious Thoughts on	171
,, Hymns Occasioned by the	148, 148A
Earthquakes, Cause and Cure of	141
Ecclesiastical History	355
E. J., Experience of	262
Electricity made Plain (Desideratum)	202

INDEX

Election and Reprobation, Considerations on	16
Elegy on Death of Robert Jones	39
„ on Whitefield	278
England, Calm Address to Inhabitants of	316
„ Serious Address to People of	327
„ History of	313
English Dictionary	162
„ Grammar, A Short	113
Englishman, A Word to an	76
Enthusiasm of Methodists and Papists compared, Letter to Author of	140
Enthusiasm of Methodists and Papists compared, Second Letter to Author of	152
Epistle to J. Wesley (C. W.)	173
„ to Whitefield	277
Erasmi Colloquia Selecta	146
Estimate of Manners	360
Excerpta ex Ovidio, etc.	130
Exeter, Second Letter to Bishop of	154
Experience of E. J, Some Account of	262
Exposition of Commandments (Hopkins)	193
Extract of Baxter's Aphorisms of Justification	67
„ „ Cadogan on the Gout	303
„ „ Christian's Pattern	26
„ „ Doctrine of Original Sin	373
„ „ John Nelson's Journal	361
„ „ Journal of Eliz. Harper	256
„ „ Law's Works	252
„ „ Letter to Viscount Howe	353
„ „ Letters of Mrs. L * * *	257
„ „ Life of Brainerd	253
„ „ Life of Mdme. Guion	314
„ „ Life of T. Haliburton	10
„ „ Life of John Janeway	159
„ „ Life of M. De Renty	21
„ „ Mary Gilbert's Journal	250
„ „ Nature and Design of Christianity	17
„ „ Paradise Lost	222
„ „ Reply to Sir Wm. Howe	352
„ „ Treatise on Religious Affections (Edwards)	294
„ „ Two Discourses on Conflagration, &c.	293
„ „ Young's Night Thoughts	269
„ „ Zinzendorf's Discourses	50
Extracts from Wesley's Journal—see Journal.	
Families, Hymns for Use of	245

INDEX 263

Families, Prayers for 74
Farrago Double Distilled, Remarks on . . . 287
Fast-Day, Hymns for the (1756) 181
Fear of Man, Treatise on (Nicodemus) . . . 12
Festivals, Hymns on the Great 94
Fletcher, Life of 389
  „ Sermon on Death of 382
Fletcher's *Equal Check*, Extract of . . . 304
Fleury, Letter to Mr. 272
Forms of Prayer for Every Day of the Week, Collection of 1
Foundery, Tunes Sung at the 38
Free, Dr., Letter to 186
  „   „   „ A Second 187
Free Grace, Sermon on 11
Freeholder, A Word to a 104
Freemen of the Church, A Word to . . . 180
French Grammar 151
Friend, Letter to a, on Tea 119
Funeral Hymns (First Series) 96
  „   „ (Second Series) 197

Gair I'r Methodist 109
Gentleman, Letter to a 184
Gesture and Pronunciation, Directions for . . 125
Gilbert, Alice, Account of 292
  „ Mary, Extract from Journal of . . . 250
Gill, Dr., Answer to 167
Gloucester, Letter to Bp. of 216
  „ Account of Trial at 52
God in the Soul of Man, Life of . . . 51
Godfathers and Godmothers, Thoughts concerning . 157
God's Dealings with Mr. Thomas Hogg, Short Account of 144
  „ Everlasting Love, Hymns on . . . 31, 32
  „ Sovereignty, Thoughts on 319
Gout, Cadogan on 303
Graces before Meat (Hymns) 98
Grammar, English 113
  „ French 151
  „ Greek 233
  „ Hebrew 150
  „ Latin 112
Great Britain, Address to Inhabitants of . . 311
Greek Grammar 233
Grounds of Vocal Music 207
Guion, Extract of Life of Madame . . . 314

Haime, John, Account of	379
Haliburton, Abstract of Life of	10
,, Extract of Life of	10
Hamilton, Dr., Sermon by	407
Happiness, Conjectures on Future (Bonnet)	392
Harmony, Sacred (Musical)	358
Harper, Elizabeth, Extract of Journal of	256
Health, Advices with respect to	255
Hebrew Grammar, A Short	150
Herbert's Poems, Parts of	297
Hervey, Answer to Letters of	227
Hill's *Farrago*, Remarks on	287
,, *Imposture Detected*, Answer to	320
,, Review of Wesley's Doctrines, Remarks on	283
Hindmarsh, Elizabeth, Account of	323
Historiæ et Præcepta Selecta	116
History, Ecclesiastical	355
,, of England	313
,, of Henry, Earl of Moreland	351
,, of Methodism, A Short	229
,, A Short Roman	289
Hitchens, Samuel, Account of	89
,, Thomas, Account of	102
Hogg, Thomas, Account of	144
Holy Life, Serious Call to a	48
Horne, Mr., Letter to	209
H * * e, Extract of Letter to Viscount	353
Howe, Reply to Sir W.	352
Human Life, Reflections on (Norris)	25
,, Nature, The Dignity of	210
Humane Society, A Sermon Preached before the	324
Hymn at the Sacrament	61
Hymns, A Collection of Psalms and (1737)	6
,, ,, ,, ,, (1738)	7
,, and Sacred Poems (1739)	15
,, ,, ,, ,, (1740)	19
,, A Collection of Psalms and (1741)	30
,, on God's Everlasting Love	31, 32
,, and Sacred Poems (1742)	40
,, A Collection of (1742)	41
,, for Times of Trouble and Persecution (1744)	59
,, for Times of Trouble	60
,, on the Lord's Supper (1745)	83
,, for the Nativity	84
,, for our Lord's Resurrection (1746)	90
,, for Ascension Day ,,	91
,, of Petition and Thanksgiving ,,	92

Hymns to the Trinity (Gloria Patri, &c.) 1746 . . 93
" on the Great Festivals " . . 94
" for the Thanksgiving Day " . . 95
" Funeral (First Series) " . . 96
" for the Watchnight " . . 97
" Graces before at and after Meat " . . 98
" for Children " . . 99
" Redemption (1747) 105
" and Sacred Poems " . . . 106
" for the use of the Brethren (1749) . . 137
" and Sacred Poems " . . . 138
" for New Year's Day (1750) . . . 147
" on the Earthquake " . . 148, 148A
" and Spiritual Songs (1753) . . . 165
" for the Year 1756 181
" of Intercession (1758) 192
" Funeral (Second Series : 1759) . . . 197
" on the Expected Invasion " . . . 198
" for Thanksgiving Day " . . . 199
" for those to whom Christ is All in All (1761) . 204
" Select, with Tunes Annext " . 205
" Select, for Christians of all Denominations (1761) 208
" on Select Passages of Scripture (1762) . . 214
" for Children (1763) 223
" for Families (1767) 245
" on the Trinity " 246
" on Preparation for Death (1772) . . . 285
" for Times of Tumult (1780) . . . 347
" Collection of, for Methodists (Large Hymn Book :
   1780) 348
" on the Protestant Association (1781) . . 357
" for the National Fast (1782) . . . 366
" for the Nation " . . 367, 368
" A Collection of Psalms and, for the Lord's Day
   (1784) 378
" for Condemned Malefactors (1785) . . 384
" The Pocket Hymn Book " . . 385
" " " " " (1787) . . 396
" for Children (1790) 414

Imposture Detected (Rowland Hill), Answer to . 320
Imputed Righteousness, Thoughts on . . 211
Infant Baptism, Thoughts upon . . . 149
Instructiones Pueriles 117
Instructions for Children 62
    " for Religious Societies . . 296

266 INDEX

Intercession, Hymns of 192
Invasion, Hymns on the Expected . . 198
Ireland, Address to Inhabitants of . . 133
  „ Short Method of Converting the Catholics of   156
  „ Compassionate Address to Inhabitants of   328

Janeway, John, Extract of Life of . . . 159
Johnson, Ann, Account of 284
Jones, Robert, Elegy on Death of . . . 39
Journal, Answer to Church's Remarks on Wesley's . 65
  „ Extract from Mary Gilbert's . . . 250
  „ John Nelson's 361
  „ Extract of Wesley's, part i. 13 ; ii. 18 ; iii. 37 ; iv. 53 ; v. 120 ; vi. 160 ; vii. 166 ; viii. 176 ; ix. 194 ; x. 203 ; xi. 224 ; xii. 240 ; xiii. 247; xiv. 270; xv. 301; xvi. 318; xvii. 335 ; xviii. 369; xix. 386 ; xx. 401 ; xxi. 415 ; relating to Affidavit, 20 ; Wheatley, 176A.
Justification, Baxter's Aphorisms on . . 67
  „ Treatise on (Goodwin) . . 226

Kempis, T. à, de Christo Imitando   114
Kingswood School, Short Account of   127

Langson, Mary, Account of   259
Latin Books :
    Caii Sallustii Crispi Bell. etc. 128; Cornelii Nepotis, etc. 129; Desiderii Erasmi, etc. 146; Excerpta ex Ovidio, etc. 130 ; Historiæ, etc. 116; Instructiones Pueriles, 117 ; Mathurini Colloquia Selecta, 115; Phædri Fabulæ, 145; Thomæ à Kempis, 114.
Latin Grammar, A Short 112
Law, Mr., Extract from Works of . . . 252
  „ „ Letter to 174
Lee, Matthew, Account of 158
Leeds, A Sermon preached at (Dr. Hamilton) . . 407
L * * * [Lefevre] Mrs., Extract of Letters of . . 257
Lessons for Children, Part i. 85
  „ „ Part ii. 100
  „ „ Part iii. 111
  „ „ Part iv. 168
Letter in *Bath Journal*, Answer to a . . . 132
  „ to Author of *Craftsman* 75

INDEX

Letter to Author of *Enthusiasm of Methodists*, etc. . 140
„   „   „   „   „   Second   152
„   „ Author of *Theron and Aspasio* . . . 183
„   „ Bp. of Exeter 154
„   „ Bp. of Gloucester 216
„   „ Bp. of London 103
„   „ a Clergyman 110
„   „ Dr. Conyers Middleton 121
„   „ Dr. Free 186
„   „ Dr. Free (Second) 187
„   „ Dr. Rutherforth 249
„   „ a Friend on Tea 119
„   „ a Gentleman 184
„   „ Mr. Baily 143
„   „ Mr. Downes 195
„   „ Mr. Fleury 272
„   „ Mr. Horne 209
„   „ Mr. Law 174
„   „ Mr. Maxfield 326
„   „ Mr. Potter 189
„   „ Mr. Whittingham 342
„   „ *Public Advertiser* 339, 349
„   „ a Quaker 108
„   „ a Roman Catholic 134
Letters, Christian (Alleine) 241
„   by Jane Cooper 225
„   Answer to Hervey's 227
„   to a Nobleman, Extract from Reply to Sir W.
        Howe on 352
Liberty, Observations on 310
„   Thoughts upon 279
Library, A Christian 131
Life of God in Soul of Man (Scougall) . . . 51
Life, Thoughts on a Single 228
Life of Brainerd, David, Extract of . . . 253
„   „ Guion, Madame, Extract of . . . 314
„   „ de Renty, Monsieur, Extract of . . . 21
„   „ Mitchell, Thomas, Short Account of . . 350
„   „ Told, Silas,   „   „   „   . . 406
Life and Death of Fletcher, Rev. John, Short Account of 389
„   „   „   „ Gilbert, Alice,   „   „   „ 292
„   „   „   „ Haliburton, Thomas, Abstract of . 10
„   „   „   „   „   „   Extract of . 10
„   „   „   „ Janeway, John,   „   „   . 159
„   „   „   „ Lee, Matthew, Some Account of . 158
„   „   „   „ Mooney, Nicholas, Some Account of . 288
„   „   „   „ Newland, Jane, Short Account of . 408

INDEX

Life and Death of Othen, Nathanael, Short Account of . 188
„ „ „ „ Walsh, Thomas, . . . 215
Lisbon, Thoughts on Earthquake at . . . 171
Logic, Compendium of 142
Lord's Day, Collection of Psalms and Hymns for . 378
„ Supper, Hymns on the 83

Magazine, Answer to Objections to Arminian . . 334
„ Proposals for 322
„ The Arminian, Vol. i. (1778) 333; Vol. ii. (1779) 338; Vol. iii. (1780) 346; Vol. iv. (1781) 356; Vol. v. (1782) 365; Vol. vi. (1783) 372; Vol. vii. (1784) 377; Vol. viii. (1785) 383; Vol. ix. (1786) 391; Vol. x. (1787) 395: Vol. xi. (1788) 400; Vol. xii. (1789) 405; Vol. xiii. (1790) 412; Vol. xiv. (1791) 417.
Malefactor, A Word to a Condemned . . . 81
Malefactors, Prayers for (Hymns) . . . 384
Manners of Antient Christians 123
„ of the Present Times, Estimate of . . 360
Marks of a Work of the Spirit, The Distinguishing . 49
Marriage and a Single Life, Thoughts on . . 42
Married Persons, Directions for 163
Mathurini Colloquia Selecta 115
Maxfield, Thomas, Letter to 326
Melody, Sacred, (Tunes) 206
Method of Converting Roman Catholics in Ireland, A Short 156
Methodism, A Short History of 229
Methodist, Character of a 34
„ Principles of a 35
„ Principles of a, Farther Explained . . 87
„ A Word to a (Welsh) 109
Methodists, Advice to 73
„ Collection of Hymns for Use of . . 348
„ and Papists Compared, Letter to Author of Enthusiasm of 140
„ and Papists Compared, Letter to Author of Enthusiasm of, Second. . . 152
„ Plain Account of People called . . 126
„ Sunday Service of . . . 376, 390
Middleton, Dr. Conyers, Letter to . . . 121
Milton's Paradise Lost, Extract from . . . 222
Minute of 1770, Defence of 273
Minutes of Conference, (1749), 135, 136; (1765), 232; (1766), 237; (1767), 244; (1768), 254; (1769) 258; (1770), 267; (1771), 275; (1772), 282;

(1773), 291; (1774), 302; (1775), 307; (1776), 312; (1777), 321; (1778), 332; (1779), 337; (1780), 343; (1781), 354; (1782), 364; (1783), 371; (1784), 375; (1785), 381; (1786), 388; (1787), 394; (1788), 399; (1789), 403; (1790), 410; (1791), 416.
Minutes, The Large, 1st edition, 164; 2nd ed., 221; 3rd ed., 268; 4th ed., 285; 5th ed., 344; 6th ed., 404.
Minutes, Irish, (1778), 332A; (1783), 370; (1784), 374; (1785), 380; (1786), 387; (1787), 393; (1788), 398; (1789), 402; (1790), 409.

Mitchell, Thomas, Account of	350
Modern Christianity at Wednesbury	72
Mooney, Nicolas, Account of	288
Moore, Richard, Account of	177
Moral and Sacred Poems, A Collection of	58
Moravians and J. & C. Wesley, Difference between	68
Moreland, Henry, Earl of	351
Music, Grounds of Vocal	207
Musical Works :—	
Hymns for the Great Festivals (Lampe's Tunes)	94
Sacred Harmony	358
Sacred Melody	206
Tunes sung at the Foundery, Collection of	38
Narrative of Revival in Virginia	330
,, of Work of God at Northampton (Edwards)	54
Nation, Hymns for the (1782)	367, 368
,, Serious Address on the State of	327
National Fast, Hymns for the (1782)	366
,, Sins and Miseries, A Sermon on	309
Nativity, Hymns for the	84
Natural Philosophy—see Survey	
Nature and Design of Christianity (Law)	17
,, Design, and Rules of United Societies	43
Necessity, Thoughts upon	300
Nelson, John, Case of	56
,, ,, Extract of Journal of	361
Nepotis, Cornelii, Excellentium Imperatorum Vitæ	129
New England, Thoughts on Revival in	66
New Testament, Notes on	172
,, ,, Text of	411
New Year's Day, Hymns for	147
Newland, Jane, Account of	408
Nicodemus, or a Treatise on the Fear of Man	12
Night Thoughts, Extract of Young's	269

Norris, on Christian Prudence, Extract of . . 2
Northampton, Narrative of Work of God at . . 54
Notes on New Testament 172
„ „ Old „ 234

Observations on Liberty . . . 310
Old Testament, Notes on . . 234
Onan, Thoughts on Sin of . . 243
Origin of Power, Thoughts on . . 280
Original Sin, Doctrine of . . 182
„ „ „ Extract of . 373
„ „ Sermon on . . 196
Othen, Nathanael, Account of . . 188
Ovidio, etc., Excerpta ex . . 130

Paradise Lost, Extract from . . . 222
Pattern, The Christian's (à Kempis) . . . 3
Perfection, Christian, Plain Account of . . . 238
„ „ Sermon on 29
„ „ Treatise on (Law) . . . 45
„ „ Farther Thoughts upon . . 219
Perseverance, Answer to Dr. Gill on Final . . 167
„ of Saints, Serious Thoughts on . . 153
Petition and Thanksgiving, Hymns of . . . 92
Phædri Fabulæ 145
Pharisaism and Antinomianism, First Part of Check to
    (Fletcher) 304
Physick, Primitive 101
Pilgrim's Progress, The 46
Plain Account of Christian Perfection . . . 238
Pocket Companion, The Christian's (Barnes) . . 231
Poems, Herbert's 297
„ Hymns and Sacred (1747) . . . 106
„ „ „ „ (1749) . . . 138
Poetry and Poetical Works.—See Hymns, &c.
Poor, Collection of Receipts for Use of the . 69
Popery Calmly Considered . . . 336
Potter, Mr., Letter to 189
Power, Thoughts concerning the Origin of . 280
Prayer for every Day in the Week, Forms of . 1
Prayers for Children 281
„ „ Condemned Malefactors (Hymns) . 384
„ „ Families 74
Predestinarian and Friend, Dialogue between . 24
Predestination Calmly Considered . . 155

INDEX

Predestination, Doctrine of, Stated and Asserted by A—T—	261
„ Election and Reprobation, Doctrine of	27
„ Serious Considerations on Absolute	22
„ Sermon on	290
Preface to *Aspasio Vindicated*, Remarks on Defence of	236
Preparation for Death in Several Hymns	285
Present Times, An Estimate of the Manners of	360
Preservative Against Unsettled Notions in Religion	191
Primitive Physick	101
Principles of a Methodist	35
„ „ „ Farther Explained	87
Professors, Cautions and Directions to the Greatest	213
Pronunciation and Gesture, Directions for	125
Proposals for Arminian Magazine	322
Protestant, A Word to a	82
„ Association, The	357
Provisions, Thoughts on Scarcity of	286
Prudence, Christian	2
Psalms and Hymns, A Collection of, (Charlestown, 1737)	6
„ „ „ „ „ (London, 1738)	7
Public Advertiser, Letter to the Printer of the	339, 349
Quaker, Letter to a	108
Queries proposed to Count Zinzendorf	169
Question, The, What is an Arminian? Answered	260
„ The Important, A Sermon on	308
Reasons against Separation from the Church	201
Rebellion, Reflections on the American	341
Receits, A Collection of	69
Redemption, Hymns for Those that Seek, etc.	105
Reflections, Christian	295
„ on American Rebellion	341
„ on Conduct of Human Life (Norris)	25
Reformation of Manners, Sermon preached before the Society for	217
Religion in Virginia, Narrative of Revival of	330
„ Preservative against Unsettled Notions in	191
„ in New England, Thoughts on Revival of	66
Religious Affections, Extract from Treatise on (Edwards)	294
„ Societies, Instructions for Members of	296
Remarks on Defence of Preface to *Aspasio Vindicated*	236
„ on Hill's *Farrago*	287
„ „ „ Review of Wesley's Doctrines	283
Renty, M. de, Extract of Life of	21

INDEX

Repentance of Believers, A Sermon on	248
Reply to Sir W. Howe on *Letters to A Nobleman*, Extract	352
Resurrection, Hymns for our Lord's	90
Revival of Religion in New England, Thoughts on	66
„ „ in Virginia, Narrative of	330
Richardson, Mrs. H., Account of	23
Righteous Overmuch, Answer to Trapp's Sermons on being	118
Righteousness, The Lord our, Sermon on	235
„ of Christ, Thoughts on the Imputed	211
Rogers, Ann, Account of	263
Roman Catechism, A	179
„ Catholic, Letter to a	134
„ Catholics, Short Method of Converting	156
„ History, A Short	289
Rome, Advantage of Church of England over Church of	161
Root, A Blow at the	212
Rules of the Band Societies	57
„ „ Strangers' Friend Society in Bristol	413
„ „ United Societies	43
Rutherforth, Dr., Letter to	249
Sabbath Breaker, A Word to a	79
Sacred Harmony (Tunes)	358
„ Melody (Tunes)	206
Sacrament, a Hymn at the	61
St. Matthew's, Bethnal-Green, Sermon preached at	309
Saints and Sinners, A Word to	86
„ Serious Thoughts on Perseverance of	153
Sallustii, Caii, Bellum	128
Salvation by Faith, A Sermon on	8
„ Faith and Good Works, The Doctrine of, from the Homilies	9
„ The Scripture Way of, A Sermon on	230
Scarcity of Provisions, Thoughts on	286
Scougall, Henry, Life of God in the Soul of Man	51
Scriptural Christianity, A Sermon on	55
Separation from the Church of England, Reasons against	201
Serious Call to a Holy Life (Law)	48

Sermon on Trouble and Rest of Good Men, 5; Salvation by Faith, 8; Free Grace, 11; The Almost Christian, 28; Christian Perfection, 29; Awake thou that Sleepest, (C. W.), 33; Scriptural Christianity, 55; Catholic Spirit, 170; The Good Soldier, 178; The Great Assize, 185; Original Sin, 196; Reformation of Manners, 217; Sin in Believers, 218; The Scripture-Way of Salvation,

230; The Lord our Righteousness, 235; The Witness of the Spirit, 242; The Repentance of Believers, 248; The Good Steward, 251; The Death of Whitefield, 266; Romans viii. 29, 30, (on Predestination), 290; 1 Cor. i. 23, 24, (Preached at Wakefield), 299; 1 John v. 7, (on the Trinity), 306; The Important Question, 308; National Sin and Miseries, 309; Numbers xxiii. 23, (Preached at Opening of City Road Chapel), 317; Matthew xxv. 34, (Preached before the Humane Society), 324; A Call to Backsliders, 329; Death of Fletcher, 382.

Sermon on Jeremiah vii. 4, by Dr. Hamilton	407
Sermons on Several Occasions, Vol. i.	88
,, ,, ,, ,, Vol. ii.	107
,, ,, ,, ,, Vol. iii.	139
,, ,, ,, ,, Vol. iv.	200
,, ,, ,, ,, Vols. v. vi. vii. viii.	397
,, Answer to Dr. Trapp's	118
Service, Sunday, for H. M. Dominions	390
,, ,, for United States	376
Silas Told, Life of	406
Sin, The Doctrine of Original	182
,, in Believers, A Discourse on	218
,, Sermon on Original	196
Single Life, Thoughts on	228
Sinners, Alarm to Unconverted (Alleine)	362
Slavery, Thoughts upon	298
Smuggler, A Word to a	239
Societies, Rules of the Band	57
,, Rules of the United	43
Society, Rules of Strangers' Friend	413
,, for Reformation of Manners, Sermon before	217
Soldier, A Word to a	44
,, The Good, Extract from a Sermon on	178
Spirit, Marks of the Work of the	49
,, Witness of the, A Sermon on	242
Strangers' Friend Society, Rules of	413
Steward, The Good, A Sermon on	251
Street Walker, A Word to a	80
Sunday Service for H.M. Dominions	390
,, ,, for United States	376
Survey of the Wisdom of God in the Creation (2 vols.)	220
,, ,, ,, ,, (3 vols.)	265
,, ,, ,, ,, (5 vols.)	325
Swearer, A Word to a, ("Swear not at all")	78

Tea, Letter to a Friend on	119
Testament, New, with Analysis	411
,, New, Notes on	172
,, Old, ,,	234
,, Old and New, Concordance to	359
Thanksgiving-Day, Hymns for	95, 199
The Consequence Proved	274
Theron and Aspasio, Answer to Letters to Author of	183
Thoughts on a Single Life	228
,, on Earthquake at Lisbon	171
,, on Godfathers and Godmothers	157
,, on God's Sovereignty	319
,, on Imputed Righteousness of Christ	211
,, on Infant Baptism	149
,, on Liberty	279
,, on Marriage and a Single Life	42
,, on Necessity	300
,, on Origin of Power	280
,, on Perseverance of the Saints	153
,, on Revival in New England	66
,, on Scarcity of Provisions	286
,, on Sin of Onan	243
,, on Slavery	298
,, on State of Public Affairs	264
,, Farther, on Christian Perfection	219
Token for Children	124
Told, Life of Silas	406
Trapp, Dr., Answer to Sermons of	118
Treatise on Christian Perfection (Law)	45
,, on Christian Prudence (Norris)	2
,, on Fear of Man (Franck)	12
,, on Justification (Goodwin)	226
Treatises, Two (Barnes)	14
Trial at Gloucester, Account of	52
Trinity, A Sermon on the	306
,, Hymns to the	93
,, Hymns on the	246
Tune Books:	
Hymns with Tunes Annext	205
Grounds of Vocal Music	207
Sacred Harmony	358
Sacred Melody	206
Tunes Sung at the Foundery, Collection of	38
Trouble and Rest of Good Men, A Sermon on	5
,, Hymns for Times of	60
,, and Persecution, Hymns for Times of	59
Tumults, Hymns Written in the Time of the	347

Unconverted, A Call to the (Baxter) . . 363
United States, Sunday Service for . . . 376
Unsettled Notions in Religion, A Preservative against 191

View of Differences between the Moravians and J. and C.
    Wesley, A Short 68
Virginia, Narrative of Revival in 330

Wakefield, Sermon preached at, taken down in Shorthand 299
Walsh, Thomas, Life and Death of (Morgan) . . 215
War in the Middle Colonies, Account of Conduct of . 340
Watchnight, Hymns for the 97
Wednesbury, Modern Christianity exemplified at . . 72
Wesley, J., Epistle to, by C. W. 173
  ,,   Collected Works of 276
Whitefield, Rev. G., Epistle to (C.W.) . . . 277
  ,,   Elegy on 278
  ,,   Sermon on Death of 266
Whit-Sunday, Hymns for 92
Whittingham, Letter to Mr. J. 342
Witness of the Spirit, A Sermon on . . . 242
Word of Advice to Saints and Sinners . . . 86
  ,, to a Condemned Malefactor . . . 81
  ,, to a Drunkard 77
  ,, to an Englishman 76
  ,, to a Freeholder 104
  ,, to Freemen of Established Church . . 180
  ,, to a Methodist (Welsh) 109
  ,, to a Protestant 82
  ,, to a Sabbath-breaker 79
  ,, to a Smuggler 239
  ,, to a Soldier 44
  ,, to a Street-Walker 80
  ,, to a Swearer 78
Work of God at Northampton, Narrative of, (Edwards) . 54
  ,,   ,, in North America, Some Account of . 331
  ,, of the Spirit of God, Marks of . . . 49
Works, The Collected, of John Wesley—see Wesley

Young's Night Thoughts, Extract of 269

Zinzendorf, Queries Proposed to . . 169
Zinzendorf's Discourses, Extract of . 50

INDEX TO THE NOTES.

The figures refer to the pages.

A—— T——, 148, 155.
Abridgement of Prayer-Book, Wesley's, 232.
Account, A Strange, 228.
Account of the Ejected Ministers, 216.
Acta Fratrum Unitatis in Anglia, 71.
Action and Utterance, Rules for, 59.
Acts and Monuments, Fox's, 74.
Acts of the Apostles, Hymns on, 251.
Adams, Rev. Thomas, 201.
Address to American Colonies, A Vindication of Wesley's, 181.
Address to the City, (London), 214; to the Inhabitants of England, 180, 188.
Adultery and Murder, God's Revenge against, 235, 239.
Advice to an Englishman, 163; to a Sailor, 27; to Electors of Bristol, 102.
Æmilius Probus de Viris Illustribus, 61.
Affairs, Free Thoughts on present state of Public, 173.
Aleppo to Jerusalem, A Journey from, 228, 233.
Allan Library, viii, 203.
Alleine, Joseph, *Alarm*, 217; author of Covenant Service, 84; Letters of, 140; Life of, 84.
Alleine, Richard, Works of, 85, 88, 94, 204.
Altar, Companion for the, 44.
Ambrose, Isaac, Life and Works of, 78.
America, Societies in, 223, 226; Wesley's Letter on ordaining Ministers for, 226.
American Patriotism, 181; War, Account of Rise and Progress of the, 201.
Americanus, A Calm Address to, 180; Letter by, 181.

Amsterdam, 231.
Ancient Mythology, Bryant on, 222.
Angels, Discourse on Preservation by, 235.
Annesley, Dr. S., Sermons by, 88, 93, 94.
Answer to Mr. Rowland Hill's Tract, 188.
Anthems, Wesley's Objection to, 234.
Antinomian and Friend, Dialogue between, 108, 173.
Antinomianism, Antidotes to, 37, 53; Fletcher's Second Check to, 161; Picture of, 198.
Aphorisms of Justification, by Baxter, 173.
Apocrypha, 45.
Appeal from the Protestant Association, 201; to Men of Reason and Religion, 120, 164; A Farther ditto, 164.
Armelle, Nicholas, 205.
Arminius, Life and Works of, 197.
Arndt's True Christianity, 63, 74.
Asbury, Francis, 156, 194, 226, 239.
Aspasio Vindicated, Remarks on Defence of Preface to, 172.
Assurance, Letters on, 115.
Athenæ Oxonienses, 10.
Atlay, John, 185, 245.
Atmore, Charles, 244.
Austin's Devotions, 93.

Bailey, Mr., 191.
Baily, Rev. Mr., 172.
Band Meetings, 117.
Band Societies, 27, 33.
Baptism, Treatise on, 107, 172.
Baptism, Thoughts on Infant, 172.
Barclay, Robert, Writings of, 53.
Bards of Epworth, 25.
Barnardiston, Sir N., Life of, 85.
Barnes, Rev. Mr., 131.
Barrow, Isaac, Writings of, 88.

Bath Journal, 63.
Baxter's Aphorisms of Justification, 173 ; Certainty of World of Spirits, 222.
Beard, Thomas, 111.
Bedell, Bp., Life of, 85, 198, 200.
Beecham, Rev. John, D.D., 252.
Behmen, Jacob, 213 ; Divinity and Philosophy of, 218.
Bell, George, 121, 130, 140.
Bengel's *Gnomon Novi Testamenti*, 91.
Bennet, John, MS. Minutes by, 65.
Benson, Rev. Joseph, 156, 160, 222, 252.
Berridge, Rev. Mr., 36, 128.
Bertius, Rev. Peter, 197.
Beveridge, Bp., Writings of, 94.
Bibliography, Osborn's Outlines of, viii ; see also Osborn.
Bicêtre, Prison of, 233.
Binning, Hugh, Writings of, 85.
Bird's *Fate and Destiny*, 22, 205.
Birstal Preaching House, The Case of, 218, 238.
Bishop, Miss, of Bath, 155, 209.
Bishops, American, 239.
Bisveal, 50.
Blackerby, Life of, 85.
Blackwell, Mr., 62.
Blow at the Root, A, 173.
Boardman, Richard, 147, 156.
Bodleian MSS., 10.
Böhler, Peter, 38.
Bolton, Robert, Life and Works of, 75.
Bonnet on the Contemplation of Nature, 191.
Book of Common Prayer, 223.
Book-Room, Library of, viii., 99.
Bosanquet, Miss, 149, 164.
Boston's *Fourfold State of Man*, 222.
Bourignon's *Treatise of Solid Virtue*, 88.
Bradburn, Samuel, 196, 244.
Bradford, Joseph, 185, 247.
„ Publisher, Philadelphia, 25.
Brainerd, David, Life, Letters, &c., of, 144, 163.
Brandt's History of the Reformation, 197.
Brevint's *Christian Sacrament and Sacrifice*, 44, 174, 249.
Bride Bush, A Wedding Sermon, 84.
Brooke, Mr Councillor Henry, 209.
Brooke, Mr. Henry, 209.
Brooke, Rev. R. Sinclair, 209.

Brown, John, Writings of, 88.
Bruen, John, Life of, 85.
Bryant's Ancient Mythology, 222, 225.
Buddæus, Latin work of, 125.
Buffon's Natural History, 218.
Bunyan's Holy War, &c., 85.
Burnet, Bp., 30.
Butts, Mr. Thomas, 250; Collection of Psalm and Hymn-Tunes, *ib.*

Cadogan on Gout, 178, 195.
Calamy, Dr., Sermons by, 88.
Calverwell, N., 79.
Calvin, 22 ; Life of, 85.
Calvinism, Minute on (1770), 152, 155, 156.
Calvinistic Methodists, 14.
Calvinists, 156.
Camelford, 231.
Carleton, Bp., 198.
Castellio, and Servetus, Account of, 198.
Castellio, Sebastian,'Dialogues of, 212, 219.
Cataret, Lady Elizabeth, 44.
Catechism, Roman, 80.
Catholic Disabilities Act, 201.
Catholic Love, Hymn on, 89.
Cawton, Mr. T., 95.
Cave, Dr. W., 85.
Chandler's History of Persecution, 198.
Character of a Methodist, 153.
Charlemagne, 212.
Charnock's Works, 88.
Cheyne, Dr., On Preservation of Health, 50.
Child, Directions for a, 250; Exhortation for, *ib* ; Morning and Evening Prayer for, *ib.*
Children, On educating, 222 ; a small Pocket Hymn-book for, 236 ; Hymns for, 236 ; Instructions for, 42, 56, 127, 171, 174, 217 ; Token for, 217.
Christian Library, 41, 62, 63, 65, 74, 75, 78, 79, 81, 83, 87, 88, 93, 94, 95, 109, 156, 187, 204, 205, 216, 229, 254.
Christian Minister preaching politics, On a, 218 ; Magazine, 153 ; Reflections, 113, 171, 174 ; Instructions, 113 ; Prudence, Norris on, 10, 162 ; Festivals observed by the Wesleys, 47 ;

278 INDEX

Christian Sacrament and Sacrifice, The, 249.
Christian Perfection, Doctrine of, 25, 135, 146, 201; Hymns on, 122; Law's, 16, 27, 29, 56, 82, 143, 157; Plain Account of, 17, 20, 23, 113, 121, 125, 128, 135, 174, 192; Brief Thoughts on, 125; Thoughts on, 113, 124; Trapp's writings against, 56.
Christianity, Nature and Design of, 217; As old as the Creation, .162; A Plain Account of Genuine, 83, 172.
Christians, Instructions for, 174.
Church, Rev. Mr. Thomas, 35, 36, 45, 165.
Church, On the, 233; Difficulties with regard to the, 200; On leaving the, 201; Advices concerning the, 201; On Separation from, 92, 108, 114, 173, 174, 196, 231, 233, 241, 245; Wesley's relation to the, 114, 249; Advantage of Church of England over Church of Rome, 172.
Churches, Thoughts on consecration of, 239.
Churchmanship of John Wesley, by Dr. Rigg, 114.
City-Road Chapel, Stevenson's History of, 188.
Clark, Mr. James, Author of *Montanus Redivivus*, 116.
Clark's Martyrology, 75.
Clark, Samuel, Autobiography of, 85; Lives of Eminent Persons by, *ib*.
Clarke, Rev. Mr., 201.
Clarke, Dr. Adam, 181; Commentary of, 132; *Wesley Family*, 222.
Clemens Romanus, 13; Epistle to Corinthians by, 63.
Clergy, Qualifications of, 97; Address to, 163.
Clergyman, Letter to a, 154, 165.
Clive, Sir Ed., Knt., 103.
Clonfert and Killmacduagh, Bp. of, 116.
Code of Laws, Methodist, 241.
Coke, Rev. Dr., 221, 224, 225, 226, 239, 240, 247.
Coleman, Dr., Letters to Dr. Watts, 29; Jonathan Edwards' letter to, 172.

Colestock, 51.
Committee for West Indies, 244; Building, 244.
Companion for the Altar, 44, 249.
Comparative Religion, 84.
Concordance by John Fisher, 115; by Thomas Taylor, 215.
Condemned Malefactors, Wesley's care for, 78.
Conference, The, 227, 240; First Printed Minutes of, 64, 65; Second Conference, 38; Wesley's Last Directions to, 244; Minutes of—see Minutes.
Consequence Proved, The, 173.
Constantine the Great, 212.
Conversation between R. Hill, Madan, etc., 156.
Cooper, Jane, Letters of, 142, 164, 174; Life of, 164.
Cooper, Rev. Mr., of Boston, 29.
Cork, Bp. of, 192.
Cotton Mather, 95.
Covenant Service, Original form of, 84.
Covenants, The Two, 245.
Cowley's Essays, 86.
Craftsman, The, 41.
Creation, Thoughts on, 233.
Crowther's Portraiture of Methodism, 33.
Cruden's Concordance, 215.
Cry of a Reprobate, 21.
Cudworth, R., B.D., Sermon by, 79.
Cudworth, William, 107, 108.
Culloden, Thanksgiving for Victory at, 48.

Daillé on the Right Use of the Fathers, 58.
Daily Advertiser, 89.
D'Avila, Don Juan, Spiritual Letters by, 94.
Death, Judgment, &c., Sermons on, 242, 245.
Decrees, Absolute or Conditional, 242; Discourse on the, 198; A Vindication of the, 155.
Deed of Declaration, 223, 227, 238, 241, 247.
Deists, Leslie's Short and Easy Method with, 106, 172.
Dell, William, Works of, 75.
De Renty, M., Life of, 17.
Desideratum, The, 174.
Devil of Mascon, The, 144, 219.
Devout Meditations by Lord Howe, 94.

Devotional Tracts from the French, 88.
Dew on Coach Glasses, Question concerning, 228.
Dewsbury House, Case of, 240, 245.
Didsbury College Library, viii., 12, 41, 97.
Dillon, Mr. John, Account of, 174.
Discipline, The Form of, 241.
Directions to Children and to Servants, 82, 157; to Preserve Fervency of Spirit, 170.
Discourses on Sermon on the Mount, 53; Two, on Conflagration and Renovation of the World, 173.
Dissent from Church of England, 107, 172.
Dissipation, Thoughts upon, 228.
Districts, Kingdom divided into, 247.
Divine Legation of Moses, Warburton's, 162.
Dobson, Mr. John, 214.
Doctrinal Standards of Methodism, 126, 157.
Doctrine of Salvation, etc., from the Homilies, 162.
Dodd, Dr., 153, 201, 218, 222.
Doddridge, Dr., and the Christian Library, 95; Family Expositor, 92.
Donne, Dr., Life of, 85, 200.
Dort, Synod of, 197, 198.
Downes, Rev. Mr., on Methodism, 110; Letter to, 171.
Dress, Thoughts on, 239.
Du Moulin, Dr. P., 144.
Duties of Husbands and Wives, 82, 113, 157.
Duten's Enquiry, etc., 192.
Dutton, W. E., 249.

Early Puritan Writers, Remarks on, 75.
Earthquake in London, 1750, 68; at Lisbon, 90, 163; Hymns on, 70.
Easter Hymn, The, 46.
Echard, Mr., 211.
Edwards, Rev. President, 37, 163, 172, 174, 176, 228.
E. J., Account of, 164.
Election and Reprobation, Considerations on, 173, 219; Treatise on, 200.
Electrical Machines provided for the poor, 115.
Electricity, 50, 115, 174.

Elegy on Death of Wesley, 147.
Encyclopædia, Chambers', 209.
England, Address to Inhabitants of, 180.
English Grammar, A Penny, 55; Liturgy, 223.
Enthusiasm of Methodists and Papists compared, Letters on, 165.
Ephesians, St. Ignatius' Epistle to, 63.
Episcopacy, Letters on Divine right of, 116.
Epistles to Moravians, Presbyterians, etc., Poetic, (C. W.), 158.
Epworth, Work of God at, 224; Disturbances at, 225.
Erasmus, Life of, 70.
Erskine, Dr., attacks Wesley, 134; reprints Hervey's Letters, *ib.*
Eucharistic Manuals, 44, 249.
Evans, Caleb, 181, 199.
Exeter, Bp. of, 63; Letter to, 171.
Exposition of Seventh Chapter of Romans, 205.

F——, the Rev. Mr., Letter to, 213.
Faerie Queene, Spenser's, 209.
Fairclough, Samuel, Life of, 85.
Farrago Double Distilled, 166, 174.
Fate and Destiny inconsistent with Christianity, 205.
Fathers, Daillé on the Right Use of the, 58.
Fénelon, Abp., 88.
Firmin, Mr. Thomas, 233.
Fisher John, Concordance of, 115.
Five Points, Whitby's Discourses on the, 228, 233, 239, 242.
Flavel, Works of, 93; Preface by Caryl, *ib.*
Fletcher, Rev. John, 10, 146, 152, 217, 230, 232; Works of, 14, 37, 181; Wesley's Designated Successor, 232; Wesley's Life of, 10.
Fletcher, Mrs., Author of *Jesus altogether lovely*, 127; Letter of, to Wesley, 128, 164.
Fleury, Abbé, Translations from, 35.
Fleury, Rev. Mr., 154.
Floyd, William, Depositions of, 222.
Fool of Quality, 209.
Foreknowledge of God, On the, 228.
Fowler, Bp. Edward, 84.
Fox's *Acts and Monuments*, 63, 74, 75.

Franke, Aug. Herm., 14.
Franklin on Electricity, 115.
Fraser, Life of Mr. James, 95.
Free, Dr., writings against the Methodists, 104; A letter to, 171.
Free Grace Indeed, A Sermon on, 14.
Freeman's Journal, 208.
French Language, Wesley's Opinion of, 73.
French Mercy, 218; *Liberty*, 233.
Funeral Hymns, 161; Third Series of, so called, 49.

G—— C——, Journal of Mr., 219, 222.
Galeacius Carraciolus, Life of, 85.
Galloway, Mr., 210.
"Gamut or Scale of Music," 117, 250.
Genius, Thoughts on, 238.
Gentlewoman, Letter to Wesley by a, 128, 164.
Gent's Life of M. de Renty, 17.
German Hymns, Wesley's First Translation of, 11.
Gesture, Rules for, 60, 179.
Gibson, Bp. of London, 20.
Gilbert, Mary, Journal of, 164.
,, Mr. Nathaniel, 169.
Gill, Dr., On the Pentateuch, 122; Thoughts in the Short Hymns borrowed from, *ib.*; Wesley's controversy with, 77, 87.
Gilpin, Bernard, Life of, 85.
,, Rev. Prebendary William, 198.
Glaucha, 14.
Gloria Patri, 21, 49.
Gloucester, Account of Trial at, 172.
,, Bp. of, 172, 188; Dean of, 193.
Glynne, Mrs., of Shrewsbury, Fletcher's letter to, 146.
Goad, Dr. Thomas, 198.
Godfathers and Godmothers, Serious Thoughts on, 173.
God's eyes over all the earth, 233.
Goldsmith's History of England, 185; History of Animated Nature, 191.
Goodman's, Dr., Winter Evening Conference, 87.
Goodwin, Dr. Thomas, Works of, 75.
,, John, on Justification, 173; on Rom. ix., 205.
Golden Treasury, 131.

Gordon Anti-Papal Riots, 206.
Gospel Glass, A, 86; Magazine, 197; Ministers, Thoughts on, 225.
Göttingen, University of, 211.
Grace, Remarkable work of, 136.
Graces before and after meat, 138, 250.
Grammars prepared for Kingswood School, 61.
Grammar, A Short English, included in collected Works, 179.
Grantham's Dialogue between a Presbyterian and a Baptist, 18.
Gresley, Rev. W., 249.
Gurney, Joseph, 18.
Guyon, Madame, 174.
Gwennap, 50.
Gwynne, Sarah, 66.

Haime, John, 205.
Hale, Lord Chief Justice, 85, 192, 235.
Haliburton, Thomas, Memoirs of, 13, 163.
Hall, Bp., Meditations of, 75.
,, Rev. S. Romilly, viii.
Halle, University of, 14.
Hamilton, Dr. James, 243.
Hammond, Dr., Life of, 95.
Hampson, Rev. J., Life of Wesley by, 77.
Hanoverian, *An Old Fox Tarr'd and Feathered* by, 181.
Hardcastle, Mr. C. D., 38, 108, 236.
Harmonia Sacra, 250.
Harper, Elizabeth, Journal of, 164.
Harris, Rev. Howell, 158.
Health, Advices with respect to, 171, 174.
Henrics, Mary, 88.
Henry, Matthew, Commentary of, 122, 132.
,, Philip, Life of, 95.
Herbert, George, 85, 206.
Hernnschmid, John D., 197.
Hervey, Rev. James, 108, 111, 129, 174; Letter to, 173.
Heylin's List of the Wesley Writings, viii., 11, 18, 21, 32, 34, 48, 49, 79, 83, 90, 98, 105, 113, 116, 119, 130, 140, 144, 160, 161, 169, 170, 177, 187, 214, 230, 236, 245, 249.
Heylin, Dr., Theological Lectures of, 92.
Hickes's Reformed Devotions, 93.

Hildrop, Dr. John, 222.
Hill, Sir Richard and Rev. Rowland, 152; Review of Wesley's doctrines, 161, 166, 173; *Farrago*, 174.
Hindmarsh, James, 190.
Historical Society, The Wesley, v., 65.
History of Methodism, Smith's and Stevens'—see Methodism.
History of the Human Heart, by Henry Brooke, 209.
Hitchens, Samuel, Account of, 163.
,, Thomas, 46, 163.
Hoard, Mr. Samuel, 198, 200.
Hockin, Frederick, 249.
Hoffman, Dr., 178.
Holy Spirit, Bp. of Gloucester on, 172.
Homilies, Extract from the, 10, 13, 162; of Macarius, 63.
Hooke's Roman History, 168.
Hooker, Richard, Life of, 85.
Hoole, Rev. Mr. Nathaniel, 11.
Hopkins, Bp., 109.
Horne, Bp., 120, 139, 172.
Horneck, Dr., 85.
"Horrible Decree, The", 22, 76.
Howe, John, Life and Works of, 94.
,, Lord, On Religious and Philosophical Subjects, 94.
Huntingdon, Countess of, 14, 33, 152; Connexion of, 14.
Husbands and Wives, The Duties of, 157.
Hutton, James, 65; Memoirs of, 89.
Hymnology, Julian's, 48, 109, 229.
Hymn,—After the Defeat at Chesapeak, 219; An Act of Devotion, 35; An Evening, 250; A Prayer for the Congress, 219; A Prayer for those who are convinced of Sin, 26; Catholic Love, 67; "Christ the Lord is risen to-day," 46; "Come let us anew our journey pursue," 49; "Father of boundless grace," 243; For a person called to bear his Testimony, 28, 66; For Ascension Day, 46; For Concord, 219; For Her Majesty, 220; For His Majesty King George, 30, 41, 172, 219; For Peace, 219; For the Conversion of the French, 220; For the Royal Family, 220; For the Watch night, 70; "Gentle Jesus, meek and mild," 25; "God of boundless pity, spare," 105; "Happy soul, thy days are ended," 147, 164; "Jesu lover of my soul,' 17; "Jesu the all-restoring Word," 250; Life and Eternity, 249; "Lo! He comes with clouds descending," 108; "O Thou God of my salvation," 147; On the death of Rev. Mr. Whitefield, 151; Primitive Christianity, 28; "Regard, Thou righteous God and true," 41; "Servant of God, well done," 151; Thanksgiving for success of the Gospel in America, 220; The bloody issue, 179; "Thee we adore, eternal Name," 249; "The God of Abraham praise," 147, 214, 217, 229; The just shall live by faith, 17; "The Lord of Sabbath let us praise," 250; The Means of Grace, 179; The Preacher's Prayer for the Flock, 114; The Promise of Sanctification, 20; The Whole Armour of God, 23, 165; Thy Kingdom come, 219; Universal Redemption, 14; Wrestling Jacob, 25, 237.
Hymn-book for children, A Small, 236; The Large, 46, 47, 83, 229; The Methodist, by Stevenson, 66; The Morning, 225; The York, 236; Prepared for the Poor, 26; A Pocket, 236.
Hymns, First of C.W.'s published, 15; first printed anonymously, 22; for Children, 25, 160, 236, 246; for Christian Friends, 66; for the English in America, 71; for Families, 138, 139; for the Fast Day, 100; for the Festivals, 49, 52, 138, 139; for Girls, 127; for the Lord's Day, 232; for the Lord's Supper, 44, 48, 117, 174, 249; for the Nativity, 44; for New Year's Day, 70; for the Preachers, 114; for Times of Trouble

and Persecution, 30, 48, 49, 99, 100; for Whit-Sunday, 47; for the Youngest, 246; A Collection of, 66, 206, 217, 218; Spence's, 236; and Sacred Poems, 20, 23, 24, 26, 48, 52, 65, 66, 99, 117, 127, 249, 250; and Spiritual Songs, 83, 99, 119, 206; of Intercession, 108, 138; on the Earthquake, 68, 99; on God's Everlasting Love, 87; on the Gospels and the Acts of the Apostles, 242, 251; on the Trinity, 47, 138, 139; Funeral, 48; Moravian, 65; Nativity, 70; Psalms and, 99, 206; Redemption, 83, 117; Select, 117, 206, 214; Amos viii. 2., Habakkuk i., Mal. iv. i, 219; Rev. xvi., xvii., 70; Revisions of, 251.
Hymn-tracts on the Christian Festivals, 47, 48, 49.

Ignatius, 13, 63.
Ilchester, 137.
Image-Worship, 242.
Imposture Detected, by Rowland Hill, 188, 189; Wesley's Answer to, 189.
Imputed Righteousness, Doctrine of, 120, 129, 133.
Indenture, or Model-Deed, 126; when first published, 157.
Infant Baptism, 72; Wall's Hist. of, *ib.*
Instructions for Children, 42, 56, 127, 171, 174, 217; for Christians, 171; for Members of Religious Societies, 171, 174.
Instructiones pueriles, 35.
Ireland, Wesley's Last Visit to, 240.

Jackson, Mr. Edward, 149.
 ,, Elizabeth, 149.
 ,, Rev. Thomas, 100, 252; *Recollections, etc., of*, 147, 180, 181, 250.
Janeway's Token for Children, 59; *Invisibles, Realities, Demonstrated*, etc., 80.
Janeway, John, Life and Death of, 80, 163, 217.
Jarratt, Rev. Devereux, of Virginia, 194.
Jerusalem, Church at, 59.

Jesus altogether lovely, 127; wrongly ascribed to Wesley, 130.
Jesus Christ, A Treatise on Godhead of, 106, 172.
Johnson, Ann, 164.
 ,, Dr. Samuel, 81, 180.
 ,, John, 149, 164.
 ,, Mrs. Elizabeth, 251.
Jones, R., Elegy on Death of, 33.
Joshua Redivivus, by Samuel Rutherfoord, 140.
Journal, C. Wesley's,—See Wesley, C., Journal of.
Journal, Wesley's — See Wesley, Journal of; Extracts from, 179.
Jubilee, Year of (1750), 70.
Julian's Hymnology, 48, 229.
Junius, Letters of, 159.
Justification, A Treatise on, by Goodwin, 174.

Keene, Mr. Arthur, 234.
Keighley Visitor, Notes on Hymnbooks in, 49, 236.
Ken, Bp., on Catechism, 85; Wesley's opinion of writing of, 109.
Kershaw, James, 134.
Kingsley, Rev. Charles, 209.
Kingswood School, 56, 61, 71, 97, 126, 131, 156, 168, 213, 221.
Kirk, Rev. John, 147.
Knight, Rev. James, Discourses by, 173.
Koker, John de, Letter from, 60.

Lampe, J. F., 48, 138; Tunes by, 48.
 ,, Mrs , 47.
Langson, Mary, 164.
Large Minutes.—See Minutes.
Larwood, Mr. Samuel, 98.
Latin Books for Kingswood School, 55, 69.
 ,, Grammar, Holmes', 54.
Lavington, Bp. of Exeter, 67, 76.
Law, Mr. W., 96, 97, 106, 136; Letter to, 172; Mystic writings of, 56, 143; Treatise on Christian Perfection, 16, 27, 29, 143, 157; Serious Call, 27, 29, 143; Spirit of Love, 162; Spirit of Prayer, 217; Works of, 143, 218.
Lay-Preachers, 54.
Lee, Matthew, 163.
 ,, Mr. Thomas, 204, 205.

INDEX   283

Lefevre, Mons. Isaac, 218.
  ,,   Mrs., 111, 146, 164.
Leighton, Abp., Exposition of Creed, 88.
Lesley on Predestination, 198.
Leslie's Method with Deists, 106.
Letter, S. W. to J. W., 11; to Wesley by a Gentlewoman, 164.
Letters between Wesley and Thompson, 115; of Jane Cooper, 128, 164; of Junius, 159; to a Nobleman, 210; on Popery, 213; to a Friend, 213; Old Methodist custom of meeting to read, 80.
Lettsome and Cooke's *Preacher's Assistant*, 11.
Lewisham, 49, 165.
Leyden, University of, 197.
Liberty, Free Thoughts on, 173; and Necessity, Essay on, 176.
Library, Allan, viii., 203; Archiepiscopal, Lambeth, 12; Didsbury College, viii., 12, 41,97; Methodist Book-room, viii., 41, 99, 201, 203; Richmond College, 95, 168, 196.
Library, The Christian—see Christian Library; The Family, 191; The Home, 249.
Life of Alleine, Joseph, 84; Ambrose, Isaac, 78; Armelle, Nicholas, 205; Atling, Henry, 85; Baxter, Richard, 85; Bedell, Bp., 85, 198, 200; Barnardiston, Sir N., 85; Blackerby, Richard, 85; Bolton, Robert, 75; Brainerd, David, 163; Bruen, John, 85; Cooper, Jane, 164; De Renty, 163; Donne, Dr., 200; Firmin, Thomas, 233; Gilpin, Bernard, 198; Haliburton, T., 13, 163; Herbert, George, 85; Janeway, John, 163, 217; Law, W., 29; Lee, Matthew, 163; Leverton, Nicholas, 85; Martyr, Peter, 85; Mather, Richard, 85; Mornay, Philip de, 85; Othen, N., 163; Row, John, 85; Sidney, Sir Philip, 85; Spanheim, F., 85; Usher, 85, 200; Walsh, Thomas, 163; Watton, Sir Henry, 85; Whitaker, John, 85; Woodward, Joseph, 85.
Lichfield and Coventry, Bp. of, 35.

Life of God in the Soul of Man, 162.
Limerick, First Irish Conference held in, 76.
Lisbon, Serious Thoughts on Earthquake at, 163.
Liturgy, The, 223, 224, 237.
Lloyd's Evening Post, Letters by Wesley in, 132, 136, 137, 153, 199.
Locke's Essay on Human Understanding, 218, 222, 225.
Logica Wesleiensis, 166.
Logic, Sanderson's Method of using, 68.
Logicæ, Aldrich's *Artis*, 68.
London, Bp. of, 35, 165.
  ,,   *Chronicle*, Letters by Wesley in, 120, 136, 137; *Daily Advertiser*, 89; Magazine, The, 41, 116.
Lopez, Gregory, 205, 229, 230.
Lovefeasts, The first held in London, 57.
Love, Mr., 44.
Lucas, Dr., Writings of, 89.
Lukins, George, Account of, 242.
Luther on Creed, 30, 212.

Mac Allester, Mr. Oliver, 233.
Macarius, Homilies of, 63.
Maclaine, Dr., 212.
Madan, 108; on Polygamy and Marriage, 222.
Magazine, The Arminian, 145, 162, 175, 190, 199, 207, 208, 209, 215, 217, 218, 221, 229, 230, 237, 248, 254; The Methodist, 182, 244, 248; The Spiritual, 199; The Wesleyan Methodist, 215, 217, 248.
Magnesians, St. Ignatius' Epistle to, 63.
Man, The Whole Duty of, 84.
Manchester, 234.
Manners of the Times, On the, 242.
Manners of the Ancient Christians, 162.
Manton, Dr., Sermons by, 75, 78.
Marriage, A Thought upon, 228.
Marsh, Mrs. Elizabeth, 213.
Mascon, The Devil of, 144, 219.
Mather, Alexander, 205; Cotton, 95; Richard, 85.
Maund G. Sculpt., 214.
Maundrell, Henry, 228, 233, 235.
Maxfield, Thomas, 193; Fanatical teaching of, 130.

Melancthon, Life of, 85.
Memory, Thoughts on, 245.
Meriton, Mr. John, 32, 111.
Methodism, Attack on, 41; early difficulties of, 57; early history of, in Ireland, 221; "examined and exposed" by Downes, 110, 172; Constitution and Polity of, 227, 241; Relation to Church of England, 249; Short History of, 165, 212; Smith's History of, viii., 133, 144, 155, 181, 197, 247; Stevens' History of, viii., 63, 108, 111, 152, 155, 169, 181, 198, 211, 216, 225, 229, 245, 247; thoughts upon, 235.
Methodist, defined, 81; Book-Room, Library of, viii., 99; Character of a, 153, 165; Church, Standard doctrinal writings of, 53, 126; Episcopal Church of America, 19, 194; Preachers, Lives of early, 123, 147; Principles of a, 165; Word to a (Welsh), 54; Work, Defence of, 36.
Methodists, Advice to, 157, 165; Cautioned, 121; Caveat against, 137; Charges against answered, 131; Chronological History of, 169, 196, 246; Economy of, 60; Enthusiasm of, 165; Oxford, 213; Plain Account of, 164; Public Prayers and Services of, 232; Short History of, 212; Treatment of, 36, 40, 97; Who are the true, 40; Welsh, 54.
Middleton, Rev. Dr. Conyers, 58, 63, 172.
Minchin-Hampton, 31.
"Ministerial Methodism," 41.
Minute on Calvinism, 152, 155, 156, 161.
Minutes, Annual, 131, 144, 160, 179, 200, 205, 208, 213, 219, 222, 224, 225, 228, 230, 233, 235, 239, 242, 245; Doctrinal and Disciplinary, 65, 165; first printed, 64; Irish, 195, 196; Large, 19, 47, 65, 157, 165, 179, 203, 230, 238, 241; MSS. of early, 65; Octavo editions, 65; Why Called "the Penny," 131; Revised, 65, 76, 153, 169, 203, 238; of 1744, 33; of 1745, 39; of 1749, 27.
Miscellany of Divine Meditations, 85.
Misery of Man, Thoughts on, 235.
Mitchell, Thomas, 205.
Model-Deed, The, 126, 157, 221, 230, 238, 241; called the Conference-Plan, 238; and the General Deed, 230.
Molinos' Spiritual Guide, 88.
Montanus Redivivus, 116.
Montesquieu's Spirit of Laws, 213.
Monthly Review, 210, 213.
Moore, Dr. Henry, Sermons of, 88.
 ,, Rev. Henry, Smith's Life of, 62; Life of Wesley—see Wesley, Life of.
Moorfields, 51.
Moral Agents, On the Liberty of, 248.
Moravian Church, 16, 31.
Moravians, 16, 97; Difference between the Wesleys and, 38, 173, 249; Doctrines of, 16; History of, 71; Hymns of, 65; Strictures on teaching of, 51; Wesley's relations with, 31.
More, Dr. Henry, 206.
Morgan, Rev. James, 163.
Morley, Dr. George, 38.
Mornay, Philip de, Life of, 85.
Mosheim, Dr. J. L., 211.
Motives to Conversion, Baxter, 216.
Murder and Adultery, God's Revenge against, 239.
Music, Thoughts on power of, 213.
Myles' Chronological History of Meth., 169, 196, 246.
Mystic Divines, The, 15.

Narrative of Conference of 1771, Shirley's, 156.
Nation, Moral State of, 36.
Necessity, Thought on, 205.
Nelson, John, The Case of, 172.
N——., Mr., 201.
Nervous Disorders, Thoughts on, 233.
New Covenant, The, by John Preston, 75.
New Jersey, College of, 174.
 ,, Review, Mr. Maty's, 228.
 ,, Testament, Notes on,—see Testament.
 ,, York, 147.

INDEX 285

Nicodemus; or The Fear of Man, 162.
North, Lord, Letter to, 181.
Norris, Mr., 162.

Old Methodist Tunes, 24.
O'Leary, Father, 208.
Olivers, Thomas, 147, 164, 185, 188.
Origin of the Soul, 218.
Original Sin, Dr. Taylor on, 100; Doctrine of, 101, 173, 222, 223.
Osborn's Bibliography, viii., 9, 12, 25, 26, 43, 48, 49, 65, 68, 79, 82, 87, 90, 98, 99, 105, 113, 116, 119, 122, 124, 135, 140, 144, 169, 170, 171, 177, 187, 207, 214, 219, 229, 236, 252.
Othen, Nathanael, 163.
Overton, Canon, Life of W. Law, 29; Life of John Wesley, 227.
Owen, Dr. John, Work and Life of, 79.
Oxford, Bodleian MSS., 10; University of, 12, 104.

Palmer, Herbert, Works of, 84.
Papists, A Disavowal of persecuting the, 218.
Paradise Lost, 125.
Pascal's Thoughts on Religion, 84.
Passions, The, 219, 222.
Patrick, Bp., Extracts of, 86, 198; Sermon by, 84.
Pelew Islands, Account of the, 245, 248.
Pennington, John, 11.
Pereaud, Mr. Francis, 144.
Perronet, Mr. C., 60, 83.
,, Rev. Vincent, Vicar of Shoreham, 67.
Perseverance of Saints, Dr. Gill on the, 77; Serious Thoughts on, 173.
Peters, Sarah, Account of, 218.
Phenomenon, Thoughts on a late, 241.
Philippians, St. Polycarp's Epistle to the, 63.
Philodemas alias etc., Letter to, 116.
Philosophical Necessity, Dr. Priestley on, 238, 242, 245.
Philosophy, A System of, 156, 192.
Piers, Mr., 32.
Pietas Oxoniensis, 161.
Pious Communicant, by S. Wesley, sen., 107.

Pilgrim's Progress, 162, 171.
Pilmoor, Joseph, 147, 156.
Plaifere on Predestination, 198, 200.
Pocket Companion, The Christian's, 130.
Poem on the Last Day, Dr. Young's, 153.
Poems, A Collection of Moral and Sacred, 25, 153.
Poetical Works—see Wesley, J. and C., Poetical Works of.
Poll-Deed, The, 223, 227, 238, 241, 247.
Poiret, M., Translations from, 35, 174.
Polycarp, Remains of, 13; Address of, to the Philippians, 63; Martyrdom of, *ib*; St. Ignatius' Epistle to, 63.
Polygamy and Marriage, Madan on, 222.
Poole's Annotations, 132.
Popery, Antidote against, 103; Exposed and J. Wesley Vindicated, by Philalethes, 203.
Portraiture of Methodism, Crowther's, 33.
Potter, Rev. Mr., A Letter to, 171.
Power, Thoughts on Origin of, 173.
Prayer, An Old Man's, 162.
Prayers, Collection of Forms of, 9, 10, 163; For Condemned Malefactors, 42; For Families, 84, 163.
Preacher's Assistant, The, 11.
Preachers, Lives of Early Methodist, 147.
Preaching Christ, On, 200.
Predestinarian and Friend, Dialogue between, 173.
Predestination, 212; Toplady on, 148, 155; Calmly considered, 173, 200; Considerations on, 173; Sermon on, 168; Scripture Doctrine of, 173, 200.
Prelectiones Pueriles, 56.
Preservative against Unsettled Notions in Religion, 19, 38, 39, 53, 78, 96, 108, 114, 119, 172, 174.
Press, Wesley's, in London, 240.
Preston, Life and Works of Dr. John 75.
Price, Dr., Observations on Civil Liberty by, 183.
Priestley, Dr., 238, 242, 245.
Primitive Physick, 174.

Principes solides de la religion, etc., 174.
Prior, Thoughts on Character and Writings of, 218.
Pronunciation and Gesture, Directions for, 179.
Prostitute, A Word to a, 42.
Protestant Association, 201, 203, 208.
Providence, A remarkable, 233.
Psalmody, Introduction to, 250.
Psalm civ. Paraphrased, 198.
Psalms and Hymns, A Collection of, (1737), 10; (1741), 206; for the Lord's Day, 232.
Public Advertiser, The, 202, 213.
Public Prayers, etc., Book of, 232.
Puritan Writers, Remarks on, 75.

Quaker, Letter to a, 107, 172.
Question, Answer to an Important, 238.

Raikes, Mr. Robert, 228.
Rankin, Mr. Thomas, 194.
Rapin's Hist. of England, 185.
Rawlinson's Continuation of Wood's *Athenæ Oxonienses*, 10.
Redemption, General, 242; Hymns, Wesley's estimate of, 52.
Reflections on the Conduct of Human Life, 162.
Refined Courtier, The, 238, 242.
Religious Affections, Treatise on, 174.
,, Tract Society, The, 170.
Renty, M. de, 163, 230.
Revelation, Book of the, 245.
Review of Wesley's Doctrines, by Hill, 161, 166, 173.
Revival in New England, Thoughts on, 172.
Reynolds, Works of Dr., 89, 93.
,, Mr. T. W., 235.
Richardson, Mrs. Hannah, 164.
Richmond College Library, 168, 196.
Rigg, Dr., on Wesley's relation to William Law, 143; to Church of England, 114, 249.
Righteousness of Christ, On Imputed, 173.
Ritchie, Miss, 186, 251.
Rod for a Reviler, by T. Olivers, 186, 188, 190.
Rogers, Ann, 164.
Roman Catechism, 172; Catholic, Letter to a, 172; Catholics, Short Method of Converting,
172; History, A Short, 71; do., by N. Hook, 168.
Romans, Goodwin's Exposition of Epistle to the, 205; St. Ignatius' Epistle to the, 63.
Rouse, Francis, 79.
Row, John, Life of, 85.
Rules of Band Societies, 27; of the United Societies, 165; Changes in, 27.
"Rusticulus, or Dr. Dodd," 153.
Rutherford, Samuel, Letters of, 137, 140.
Rutherforth, Dr., Charges to the Clergy by, 141; Letter to, 172.
Ryan, Mrs. Sarah, 200.

Sacrament and Sacrifice, The Christian, by Brevint, 44, 174, 249.
Sacrifice, The Christian, by Bp. Patrick, 86.
Sacred Harmony, 214.
Sacred Melody, 214.
Saints' Everlasting Rest, Baxter's, 187.
Salvation by Faith, Thoughts on, 200.
Sandemanians, 102.
Sanderson, Bp., Works of, 84.
Savannah, 17.
Scougall, Rev. Henry, 30; Discourses by, 93.
,, Bp., 30.
Scripture, Divine Inspiration of, 242.
Self-Examination, A Scheme of, 213; Questions for, by Wesley, 9.
Serious Call, Law's, 27, 29, 56, 217.
Sermon before the Society for the Recovery of Drowned Persons, 191; by Dr. Hamilton, 243; Awake thou that sleepest, 217; Caution against False Prophets, 67; Christian Perfection, 23; Death of Whitefield, 157; Discovery of False Prophets, 104; Family Religion, 160; Free Grace, 10, 22, 173; God is Love, 228; The Good Steward, 157, 220; National Sins and Miseries, 183; Obedience to Parents, 160; Original Sin, 217; Reformation of Manners, 157; The Almost Christian, 20, 217; The Lord our Righteousness, 53, 157; Predestination, 168;

Repentance of Believers, 157;
Sin in Believers, 141, 157;
The Circumcision of the
Heart, 220; Salvation by
Faith, 130, 217; The Great
Assize, 157, 217, 220; The
Important Question, 217;
The New Birth, 217; The
Scripture-Way of Salvation,
133, 141, 157; The Trinity,
181, 217; The Use of Money,
220; The Way to the Kingdom, 217; The Witness of
the Spirit, A Second, 137,
157; The Korah, 245;
Wandering Thoughts, 157.
Sermons on Death, Judgment, etc.,
242, 245; on Several Occasions, by Wesley, 110, 157,
168, 181; Proposals for printing the First Series, 40, 46; the
Second Series, 237; Jackson's
edition of, in 2 vols., 195,
245; Original in Magazine,
213, 219, 222, 224, 228, 233,
235, 238, 241, 245, 248;
Separately re-printed, 67.
Service in Church-hours, 231.
Shaw, Samuel, Life and Writings
of, 85.
Sheridan's Lectures on Elocution,
60.
Shirley, Rev. Walter, 152, 155, 156.
Sibs, Richard, Life and Writings of,
75.
Sidney, Sir Philip, Life of, 85.
Silas Told, 229, 235.
Singing, Directions for, 117.
Single Life, Thoughts on a, 174.
Smollett's Hist. of England, 185.
Smith, Rev. John, Works of, 79,
84; Hist. of Methodism—
see Methodism.
Smuggling, Efforts to prevent, 136.
Smyrna, Epistle to the Church of,
63.
Smyth, Rev. Edward, 196.
Societies in Europe and America,
248.
Society, Methodist, First Ticket of,
10; Rules of, 165; for
Reformation of Manners,
124; for Distribution of
Religious Tracts among the
poor, 217.
Soldier, Advice to a, 163.
Soliloquy for an Unregenerate
Sinner, by Baxter, 216.

Sophronius and Callistus, Dialogues
between, 235.
Soul, The Origin of the, 218.
Southey's Life of Wesley—See
Wesley, Life of.
South's Sermons, 93.
Spangenberg, 38, 66.
Spanheim, Frederick, Life of, 85.
Spence, Mr., of York, 215, 236.
Spira, The Second, 222.
Spirit of God, Marks of the Work
of the, 172.
,, of Prayer, The, 96, 217.
St. Bartholomew's Day, 32.
St. Just, Revival at, 225.
St. Mary's, Oxford, 20, 32.
Staffordshire, Riots in, 40.
Stanhope's Translation of Thomas
a Kempis, 10.
Stevens' History of Methodism,—
see Methodism.
Stevinson, Mr. G. J., 48, 114, 180,
188.
Stonehouse, Rev. Mr., 158.
Study, A Method of, 60.
Sugden, Mr. William, 215.
Suicide, Thoughts on, 245.
Sunday Charity Schools, 228;
Service, The, 21, 224, 225,
232.
Superstition and Religion, 235.
Supplement to Large Hymn-Book,
34.
Sure Guide to Heaven, 216.
Survey of Wisdom of God in the
Creation, 179, 213, 222, 224,
233, 239, 242, 245.
Swaddlers, Title given to Methodists
in Ireland, 64, 116.
Swedenborg, Thoughts on the
Writings of, 222.
Swindells, Mr., 54.

Taste, Thoughts upon, 205.
Taxation no Tyranny, by Dr.
Johnson, 180.
Taylor, Dr., of Norwich, 100, 102,
128.
Taylor, Jeremy, Works of, 79, 135.
,, Mr. Thomas, 215.
,, ,, ,, A.M, 245.
Tea, Ill effects of, 57; Letter on, 174.
Tedworth, The Drummer of, 228.
Telford's Life of Wesley—see Wesley.
The Temple, by Herbert, 171.
Testament, Notes on New, 156, 157,
179, 245, 252; Part of
the Doctrinal Standards of

Methodism, 53; Text of, 234, 244; Notes on Old, 156; Why so meagre, 132; few sold, 133, 179.
T. H., Letter to, by Wesley, 116.
Thecla, Sufferings of, 242.
Theron and Aspasio, 121, 129; Letter to Author of, 173.
Thessalonians, Thoughts on an Expression in, 233.
The Spiritual Bee, 85.
Thompson, R., Letters between Wesley and, 115.
Thompson, William, 247.
Thoughts on Marriage and Celibacy, 26; on late Occurrences, 228; on Nervous Disorders, 177; on an Important Question, 218; on Religion, by Beveridge, 94; on Revival in New England, 172; on the Brute Creation, 222.
Three Dialogues, Extract from, 233, 235.
Thriving, Surest way of, 238, 242.
Tilenus, The Examination of, 197.
Tillotson, Abp., Works of, 93; Wesley's Preface to, 94.
Time, On the folly of mis-spending, 238; On the swiftness of, 238.
Tissot, Dr., 138, 145.
Token for Children, 217.
Toplady, Mr. A., 148, 152, 181, 190.
Towgood, A Letter to Mr., on Dissent, 107, 172.
Trallians, St. Ignatius' Epistle to the, 63.
Trapp, Dr., Sermons by, 162.
Tregoss, Mr. Thomas, Life of, 95.
Trench, Dean, 245.
Trevecca College, 156.
Trial of Spirits, The, by C. Perronet, 83; wrongly ascribed to Wesley, *ib*.
Trinity, Hymns and Prayers to the, 139; Doctrine of, *ib*.
Trosse, Mr. G., Life of, 95.
True Christianity, Arndt's, 63, 74.
Trust-Deeds, Sermons referred to in, 53, 157.
Trustees, Appointment of New, 182.
T.S., *A Cool Reply to a Calm Address* by, 181.
Tune-Book, The first Methodist, 24.
Tunes, Collection of, 214.

Tyerman's Life of Wesley—see Wesley, Life of.

Unhappy Woman, Word to an, 42.
Universal Redemption, Hymn on, 14.
Unsettled Notions in Religion, Preservative against—see Preservative.
Urlin, R. Denny, 249.
Usher, Abp., Life of, 85, 200.

Vasey, Mr. Thomas, 224, 239.
Verheyen, Dr. Philip, 225.
Vial, Hymn on the Seventh, 70.
Vindication of Godliness, Alleine's, 204.
Voice, Lessons for exercising the, 119.

Walker, Rev. Mr., 200, 201.
Walsall, 40.
Walsh, Thomas, 111; Life of, 122, 163; Learning of, 123.
Warburton, Bp., 123; *Divine Legation of Moses* by, 143, 162.
Ward, Bp., Sermon by, 85.
Waterford, 154.
Watton, Sir Henry, Life of, 85.
Watts' *Bibliotheca Britannica*, 11; Dr. Isaac, 13, 237.
Wedgwood, Julia, Life of Wesley by, 67.
Weekly History, (Whitefield), 17, 22, 29.
Wednesbury, 40, 43, 57; Modern Christianity at, 43, 172.
Welsh, *A Word to a Methodist*, translated into, 54.
Wesley Family, by Dr. Clarke, 222.
Wesley, Charles, printed Sermons of, 11; First printed hymns of, 15; preaches before the University, 22; spirit of the ministry of, 51; persecution of, 52; accused of Calvinism, 76; special work in time of national distress, 100; in sickness writes *Short Hymns on Select Passages of Scripture*, 122; composes hymns to Lampe's tunes, 138; careless in editing his hymn-books, 139; sorrow on death of Whitefield, 152; unpublished poems, 158, 162, 251, 253; attachment to Whitefield,

158, 159; clearness and force of his writing, 164; signed the second edition of the Rules, 163; short hymns in Magazine, 205, 242; on the Gordon riots, 206, 213; large number of his hymns in the large hymn-book, 206; his last publication, 228; visitations to the prisons, 229; record of his death, 237; hymns for Children, 246; wrote large number of hymns on the Gospels and the Acts of the Apostles, 251; the same revised by J. W., *ib*; Poetical Works of, 252; total original prose and poetical publications of, 254; Journal of, 18, 25, 27, 32, 48, 49, 52, 69, 70, 114, 158, 206, 229; Life of, by Jackson, 13, 17, 18, 21, 23, 25, 32, 34, 44, 48, 51, 66, 68, 92, 97, 100, 107, 112, 114, 122, 127, 139, 152, 158, 206.

Wesley, Charles, Esq., 214.

,, John, First publications of, 9; early letter of, 10; earliest translations of German hymns by, 11; mistakes respecting his writings, 12; studies the Homilies on Justification by faith, 13; high estimate of Life of Haliburton, 13; cause of difference between, and Whitefield, 14, 173; beginning of his great work, 15; Missionary Life, *ib.*; visits Moravians in Germany, 16; Conversion, *ib.*; preaches before the University, 20, 32; converses with Bp. of London on Christian Perfection, 20; cares for the poor, 26, 42; influence of Law's writings on, 27; reads while walking, 31; vindicates his teaching, 35; visits the prisons, 42; observes the Christian Festivals, 47; appeals to Bp. of London, 51; ethical teaching of, 53; preaches from his father's tomb, 57; denied the Sacrament at Epworth, *ib.*; opinion of Sheridan's Lectures, 60; carries books when travelling, 62; urges the use of the Christian Library, 63; tries to conciliate the Catholics of Ireland, 64; skilled in logic, 68; great labour of, 69, 103, 133; opinion of the French language, 73; charity of, 85, 90; controversy with Dr. Gill, 87; always called Rev. *Mr.* Wesley, 87; portrait of, by Williams, 92; revises the Christian Library, 95; proposes to raise 200 Volunteers, 98; Roman Catechism wrongly attributed to, 99; accused of connexion with popery, *ib.*; anti-popish publications of, *ib.*; meets the voters of Bristol, *ib.*; severe writing of, 102; defence of *Theron and Aspasio*, *ib.*; replies to Dr. Free, 104; during illness writes his own epitaph, 109; purpose in publishing the *Desideratum* and the *Primitive Physick*, 115; letters of, to Thompson on Assurance, 115; curious defence of, 116; has difficulty in providing good tune-books, 118; hampered by false teachers, 121; opinion of the *Short Hymns* (No. 214), 122; refutes Bp. Warburton, 123; purpose of, in preparing the *Survey* (No. 220), 125; reads the *Survey* with his preachers, 126; portrait of, by Hone, 132; charged with inconsistency, 133; "power" of, explained, 134; how led to embrace doctrine of Christian Perfection, 135; strives to prevent smuggling, 136; writes to several public Journals in defence of his work, 136-7; appeals to the clergy, 140; opinion of Mary Gilbert's *Journal*, 142; views on Law's writings, 143; on Brainerd's Life, *ib.*; on Tissot's works, 145; defines Christian Perfection, 146; controversy with Toplady, 148, 155; commends the Experience of E. J., 149; writes on public affairs, *ib.*, 159, 187, 193; Sermon on death of Whitefield, 151; controversy on Calvinism, 152; abridges Young's Night Thoughts, 153; assailed by Rev. Mr. Fleury, 154; publishes a collection of his Works, 156; care for children, 160; *ex tempore* sermon, 175; writings on the American War, 180, 183, 184, 201, 202, 210; opens City Road Chapel, 188; proposes to publish a Magazine, 190; violent press persecution, 192; advices to preachers, 195; his first Conferences in Ireland, 195; publishes his Magazine, 196; writes on popery, 201; issues the large Hymn-Book, 206; controversy with O'Leary, 208; founds a Tract Society, 217; thoughts on his own Sermons, 220; abridges Liturgy and ordains Superintendents and Elders for America, 223, 224, 226, 232, 239; objects to the term Bishop, 239; Sermon on death of Fletcher, 227; enrols Deed of Declaration, 227; last visit to Ireland, 240; last publication of, 244; establishes a Strangers' Friend Society, 246; reflections on entering his 88th year, 246; death, 247; *More Work for, or a Vindication of the Decrees, etc.*, 155; Sermon on Pleasantness of a Religious Life, wrongly ascribed to, 11; Sermons, 195; Works, Errors in, 23, 28; total number of, 254; Churchmanship of, by Dr. Rigg, 114, 249; his designated Successor, 232.

Wesley, Journal of, 17, 18, 20, 22, 27, 30, 31, 36, 40, 42, 48, 49, 50, 51, 54, 58, 60, 61, 62, 63, 67, 68, 69, 71, 72, 73, 74, 86, 89, 90, 92, 99, 100, 102, 103, 104, 114, 115, 116, 120, 123, 124, 126, 128, 129, 133, 134, 143, 147, 151, 156, 165, 175, 177, 180, 182, 183, 185, 188, 189, 190, 201, 203, 218, 220, 224, 231, 232, 234, 243, 246, 248, 251.

Wesley, Life of, Beecham's, 252; The Churchman's, 249; Hampson's, 77; Moore's, 10, 51, 58, 139, 227, 237; Canon Overton's, 227; Southey's, 14, 96, 181, 184, 208, 216, 227, 229; Telford's, 28, 92; Tyerman's, viii., 14, 17, 20, 41, 61, 63, 72, 77, 79, 89, 97, 98, 108, 114, 120, 123, 127, 129, 130, 133, 181, 190, 192, 201, 221, 246, 252; Watson's, 90, 156; Wedgwood's, 67; Whitehead's, 150; list of Works, by Heylin and Smith, viii.; Works of, own edition (1771-4), 16, 28, 43, 53, 59, 80, 119, 122, 142, 147, 150, 154, 157, 160, 162, 163, 164, 165, 171, 177, 252; Benson's edition (1809-13), 160, 180, 195, 252; Jackson's edition (1829-31), 16, 18, 19, 21, 27, 29, 31, 33, 35, 44, 53, 59, 60, 62, 63, 66, 68, 80, 95, 102, 103, 107, 115, 125, 129, 133, 136, 140, 143, 149, 155, 160, 175, 180, 186, 192, 209, 218, 221, 231, 232, 239, 252.

Wesley, J. and C., Poetical Works of, viii., 11, 12, 21, 22, 34, 44, 49, 69, 105, 119, 140, 151, 158, 161, 198, 228, 251, 252.

,, Samuel, Letters and Life of, 11; Sermon by, 124; Hymn of, 206.

,, Samuel, Jun., Hymns of, 206, 250.

,, Susannah, 57.

,, Historical Society, v., 65

Westminster Journal, 137.

Wheatley, Mr. James, 98.

Wilson, Captain Henry, 248

West Indies, Missionaries for, 238.

Whatcoat, Richard, 213, 224, 226, 239.

Whitaker, William, Life of, 85.

Wheatley, James, Life of Janeway by, 79.

Whitby, Dr., 228, 233, 235.

Whitefield, Rev. George, 13, 14, 18, 29, 30, 31, 61, 107, 151, 158, 189, 232; Letters by, 13, 14. 31; Teaching of, defended,

INDEX

51; *Weekly History*, 17, 22, 29; Tyerman's Life of, 30, 159.
Whitfield, G., (Book-Steward), 206, 214.
Whitehead, Dr., 150, 157, 185.
Wilkes, John, 159.
Wilcocks, Thomas, Works of, 45.
Williams, Rev. Dr. H. W., 227, 241.
Wilson, Captn. Henry, 248.
  ,,   Mr. Thomas, Life of, 95.
Winter, Dr. Samuel, Life of, 95.
Womack, Bp. Lawrence, 197, 198.
Wood's *Athenæ Oxonienses*, 10.
Woodhead, Abraham, 230.
Woolmer, Rev. T., 11.
Woodward, Joseph, Life of, 85.

"Words," 27, 42, 43, 217.
Word, A, To whom it may concern, 42, 138.
Worthington, John, 84.
Wotton-under-Edge, 189.
Wright, Richard, 156.
Wroot, 11.

Young, Dean of Sarum, Works of, 94.
York Hymn-Book, 236.

Zanchius, on Predestination, 148.
Zinzendorf, Count, 38, 107; Hymns of, 65; Life of, by Spangenberg, 66, 158.

ERRATA.

p   9, l. 37, *for* Grey *read* Gray.
p. 12, l. 3, *substitute* the book was sold by auction for £20.
p. 13, l. 39, *for* J. Watts *read* I. Watts.
p. 14, l. 20, *for* Frank *read* Franck.
p. 17, l. 28, *for* 14 *read* 13.
p. 39, l. 39, *for* each *read* the former.
p. 48, l. 5, *for* 139 *read* 138.
p. 59, l. 23, *for* see No. 63 *read* James Janeway.
p. 68, l. 43, *for* Saunderson *read* Sanderson.
p. 85, l. 25, *for* Barardiston *read* Barnardiston.
p. 108, l. 29, *for* Jackson's *read* Tyerman's.
p. 164, l. 21, *for* one sermon *read* two sermons.
p. 254, l. 14, *for* 326 *read* 315.
p. 254, l. 16, *for* 61 *read* 62.

www.ingramcontent.com/pod-product-compliance
Lightning Source LLC
Chambersburg PA
CBHW032102220426
43664CB00008B/1099